Social Justice

BLACKWELL READINGS IN PHILOSOPHY

Series Editor: Steven M. Cahn

———

Blackwell Readings in Philosophy are concise, chronologically arranged collections of primary readings from classical and contemporary sources. They represent core positions and important developments with respect to key philosophical concepts. Edited and introduced by leading philosophers, these volumes provide valuable resources for teachers and students of philosophy, and for all those interested in gaining a solid understanding of central topics in philosophy.

Social Justice

Edited by
Matthew Clayton and Andrew Williams

Blackwell Publishing

Editorial material and organization © 2004 by Blackwell Publishing Ltd

BLACKWELL PUBLISHING
350 Main Street, Malden, MA 02148-5020, USA
108 Cowley Road, Oxford OX4 1JF, UK
550 Swanston Street, Carlton, Victoria 3053, Australia

The right of Matthew Clayton and Andrew Williams to be identified as the Authors of the Editorial Material in this Work has been asserted in accordance with the UK Copyright, Designs, and Patents Act 1988.

First published 2004 by Blackwell Publishing Ltd
Reprinted 2004

Library of Congress Cataloging-in-Publication Data

Social justice / edited by Matthew Clayton and Andrew Williams.
p. cm. — (Blackwell readings in philosophy)
Includes bibliographical references and index.
ISBN 1-4051-1109-7 (hardcover: alk. paper) — ISBN 1-4051-1146-1
(pbk.: alk. paper)
1. Social justice.   I. Clayton, Matthew, 1966–   II. Williams, Andrew, 1963–   III. Series.

HM681.S63 2004
303.3′72 — dc21

2003013914

A catalogue record for this title is available from the British Library.

Set in 10/12.5pt Palatino
by Kolam Information Services Pvt. Ltd, Pondicherry, India
Printed and bound in the United Kingdom
by MPG Books Ltd, Bodmin, Cornwall

The publisher's policy is to use permanent paper from mills that operate a sustainable forestry policy, and which has been manufactured from pulp processed using acid-free and elementary chlorine-free practices. Furthermore, the publisher ensures that the text paper and cover board used have met acceptable environmental accreditation standards.

For further information on
Blackwell Publishing, visit our website:
www.blackwellpublishing.com

Contents

Acknowledgements

For assistance in preparing the volume, the editors are very grateful to Elizabeth S. Anderson, Nick Bellorini, Harry Brighouse, Paula Casal, Dario Castiglione, Joseph Chan, Jeff Dean, Alison Dunnett, Simon Eckley, Andrew Mason, Kelvin Matthews, David Miller, Janet Moth, Serena Olsaretti, Mark Philip, Thomas W. Pogge, Jonathan Riley, Andrew Reeve, David Stevens, and Peter Vallentyne.

Both the editors and publisher gratefully acknowledge the following permissions granted to reproduce the copyright material in this volume:

Chapter 1: John Locke, 'Of Property', chapter V, (sections 25–51), from *Second Treatise of Government* (section numbers retained), and 'Of Adam's Title to Sovereignty by Donation, *Gen. 1.28*' (section 42), from *First Treatise of Government*, in *Two Treatises of Government*, ed. Peter Laslett (Cambridge: Cambridge University Press, 1988), pp. 285–302, 170 (editorial notes omitted). Copyright © Cambridge University Press, 1960, 1967, 1988. Reprinted by permission of the publisher.

Chapter 2: David Hume, 'Of Justice' (section 3), from *An Enquiry Concerning the Principles of Morals*, ed. T. Beauchamp (Oxford: Oxford University Press, 1998), pp. 13–27. Reprinted by permission of Oxford University Press.

Chapter 3: extracts from John Rawls, *A Theory of Justice*, revised edition (Cambridge, MA: The Belknap Press of Harvard University Press, 1999), pp. 6–9, 10–19, 52–58, 61–73, 130–39. Copyright © 1971, 1999 by the President and Fellows of Harvard College. Reprinted by permission of Harvard University Press.

Chapter 4: extracts from Robert Nozick, *Anarchy, State, and Utopia* (New York: Basic Books, 1974), pp. 149–64, 167–82. Copyright © 1974 by Basic Books, Inc. Reprinted by permission of Basic Books, a member of Perseus Books. LLC.

Chapter 5: Ronald Dworkin, 'What is Equality? Part 2: Equality of Resources', pp. 283–314, from *Philosophy and Public Affairs*, 10: 4 (1981), pp. 283–345. Copyright © 1981 by Princeton University Press. Reprinted by permission of Princeton University Press.

Chapter 6: G. A. Cohen, 'On the Currency of Egalitarian Justice', pp. 916–34 (section IV), from *Ethics* 99 (1989), pp. 906–44. Copyright © 1989 by The University of Chicago. Reprinted by permission of the publisher.

Chapter 7: extracts from Elizabeth S. Anderson, 'What Is the Point of Equality?' from *Ethics* 109 (1999), pp. 287–326 and 336–7 (abridged by the author). Copyright © 1999 by The University of Chicago. Reprinted by permission of the publisher.

Chapter 8: David Miller, 'The Concept of Desert', abridged and revised by the author from chapter 7 in his *Principles of Social Justice* (Cambridge, MA: Harvard University Press, 1999). Copyright © 1999 by the President and Fellows of Harvard College. Adapted and reprinted by permission of Harvard University Press.

Chapter 9: extracts from Susan Moller Okin, *Justice, Gender, and the Family* (New York: Basic Books, 1989), pp. 3–6, 89, 103–5, 170–2, 173, 175–7, 180–2, 183–86, 187 (notes), 197 (notes). Copyright © 1989 by Basic Books, Inc. Reprinted by permission of Basic Books, a member of Perseus Books. LLC.

Chapter 10: G. A. Cohen, 'Where the Action Is: On the Site of Distributive Justice', from *Philosophy and Public Affairs* 26 (1997), pp. 3–30. Copyright © 1997 by Princeton University Press. Reprinted by permission of Princeton University Press.

Chapter 11: Paula Casal, 'Animals and Accommodation', revised by the author from her 'Is Multiculturalism Bad for Animals?' in *Journal of Political Philosophy* 11:1 (2003), pp. 1–22. Copyright © 2003 by Blackwell Publishing.

Chapter 12: Thomas W. Pogge, 'Brief for a Global Resources Dividend', revised and updated by the author from his 'Eradicating Systemic Poverty: Brief for a Global Resources Dividend', in *Journal of Human Development* 2 (2001), pp. 59–77. Copyright © 2001 by Taylor & Francis Ltd (http://www.tandf.co.uk/journals). Reprinted by permission of the publisher.

Chapter 13: Derek Parfit, 'The Non-Identity Problem' from *Reasons and Persons* (Oxford: Clarendon Press, 1984), pp. 355–77 (sections 120–6). Reprinted by permission of Oxford University Press.

Every effort has been made to trace copyright holders and to obtain their permission for the use of copyright material. The publisher apologizes for any errors or omissions in the above list and would be grateful if notified of any corrections that should be incorporated in future reprints or editions of this book.

All editorial royalties from the sale of this book go to Oxfam. We are particularly grateful to those publishers who consequently reduced their fees.

Introduction

Matthew Clayton and Andrew Williams

I

Issues of social justice, in the broadest sense, arise when decisions affect the
distribution of benefits and burdens between different individuals or groups.
These issues have exercised past philosophers and dominated the study of
political philosophy since the publication of Rawls's *A Theory of Justice* in 1971.[1]
The papers, chapters, and extracts selected for this volume are, in our view,
some of the most philosophically interesting and provocative contributions to
the ongoing debate about justice.

The collection begins with two classic discussions of justice by Locke and
Hume respectively. Both view justice in terms of respect for private property.
Locke's discussion is perhaps the most interpreted and discussed defence of
the right to private property in the history of political philosophy and, in its
essentials, remains attractive to many modern readers.[2] The discussion proposes certain conditions under which an individual can justifiably lay exclusive claim to a part of the world, which was originally held in common by
humankind, without the consent of those co-owners. In defending such property rights, Locke attends to a number of issues and offers various arguments
that have been developed by subsequent philosophers. One issue concerns the
legitimacy of the institution of private property, which he takes to be necessary
for our self-preservation given the nature of the world as replete with low-
value resources whose value can be enhanced by labour. A second concerns
the conditions that must be satisfied if an individual is to appropriate a
common resource without the consent of others. He argues that an individual
may privatize such a resource by labouring on it if such privatization leaves
'enough and as good' for others. A third feature of Locke's account is his
interest in the question of the legitimate retention of private property, which,
he argues, is conditional upon not spoiling the resource at stake. Note also that
he regards all of us as subject to a duty of charity, a duty, that is, to provide

adequate opportunity for others to work for their subsistence or to provide it in the case of those unable to work (see the *First Treatise*, sect. 42). In Locke's view, unlike those of contemporary neo-Lockeans like Robert Nozick (see chapter 4), such constraints constitute limits to the rights we enjoy over our private property.

Locke's discussion also attends to the question of justifiable economic inequality, which has been a preoccupation of philosophers concerned with social justice. He claims that in societies lacking the institution of money his non-spoilage condition on legitimate retention would effectively limit the extent of legitimate inequality because individuals would lack the means of accumulating resources without waste. However, in monetarized societies that condition is rendered ineffective as a limit on individual accumulation by the possibility, through exchange, of converting perishable resources into money, which, by convention, is invested with economic value. Consequently, Locke's account is often read as a defence of inequality. Given the multiple questions and different lines of argument Locke supplies in so short a discussion, it is unsurprising that his view has been interpreted and deployed in some strikingly different ways.[3]

Whereas Locke's account of justice rests on the right of self-preservation through labour, Hume's is premised on justice as a facilitator of mutually beneficial cooperation. Like Locke, Hume theorizes justice as respect for (appropriate) rules for the distribution of private property. The primary value of respecting such rules is that doing so facilitates stable cooperation for creatures like us, living in worlds similar to ours. Such worlds exhibit moderate scarcity, in which reciprocal cooperation brings mutual gains, and are also populated by individuals with partial sympathies who, therefore, compete over the distribution of cooperatively produced resources. For Hume, the 'cautious, jealous virtue' of justice has its origins in each individual's recognition that she would gain from following conventions for the determination and protection of private property. These gains might be cashed out in various terms. Hume emphasizes the beneficial consequences for cooperation that follow from having a set of determinate rules for the distribution and regulation of private property and the benefits of having stable expectations about reaping the fruits of one's labour. This kind of account has been labelled a conception of *justice as mutual advantage*.[4] As Hume shows, if the point of justice is to serve mutually beneficial cooperation, then we must acknowledge that the rules for determining the manner in which property is distributed must be ones that facilitate that end. Consequently, Hume famously criticizes desert-based arguments and egalitarian conceptions of social justice. He favours, instead, a conception in which, among other things, private property is arranged in such a way as to reward industry, allow exchange, facilitate inheritance, and enforce contracts.

Humean conceptions of justice are often criticized for failing to acknowledge that we have fundamental reasons to treat others justly or impartially, even at the expense of our long-term interests. Hume's account of the circumstances of justice is an illustration of the problems with the view. On his view, we owe no duties of justice, as opposed to duties of humanity, to non-human animals or powerless humans because in these relationships we can satisfy our interests without the restraint of justice. In addition, he claims that considerations of justice do not hold in situations of extreme scarcity arising, for example, when there are too few lifeboats to provide places for the passengers. In these cases, the strong fare better by not respecting rules of justice. For many, however, such cases point to the inadequacy of the Humean conception: since the rationing of scarce life-saving resources and our treatment of the powerless and vulnerable are central areas where considerations of justice apply, we ought to move beyond Hume's overly restrictive understanding of the reach of justice.

II

Part II turns to contemporary debates about social justice, starting with extracts from the revised edition of *A Theory of Justice*, the work of twentieth-century moral and political philosophy most likely to achieve the abiding importance secured by the writings of Locke and Hume. On Rawls's understanding, principles of social justice are especially stringent normative standards that apply to what he terms the *basic structure* of a society, or those major social, political, and economic institutions that exert a profound and unavoidable impact on its members' life prospects and motivations. Thus, as Rawls's remark that 'Justice is the first virtue of social institutions' indicates, such principles are distinguished by their special force and subject matter.[5] According to utilitarianism, the most plausible principle of social justice requires institutions that maximize the sum of benefits and burdens. One of Rawls's main ambitions in writing *A Theory of Justice* was to develop a superior alternative to this influential view.[6] Focusing on its core assumption, he argues that we should reject utilitarian aggregation because it fails to provide a secure foundation for liberal, democratic freedoms, or to accommodate the conviction that individual rights, and distributive considerations, have fundamental rather than merely derivative moral importance.

Unlike *intuitionist* critics of utilitarianism, who appeal to an irreducible and unordered plurality of first principles, Rawls provides a more systematic alternative. In place of a utility maximizing principle, he defends a set of liberal egalitarian principles that share a common foundation, and are *lexically ordered* in the sense that prior principles cannot be compromised in order better to satisfy subordinate principles. Once society has reached a certain level of development, Rawls's first *basic liberty principle* attaches such priority to a set of specific civil liberties, such as freedom of conscience, expression, association and occupational choice, and rights to democratic political participation. His second more distinctive and radical principle of *democratic equality* governs the distribution of opportunities to compete for jobs and political offices and of material expectations, and contains two sub-principles. The former *principle of fair equality of opportunity* requires the elimination not only of formal discrimination, but also of certain inequalities in occupational opportunity that originate from the *social lottery*, including variations in individuals' family or class background. The latter *difference principle* is a test for just differences in income and wealth, including those arising from variations in productive potential caused by the *natural lottery*. It requires that such inequalities be arranged to benefit the least advantaged members of society as much as possible.

As well as showing the intuitive plausibility of his two principles, Rawls defends them by employing a hypothetical contractarian argument. He argues that his two principles are sound because they would be the object of rational agreement for parties in an *original position*, who aim to advance the good of the particular individuals they represent, but who are fairly situated behind a *veil of ignorance*.[7] Thus, they are oblivious to the specific conceptions of the good, and the particular fortunes or misfortunes of those individuals, and aware only of their needs as *free and equal citizens*, and of suitably general facts about, for example, human psychology and society. In assessing competing principles, the parties proceed via two stages. They first consider the possible effects of instituting those principles on individuals' shares of *social primary goods*, including basic liberties, occupational opportunities, income and wealth, and the social bases of self-respect. Since Rawls assumes that principles of social justice are more plausible to the extent that they secure *well-ordered social cooperation* according to publicly shared principles, the parties also consider the ways in which competing principles would shape individual motivation, and generate their own support once implemented.[8]

Though chapter 3 contains Rawls's intuitive explanation of the appeal of democratic equality, and the first stage of his argument for the superiority of his two principles over a utilitarian principle, readers should bear in mind that it is merely an extract. Rawls has many further arguments against other rival non-utilitarian principles, including hybrids that incorporate civil liberties and a social minimum as constraints on utility maximization. In work published since 1971 he has also elaborated, extended, and criticized his earlier statement of justice as fairness in considerable depth.[9] In addition, there is a vast critical literature on Rawls's conception of justice, challenging such central features as his primary focus of the basic structure of nation states, and his description of the original position and the parties' grounds for accepting the two principles.[10] Critics have also questioned both the form and the content of Rawls's second principle in ways worth briefly rehearsing.

To understand some of the main form-based objections, it is useful to distinguish between three types of distributive principle. *Relational egalitarian principles* require that no individual enjoy a higher level of advantage than any other individual. *Non-relational egalitarian*, or *prioritarian*, *principles* assume our reasons to improve an individual's level of advantage diminish as she becomes better off, and so give priority to less advantaged over more advantaged individuals.[11] *Sufficientarian principles* require that each individual is capable of attaining a certain threshold of advantage. Because of its concern with fair equality of opportunity and with maximizing the prospects of those with least income and wealth, democratic equality combines both relational egalitarian and prioritarian elements. As such, it can be criticized from various opposing perspectives. For example, *anti-egalitarian sufficientarians* deny we should care about equality, or attach priority to the less advantaged, once everyone has 'enough'.[12] Opponents of *extreme prioritarianism* deny we should attach overriding priority to improving the condition of the least advantaged when doing so produces few benefits for them at considerable cost to the more advantaged.[13] *Pluralist relational egalitarians* claim that since inequality as such is unfair, there are reasons to eliminate it even if doing so would be to the detriment of everyone, including the least advantaged. Democratic equality, therefore, provides an incomplete account of distributive justice because it fails to acknowledge that such reasons exist, and must be balanced against competing considerations of efficiency or priority.

Content-based objections to Rawls's second principle challenge his use of social primary goods as a standard of interpersonal comparison to determine different individuals' levels of advantage. One especially influential objection claims that the Rawlsian standard is blind to various inequalities any adequate conception of social justice must address; for example, an individual might enjoy the same share of social primary goods as others, but unlike them still suffer from a severe physical disability that clearly strengthens her claim on additional resources. Elaborating on such cases, Sen has argued they reveal a deeper problem, namely that the Rawlsian standard is *fetishistic* in so far as it mistakenly focuses on means rather than individuals' *capabilities*, which interpersonal comparisons should ultimately focus upon.[14] Another objection claims that the Rawlsian approach is insufficiently determinate because it fails to solve the *indexing problem* that arises when comparing different primary goods. It is far from obvious how the approach enables us to choose between, for example, one set of economic institutions that provide a lower level of income for the least advantaged but more valuable opportunities to exercise authority and influence within the workplace and another set offering higher levels of income but at the expense of the latter good.

III

Nozick's *historical entitlement* conception of justice, outlined in chapter 4, offers a radical, as well as politically and philosophically influential, alternative to justice as fairness. In his book *Anarchy, State, and Utopia*, Nozick aims to show that a state might be just even if it performs only such minimal functions as protecting individuals against theft, fraud, and breach of contract, and fails to pursue other familiar political objectives, such as ensuring that public goods are supplied efficiently, or that basic needs can be met.[15] Though he fully shares Rawls's opposition to utilitarianism, Nozick not only denies that justice requires democratic equality, but also claims that justice prohibits enforcing its redistributive principles without individuals' consent, unless doing so can be justified as a temporary corrective for past injustice.

While Rawls lets the choice between his favoured forms of capitalism and market socialism depend on local circumstances and social scientific conjectures about which set of economic institutions is the most effective instrument in satisfying his two principles, Nozick echoes earlier theorists in assuming that private property in the means of production plays a fundamental role in understanding distributive justice.[16] Thus, chapter 4 begins by taking for granted that principles of justice apply to the distribution of *entitlements*, which confer enforceable claims and powers on their bearers to control, alienate, and benefit from their holdings. The central task of a theory of justice, then, is to explain why individuals possess such entitlements, or how they can acquire them. Nozick also takes for granted a principle of *self-ownership*, according to which normal adults possess alienable entitlements over their own bodies and labour. Discussing ownership rights in external objects, he argues that entitlements can be justified by appeal to three further types of principles governing the *acquisition* of unowned resources, the *transfer* of owned resources, and the *rectification* of past injustice.

Given this framework, and in particular the extensive decision-making powers it awards property-owners, Nozick draws some important critical conclusions. In particular, he concludes that sound principles of justice must be *historical*, and so make the justice of a distribution dependent on its origins; thus, if it was cleanly generated by a suitably voluntary process, even slavery might be just. Furthermore, familiar *patterned* principles, such as those requiring distribution according to moral merit, or productivity, or need, cannot be sound since they require distributions that can be preserved only by denying individuals liberty to transfer their holdings as they see fit. Offering a construal of Locke's famous remark about appropriators leaving 'enough and as good' for others, Nozick also defends a specific principle of acquisition, according to which individuals can unilaterally acquire entitlements in unowned resources if doing so does not make others worse off than they would have been had those resources continued to be unowned. Given that the absence of ownership rights is likely to generate highly inefficient outcomes, he infers that enormously unequal distributions, including ones produced by actual capitalist economies, are quite consistent with justice since they may still satisfy the Lockean proviso, thus construed.

Though Thomas Nagel once dubbed Nozick's view 'Libertarianism without Foundations', others have attempted to work within Nozick's framework and develop more plausible historical entitlement theories.[17] Amongst these fellow travellers, some *left-libertarians* favour more egalitarian principles of acquisition, which grant each individual an equally valuable share of private property in non-produced resources.[18] It remains debatable, however, whether such amendments address the fundamental question of why entitlement, rather than some account of morally urgent individual interests, should play such a basic role in a theory of justice.

Ronald Dworkin provides the third influential approach to social justice sampled in part II. Like Nozick's view, Dworkin's conception of *equality of resources* assumes that liberty plays a central role in understanding economic justice, and endorses private ownership in the means of production as well as personal property. Thus, Dworkin does not construe liberty purely by reference to a list of basic civil liberties, or regard the choice between liberal democratic forms of capitalism and socialism as contingently grounded. Unlike Nozick, however, Dworkin sides firmly with Rawls in rejecting the conclusion that liberty requires us to abandon, or severely restrict, the pursuit of economic equality. He escapes the anti-egalitarian conclusion by questioning the common assumption – shared by Rawls, Nozick, and many others – that liberty and equality are distinct and potentially antagonistic values. Instead, equality of resources assumes economic equality itself requires respect not only for civil liberties but also for private property and market procedures. So, liberty and equality are interdependent elements of a single political ideal.

Dworkin defends his optimistic stance by arguing that whether a distribution of privately owned resources is just depends upon the possibility of that distribution emerging from a particular type of market process. He illustrates his proposal by asking us to imagine a group of castaways faced with the task of distributing private ownership rights over a desert island. While the Nozickian proviso would permit some castaways unilaterally to appropriate more valuable shares than others, Dworkin insists that they should attempt to satisfy an appropriate version of what economists (misleadingly) term the 'envy test', a standard which treats distributions as fair only if no individual prefers any other individual's holdings. Dworkin argues that the elimination of envy is best secured by an auction in which each bidder has equal purchasing power, and lots are continuously divided until the market clears, and no bidder wishes to repeat the process. He then asks whether his market-orientated approach remains appropriate once production, investment, trade, illness, disability, and variations in talent complicate the island's economy, and the castaways' prospects are shaped by differences in luck as well as ambition.

At this stage, Dworkin draws some important distinctions between various types of economic inequality. In cases where inequalities are due to differences in choice rather than luck, as when two equally talented castaways pursue unequally remunerative occupations, Dworkin argues that justice not merely permits but requires such inequality. He draws a further distinction between economic inequalities produced by variations in individuals' *option luck* and their *brute luck*. The former varies, for example, when some castaways are wealthier than others as a result of winning a fair lottery that everyone had the opportunity to enter, whilst the latter varies when the inequality is a result of their receiving more valuable bequests, or genetic endowments. Like historical entitlement theorists, Dworkin assumes that competent, well-informed individuals are entitled to expose themselves to differing degrees of option luck, and infers that if some castaways choose to gamble, and have good option luck, then there is little reason to deny them more resources than others who declined to gamble, or who chose to gamble and had worse option luck. Extending this line of argument to brute luck inequalities, he crucially argues that the victims of brute luck are entitled to as much compensation as would be provided by a fair insurance market in which purchasers make decisions based on their own conceptions of the good and attitudes to risk, but an awareness only of the overall distribution of brute luck rather than their own good or bad luck. Dworkin concludes that the castaways should attempt to mimic the operation of such a market by introducing a compensatory scheme to redress brute luck inequalities financed by a system of progressive taxation.

In describing how distributive institutions might achieve not only what he terms *endowment-insensitivity* but also *ambition-sensitivity*, Dworkin has produced a conception of social justice that combines elements from justice as fairness and historical entitlement theory. Thus, as well as incorporating convictions about the importance of regulating economic inequalities arising from the social and natural lottery that are central to democratic equality, equality of resources accommodates convictions about choice and responsibility that account for the appeal of entitlement theories.[19] For example, unlike the difference principle, Dworkin's appeal to hypothetical insurance incorporates both of these considerations by requiring individuals to share each other's misfortunes in a way which is sensitive to each individual's actual values and attitude to risk. It is also striking how Dworkin's view addresses some of the problems associated with Rawls's view.

Consider, for instance, the dilemma generated by individuals with severe physical or mental disabilities, whose condition can be improved only slightly but at considerable cost to those who are more fortunate. Rawlsians may respond by maintaining the extreme priority view but attempting to reduce its counterintuitive consequences; for example, by arguing that disabled individuals are not distinctively disadvantaged since interpersonal comparison should focus exclusively upon social primary goods. Many, however, will doubt whether this is an acceptable price to pay for saving the extreme view. Rawlsians might instead concede that interpersonal comparisons should focus upon additional factors, including severe disabilities, and attempt to avoid embarrassing results in some other way; for example, by adopting a *moderate* prioritarian view, which denies absolute priority to the least advantaged, or by insisting only that disabled individuals reach some threshold of basic capabilities. However, both these responses rely on ideas about which Rawlsians are rightly suspicious: a vague form of intuitionist balancing in the former case, and an apparently arbitrary threshold in the latter. Moreover, in cases where securing even basic capabilities is extremely costly, the latter sufficientarian solution is vulnerable to similar problems of cost as extreme prioritarianism.

Now compare the resource egalitarian response. By arguing that misfortune should be shared in an ambition-sensitive manner that mimics the operation of a fair insurance market rather than maximizes the expectations of any particular group, Dworkin's view can explain why justice sometimes permits denying absolute priority to the worst off. For example, if disabilities are sufficiently grave and costly to redress that, given our values and attitudes to risk, we would refuse to purchase a maximinimizing policy, then equality of resources implies we should not be taxed to fund such a policy. The view does not, however, secure this result by overlooking inequalities other than those in social primary goods, but accepts that *personal resources*, such as health and talent, should figure in interpersonal comparison as well as *impersonal resources*, such as occupation and wealth. It would be too hasty, however, to conclude that Dworkin's attempt to achieve endowment-insensitivity in an ambition-sensitive manner does not encounter problems of its own. Some may still balk at the thought that whether justice demands that the blind obtain redress, or hip replacements receive funding before cosmetic surgery, is contingent on hypothetical market behaviour informed by individuals' personal evaluations.

IV

The remaining contributors to part II articulate important objections to the views canvassed in the previous two sections. In his discussion of equality of resources in chapter 6, Cohen challenges Rawls's and Dworkin's denial that interpersonal comparisons of *welfare* can play a legitimate role within conceptions of social justice. Defending the relevance of comparisons based upon experiential quality, Cohen argues that equality of resources cannot accommodate our conviction that individuals whose movement is accompanied by severe pain are fitting objects of egalitarian concern without itself invoking comparative considerations about welfare. Turning to comparisons based on preference-satisfaction, Cohen focuses on Dworkin's central anti-welfarist dilemma, according to which egalitarians who attend to individuals' levels of satisfaction will have either to pander unfairly to individuals who voluntarily acquire relatively expensive preferences, or unfairly penalize individuals who are initially endowed with relatively inexpensive preferences.[20]

Cohen's response is to insist that we should ask whether or not an individual has a lower level of satisfaction than others due to factors beyond his control. He argues that if the individual could not have avoided having preferences that are relatively expensive to satisfy, then justice requires attending to his welfare deficit. So, for example, if Paul's leisure preferences are more costly to satisfy than Fred's, and Paul could not have avoided having more costly preferences than Fred, there are reasons of justice to grant him a larger share of resources. If, however, Paul could have avoided those preferences, then justice does not require such attention. Having shown how an appeal to personal responsibility enables a welfarist to avoid pandering to voluntarily acquired expensive ambitions, Cohen acknowledges that the second horn of the anti-welfarist dilemma presents a greater challenge. He concedes that it is implausible to suppose that individuals who are endowed with inexpensive preferences and then voluntarily acquire preferences as expensive as others are not entitled to any additional resources whatsoever. Though this concession threatens Arneson's principle of *equality of opportunity for welfare*, Cohen argues that it does not undermine his favoured welfarist principle, *equality of access to advantage*.[21] Because this hybrid principle assumes welfare, capabilities, *and* resources should all play some role in interpersonal comparison, it does not entail that individuals who have the (alleged) good fortune to be endowed with inexpensive preferences are entitled only to those resources they need to secure equality of opportunity for welfare. Instead it merely implies that such individuals are not entitled to as many resources as others. Cohen's argument, therefore, suggests that we should be willing to deny Fred as many resources as Paul if he voluntarily chooses to abandon inexpensive fishing in favour of more expensive photography. If that claim is plausible, then Dworkin's dilemma does not refute principles of justice that rely, in part, on interpersonal comparisons of welfare.

In addition to Cohen and Arneson, many other notable theorists, including Eric Rakowski, John Roemer, Hillel Steiner, and Philippe Van Parijs, have followed Dworkin's lead in assuming that there is a fundamental difference between inequalities that originate from luck and those that originate from choice. In chapter 7, Elizabeth Anderson subjects the resulting philosophical movement, which she dubs 'luck egalitarianism', to a forceful and wide-ranging critique.[22] Alleging that egalitarian theorists have paid insufficient attention to the demands of actual egalitarian movements, she argues that luck egalitarians should recognize that the fundamental egalitarian aim is not to compensate individuals for undeserved social and natural misfortune but rather to eliminate oppression, and to create certain types of egalitarian social relations.

As well as claiming that the pursuit of the luck egalitarian aim relies upon intrusive means, and has demeaning implications for its supposed beneficiaries, Anderson raises a host of fundamental objections. Some claim that luck egalitarianism makes individuals' entitlements dependent on their choices to an excessive degree; for example, it permits extreme inequalities that arise through voluntary choices against an equal background.[23] Others allege that both welfarist and resourcist forms of luck egalitarianism are excessively concerned to share the effects of luck. In contrast, according to Anderson, there are many brute luck-based inequalities in welfare, personal, and impersonal resources that are not unjust including, for example, ones deriving from differences in personal appearance or productive potential. As an alternative to luck egalitarianism, Anderson proposes a complex version of Sen's capability view, in which the capacities for citizenship play a central but not exclusive role. Though, like Rawls, she describes her alternative as 'democratic equality', it is notable that she does not endorse his principle of fair equality of opportunity, and explicitly rejects his difference principle in favour of a sufficientarian approach more hospitable to inequalities in income and wealth.

Some may regard this as an over-reaction to the philosophical excesses of luck egalitarianism.

Though Anderson's suggestion that desert plays a role within luck egalitarian arguments is debatable, it is clearly true that a revival of interest in desert has taken place amongst philosophers, and that ordinary judgements about social justice are often expressed using the language of desert.[24] In chapter 8, David Miller, one of the most persistent and distinguished advocates of desert principles of social justice, attempts to clarify what is involved in desert judgements, and to respond to various doubts about their importance and validity. For example, influenced by Rawls's discussion in *A Theory of Justice*, many are convinced that, despite their frequency, judgements about desert can play at most a derivative rather than a fundamental role in understanding social justice. On this view, individuals deserve certain goods only because more fundamental principles of justice require institutions assigning those goods to them; those institutions are not themselves just because they treat individuals as they deserve. Other critics have concluded that desert principles of economic justice which make fair shares depend upon productive contributions are flawed because of their inegalitarian implications. Suppose, for example, that one individual produces far less than another no more diligent worker merely because she has been endowed with an inferior technology. Surely, the critics argue, it is implausible to assume that their unequal productive contribution suffices to justify any substantial inequality in their material expectations. If so, they conclude, desert principles should be rejected because they require economic inequalities arising from comparably arbitrary factors, such as differences in educational investment or natural aptitude. Miller's contribution engages with both of these influential objections, as well as attempting to show that desert judgements have sufficient determinacy to serve as practical standards.

V

Philosophical discussions of social justice proceed at differing levels of abstraction and generality. In selecting papers for the volume's final section we have chosen ones that discuss more concrete or specific issues in a way that is provocative, and extends our understanding of social justice itself.

One fertile area of recent philosophical reflection concerns what G. A. Cohen has termed the *site* of distributive justice: in assessing items as socially just or unjust, which items do we have in mind? As mentioned, one prominent liberal answer is offered by Rawls, whose primary focus is on a society's basic structure. On his view justice requires, among other things, constitutional and legal arrangements that fairly regulate democratic politics and individual freedoms, arrangements for education and employment that ensure fair equality of opportunity, and a system of property, taxation, and public spending that prioritizes the interests of the least advantaged in society. To be sure, norms of justice also apply to individuals who are duty-bound to bear a fair share of the burden of realizing such social and political institutions. Nevertheless, in Rawls's view the duties of social justice that apply to individuals are derived from an account of a just basic structure.

In focusing primarily on the basic structure, Rawls's view diverges from two influential alternatives. Thus, Rawls rejects the *individualist* assumption, which he associates with Nozick's version of libertarianism, that the demands of justice are exhausted by general principles that regulate each individual's conduct.[25] Instead he assumes that any adequate theory of social justice must contain principles guiding institutional design and the decisions of collective agents charged with special responsibility for preserving background fairness. In focusing primarily on the basic structure, however, Rawls does not merely make the sociologically realistic claim that principles for individual decision-making are insufficient to characterize social justice. He also rejects the *monist* assumption that all of the types of consideration relevant to institutional design should also govern everyday individual decision-making.[26] Many find this second aspect of Rawls's view attractive because it produces a moral division of labour regarding the duties that free and equal persons owe to each other. If these duties can be externalized in a set of institutional rules which we fight for and respect, then, in the rest of our lives, we are free to pursue our personal projects and relationships in the knowledge that what we owe to each other from the point of view of justice is satisfied by the institutions that constrain us.[27]

This familiar liberal attitude to social justice is not without its critics. Certain egalitarians and feminists, for example, have criticized it for permitting too much economic or sexual inequality. Some, like Okin, have argued that the fundamental liberal ideals of freedom and equality support the inclusion of the family within the basic structure, and its regulation by the two principles of justice. The gendered way in which family life is traditionally organized and related to the workplace has a profound effect on the life-chances of men and women respectively. Moreover, the gendered family, into which we are born and socialized, has significant implications for our self-conception as agents. Consequently, if we value fair cooperation between individuals understood as free and equal, then the distribution of power, wealth, and responsibility within the family must be rendered more equal.

Okin's remarks in chapter 9 suggest various ways in which these claims might be developed. First, we might argue that family life should ideally be governed by a gender egalitarian ethos that prohibits treating gender as a reason for unequally dividing benefits and burdens, including responsibility for childcare, amongst family members. To support such an ethos, public policies regulating child-care, education, and paid employment might be reformed, thereby enabling women and men to combine both paid and domestic labour on an egalitarian basis. Second, we might recognize that some sections of culturally diverse societies will not conform with a gender egalitarian ethos, and accept that such conduct should be tolerated. Consequently we might, among other things, attempt to ensure that public policies protect women from the disadvantages arising from the continued existence of the traditional division of domestic labour. Various of Okin's proposals concern this question, including changes to employment law that require an equal split of earned family income.

The issue of the site of distributive justice is also addressed in chapter 10 by Cohen, who criticizes the justice of incentive-generating economic inequalities. Liberal conceptions of justice require us to vote for tax-and-spend policies that favour the disadvantaged, but they also permit us to make everyday economic decisions that fail to benefit the disadvantaged. We may, for example, demand higher salaries without taking into consideration the impact of our demands upon those less fortunate; or we might decide to enjoy more leisure, or pursue a less productive occupation, thereby failing to produce wealth that could be used to their benefit. Taking it for granted that such behaviour is permissible, liberals have frequently accepted substantial income inequalities when they prove necessary to attract potentially productive individuals into socially beneficial occupations, or to induce them to work harder.

Cohen argues that to the extent that Rawls's difference principle is a sound principle of economic justice it must govern not merely the coercive institutional rules of the basic structure but also our everyday market behaviour. If, as free and equal individuals with a sense of justice, the productive acknowledge the claims of the less advantaged, then it is incoherent for them to demand more than an equal share of advantage as a condition for deploying their talents. The basis of Cohen's critique of Rawlsian justice is that its restricted focus on the basic structure is unsustainable. The radical alternative he envisages is that all decisions with profound distributive effects fall within the purview of social justice. If we accept that alternative, then there are powerful reasons to doubt whether the self-serving behaviour characteristic of contemporary market societies is consistent with social justice.

One worry about feminist and more general egalitarian departures from liberal conceptions of justice is their apparent sectarianism. We have already noted, for example, Okin's acknowledgement that even in liberal societies many individuals uphold the traditional gender-based division of domestic labour. The existence of cultural pluralism has raised a number of further questions concerning social justice. One prominent issue is whether justice requires or permits exempting individuals or groups from the observance of generally applicable social norms in order to respect particular cultural practices. Is it just to exempt Sikhs from laws requiring citizens to wear protective headgear when riding motorcycles? Does justice require, permit, or condemn state funding for religious schools?

There are many other questions about the relationship between minority cultural practices and the wider society in which they exist. The issue of justice between cultures is sometimes complicated by questions concerning how individuals are treated within minority cultures. For example, particular groups demand not merely freedom from interference by the dominant culture, but also freedom to regulate the lives of their members. Under what circumstances is it just to allow minority cultures to uphold and preserve their long-standing traditions when doing so conflicts with the dominant culture's understanding of what it is to treat individuals as free and equal citizens? Some arguments for cultural exemptions appeal to the religious significance of the practice for the group in question. Another appeals to considerations of fairness in the treatment of different practices: if Christian schools receive state subsidies, then surely fairness also requires providing them to Muslim schools.

As well as exploring our duties to non-human animals, in chapter 11 Casal offers a critique of the justice of cultural exemptions, focusing on the practice of ritual animal sacrifice involved in the Santería religion. Amongst other reasons, the discussion is illuminating because our duties to non-human animals are generally considered to be less extensive, or stringent, than our duties to vulnerable human beings, the violation of which critics of cultural rights normally focus upon.[28] If Casal is correct to criticize the arguments for cultural exemptions in cases involving harm to animals, then it would appear that we have reason to call into question arguments for cultural exemptions more generally.

The volume's final two chapters address perhaps the most important moral issues facing humanity today: the widespread incidence of poverty across the globe, and the process of rapid environmental degradation now threatening the standard of living of future generations. Many react to global poverty by reaching for their chequebook, believing themselves to be under a duty of charity to aid victims of poverty. From the point of view of justice, however, the question is whether the world's poor are unjustly treated, or fail to receive what they are owed, if the rich refuse to redistribute. Few believe that there are no principles of justice that apply globally: no one seriously supposes that the right to be free from torture does not have worldwide application. The task, then, is to characterize and defend a set of principles that can constitute a plausible basis for global justice.

This challenge has engaged an increasing number of political philosophers in recent years. In considering their claims, it is necessary to draw a distinction between ideal and non-ideal political theory. The distinction depends on how many of the current global political arrangements are taken as given for the purposes of fashioning a conception of global justice. In characterizing ideal global principles, our conception of justice must avoid *utopianism*, and so not describe an ideal that is unrealizable given a plausible understanding of human capacities, reasonable human motivations, and possible social institutions.[29] Nevertheless, there are many highly radical suggestions for global reform which avoid utopianism so construed but which are not remotely on the international agenda. It is in that context that Pogge proposes the idea of a *global resources dividend*, a tax on the use of the world's natural resources, the proceeds from which are then deployed in the fight against poverty. Pogge's proposal is, so he argues, ecumenical in so far as it may be defended by appeal to a variety of otherwise competing philosophical approaches to justice, and its application requires only modest reform of global political arrangements. Pogge's paper, like Okin's, shows brilliantly how theorists of justice can engage with, and develop feasible proposals for reform of, the non-ideal world.

The issue of justice with respect to future people involves practical issues concerning environmental conservation and improvement. It has also been the subject of a fundamental philosophical debate about how we understand the ideal of social justice. Recall Hume's conception of justice, in which individuals accept restraints on the pursuit of their self-interest where such restraints are necessary for mutually beneficial social cooperation. As Hume himself notes, such a conception effectively excludes the relationship between human and non-human animals from the purview of social justice. It also precludes a justice-based assessment of our decisions affecting the lives of future generations. Assuming neither non-human animals nor future people have the power to affect us for better or worse, we lack adequate reason, in Hume's view, to restrain ourselves by norms of justice. Most theorists of justice now reject Hume's conception of the circumstances of justice. Nevertheless, as Parfit shows, the particular relationship we have with future people may require further revisions to our understanding of morality and justice.

It is commonly thought, for example, that to establish an injustice we must, minimally, show how the victim of the alleged injustice is harmed, or made worse off than they otherwise would have been, by our decision. However, in the case of future people, that claim often cannot be established. The decisions we take that have long-term ramifications for future living standards also affect *who* will live in the distant future. Parfit argues that, if future people have lives worth living, then resource depletion cannot plausibly be thought to be harmful to them. *They* will not be better off if we conserve resources since conservation would have the effect of bringing a different set of individuals into existence. If this is correct, then we have a choice. We might retain our belief that the primary concern of justice is to ensure that people avoid various kinds of harm, or that they are not made worse off in their enjoyment of particular goods than they might be. If we retain what Parfit terms that *person-affecting principle*, then we must accept that conceptions of justice cannot be employed to address a number of decisions that affect the lives of future generations (though we might criticize those decisions on grounds other than justice). Alternatively, we might, as he argues, reject the person-affecting principle and theorize our obligations to future generations in impersonal terms. We might say, for instance, that outcomes can be morally bad even when they are bad for no particular person. A future world in which people fare badly is, to that extent, worse than a future world in which people fare well, even when there is no one who would be made worse off by a decision to produce the first world.

Notes

1   See *A Theory of Justice* (Cambridge, MA: The Belknap Press of Harvard University Press, 1971). Ch. 3 contains extracts from *A Theory of Justice*, rev. edn. (Cambridge, MA: The Belknap Press of Harvard University Press, 1999). All page references below cite the revised edition.

2   See, for example, Nozick's entitlement theory (ch. 4), which draws on Locke's account. One of Pogge's justifications for a *global resources dividend* as a means of eradicating world poverty (ch. 12) also appeals to Lockean considerations.

3   For two contrasting interpretations, see James Tully, *A Discourse on Property* (Cambridge: Cambridge University Press, 1980), and Jeremy Waldron, *The Right to Private Property* (Oxford: Oxford University Press, 1988).

4   See Brian Barry's *Theories of Justice* (Berkeley: California University Press, 1989) for the distinction between *justice as mutual advantage* and *justice as impartiality*. Drawing on Hume's earlier and lengthier discussion of justice in *A Treatise of Human Nature*, Barry interprets Hume's account as displaying elements from both views. For an interpretation of Hume as a mutual advantage theorist, see David Gauthier's 'David Hume, Contractarian', *Philosophical Review*, 88 (1979), 3–38.

5   See *A Theory of Justice*, p. 3.

6   See, for example, ibid., pp. xi–xii.

7   Rawls embeds his contractarian argument within a more general coherentist conception of moral justification, as well as a particular liberal account of the standards political arguments should satisfy in order to legitimize the exercise of power in democratic societies. For further discussion, see T. M. Scanlon, 'Rawls on Justification', in Samuel Freeman (ed.), *The Cambridge Companion to Rawls* (Cambridge: Cambridge University Press, 2002).

8   See *A Theory of Justice*, Part III.

9   For this later work, see: John Rawls, *Political Liberalism*, pbk edn. (New York: Columbia University Press, 1996); *Collected Papers*, ed. Samuel Freeman (Cambridge, MA: Harvard University Press, 1999); *The Law of Peoples* (Cambridge, MA: Harvard University Press, 1999); and *Justice as Fairness: A Restatement*, ed. Erin Kelly (Cambridge, MA: The Belknap Press of Harvard University Press, 1999).

10   For a survey of that literature, see Henry Richardson and Paul Weithman (eds.), *The Philosophy of Rawls: A Collection of Essays* (New York: Garland, 1999), vols. 1–5.

11   For a discussion of the two forms of egalitarian principle, and for a defence of pluralist relational egalitarianism, see respectively Derek Parfit, 'Equality or Priority?' and Larry Temkin, 'Equality, Priority, and the Levelling Down Objection', in Matthew Clayton and Andrew Williams (eds.), *The Ideal of Equality* (London: Palgrave, 2000). Our terminology derives from Parfit's classic paper, though the label 'sufficientarian' is due to Paula Casal.

12   For one example of this type of response, see Harry Frankfurt, 'Equality as a Moral Ideal', *Ethics*, 98 (1987), pp. 21–43. For possible replies to this line of criticism, see *A Theory of Justice*, sect. 49. The appeal of fair equality of opportunity suggests another immediate reply: even if everyone has *sufficient* occupational opportunities, many accept that if some similarly talented and ambitious individuals have *fewer* opportunities than others merely because their parents are less wealthy, then that inequality is unfair, at least assuming its removal would not leave the disadvantaged with

even fewer valuable opportunities. (Note the final proviso is necessary to accommodate Rawls's recognition that inequalities in opportunity, like inequalities in income and wealth, might, in principle, be justified by a concern with the least advantaged. See *A Theory of Justice*, pp. 264–5, and the final statement of Rawls's two principles on pp. 266–7, which refines the statement reproduced in this volume.)

13 The final section of ch. 3 provides a reply to this common objection, as does *Justice as Fairness: A Restatement*, sect. 19.

14 See, for example, Amartya Sen, 'Justice: Means versus Freedoms', *Philosophy and Public Affairs*, 19 (1990), pp. 111–21, and, for Rawls's reply, *Justice as Fairness: A Restatement*, sect. 51.

15 See Robert Nozick, *Anarchy, State, and Utopia* (New York: Basic Books, 1974).

16 For Rawls's view, see *Justice as Fairness: A Restatement*, p. 114.

17 For Nagel's essay of that title, see Jeffrey Paul (ed.), *Reading Nozick* (Oxford: Blackwell, 1981), ch. 10.

18 For critical discussion of Nozick's conception, see G. A. Cohen, *Self-Ownership, Freedom, and Equality* (Cambridge: Cambridge University Press, 1995), and for statements of left-libertarianism, see Hillel Steiner, *An Essay on Rights* (Oxford: Blackwell, 1994), and Michael Otsuka, *Libertarianism without Inequality* (Oxford: Clarendon Press, 2003).

19 As G. A. Cohen notes in the penultimate section of chapter 6, 'Dworkin has, in effect, performed for egalitarianism the considerable service of incorporating within it the most powerful idea in the arsenal of the anti-egalitarian right: the idea of choice and responsibility.'

20 For his critique of welfare egalitarianism, see Ronald Dworkin, 'What is Equality? Part 1: Equality of Welfare', *Philosophy and Public Affairs*, 10 (1981), pp. 185–246, repr. as ch. 1 in *Sovereign Virtue* (Cambridge, MA: Harvard University Press, 2000), ch. 7 of which contains Dworkin's reply to Cohen. For discussion of their debate see Matthew Clayton, 'The Resources of Liberal Equality', *Imprints*, 5 (2000), pp. 63–82, and Andrew Williams, 'Equality for the Ambitious', *Philosophical Quarterly*, 52 (2002), pp. 377–89.

21 See Richard Arneson, 'Equality and Equal Opportunity for Welfare', *Philosophical Studies*, 56 (1989), pp. 77–93.

22 For discussion of this and many other recent developments in contemporary egalitarianism, see the Equality Network website: <http://aran.univ-pau.fr/ee/index.html>.

23 Cp. Dworkin's treatment of individuals with bad option luck who decline insurance against blindness in ch. 5, sect. III, and Cohen's remark in ch. 6, sect. II that 'When deciding whether or not justice (as opposed to charity) requires redistribution, the egalitarian asks if someone with a disadvantage could have avoided it or could now overcome it. If he could have avoided it, he has no claim to compensation, from an egalitarian point of view.'

24 For an example of the revival, see Serena Olsaretti (ed.), *Justice and Desert* (Oxford: Oxford University Press, 2003).

25 For elaboration, see 'The Basic Structure as Subject', sects. 3 and 4 in Rawls's second book, *Political Liberalism*. According to Brian Barry, Rawls's focus on the basic structure 'represents the coming of age of liberal political philosophy' because for 'the first time, a major figure in the broadly individualistic tradition has taken account of the legacy of Marx and Weber by recognizing explicitly that societies

have patterns of inequality that persist over time and systematic ways of allocating people to positions within these hierarchies of power, status and money'. See *Justice as Impartiality* (Oxford: Clarendon Press, 1995), p. 214.

26 Liam Murphy suggests the term 'monist' in 'Institutions and the Demands of Justice', *Philosophy and Public Affairs*, 27 (1998), pp. 251–91.

27 For discussion of such a moral division of labour, see Thomas Nagel, *Equality and Partiality* (Oxford: Oxford University Press, 1991), ch. 6.

28 See, for example, Susan Okin's contributions to Joshua Cohen et al. (eds.), *Is Multiculturalism Bad for Women?* (Princeton: Princeton University Press, 1999), and Brian Barry, *Culture and Equality* (Cambridge, MA: Harvard University Press, 2001).

29 On the problem of utopianism in political philosophy, see Nagel's *Equality and Partiality*, ch. 3, and for related discussion in the field of international political philosophy, see Rawls's *The Law of Peoples*.

Part I

Historical Essays

1

Of Property

John Locke

25.   Whether we consider natural *Reason*, which tells us, that Men, being once born, have a right to their Preservation, and consequently to Meat and Drink, and such other things, as Nature affords for their Subsistence: Or *Revelation*, which gives us an account of those Grants God made of the World to *Adam*, and to *Noah*, and his Sons, 'tis very clear, that God, as King *David* says, *Psal.* CXV. xvj. *has given the Earth to the Children of Men*, given it to Mankind in common. But this being supposed, it seems to some a very great difficulty, how any one should ever come to have a *Property* in any thing: I will not content my self to answer, That if it be difficult to make out *Property*, upon a supposition, that God gave the World to *Adam* and his Posterity in common; it is impossible that any Man, but one universal Monarch, should have any *Property*, upon a supposition, that God gave the World to *Adam*, and his Heirs in Succession, exclusive of all the rest of his Posterity. But I shall endeavour to shew, how Men might come to have a *property* in several parts of that which God gave to Mankind in common, and that without any express Compact of all the Commoners.

   26.   God, who hath given the World to Men in common, hath also given them reason to make use of it to the best advantage of Life, and convenience. The Earth, and all that is therein, is given to Men for the Support and Comfort of their being. And though all the Fruits it naturally produces, and Beasts it feeds, belong to Mankind in common, as they are produced by the spontaneous hand of Nature; and no body has originally a private Dominion, exclusive of the rest of Mankind, in any of them, as they are thus in their natural state: yet being given for the use of Men, there must of necessity be a means *to appropriate*

John Locke, 'Of Property', chapter V, (sections 25–51), from *Second Treatise of Government* (section numbers retained), and 'Of Adam's Title to Sovereignty by Donation, *Gen. 1.28*', (section 42) from the *First Treatise of Government*, in *Two Treatises of Government*, ed. Peter Laslett (Cambridge: Cambridge University Press, 1960, 1967, 1988), pp. 285–302 and 170 (editorial notes omitted).

them some way or other before they can be of any use, or at all beneficial to any particular Man. The Fruit, or Venison, which nourishes the wild *Indian*, who knows no Inclosure, and is still a Tenant in common, must be his, and so his, *i.e.* a part of him, that another can no longer have any right to it, before it can do him any good for the support of his Life.

27.   Though the Earth, and all inferior Creatures be common to all Men, yet every Man has a *Property* in his own *Person*. This no Body has any Right to but himself. The *Labour* of his Body, and the *Work* of his Hands, we may say, are properly his. Whatsoever then he removes out of the State that Nature hath provided, and left it in, he hath mixed his *Labour* with, and joyned to it something that is his own, and thereby makes it his *Property*. It being by him removed from the common state Nature placed it in, it hath by this *labour* something annexed to it, that excludes the common right of other Men. For this *Labour* being the unquestionable Property of the Labourer, no Man but he can have a right to what that is once joyned to, at least where there is enough, and as good left in common for others.

28.   He that is nourished by the Acorns he pickt up under an Oak, or the Apples he gathered from the Trees in the Wood, has certainly appropriated them to himself. No Body can deny but the nourishment is his. I ask then, When did they begin to be his? When he digested? Or when he eat? Or when he boiled? Or when he brought them home? Or when he pickt them up? And 'tis plain, if the first gathering made them not his, nothing else could. That *labour* put a distinction between them and common. That added something to them more than Nature, the common Mother of all, had done; and so they became his private right. And will any one say he had no right to those Acorns or Apples he thus appropriated, because he had not the consent of all Mankind to make them his? Was it a Robbery thus to assume to himself what belonged to all in Common? If such a consent as that was necessary, Man had starved, notwithstanding the Plenty God had given him. We see in *Commons*, which remain so by Compact, that 'tis the taking any part of what is common, and removing it out of the state Nature leaves it in, which *begins the Property*; without which the Common is of no use. And the taking of this or that part, does not depend on the express consent of all the Commoners. Thus the Grass my Horse has bit; the Turfs my Servant has cut; and the Ore I have digg'd in any place where I have a right to them in common with others, become my *Property*, without the assignation or consent of any body. The *labour* that was mine, removing them out of that common state they were in, hath *fixed* my *Property* in them.

29.   By making an explicit consent of every Commoner, necessary to any ones appropriating to himself any part of what is given in common, Children or Servants could not cut the Meat which their Father or Master had provided for them in common, without assigning to every one his peculiar part. Though the Water running in the Fountain be every ones, yet who can doubt, but that in the Pitcher is his only who drew it out? His *labour* hath taken it out of the hands of Nature, where it was common, and belong'd equally to all her Children, and *hath* thereby *appropriated* it to himself.

30.   Thus this Law of reason makes the Deer, that *Indian's* who hath killed it; 'tis allowed to be his goods who hath bestowed his labour upon it, though before, it was the common right of every one. And amongst those who are counted the Civiliz'd part of Mankind, who have made and multiplied positive Laws to determine Property, this original Law of Nature for the *beginning of Property*, in what was before common, still takes place; and by vertue thereof, what Fish any one catches in the Ocean, that great and still remaining Common of Mankind; or what Ambergriese any one takes up here, is *by* the *Labour* that removes it out of that common state Nature left it in, *made* his *Property* who takes that pains about it. And even amongst us the Hare that any one is Hunting, is thought his who pursues her during the Chase. For being a Beast that is still looked upon as common, and no Man's private Possession; whoever has imploy'd so much *labour* about any of that kind, as to find and pursue her, has thereby removed her from the state of Nature, wherein she was common, and hath *begun a Property*.

31.   It will perhaps be objected to this, That if gathering the Acorns, or other Fruits of the Earth, &c. makes a right to them, then any one may *ingross* as much as he will. To which I Answer, Not so. The same Law of Nature, that does by this means give us Property, does also *bound* that *Property* too. *God has given us all things richly*, 1 Tim. vi. 17. is the Voice of Reason confirmed by Inspiration. But how far has he given it us? *To enjoy.* As much as any one can make use of to any advantage of life before it spoils; so much he may by his labour fix a Property in. Whatever is beyond this, is more than his share, and belongs to others. Nothing was made by God for Man to spoil or destroy. And thus considering the plenty of natural Provisions there was a long time in the World, and the few spenders, and to how small a part of that provision the industry of one Man could extend it self, and ingross it to the prejudice of others; especially keeping within the *bounds*, set by reason of what might serve for his *use*; there could be then little room for Quarrels or Contentions about Property so establish'd.

32.   But the *chief matter of Property* being now not the Fruits of the Earth, and the Beasts that subsist on it, but the *Earth it self*; as that which takes in and carries with it all the rest: I think it is plain, that *Property* in that too is acquired as the former. *As much Land* as a Man Tills, Plants, Improves, Cultivates, and can use the Product of, so much is his *Property*. He by his Labour does, as it were, inclose it from the Common. Nor will it invalidate his right to say, Every body else has an equal Title to it; and therefore he cannot appropriate, he cannot inclose, without the Consent of all his Fellow-Commoners, all Mankind. God, when he gave the World in common to all Mankind, commanded Man also to labour, and the penury of his Condition required it of him. God and his Reason commanded him to subdue the Earth, *i.e.* improve it for the benefit of Life, and therein lay out something upon it that was his own, his labour. He that in Obedience to this Command of God, subdued, tilled and sowed any part of it, thereby annexed to it something that was his *Property*, which another had no Title to, nor could without injury take from him.

33. Nor was this *appropriation* of any parcel of *Land*, by improving it, any prejudice to any other Man, since there was still enough, and as good left; and more than the yet unprovided could use. So that in effect, there was never the less left for others because of his inclosure for himself. For he that leaves as much as another can make use of, does as good as take nothing at all. No Body could think himself injur'd by the drinking of another Man, though he took a good Draught, who had a whole River of the same Water left him to quench his thirst. And the Case of Land and Water, where there is enough of both, is perfectly the same.

34. God gave the World to Men in Common; but since he gave it them for their benefit, and the greatest Conveniencies of Life they were capable to draw from it, it cannot be supposed he meant it should always remain common and uncultivated. He gave it to the use of the Industrious and Rational, (and *Labour* was to be *his Title* to it;) not to the Fancy or Covetousness of the Quarrelsom and Contentious. He that had as good left for his Improvement, as was already taken up, needed not complain, ought not to meddle with what was already improved by another's Labour: If he did, 'tis plain he desired the benefit of another's Pains, which he had no right to, and not the Ground which God had given him in common with others to labour on, and whereof there was as good left, as that already possessed, and more than he knew what to do with, or his Industry could reach to.

35. 'Tis true, in *Land* that is *common* in *England*, or any other Country, where there is Plenty of People under Government, who have Money and Commerce, no one can inclose or appropriate any part, without the consent of all his Fellow-Commoners: Because this is left common by Compact, *i.e.* by the Law of the Land, which is not to be violated. And though it be Common, in respect of some Men, it is not so to all Mankind; but is the joint property of this Country, or this Parish. Besides, the remainder, after such inclosure, would not be as good to the rest of the Commoners as the whole was, when they could all make use of the whole: whereas in the beginning and first peopling of the great Common of the World, it was quite otherwise. The Law Man was under, was rather for *appropriating*. God Commanded, and his Wants forced him to *labour*. That was his *Property* which could not be taken from him where-ever he had fixed it. And hence subduing or cultivating the Earth, and having Dominion, we see are joyned together. The one gave Title to the other. So that God, by commanding to subdue, gave Authority so far to *appropriate*. And the Condition of Humane Life, which requires Labour and Materials to work on, necessarily introduces *private Possessions*.

36. The measure of Property, Nature has well set, by the Extent of Mens *Labour, and the Conveniency of Life*: No Mans Labour could subdue, or appropriate all: nor could his Enjoyment consume more than a small part; so that it was impossible for any Man, this way, to intrench upon the right of another, or acquire, to himself, a Property, to the Prejudice of his Neighbour, who would still have room, for as good, and as large a Possession (after the other had taken out his) as before it was appropriated. This *measure* did confine every Man's

Possession, to a very moderate Proportion, and such as he might appropriate to himself, without Injury to any Body in the first Ages of the World, when Men were more in danger to be lost, by wandering from their Company, in the then vast Wilderness of the Earth, than to be straitned for want of room to plant in. And the same *measure* may be allowed still, without prejudice to any Body, as full as the World seems. For supposing a Man, or Family, in the state they were, at first peopling of the World by the Children of *Adam*, or *Noah*; let him plant in some in-land, vacant places of *America*, we shall find that the *Possessions* he could make himself upon the *measures* we have given, would not be very large, nor, even to this day, prejudice the rest of Mankind, or give them reason to complain, or think themselves injured by this Man's Incroachment, though the Race of Men have now spread themselves to all the corners of the World, and do infinitely exceed the small number [which] was at the beginning. Nay, the extent of *Ground* is of so little value, *without labour*, that I have heard it affirmed, that in *Spain* it self, a Man may be permitted to plough, sow, and reap, without being disturbed, upon Land he has no other Title to, but only his making use of it. But, on the contrary, the Inhabitants think themselves beholden to him, who, by his Industry on neglected, and consequently waste Land, has increased the stock of Corn, which they wanted. But be this as it will, which I lay no stress on; This I dare boldly affirm, That the same *Rule of Propriety*, (*viz.*) that every Man should have as much as he could make use of, would hold still in the World, without straitning any body, since there is Land enough in the World to suffice double the Inhabitants had not the *Invention of Money*, and the tacit Agreement of Men to put a value on it, introduced (by Consent) larger Possessions, and a Right to them; which, how it has done, I shall, by and by, shew more at large.

37.   This is certain, That in the beginning, before the desire of having more than Men needed, had altered the intrinsick value of things, which depends only on their usefulness to the Life of Man; or [Men] had *agreed, that a little piece of yellow Metal*, which would keep without wasting or decay, should be worth a great piece of Flesh, or a whole heap of Corn; though Men had a Right to appropriate, by their Labour, each one to himself, as much of the things of Nature, as he could use: Yet this could not be much, nor to the Prejudice of others, where the same plenty was still left, to those who would use the same Industry. To which let me add, that he who appropriates land to himself by his labour, does not lessen but increase the common stock of mankind. For the provisions serving to the support of humane life, produced by one acre of inclosed and cultivated land, are (to speak much within compasse) ten times more, than those, which are yielded by an acre of Land, of an equal richnesse, lyeing wast in common. And therefor he, that incloses Land and has a greater plenty of the conveniencys of life from ten acres, than he could have from an hundred left to Nature, may truly be said, to give ninety acres to Mankind. For his labour now supplys him with provisions out of ten acres, which were but the product of an hundred lying in common. I have here rated the improved land very low in making its product but as ten to one, when it is much nearer

an hundred to one. For I aske whether in the wild woods and uncultivated wast of America left to Nature, without any improvement, tillage or husbandry, a thousand acres will yield the needy and wretched inhabitants as many conveniencies of life as ten acres of equally fertile land doe in Devonshire where they are well cultivated?

Before the Appropriation of Land, he who gathered as much of the wild Fruit, killed, caught, or tamed, as many of the Beasts as he could; he that so employed his Pains about any of the spontaneous Products of Nature, as any way to alter them, from the state which Nature put them in, *by* placing any of his *Labour* on them, did thereby *acquire a Propriety in them*: But if they perished, in his Possession, without their due use; if the Fruits rotted, or the Venison putrified, before he could spend it, he offended against the common Law of Nature, and was liable to be punished; he invaded his Neighbour's share, for he had *no Right, farther than his Use* called for any of them, and they might serve to afford him Conveniencies of Life.

38. The same *measures* governed the *Possession of Land* too: Whatsoever he tilled and reaped, laid up and made use of, before it spoiled, that was his peculiar Right; whatsoever he enclosed, and could feed, and make use of, the Cattle and Product was also his. But if either the Grass of his Inclosure rotted on the Ground, or the Fruit of his planting perished without gathering, and laying up, this part of the Earth, notwithstanding his Inclosure, was still to be looked on as Waste, and might be the Possession of any other. Thus, at the beginning, *Cain* might take as much Ground as he could till, and make it his own Land, and yet leave enough to *Abel's* Sheep to feed on; a few Acres would serve for both their Possessions. But as Families increased, and Industry inlarged their Stocks, their *Possessions inlarged* with the need of them; but yet it was commonly *without any fixed property in the ground* they made use of, till they incorporated, settled themselves together, and built Cities, and then, by consent, they came in time, to set out the *bounds of their distinct Territories*, and agree on limits between them and their Neighbours, and by Laws within themselves, settled the *Properties* of those of the same Society. For we see, that in that part of the World which was first inhabited, and therefore like to be best peopled, even as low down as *Abraham's* time, they wandred with their Flocks, and their Herds, which was their substance, freely up and down; and this *Abraham* did, in a Country where he was a Stranger. Whence it is plain, that at least, a great part of the *Land lay in common*; that the Inhabitants valued it not, nor claimed Property in any more than they made use of. But when there was not room enough in the same place, for their Herds to feed together, they, by consent, as *Abraham* and *Lot* did, *Gen.* xiii. 5. separated and inlarged their pasture, where it best liked them. And for the same Reason *Esau* went from his Father, and his Brother, and planted in *Mount Seir*, Gen. xxxvi. 6.

39. And thus, without supposing any private Dominion, and property in *Adam*, over all the World, exclusive of all other Men, which can no way be proved, nor any ones Property be made out from it; but supposing the *World* given as it was to the Children of Men *in common*, we see how *labour* could make Men distinct titles to several parcels of it, for their private uses; wherein there could be no doubt of Right, no room for quarrel.

40.   Nor is it so strange, as perhaps before consideration it may appear, that the *Property of labour* should be able to over-ballance the Community of Land. For 'tis *Labour* indeed that *puts the difference of value* on every thing; and let any one consider, what the difference is between an Acre of Land planted with Tobacco, or Sugar, sown with Wheat or Barley; and an Acre of the same Land lying in common, without any Husbandry upon it, and he will find, that the improvement of *labour makes* the far greater part of *the value*. I think it will be but a very modest Computation to say, that of the *Products* of the Earth useful to the Life of Man $\frac{9}{10}$ are the *effects of labour*: nay, if we will rightly estimate things as they come to our use, and cast up the several Expences about them, what in them is purely owing to *Nature*, and what to *labour*, we shall find, that in most of them $\frac{99}{100}$ are wholly to be put on the account of *labour*.

41.   There cannot be a clearer demonstration of any thing, than several Nations of the *Americans* are of this, who are rich in Land, and poor in all the Comforts of Life; whom Nature having furnished as liberally as any other people, with the materials of Plenty, *i.e.* a fruitful Soil, apt to produce in abundance, what might serve for food, rayment, and delight; yet for want of improving it by labour, have not one hundreth part of the Conveniencies we enjoy: And a King of a large and fruitful Territory there feeds, lodges, and is clad worse than a day Labourer in *England*.

42.   To make this a little clearer, let us but trace some of the ordinary provisions of Life, through their several progresses, before they come to our use, and see how much they receive of their *value from Humane Industry*. Bread, Wine and Cloth, are things of daily use, and great plenty, yet notwithstanding, Acorns, Water, and Leaves, or Skins, must be our Bread, Drink and Clothing, did not *labour* furnish us with these more useful Commodities. For whatever *Bread* is more worth than Acorns, *Wine* than Water, and *Cloth* or *Silk* than Leaves, Skins, or Moss, that is wholly *owing to labour* and industry. The one of these being the Food and Rayment which unassisted Nature furnishes us with; the other provisions which our industry and pains prepare for us, which how much they exceed the other in value, when any one hath computed, he will then see, how much *labour makes the far greatest part of the value* of things, we enjoy in this World: And the ground which produces the materials, is scarce to be reckon'd in, as any, or at most, but a very small, part of it; So little, that even amongst us, Land that is left wholly to Nature, that hath no improvement of Pasturage, Tillage, or Planting, is called, as indeed it is, *wast*; and we shall find the benefit of it amount to little more than nothing. This shews, how much numbers of men are to be preferd to largenesse of dominions, and that the increase of lands and the right imploying of them is the great art of government. And that Prince who shall be so wise and godlike as by established laws of liberty to secure protection and incouragement to the honest industry of Mankind against the oppression of power and narrownesse of Party will quickly be too hard for his neighbours. But this bye the bye. To return to the argument in hand.

43.   An Acre of Land that bears here Twenty Bushels of Wheat, and another in *America*, which, with the same Husbandry, would do the like, are, without doubt, of the same natural, intrinsick Value. But yet the Benefit Mankind receives from the one, in a Year, is worth 5 *l.* and from the other possibly not worth a Penny, if all the Profit an *Indian* received from it were to be valued, and sold here; at least, I may truly say, not $\frac{1}{1000}$. 'Tis *Labour* then which *puts the greatest part of Value upon Land*, without which it would scarcely be worth any thing: 'tis to that we owe the greatest part of all its useful Products: for all that the Straw, Bran, Bread, of that Acre of Wheat, is more worth than the Product of an Acre of as good Land, which lies wast, is all the Effect of Labour. For 'tis not barely the Plough-man's Pains, the Reaper's and Thresher's Toil, and the Bakers Sweat, is to be counted into the *Bread* we eat; the Labour of those who broke the Oxen, who digged and wrought the Iron and Stones, who felled and framed the Timber imployed about the Plough, Mill, Oven, or any other Utensils, which are a vast Number, requisite to this Corn, from its being seed to be sown to its being made Bread, must all be *charged on* the account of *Labour*, and received as an effect of that: Nature and the Earth furnished only the almost worthless Materials, as in themselves. 'Twould be a strange *Catalogue of things, that Industry provided and made use of, about every Loaf of Bread*, before it came to our use, if we could trace them; Iron, Wood, Leather, Bark, Timber, Stone, Bricks, Coals, Lime, Cloth, Dying-Drugs, Pitch, Tar, Masts, Ropes, and all the Materials made use of in the Ship, that brought any of the Commodities made use of by any of the Workmen, to any part of the Work, all which, 'twould be almost impossible, at least too long, to reckon up.

44.   From all which it is evident, that though the things of Nature are given in common, yet Man (by being Master of himself, and *Proprietor of his own Person*, and the Actions or *Labour* of it) had still in himself *the great Foundation of Property*; and that which made up the great part of what he applyed to the Support or Comfort of his being, when Invention and Arts had improved the conveniencies of Life, was perfectly his own, and did not belong in common to others.

45.   Thus *Labour*, in the Beginning, *gave a Right of Property*, where-ever any one was pleased to imploy it, upon what was common, which remained, a long while, the far greater part, and is yet more than Mankind makes use of. Men, at first, for the most part, contented themselves with what un-assisted Nature offered to their Necessities: and though afterwards, in some parts of the World, (where the Increase of People and Stock, with the *Use of Money*) had made Land scarce, and so of some Value, the several *Communities* settled the Bounds of their distinct Territories, and by Laws within themselves, regulated the Properties of the private Men of their Society, and so, *by Compact* and Agreement, *settled the Property* which Labour and Industry began; and the Leagues that have been made between several States and Kingdoms, either expressly or tacitly disowning all Claim and Right to the Land in the others Possession, have, by common Consent, given up their Pretences to their natural common

Right, which originally they had to those Countries, and so have, by *positive agreement, settled a Property* amongst themselves, in distinct Parts and parcels of the Earth: yet there are still *great Tracts of Ground* to be found, which (the Inhabitants thereof not having joyned with the rest of Mankind, in the consent of the Use of their common Money) *lie waste*, and are more than the People, who dwell on it, do, or can make use of, and so still lie in common. Tho' this can scarce happen amongst that part of Mankind, that have consented to the Use of Money.

46. The greatest part of *things really useful* to the Life of Man, and such as the necessity of subsisting made the first Commoners of the World look after, as it doth the *Americans* now, *are* generally things *of short duration*; such as, if they are not consumed by use, will decay and perish of themselves: Gold, Silver, and Diamonds, are things, that Fancy or Agreement hath put the Value on, more then real Use, and the necessary Support of Life. Now of those good things which Nature hath provided in common, every one had a Right (as hath been said) to as much as he could use, and had a Property in all that he could affect with his Labour: all that his Industry could extend to, to alter from the State Nature had put it in, was his. He that *gathered* a Hundred Bushels of Acorns or Apples, had thereby a *Property* in them; they were his Goods as soon as gathered. He was only to look that he used them before they spoiled; else he took more then his share, and robb'd others. And indeed it was a foolish thing, as well as dishonest, to hoard up more than he could make use of. If he gave away a part to any body else, so that it perished not uselesly in his Possession, these he also made use of. And if he also bartered away Plumbs that would have rotted in a Week, for Nuts that would last good for his eating a whole Year, he did no injury; he wasted not the common Stock; destroyed no part of the portion of Goods that belonged to others, so long as nothing perished uselesly in his hands. Again, if he would give his Nuts for a piece of Metal, pleased with its colour; or exchange his Sheep for Shells, or Wool for a sparkling Pebble or a Diamond, and keep those by him all his Life, he invaded not the Right of others, he might heap up as much of these durable things as he pleased; the *exceeding of the bounds of his* just *Property* not lying in the largeness of his Possession, but the perishing of any thing uselesly in it.

47. And thus *came in the use of Money*, some lasting thing that Men might keep without spoiling, and that by mutual consent Men would take in exchange for the truly useful, but perishable Supports of Life.

48. And as different degrees of Industry were apt to give Men Possessions in different Proportions, so this *Invention of Money* gave them the opportunity to continue and enlarge them. For supposing an Island, separate from all possible Commerce with the rest of the World, wherein there were but a hundred Families, but there were Sheep, Horses and Cows, with other useful Animals, wholsome Fruits, and Land enough for Corn for a hundred thousand times as many, but nothing in the Island, either because of its Commonness, or Perishableness, fit to supply the place of *Money*: What reason could any one have there to enlarge his Possessions beyond the use of his Family, and a

plentiful supply to its Consumption, either in what their own Industry produced, or they could barter for like perishable, useful Commodities, with
others? Where there is not something both lasting and scarce, and so valuable
to be hoarded up, there Men will not be apt to enlarge their *Possessions of Land*,
were it never so rich, never so free for them to take. For I ask, What would a
Man value Ten Thousand, or an Hundred Thousand Acres of excellent *Land*,
ready cultivated, and well stocked too with Cattle, in the middle of the in-land
Parts of *America*, where he had no hopes of Commerce with other Parts of the
World, to draw *Money* to him by the Sale of the Product? It would not be worth
the inclosing, and we should see him give up again to the wild Common of
Nature, whatever was more than would supply the Conveniencies of Life to be
had there for him and his Family.

49.   Thus in the beginning all the World was *America*, and more so than that
is now; for no such thing as *Money* was any where known. Find out something
that hath the *Use and Value of Money* amongst his Neighbours, you shall see the
same Man will begin presently to *enlarge* his *Possessions*.

50.   But since Gold and Silver, being little useful to the Life of Man in
proportion to Food, Rayment, and Carriage, has its *value* only from the consent
of Men, whereof Labour yet makes, in great part, *the measure*, it is plain, that
Men have agreed to disproportionate and unequal Possession of the Earth,
they having by a tacit and voluntary consent found out a way, how a man may
fairly possess more land than he himself can use the product of, by receiving in
exchange for the overplus, Gold and Silver, which may be hoarded up without
injury to any one, these metalls not spoileing or decaying in the hands of the
possessor. This partage of things, in an inequality of private possessions, men
have made practicable out of the bounds of Societie, and without compact,
only by putting a value on gold and silver and tacitly agreeing in the use of
Money. For in Governments the Laws regulate the right of property, and the
possession of land is determined by positive constitutions.

51.   And thus, I think, it is very easie to conceive without any difficulty, *how
Labour could at first begin a title of Property* in the common things of Nature, and
how the spending it upon our uses bounded it. So that there could then be no
reason of quarrelling about Title, nor any doubt about the largeness of Possession it gave. Right and conveniency went together; for as a Man had a Right to
all he could imploy his Labour upon, so he had no temptation to labour for
more than he could make use of. This left no room for Controversie about the
Title, nor for Incroachment on the Right of others; what Portion a Man carved
to himself, was easily seen; and it was useless as well as dishonest to carve
himself too much, or take more than he needed.

From the *First Treatise of Government*, Chapter IV

42.   But we know God hath not left one Man so to the Mercy of another, that
he may starve him if he please: God the Lord and Father of all, has given no

one of his Children such a Property, in his peculiar Portion of the things of this World, but that he has given his needy Brother a Right to the Surplusage of his Goods; so that it cannot justly be denied him, when his pressing Wants call for it. And therefore no Man could ever have a just Power over the Life of another, by Right of property in Land or Possessions; since 'twould always be a Sin in any Man of Estate, to let his Brother perish for want of affording him Relief out of his Plenty. As *Justice* gives every Man a Title to the product of his honest Industry, and the fair Acquisitions of his Ancestors descended to him; so *Charity* gives every Man a Title to so much out of another's Plenty, as will keep him from extream want, where he has no means to subsist otherwise; and a Man can no more justly make use of another's necessity, to force him to become his Vassal, by with-holding that Relief, God requires him to afford to the wants of his Brother, than he that has more strength can seize upon a weaker, master him to his Obedience, and with a Dagger at his Throat offer him Death or Slavery.

2

Of Justice

David Hume

Part 1

That justice is useful to society, and consequently that *part* of its merit, at least, must arise from that consideration, it would be a superfluous undertaking to prove. That public utility is the *sole* origin of justice, and that reflections on the beneficial consequences of this virtue are the *sole* foundation of its merit; this proposition, being more curious and important, will better deserve our examination and enquiry.

Let us suppose, that nature has bestowed on the human race such profuse *abundance* of all *external* conveniencies, that, without any uncertainty in the event, without any care or industry on our part, every individual finds himself fully provided with whatever his most voracious appetites can want, or luxurious imagination wish or desire. His natural beauty, we shall suppose, surpasses all acquired ornaments: The perpetual clemency of the seasons renders useless all cloaths or covering: The raw herbage affords him the most delicious fare; the clear fountain, the richest beverage. No laborious occupation required: No tillage: No navigation. Music, poetry, and contemplation form his sole business: Conversation, mirth, and friendship his sole amusement.

It seems evident, that, in such a happy state, every other social virtue would flourish, and receive tenfold encrease; but the cautious, jealous virtue of justice would never once have been dreamed of. For what purpose make a partition of goods, where every one has already more than enough? Why give rise to property, where there cannot possibly be any injury? Why call this object *mine*, when, upon the seizing of it by another, I need but stretch out my hand

David Hume, 'Of Justice', (section 3) from *An Enquiry Concerning the Principles of Morals*, ed. T. Beauchamp (Oxford: Oxford University Press, 1998), pp. 13–27; the second footnote has been omitted after the first two sentences.

to possess myself of what is equally valuable? Justice, in that case, being totally USELESS, would be an idle ceremonial, and could never possibly have place in the catalogue of virtues.

We see, even in the present necessitous condition of mankind, that, wherever any benefit is bestowed by nature in an unlimited abundance, we leave it always in common among the whole human race, and make no subdivisions of right and property. Water and air, though the most necessary of all objects, are not challenged as the property of individuals; nor can any man commit injustice by the most lavish use and enjoyment of these blessings. In fertile extensive countries, with few inhabitants, land is regarded on the same footing. And no topic is so much insisted on by those, who defend the liberty of the seas, as the unexhausted use of them in navigation. Were the advantages, procured by navigation, as inexhaustible, these reasoners had never had any adversaries to refute; nor had any claims ever been advanced of a separate, exclusive dominion over the ocean.

It may happen, in some countries, at some periods, that there be established a property in water, none in land;[1] if the latter be in greater abundance than can be used by the inhabitants, and the former be found, with difficulty, and in very small quantities.

Again; suppose, that, though the necessities of human race continue the same as at present, yet the mind is so enlarged, and so replete with friendship and generosity, that every man has the utmost tenderness for every man, and feels no more concern for his own interest than for that of his fellows: It seems evident, that the USE of justice would, in this case, be suspended by such an extensive benevolence, nor would the divisions and barriers of property and obligation have ever been thought of. Why should I bind another, by a deed or promise, to do me any good office, when I know that he is already prompted, by the strongest inclination, to seek my happiness, and would, of himself, perform the desired service; except the hurt, he thereby receives, be greater than the benefit accruing to me? In which case, he knows, that, from my innate humanity and friendship, I should be the first to oppose myself to his imprudent generosity. Why raise land-marks between my neighbour's field and mine, when my heart has made no division between our interests; but shares all his joys and sorrows with the same force and vivacity as if originally my own? Every man, upon this supposition, being a second self to another, would trust all his interests to the discretion of every man; without jealousy, without partition, without distinction. And the whole human race would form only one family; where all would lie in common, and be used freely, without regard to property; but cautiously too, with as entire regard to the necessities of each individual, as if our own interests were most intimately concerned.

In the present disposition of the human heart, it would, perhaps, be difficult to find compleat instances of such enlarged affections; but still we may observe, that the case of families approaches towards it; and the stronger the mutual benevolence is among the individuals, the nearer it approaches; till all distinction of property be, in a great measure, lost and confounded among them. Between married persons, the cement of friendship is by the laws supposed so strong as to abolish all division of possessions; and has often, in reality, the force ascribed to it. And it is observable, that, during the ardour of new enthusiasms, when every principle is enflamed into extravagance, the community of goods has frequently been attempted; and nothing but experience of its inconveniencies, from the returning or disguised selfishness of men, could make the imprudent fanatics adopt anew the ideas of justice and of separate property. So true is it, that this virtue derives its existence entirely from its necessary *use* to the intercourse and social state of mankind.

To make this truth more evident, let us reverse the foregoing suppositions; and carrying every thing to the opposite extreme, consider what would be the effect of these new situations. Suppose a society to fall into such want of all common necessaries, that the utmost frugality and industry cannot preserve the greater number from perishing, and the whole from extreme misery: It will readily, I believe, be admitted, that the strict laws of justice are suspended, in such a pressing emergence, and give place to the stronger motives of necessity and self-preservation. Is it any crime, after a shipwreck, to seize whatever means or instrument of safety one can lay hold of, without regard to former limitations of property? Or if a city besieged were perishing with hunger; can we imagine, that men will see any means of preservation before them, and lose their lives, from a scrupulous regard to what, in other situations, would be the rules of equity and justice? The USE and TENDENCY of that virtue is to procure happiness and security, by preserving order in society: But where the society is ready to perish from extreme necessity, no greater evil can be dreaded from violence and injustice; and every man may now provide for himself by all the means, which prudence can dictate, or humanity permit. The public, even in less urgent necessities, opens granaries, without the consent of proprietors; as justly supposing, that the authority of magistracy may, consistent with equity, extend so far: But were any number of men to assemble, without the tye of laws or civil jurisdiction; would an equal partition of bread in a famine, though effected by power and even violence, be regarded as criminal or injurious?

Suppose likewise, that it should be a virtuous man's fate to fall into the society of ruffians, remote from the protection of laws and government; what conduct must he embrace in that melancholy situation? He sees such a desperate rapaciousness prevail; such a disregard to equity, such contempt of order, such stupid blindness to future consequences, as must immediately have the most tragical conclusion, and must terminate in destruction to the greater number, and in a total dissolution of society to the rest. He, mean while, can have no other expedient than to arm himself, to whomever the sword he seizes, or the buckler, may belong: To make provision of all means of defence and security: And his particular regard to justice being no longer of USE to his own safety or that of others, he must consult the dictates of self-preservation alone, without concern for those who no longer merit his care and attention.

When any man, even in political society, renders himself, by his crimes, obnoxious to the public, he is punished by the laws in his goods and person;

that is, the ordinary rules of justice are, with regard to him, suspended for a moment, and it becomes equitable to inflict on him, for the *benefit* of society, what, otherwise, he could not suffer without wrong or injury.

The rage and violence of public war; what is it but a suspension of justice among the warring parties, who perceive, that this virtue is now no longer of any *use* or advantage to them? The laws of war, which then succeed to those of equity and justice, are rules calculated for the *advantage* and *utility* of that particular state, in which men are now placed. And were a civilized nation engaged with barbarians, who observed no rules even of war; the former must also suspend their observance of them, where they no longer serve to any purpose; and must render every action or rencounter as bloody and pernicious as possible to the first aggressors.

Thus, the rules of equity or justice depend entirely on the particular state and condition, in which men are placed, and owe their origin and existence to that UTILITY, which results to the public from their strict and regular observance. Reverse, in any considerable circumstance, the condition of men: Produce extreme abundance or extreme necessity: Implant in the human breast perfect moderation and humanity, or perfect rapaciousness and malice: By rendering justice totally *useless*, you thereby totally destroy its essence, and suspend its obligation upon mankind.

The common situation of society is a medium amidst all these extremes. We are naturally partial to ourselves, and to our friends; but are capable of learning the advantage resulting from a more equitable conduct. Few enjoyments are given us from the open and liberal hand of nature; but by art, labour, and industry, we can extract them in great abundance. Hence the ideas of property become necessary in all civil society: Hence justice derives its usefulness to the public: And hence alone arises its merit and moral obligation.

These conclusions are so natural and obvious, that they have not escaped even the poets, in their descriptions of the felicity, attending the golden age or the reign of SATURN. The seasons, in that first period of nature, were so temperate, if we credit these agreeable fictions, that there was no necessity for men to provide themselves with cloaths and houses, as a security against the violence of heat and cold: The rivers flowed with wine and milk: The oaks yielded honey; and nature spontaneously produced her greatest delicacies. Nor were these the chief advantages of that happy age. Tempests were not alone removed from nature; but those more furious tempests were unknown to human breasts, which now cause such uproar, and engender such confusion. Avarice, ambition, cruelty, selfishness, were never heard of: Cordial affection, compassion, sympathy, were the only movements with which the mind was yet acquainted. Even the punctilious distinction of *mine* and *thine* was banished from among that happy race of mortals, and carried with it the very notion of property and obligation, justice and injustice.

This *poetical* fiction of the *golden age* is, in some respects, of a piece with the *philosophical* fiction of the *state of nature*; only that the former is represented as the most charming and most peaceable condition, which can possibly be imagined; whereas the latter is painted out as a state of mutual war and violence, attended with the most extreme necessity. On the first origin of mankind, we are told, their ignorance and savage nature were so prevalent, that they could give no mutual trust, but must each depend upon himself, and his own force or cunning for protection and security. No law was heard of: No rule of justice known: No distinction of property regarded: Power was the only measure of right; and a perpetual war of all against all was the result of men's untamed selfishness and barbarity.[2]

Whether such a condition of human nature could ever exist, or if it did, could continue so long as to merit the appellation of a *state*, may justly be doubted. Men are necessarily born in a family-society, at least; and are trained up by their parents to some rule of conduct and behaviour. But this must be admitted, that, if such a state of mutual war and violence was ever real, the suspension of all laws of justice, from their absolute inutility, is a necessary and infallible consequence.

The more we vary our views of human life, and the newer and more unusual the lights are, in which we survey it, the more shall we be convinced, that the origin here assigned for the virtue of justice is real and satisfactory.

Were there a species of creatures, intermingled with men, which, though rational, were possessed of such inferior strength, both of body and mind, that they were incapable of all resistance, and could never, upon the highest provocation, make us feel the effects of their resentment; the necessary consequence, I think, is, that we should be bound, by the laws of humanity, to give gentle usage to these creatures, but should not, properly speaking, lie under any restraint of justice with regard to them, nor could they possess any right or property, exclusive of such arbitrary lords. Our intercourse with them could not be called society, which supposes a degree of equality; but absolute command on the one side, and servile obedience on the other. Whatever we covet, they must instantly resign: Our permission is the only tenure, by which they hold their possessions: Our compassion and kindness the only check, by which they curb our lawless will: And as no inconvenience ever results from the exercise of a power, so firmly established in nature, the restraints of justice and property, being totally *useless*, would never have place in so unequal a confederacy.

This is plainly the situation of men, with regard to animals; and how far these may be said to possess reason, I leave it to others to determine. The great superiority of civilized EUROPEANS above barbarous INDIANS, tempted us to imagine ourselves on the same footing with regard to them, and made us throw off all restraints of justice, and even of humanity, in our treatment of them. In many nations, the female sex are reduced to like slavery, and are rendered incapable of all property, in opposition to their lordly masters. But though the males, when united, have, in all countries, bodily force sufficient to maintain this severe tyranny; yet such are the insinuation, address, and charms of their fair companions, that women are commonly able to break the confederacy, and share with the other sex in all the rights and privileges of society.

Were the human species so framed by nature as that each individual possessed within himself every faculty, requisite both for his own preservation
and for the propagation of his kind: Were all society and intercourse cut off
between man and man, by the primary intention of the Supreme Creator: It
seems evident, that so solitary a being would be as much incapable of justice,
as of social discourse and conversation. Where mutual regards and forbear-
ance serve to no manner of purpose, they would never direct the conduct of
any reasonable man. The headlong course of the passions would be checked by
no reflection on future consequences. And as each man is here supposed to
love himself alone, and to depend only on himself and his own activity for
safety and happiness, he would, on every occasion, to the utmost of his power,
challenge the preference above every other being, to none of which he is bound
by any ties, either of nature or of interest.

But suppose the conjunction of the sexes to be established in nature,
a family immediately arises; and particular rules being found requisite for
its subsistence, these are immediately embraced; though without comprehend-
ing the rest of mankind within their prescriptions. Suppose, that several
families unite together into one society, which is totally disjoined from all
others, the rules, which preserve peace and order, enlarge themselves to
the utmost extent of that society; but becoming then entirely useless, lose
their force when carried one step farther. But again suppose, that several
distinct societies maintain a kind of intercourse for mutual convenience and
advantage, the boundaries of justice still grow larger, in proportion to
the largeness of men's views, and the force of their mutual connexions.
History, experience, reason sufficiently instruct us in this natural progress
of human sentiments, and in the gradual enlargement of our regards to
justice, in proportion as we become acquainted with the extensive utility of
that virtue.

Part 2

If we examine the *particular* laws, by which justice is directed, and property
determined; we shall still be presented with the same conclusion. The good of
mankind is the only object of all these laws and regulations. Not only it is
requisite, for the peace and interest of society, that men's possessions should
be separated; but the rules, which we follow, in making the separation, are
such as can best be contrived to serve farther the interests of society.

We shall suppose, that a creature, possessed of reason, but unacquainted
with human nature, deliberates with himself what RULES of justice or property
would best promote public interest, and establish peace and security among
mankind: His most obvious thought would be, to assign the largest possessions to the most extensive virtue, and give every one the power of doing good,
proportioned to his inclination. In a perfect theocracy, where a being, infinitely
intelligent, governs by particular volitions, this rule would certainly have

place, and might serve to the wisest purposes: But were mankind to execute such a law; so great is the uncertainty of merit, both from its natural obscurity, and from the self-conceit of each individual, that no determinate rule of conduct would ever result from it; and the total dissolution of society must be the immediate consequence. Fanatics may suppose, *that dominion is founded on grace*, and *that saints alone inherit the earth*; but the civil magistrate very justly puts these sublime theorists on the same footing with common robbers, and teaches them by the severest discipline, that a rule, which, in speculation, may seem the most advantageous to society, may yet be found, in practice, totally pernicious and destructive.

That there were *religious* fanatics of this kind in ENGLAND, during the civil wars, we learn from history; though it is probable, that the obvious *tendency* of these principles excited such horror in mankind, as soon obliged the danger-ous enthusiasts to renounce, or at least conceal their tenets. Perhaps, the *levellers*, who claimed an equal distribution of property, were a kind of *political* fanatics, which arose from the religious species, and more openly avowed their pretensions; as carrying a more plausible appearance, of being practicable in themselves, as well as useful to human society.

It must, indeed, be confessed, that nature is so liberal to mankind, that, were all her presents equally divided among the species, and improved by art and industry, every individual would enjoy all the necessaries, and even most of the comforts of life; nor would ever be liable to any ills, but such as might accidentally arise from the sickly frame and constitution of his body. It must also be confessed, that, wherever we depart from this equality, we rob the poor of more satisfaction than we add to the rich, and that the slight gratification of a frivolous vanity, in one individual, frequently costs more than bread to many families, and even provinces. It may appear withal, that the rule of equality, as it would be highly *useful*, is not altogether *impracticable*; but has taken place, at least in an imperfect degree, in some republics; particularly that of SPARTA; where it was attended, it is said, with the most beneficial consequences. Not to mention, that the AGRARIAN laws, so frequently claimed in ROME, and carried into execution in many GREEK cities, proceeded, all of them, from a general idea of the utility of this principle.

But historians, and even common sense, may inform us, that, however specious these ideas of *perfect* equality may seem, they are really, at bottom, *impracticable*; and were they not so, would be extremely *pernicious* to human society. Render possessions ever so equal, men's different degrees of art, care, and industry will immediately break that equality. Or if you check these virtues, you reduce society to the most extreme indigence; and instead of preventing want and beggary in a few, render it unavoidable to the whole community. The most rigorous inquisition too is requisite to watch every inequality on its first appearance; and the most severe jurisdiction, to punish and redress it. But besides, that so much authority must soon degenerate into tyranny, and be exerted with great partialities; who can possibly be possessed of it, in such a situation as is here supposed? Perfect equality of possessions, destroying all subordination, weakens extremely the authority of magistracy, and must reduce all power nearly to a level, as well as property.

We may conclude, therefore, that, in order to establish laws for the regulation of property, we must be acquainted with the nature and situation of man; must reject appearances, which may be false, though specious; and must search for those rules, which are, on the whole, most *useful* and *beneficial*. Vulgar sense and slight experience are sufficient for this purpose; where men give not way to too selfish avidity, or too extensive enthusiasm.

Who sees not, for instance, that whatever is produced or improved by a man's art or industry ought, for ever, to be secured to him, in order to give encouragement to such *useful* habits and accomplishments? That the property ought also to descend to children and relations, for the same *useful* purpose? That it may be alienated by consent, in order to beget that commerce and intercourse, which is so *beneficial* to human society? And that all contracts and promises ought carefully to be fulfilled, in order to secure mutual trust and confidence, by which the general *interest* of mankind is so much promoted?

Examine the writers on the laws of nature; and you will always find, that, whatever principles they set out with, they are sure to terminate here at last, and to assign, as the ultimate reason for every rule which they establish, the convenience and necessities of mankind. A concession thus extorted, in opposition to systems, has more authority, than if it had been made in prosecution of them.

What other reason, indeed, could writers ever give, why this must be *mine* and that *yours*; since uninstructed nature, surely, never made any such distinction? The objects, which receive those appellations, are, of themselves, foreign to us; they are totally disjoined and separated from us; and nothing but the general interests of society can form the connexion.

Sometimes, the interests of society may require a rule of justice in a particular case; but may not determine any particular rule, among several, which are all equally beneficial. In that case, the slightest *analogies* are laid hold of, in order to prevent that indifference and ambiguity, which would be the source of perpetual dissention. Thus possession alone, and first possession, is supposed to convey property, where no body else has any preceding claim and pretension. Many of the reasonings of lawyers are of this analogical nature, and depend on very slight connexions of the imagination.

Does any one scruple, in extraordinary cases, to violate all regard to the private property of individuals, and sacrifice to public interest a distinction, which had been established for the sake of that interest? The safety of the people is the supreme law: All other particular laws are subordinate to it, and dependent on it: And if, in the *common* course of things, they be followed and regarded; it is only because the public safety and interest *commonly* demand so equal and impartial an administration.

Sometimes both *utility* and *analogy* fail, and leave the laws of justice in total uncertainty. Thus, it is highly requisite, that prescription or long possession should convey property; but what number of days or months or years should be sufficient for that purpose, it is impossible for reason alone to determine. *Civil laws* here supply the place of the natural *code*, and assign different terms for prescription, according to the different *utilities*, proposed by the legislator. Bills of exchange and promissory notes, by the laws of most countries, prescribe sooner than bonds, and mortgages, and contracts of a more formal nature.

In general, we may observe, that all questions of property are subordinate to the authority of civil laws, which extend, restrain, modify, and alter the rules of natural justice, according to the particular *convenience* of each community. The laws have, or ought to have, a constant reference to the constitution of government, the manners, the climate, the religion, the commerce, the situation of each society. A late author of genius, as well as learning, has prosecuted this subject at large, and has established, from these principles, a system of political knowledge, which abounds in ingenious and brilliant thoughts, and is not wanting in solidity.[3]

What is a man's property? Any thing, which it is lawful for him, and for him alone, to use. *But what rule have we, by which we can distinguish these objects?* Here we must have recourse to statutes, customs, precedents, analogies, and a hundred other circumstances; some of which are constant and inflexible, some variable and arbitrary. But the ultimate point, in which they all professedly terminate, is, the interest and happiness of human society. Where this enters not into consideration, nothing can appear more whimsical, unnatural, and even superstitious, than all or most of the laws of justice and of property.

Those, who ridicule vulgar superstitions, and expose the folly of particular regards to meats, days, places, postures, apparel, have an easy task; while they consider all the qualities and relations of the objects, and discover no adequate cause for that affection or antipathy, veneration or horror, which have so mighty an influence over a considerable part of mankind. A SYRIAN would have starved rather than taste pigeon; an EGYPTIAN would not have approached bacon: But if these species of food be examined by the senses of sight, smell, or taste, or scrutinized by the sciences of chymistry, medicine, or physics; no difference is ever found between them and any other species, nor can that precise circumstance be pitched on, which may afford a just foundation for the religious passion. A fowl on Thursday is lawful food; on Friday abominable: Eggs, in this house, and in this diocese, are permitted during Lent; a hundred paces farther, to eat them is a damnable sin. This earth or building, yesterday was profane; to-day, by the muttering of certain words, it has become holy and sacred. Such reflections as these, in the mouth of a philosopher, one may safely say, are too obvious to have any influence; because they must always, to every man, occur at first sight; and where they prevail not, of themselves, they are surely obstructed by education, prejudice, and passion, not by ignorance or mistake.

It may appear to a careless view, or rather, a too abstracted reflection, that there enters a like superstition into all the sentiments of justice; and that, if a man expose its object, or what we call property, to the same scrutiny of sense and science, he will not, by the most accurate enquiry, find any foundation for the difference made by moral sentiment. I may lawfully nourish myself from this tree; but the fruit of another of the same species, ten paces off, it is criminal for me to touch. Had I worne this apparel an hour ago, I had merited the severest punishment; but a man, by pronouncing a few magical syllables, has now rendered it fit for my use and service. Were this house placed in the neighbouring territory, it had been immoral for me to dwell in it; but being built on this side the river, it is subject to a different municipal law, and, by its becoming mine, I incur no blame or censure. The same species of reasoning, it may be thought, which so successfully exposes superstition, is also applicable to justice; nor is it possible, in the one case more than in the other, to point out, in the object, that precise quality or circumstance, which is the foundation of the sentiment.

But there is this material difference between *superstition* and *justice*, that the former is frivolous, useless, and burdensome; the latter is absolutely requisite to the well-being of mankind and existence of society. When we abstract from this circumstance (for it is too apparent ever to be overlooked) it must be confessed, that all regards to right and property, seem entirely without foundation, as much as the grossest and most vulgar superstition. Were the interests of society nowise concerned, it is as unintelligible, why another's articulating certain sounds, implying consent, should change the nature of my actions with regard to a particular object, as why the reciting of a liturgy by a priest, in a certain habit and posture, should dedicate a heap of brick and timber, and render it, thenceforth and for ever, sacred.[4]

These reflections are far from weakening the obligations of justice, or diminishing any thing from the most sacred attention to property. On the contrary, such sentiments must acquire new force from the present reasoning. For what stronger foundation can be desired or conceived for any duty, than to observe, that human society, or even human nature could not subsist, without the establishment of it; and will still arrive at greater degrees of happiness and perfection, the more inviolable the regard is, which is paid to that duty?

The dilemma seems obvious: As justice evidently tends to promote public utility and to support civil society, the sentiment of justice is either derived from our reflecting on that tendency, or like hunger, thirst, and other appetites, resentment, love of life, attachment to offspring, and other passions, arises from a simple original instinct in the human breast, which nature has implanted for like salutary purposes. If the latter be the case, it follows, that property, which is the object of justice, is also distinguished by a simple, original instinct, and is not ascertained by any argument or reflection. But who is there that ever heard of such an instinct? Or is this a subject, in which new discoveries can be made? We may as well expect to discover, in the body, new senses, which had before escaped the observation of all mankind.

But farther, though it seems a very simple proposition to say, that nature, by an instinctive sentiment, distinguishes property, yet in reality we shall find, that there are required for that purpose ten thousand different instincts, and these employed about objects of the greatest intricacy and nicest discernment. For when a definition of *property* is required, that relation is found to resolve itself into any possession acquired by occupation, by industry, by prescription, by inheritance, by contract, &c. Can we think, that nature, by an original instinct, instructs us in all these methods of acquisition?

These words too, *inheritance* and *contract*, stand for ideas infinitely complicated; and to define them exactly, a hundred volumes of laws, and a thousand volumes of commentators, have not been found sufficient. Does nature, whose instincts in men are all simple, embrace such complicated and artificial objects, and create a rational creature, without trusting any thing to the operation of his reason?

But even though all this were admitted, it would not be satisfactory. Positive laws can certainly transfer property. Is it by another original instinct, that we recognize the authority of kings and senates, and mark all the boundaries of their jurisdiction? Judges too, even though their sentence be erroneous and illegal, must be allowed, for the sake of peace and order, to have decisive authority, and ultimately to determine property. Have we original, innate ideas of prætors and chancellors and juries? Who sees not, that all these institutions arise merely from the necessities of human society?

All birds of the same species, in every age and country, build their nests alike: In this we see the force of instinct. Men, in different times and places, frame their houses differently: Here we perceive the influence of reason and custom. A like inference may be drawn from comparing the instinct of generation and the institution of property.

How great soever the variety of municipal laws, it must be confessed, that their chief outlines pretty regularly concur; because the purposes, to which they tend, are every where exactly similar. In like manner, all houses have a roof and walls, windows and chimneys; though diversified in their shape, figure, and materials. The purposes of the latter, directed to the conveniencies of human life, discover not more plainly their origin from reason and reflection, than do those of the former, which point all to a like end.

I need not mention the variations, which all the rules of property receive from the finer turns and connexions of the imagination, and from the subtilties and abstractions of law-topics and reasonings. There is no possibility of reconciling this observation to the notion of original instincts.

What alone will beget a doubt concerning the theory, on which I insist, is the influence of education and acquired habits, by which we are so accustomed to blame injustice, that we are not, in every instance, conscious of any immediate reflection on the pernicious consequences of it. The views the most familiar to us are apt, for that very reason, to escape us; and what we have very frequently performed from certain motives, we are apt likewise to continue mechanically, without recalling, on every occasion, the reflections, which first determined us. The convenience, or rather necessity, which leads to justice, is so universal, and every where points so much to the same rules, that the habit takes place in all societies; and it is not without some scrutiny, that we are able to ascertain its true origin. The matter, however, is not so obscure, but that, even in common life, we have, every moment, recourse to the principle of public utility, and ask, *What must become of the world, if such practices prevail? How could society subsist under such disorders?* Were the distinction or separation of possessions entirely useless, can any one conceive, that it ever should have obtained in society?

Thus we seem, upon the whole, to have attained a knowledge of the force of that principle here insisted on, and can determine what degree of esteem or moral approbation may result from reflections on public interest and utility. The necessity of justice to the support of society is the SOLE foundation of that virtue; and since no moral excellence is more highly esteemed, we may conclude, that this circumstance of usefulness has, in general, the strongest energy, and most entire command over our sentiments. It must, therefore, be the source of a considerable part of the merit ascribed to humanity, benevolence, friendship, public spirit, and other social virtues of that stamp; as it is the SOLE source of the moral approbation paid to fidelity, justice, veracity, integrity, and those other estimable and useful qualities and principles. It is entirely agreeable to the rules of philosophy, and even of common reason; where any principle has been found to have a great force and energy in one instance, to ascribe to it a like energy in all similar instances. This indeed is NEWTON's chief rule of philosophizing.[5]

Notes

1 Genesis, chs. 13 and 21.
2 This fiction of a state of nature, as a state of war, was not first started by Mr. HOBBES, as is commonly imagined. PLATO endeavours to refute an hypothesis very like it in the 2d, 3d, and 4th books de republica. CICERO, on the contrary, supposes it certain and universally acknowledged ...
3 The author of *L'Esprit des Loix*. This illustrious writer, however, sets out with a different theory, and supposes all right to be founded on certain *rapports* or relations; which is a system, that, in my opinion, never will be reconciled with true philosophy. Father MALEBRANCHE, as far as I can learn, was the first that started this abstract theory of morals, which was afterwards adopted by CUDWORTH, CLARKE, and others; and as it excludes all sentiment, and pretends to found every thing on reason, it has not wanted followers in this philosophic age. With regard to justice, the virtue here treated of, the inference against this theory seems short and conclusive. Property is allowed to be dependent on civil laws; civil laws are allowed to have no other object, but the interest of society: This therefore must be allowed to be the sole foundation of property and justice. Not to mention, that our obligation itself to obey the magistrate and his laws is founded on nothing but the interests of society.

   If the ideas of justice, sometimes, do not follow the dispositions of civil law; we shall find, that these cases, instead of objections, are confirmations of the theory delivered above. Where a civil law is so perverse as to cross all the interests of society, it loses all its authority, and men judge by the ideas of natural justice, which are conformable to those interests. Sometimes also civil laws, for useful purposes, require a ceremony or form to any deed; and where that is wanting, their decrees run contrary to the usual tenor of justice; but one who takes advantage of such chicanes, is not commonly regarded as an honest man. Thus, the interests of society require, that contracts be fulfilled; and there is not a more material article either of natural or civil justice: But the omission of a trifling circumstance will often, by law, invalidate a contract, *in foro humano*, but not *in foro conscientiæ*, as divines express themselves. In these cases, the magistrate is supposed only to withdraw his power of enforcing the right, not to have altered the right. Where his intention extends to the right, and is conformable to the interests of society; it never fails to alter the right; a clear proof of the origin of justice and of property, as assigned above.

4   It is evident, that the will or consent alone never transfers property, nor causes the obligation of a promise, (for the same reasoning extends to both) but the will must be expressed by words or signs, in order to impose a tye upon any man. The expression being once brought in as subservient to the will, soon becomes the principal part of the promise; nor will a man be less bound by his word, though he secretly give a different direction to his intention, and with-hold the assent of his mind. But though the expression makes, on most occasions, the whole of the promise, yet it does not always so; and one who should make use of any expression, of which he knows not the meaning, and which he use without any sense of the consequences, would not certainly be bound by it. Nay, though he know its meaning, yet if he use it in jest only, and with such signs as evidently show, that he has no serious intention of binding himself, he would not lie under any obligation of performance; but it is necessary, that the words be a perfect expression of the will, without any contrary signs. Nay, even this we must not carry so far as to imagine, that one, whom, by our quickness of understanding, we conjecture, from certain signs, to have an intention of deceiving us, is not bound by his expression or verbal promise, if we accept of it; but must limit this conclusion to those cases where the signs are of a different nature from those of deceit. All these contradictions are easily accounted for, if justice arise entirely from its usefulness to society; but will never be explained on any other hypothesis.

It is remarkable, that the moral decisions of the JESUITS and other relaxed casuists, were commonly formed in prosecution of some such subtilties of reasoning as are here pointed out, and proceeded as much from the habit of scholastic refinement as from any corruption of the heart, if we may follow the authority of Mons. BAYLE. See his *Dictionary*, article LOYOLA. And why has the indignation of mankind risen so high against these casuists; but because every one perceived, that human society could not subsist were such practices authorized, and that morals must always be handled with a view to public interest, more than philosophical regularity? If the secret direction of the intention, said every man of sense, could invalidate a contract; where is our security? And yet a metaphysical schoolman might think, that, where an intention was supposed to be requisite, if that intention really had not place, no consequence ought to follow, and no obligation be imposed. The casuistical sub-tilties may not be greater than the subtilties of lawyers, hinted at above; but as the former are *pernicious*, and the latter *innocent* and even *necessary*, this is the reason of the very different reception they meet with from the world.

It is a doctrine of the church of ROME, that the priest, by a secret direction of his intention, can invalidate any sacrament. This position is derived from a strict and regular prosecution of the obvious truth, that empty words alone, without any meaning or intention in the speaker, can never be attended with any effect. If the same conclusion be not admitted in reasonings concerning civil contracts, where the affair is allowed to be of so much less consequence than the eternal salvation of thousands, it proceeds entirely from men's sense of the danger and inconvenience of the doctrine in the former case: And we may thence observe, that however positive, arrogant, and dogmatical any superstition may appear, it never can convey any thorough persuasion of the reality of its objects, or put them, in any degree, on a balance with the common incidents of life, which we learn from daily observation and experimental reasoning.

5   Principia, lib. 3.

Part II

Contemporary Theories

3

On Justice as Fairness

John Rawls

I. The Subject of Justice

Many different kinds of things are said to be just and unjust: not only
laws, institutions, and social systems, but also particular actions of many
kinds, including decisions, judgments, and imputations. We also call the
attitudes and dispositions of persons, and persons themselves, just and unjust.
Our topic, however, is that of social justice. For us the primary subject of justice
is the basic structure of society, or more exactly, the way in which the major
social institutions distribute fundamental rights and duties and determine
the division of advantages from social cooperation. By major institutions
I understand the political constitution and the principal economic and social
arrangements. Thus the legal protection of freedom of thought and liberty of
conscience, competitive markets, private property in the means of production,
and the monogamous family are examples of major social institutions. Taken
together as one scheme, the major institutions define men's rights and duties
and influence their life prospects, what they can expect to be and how well
they can hope to do. The basic structure is the primary subject of justice
because its effects are so profound and present from the start. The intuitive
notion here is that this structure contains various social positions and that men
born into different positions have different expectations of life determined,
in part, by the political system as well as by economic and social circumstances. In this way the institutions of society favor certain starting
places over others. These are especially deep inequalities. Not only are they
pervasive, but they affect men's initial chances in life; yet they cannot possibly
be justified by an appeal to the notions of merit or desert. It is these inequalities, presumably inevitable in the basic structure of any society, to which

Extracts from John Rawls, *A Theory of Justice*, revised edition (Cambridge, MA: The
Belknap Press of Harvard University Press, 1999), pp. 6–9, 10–19, 52–8, 61–73, 130–9.

the principles of social justice must in the first instance apply. These principles, then, regulate the choice of a political constitution and the main elements of the economic and social system. The justice of a social scheme depends essentially on how fundamental rights and duties are assigned and on the economic opportunities and social conditions in the various sectors of society.

The scope of our inquiry is limited in two ways. First of all, I am concerned with a special case of the problem of justice. I shall not consider the justice of institutions and social practices generally, nor except in passing the justice of the law of nations and of relations between states. Therefore, if one supposes that the concept of justice applies whenever there is an allotment of something rationally regarded as advantageous or disadvantageous, then we are interested in only one instance of its application. There is no reason to suppose ahead of time that the principles satisfactory for the basic structure hold for all cases. These principles may not work for the rules and practices of private associations or for those of less comprehensive social groups. They may be irrelevant for the various informal conventions and customs of everyday life; they may not elucidate the justice, or perhaps better, the fairness of voluntary cooperative arrangements or procedures for making contractual agreements. The conditions for the law of nations may require different principles arrived at in a somewhat different way. I shall be satisfied if it is possible to formulate a reasonable conception of justice for the basic structure of society conceived for the time being as a closed system isolated from other societies. The significance of this special case is obvious and needs no explanation. It is natural to conjecture that once we have a sound theory for this case, the remaining problems of justice will prove more tractable in the light of it. With suitable modifications such a theory should provide the key for some of these other questions.

The other limitation on our discussion is that for the most part I examine the principles of justice that would regulate a well-ordered society. Everyone is presumed to act justly and to do his part in upholding just institutions. Though justice may be, as Hume remarked, the cautious, jealous virtue, we can still ask what a perfectly just society would be like.[1] Thus I consider primarily what I call strict compliance as opposed to partial compliance theory. The latter studies the principles that govern how we are to deal with injustice. It comprises such topics as the theory of punishment, the doctrine of just war, and the justification of the various ways of opposing unjust regimes, ranging from civil disobedience and conscientious objection to militant resistance and revolution. Also included here are questions of compensatory justice and of weighing one form of institutional injustice against another. Obviously the problems of partial compliance theory are the pressing and urgent matters. These are the things that we are faced with in everyday life. The reason for beginning with ideal theory is that it provides, I believe, the only basis for the systematic grasp of these more pressing problems. At least, I shall assume that a deeper understanding can be gained in no other way, and that the nature and aims of a perfectly just society is the fundamental part of the theory of justice.

Now admittedly the concept of the basic structure is somewhat vague. It is not always clear which institutions or features thereof should be included. But it would be premature to worry about this matter here. I shall proceed by discussing principles which do apply to what is certainly a part of the basic structure as intuitively understood; I shall then try to extend the application of these principles so that they cover what would appear to be the main elements of this structure. Perhaps these principles will turn out to be perfectly general, although this is unlikely. It is sufficient that they apply to the most important cases of social justice. The point to keep in mind is that a conception of justice for the basic structure is worth having for its own sake. It should not be dismissed because its principles are not everywhere satisfactory.

A conception of social justice, then, is to be regarded as providing in the first instance a standard whereby the distributive aspects of the basic structure of society are to be assessed. This standard, however, is not to be confused with the principles defining the other virtues, for the basic structure, and social arrangements generally, may be efficient or inefficient, liberal or illiberal, and many other things, as well as just or unjust. A complete conception defining principles for all the virtues of the basic structure, together with their respective weights when they conflict, is more than a conception of justice; it is a social ideal. The principles of justice are but a part, although perhaps the most important part, of such a conception. A social ideal in turn is connected with a conception of society, a vision of the way in which the aims and purposes of social cooperation are to be understood. The various conceptions of justice are the outgrowth of different notions of society against the background of opposing views of the natural necessities and opportunities of human life. Fully to understand a conception of justice we must make explicit the conception of social cooperation from which it derives. But in doing this we should not lose sight of the special role of the principles of justice or of the primary subject to which they apply.

In these preliminary remarks I have distinguished the concept of justice as meaning a proper balance between competing claims from a conception of justice as a set of related principles for identifying the relevant considerations which determine this balance. I have also characterized justice as but one part of a social ideal, although the theory I shall propose no doubt extends its everyday sense. This theory is not offered as a description of ordinary meanings but as an account of certain distributive principles for the basic structure of society. I assume that any reasonably complete ethical theory must include principles for this fundamental problem and that these principles, whatever they are, constitute its doctrine of justice. The concept of justice I take to be defined, then, by the role of its principles in assigning rights and duties and in defining the appropriate division of social advantages. A conception of justice is an interpretation of this role. . . .

II.   The Main Idea of the Theory of Justice

My aim is to present a conception of justice which generalizes and carries to a higher level of abstraction the familiar theory of the social contract as found, say, in Locke, Rousseau, and Kant.[2] In order to do this we are not to think of the original contract as one to enter a particular society or to set up a particular form of government. Rather, the guiding idea is that the principles of justice for the basic structure of society are the object of the original agreement. They are the principles that free and rational persons concerned to further their own interests would accept in an initial position of equality as defining the funda-mental terms of their association. These principles are to regulate all further agreements; they specify the kinds of social cooperation that can be entered into and the forms of government that can be established. This way of regarding the principles of justice I shall call justice as fairness.

Thus we are to imagine that those who engage in social cooperation choose together, in one joint act, the principles which are to assign basic rights and duties and to determine the division of social benefits. Men are to decide in advance how they are to regulate their claims against one another and what is to be the foundation charter of their society. Just as each person must decide by rational reflection what constitutes his good, that is, the system of ends which it is rational for him to pursue, so a group of persons must decide once and for all what is to count among them as just and unjust. The choice which rational men would make in this hypothetical situation of equal liberty, assuming for the present that this choice problem has a solution, determines the principles of justice.

In justice as fairness the original position of equality corresponds to the state of nature in the traditional theory of the social contract. This original position is not, of course, thought of as an actual historical state of affairs, much less as a primitive condition of culture. It is understood as a purely hypothetical situ-ation characterized so as to lead to a certain conception of justice.[3] Among the essential features of this situation is that no one knows his place in society, his class position or social status, nor does any one know his fortune in the distribution of natural assets and abilities, his intelligence, strength, and the like. I shall even assume that the parties do not know their conceptions of the good or their special psychological propensities. The principles of justice are chosen behind a veil of ignorance. This ensures that no one is advantaged or disadvantaged in the choice of principles by the outcome of natural chance or the contingency of social circumstances. Since all are similarly situated and no one is able to design principles to favor his particular condition, the principles of justice are the result of a fair agreement or bargain. For given the circumstances of the original position, the symmetry of everyone's rela-tions to each other, this initial situation is fair between individuals as moral persons, that is, as rational beings with their own ends and capable, I shall assume, of a sense of justice. The original position is, one might say, the appropriate initial status quo, and thus the fundamental agreements reached in it are fair. This explains the propriety of the name "justice as fairness": it conveys the idea that the principles of justice are agreed to in an initial situation that is fair. The name does not mean that the concepts of justice and fairness are the same, any more than the phrase "poetry as metaphor" means that the concepts of poetry and metaphor are the same.

Justice as fairness begins, as I have said, with one of the most general of all choices which persons might make together, namely, with the choice of the first principles of a conception of justice which is to regulate all subsequent criticism and reform of institutions. Then, having chosen a conception of justice, we can suppose that they are to choose a constitution and a legislature to enact laws, and so on, all in accordance with the principles of justice initially agreed upon. Our social situation is just if it is such that by this sequence of hypothetical agreements we would have contracted into the general system of rules which defines it. Moreover, assuming that the original position does determine a set of principles (that is, that a particular conception of justice would be chosen), it will then be true that whenever social institutions satisfy these principles those engaged in them can say to one another that they are cooperating on terms to which they would agree if they were free and equal persons whose relations with respect to one another were fair. They could all view their arrangements as meeting the stipulations which they would acknowledge in an initial situation that embodies widely accepted and reasonable constraints on the choice of principles. The general recognition of this fact would provide the basis for a public acceptance of the corresponding principles of justice. No society can, of course, be a scheme of cooperation which men enter voluntarily in a literal sense; each person finds himself placed at birth in some particular position in some particular society, and the nature of this position materially affects his life prospects. Yet a society satisfying the principles of justice as fairness comes as close as a society can to being a voluntary scheme, for it meets the principles which free and equal persons would assent to under circumstances that are fair. In this sense its members are autonomous and the obligations they recognize self-imposed.

One feature of justice as fairness is to think of the parties in the initial situation as rational and mutually disinterested. This does not mean that the parties are egoists, that is, individuals with only certain kinds of interests, say in wealth, prestige, and domination. But they are conceived as not taking an interest in one another's interests. They are to presume that even their spiritual aims may be opposed, in the way that the aims of those of different religions may be opposed. Moreover, the concept of rationality must be interpreted as far as possible in the narrow sense, standard in economic theory, of taking the most effective means to given ends. I shall modify this concept to some extent, but one must try to avoid introducing into it any controversial ethical elements. The initial situation must be characterized by stipulations that are widely accepted.

In working out the conception of justice as fairness one main task clearly is to determine which principles of justice would be chosen in the original position.

To do this we must describe this situation in some detail and formulate with care the problem of choice which it presents. These matters I shall take up in the immediately succeeding chapters [omitted, eds.]. It may be observed, however, that once the principles of justice are thought of as arising from an original agreement in a situation of equality, it is an open question whether the principle of utility would be acknowledged. Off-hand it hardly seems likely that persons who view themselves as equals, entitled to press their claims upon one another, would agree to a principle which may require lesser life prospects for some simply for the sake of a greater sum of advantages enjoyed by others. Since each desires to protect his interests, his capacity to advance his conception of the good, no one has a reason to acquiesce in an enduring loss for himself in order to bring about a greater net balance of satisfaction. In the absence of strong and lasting benevolent impulses, a rational man would not accept a basic structure merely because it maximized the algebraic sum of advantages irrespective of its permanent effects on his own basic rights and interests. Thus it seems that the principle of utility is incompatible with the conception of social cooperation among equals for mutual advantage. It appears to be inconsistent with the idea of reciprocity implicit in the notion of a well-ordered society. Or, at any rate, so I shall argue.

I shall maintain instead that the persons in the initial situation would choose two rather different principles: the first requires equality in the assignment of basic rights and duties, while the second holds that social and economic inequalities, for example inequalities of wealth and authority, are just only if they result in compensating benefits for everyone, and in particular for the least advantaged members of society. These principles rule out justifying institutions on the grounds that the hardships of some are offset by a greater good in the aggregate. It may be expedient but it is not just that some should have less in order that others may prosper. But there is no injustice in the greater benefits earned by a few provided that the situation of persons not so fortunate is thereby improved. The intuitive idea is that since everyone's well-being depends upon a scheme of cooperation without which no one could have a satisfactory life, the division of advantages should be such as to draw forth the willing cooperation of everyone taking part in it, including those less well situated. The two principles mentioned seem to be a fair basis on which those better endowed, or more fortunate in their social position, neither of which we can be said to deserve, could expect the willing cooperation of others when some workable scheme is a necessary condition of the welfare of all.[4] Once we decide to look for a conception of justice that prevents the use of the accidents of natural endowment and the contingencies of social circumstance as counters in a quest for political and economic advantage, we are led to these principles. They express the result of leaving aside those aspects of the social world that seem arbitrary from a moral point of view.

The problem of the choice of principles, however, is extremely difficult. I do not expect the answer I shall suggest to be convincing to everyone. It is, therefore, worth noting from the outset that justice as fairness, like other contract views, consists of two parts: (1) an interpretation of the initial situation and of the problem of choice posed there, and (2) a set of principles which, it is argued, would be agreed to. One may accept the first part of the theory (or some variant thereof), but not the other, and conversely. The concept of the initial contractual situation may seem reasonable although the particular principles proposed are rejected. To be sure, I want to maintain that the most appropriate conception of this situation does lead to principles of justice contrary to utilitarianism and perfectionism, and therefore that the contract doctrine provides an alternative to these views. Still, one may dispute this contention even though one grants that the contractarian method is a useful way of studying ethical theories and of setting forth their underlying assumptions.

Justice as fairness is an example of what I have called a contract theory. Now there may be an objection to the term "contract" and related expressions, but I think it will serve reasonably well. Many words have misleading connotations which at first are likely to confuse. The terms "utility" and "utilitarianism" are surely no exception. They too have unfortunate suggestions which hostile critics have been willing to exploit; yet they are clear enough for those prepared to study utilitarian doctrine. The same should be true of the term "contract" applied to moral theories. As I have mentioned, to understand it one has to keep in mind that it implies a certain level of abstraction. In particular, the content of the relevant agreement is not to enter a given society or to adopt a given form of government, but to accept certain moral principles. Moreover, the undertakings referred to are purely hypothetical: a contract view holds that certain principles would be accepted in a well-defined initial situation.

The merit of the contract terminology is that it conveys the idea that principles of justice may be conceived as principles that would be chosen by rational persons, and that in this way conceptions of justice may be explained and justified. The theory of justice is a part, perhaps the most significant part, of the theory of rational choice. Furthermore, principles of justice deal with conflicting claims upon the advantages won by social cooperation; they apply to the relations among several persons or groups. The word "contract" suggests this plurality as well as the condition that the appropriate division of advantages must be in accordance with principles acceptable to all parties. The condition of publicity for principles of justice is also connoted by the contract phraseology. Thus, if these principles are the outcome of an agreement, citizens have a knowledge of the principles that others follow. It is characteristic of contract theories to stress the public nature of political principles. Finally there is the long tradition of the contract doctrine. Expressing the tie with this line of thought helps to define ideas and accords with natural piety. There are then several advantages in the use of the term "contract." With due precautions taken, it should not be misleading.

A final remark. Justice as fairness is not a complete contract theory. For it is clear that the contractarian idea can be extended to the choice of more or less an entire ethical system, that is, to a system including principles for all the virtues and not only for justice. Now for the most part I shall consider only principles of justice and others closely related to them; I make no attempt to discuss the virtues in a systematic way. Obviously if justice as fairness succeeds reasonably well, a next step would be to study the more general view suggested by the name "rightness as fairness." But even this wider theory fails to embrace all moral relationships, since it would seem to include only our relations with other persons and to leave out of account how we are to conduct ourselves toward animals and the rest of nature. I do not contend that the contract notion offers a way to approach these questions which are certainly of the first importance; and I shall have to put them aside. We must recognize the limited scope of justice as fairness and of the general type of view that it exemplifies. How far its conclusions must be revised once these other matters are understood cannot be decided in advance.

III.   The Original Position and Justification

I have said that the original position is the appropriate initial status quo which insures that the fundamental agreements reached in it are fair. This fact yields the name "justice as fairness." It is clear, then, that I want to say that one conception of justice is more reasonable than another, or justifiable with respect to it, if rational persons in the initial situation would choose its principles over those of the other for the role of justice. Conceptions of justice are to be ranked by their acceptability to persons so circumstanced. Understood in this way the question of justification is settled by working out a problem of deliberation: we have to ascertain which principles it would be rational to adopt given the contractual situation. This connects the theory of justice with the theory of rational choice.

If this view of the problem of justification is to succeed, we must, of course, describe in some detail the nature of this choice problem. A problem of rational decision has a definite answer only if we know the beliefs and interests of the parties, their relations with respect to one another, the alternatives between which they are to choose, the procedure whereby they make up their minds, and so on. As the circumstances are presented in different ways, correspondingly different principles are accepted. The concept of the original position, as I shall refer to it, is that of the most philosophically favored interpretation of this initial choice situation for the purposes of a theory of justice.

But how are we to decide what is the most favored interpretation? I assume, for one thing, that there is a broad measure of agreement that principles of justice should be chosen under certain conditions. To justify a particular description of the initial situation one shows that it incorporates these commonly shared presumptions. One argues from widely accepted but weak premises to more specific conclusions. Each of the presumptions should by itself be natural and plausible; some of them may seem innocuous or even trivial. The aim of the contract approach is to establish that taken together they impose significant bounds on acceptable principles of justice. The ideal outcome would be that these conditions determine a unique set of principles; but I shall be satisfied if they suffice to rank the main traditional conceptions of social justice.

One should not be misled, then, by the somewhat unusual conditions which characterize the original position. The idea here is simply to make vivid to ourselves the restrictions that it seems reasonable to impose on arguments for principles of justice, and therefore on these principles themselves. Thus it seems reasonable and generally acceptable that no one should be advantaged or disadvantaged by natural fortune or social circumstances in the choice of principles. It also seems widely agreed that it should be impossible to tailor principles to the circumstances of one's own case. We should insure further that particular inclinations and aspirations, and persons' conceptions of their good do not affect the principles adopted. The aim is to rule out those principles that it would be rational to propose for acceptance, however little the chance of success, only if one knew certain things that are irrelevant from the standpoint of justice. For example, if a man knew that he was wealthy, he might find it rational to advance the principle that various taxes for welfare measures be counted unjust; if he knew that he was poor, he would most likely propose the contrary principle. To represent the desired restrictions one imagines a situation in which everyone is deprived of this sort of information. One excludes the knowledge of those contingencies which sets men at odds and allows them to be guided by their prejudices. In this manner the veil of ignorance is arrived at in a natural way. This concept should cause no difficulty if we keep in mind the constraints on arguments that it is meant to express. At any time we can enter the original position, so to speak, simply by following a certain procedure, namely, by arguing for principles of justice in accordance with these restrictions.

It seems reasonable to suppose that the parties in the original position are equal. That is, all have the same rights in the procedure for choosing principles; each can make proposals, submit reasons for their acceptance, and so on. Obviously the purpose of these conditions is to represent equality between human beings as moral persons, as creatures having a conception of their good and capable of a sense of justice. The basis of equality is taken to be similarity in these two respects. Systems of ends are not ranked in value; and each man is presumed to have the requisite ability to understand and to act upon whatever principles are adopted. Together with the veil of ignorance, these conditions define the principles of justice as those which rational persons concerned to advance their interests would consent to as equals when none are known to be advantaged or disadvantaged by social and natural contingencies.

There is, however, another side to justifying a particular description of the original position. This is to see if the principles which would be chosen match our considered convictions of justice or extend them in an acceptable way. We can note whether applying these principles would lead us to make the same judgments about the basic structure of society which we now make intuitively and in which we have the greatest confidence; or whether, in cases where our present judgments are in doubt and given with hesitation, these principles offer a resolution which we can affirm on reflection. There are questions which we feel sure must be answered in a certain way. For example, we are confident that religious intolerance and racial discrimination are unjust. We think that we have examined these things with care and have reached what we believe is an impartial judgment not likely to be distorted by an excessive attention to our own interests. These convictions are provisional fixed points which we presume any conception of justice must fit. But we have much less assurance as to what is the correct distribution of wealth and authority. Here we may be looking for a way to remove our doubts. We can check an interpretation of the initial situation, then, by the capacity of its principles to accommodate our firmest convictions and to provide guidance where guidance is needed.

In searching for the most favored description of this situation we work from both ends. We begin by describing it so that it represents generally shared and preferably weak conditions. We then see if these conditions are strong enough to yield a significant set of principles. If not, we look for further premises equally reasonable. But if so, and these principles match our considered convictions of justice, then so far well and good. But presumably there will be discrepancies. In this case we have a choice. We can either modify the account of the initial situation or we can revise our existing judgments, for even the judgments we take provisionally as fixed points are liable to revision. By going back and forth, sometimes altering the conditions of the contractual circumstances, at others withdrawing our judgments and conforming them to principle, I assume that eventually we shall find a description of the initial situation that both expresses reasonable conditions and yields principles which match our considered judgments duly pruned and adjusted. This state of affairs I refer to as reflective equilibrium.[5] It is an equilibrium because at last our principles and judgments coincide; and it is reflective since we know to what principles our judgments conform and the premises of their derivation. At the moment everything is in order. But this equilibrium is not necessarily stable. It is liable to be upset by further examination of the conditions which should be imposed on the contractual situation and by particular cases which may lead us to revise our judgments. Yet for the time being we have done what we can to render coherent and to justify our convictions of social justice. We have reached a conception of the original position.

I shall not, of course, actually work through this process. Still, we may think of the interpretation of the original position that I shall present as the result of such a hypothetical course of reflection. It represents the attempt to accommodate within one scheme both reasonable philosophical conditions on principles as well as our considered judgments of justice. In arriving at the favored interpretation of the initial situation there is no point at which an appeal is made to self-evidence in the traditional sense either of general conceptions or particular convictions. I do not claim for the principles of justice proposed that they are necessary truths or derivable from such truths. A conception of justice cannot be deduced from self-evident premises or conditions on principles; instead, its justification is a matter of the mutual support of many considerations, of everything fitting together into one coherent view.

A final comment. We shall want to say that certain principles of justice are justified because they would be agreed to in an initial situation of equality. I have emphasized that this original position is purely hypothetical. It is natural to ask why, if this agreement is never actually entered into, we should take any interest in these principles, moral or otherwise. The answer is that the conditions embodied in the description of the original position are ones that we do in fact accept. Or if we do not, then perhaps we can be persuaded to do so by philosophical reflection. Each aspect of the contractual situation can be given supporting grounds. Thus what we shall do is to collect together into one conception a number of conditions on principles that we are ready upon due consideration to recognize as reasonable. These constraints express what we are prepared to regard as limits on fair terms of social cooperation. One way to look at the idea of the original position, therefore, is to see it as an expository device which sums up the meaning of these conditions and helps us to extract their consequences. On the other hand, this conception is also an intuitive notion that suggests its own elaboration, so that led on by it we are drawn to define more clearly the standpoint from which we can best interpret moral relationships. We need a conception that enables us to envision our objective from afar: the intuitive notion of the original position is to do this for us.[6] ...

IV. Two Principles of Justice

I shall now state in a provisional form the two principles of justice that I believe would be agreed to in the original position. The first formulation of these principles is tentative. As we go on I shall consider several formulations and approximate step by step the final statement to be given much later. I believe that doing this allows the exposition to proceed in a natural way.

The first statement of the two principles reads as follows.

First: each person is to have an equal right to the most extensive scheme of equal basic liberties compatible with a similar scheme of liberties for others.

Second: social and economic inequalities are to be arranged so that they are both (a) reasonably expected to be to everyone's advantage, and (b) attached to positions and offices open to all.

There are two ambiguous phrases in the second principle, namely "everyone's advantage" and "open to all." Determining their sense more exactly will lead to a second formulation of the principle in §VI.[7] ...

These principles primarily apply, as I have said, to the basic structure of society and govern the assignment of rights and duties and regulate the distribution of social and economic advantages. Their formulation presupposes that, for the purposes of a theory of justice, the social structure may be viewed as having two more or less distinct parts, the first principle applying to the one, the second principle to the other. Thus we distinguish between the aspects of the social system that define and secure the equal basic liberties and the aspects that specify and establish social and economic inequalities. Now it is essential to observe that the basic liberties are given by a list of such liberties. Important among these are political liberty (the right to vote and to hold public office) and freedom of speech and assembly; liberty of conscience and freedom of thought; freedom of the person, which includes freedom from psychological oppression and physical assault and dismemberment (integrity of the person); the right to hold personal property and freedom from arbitrary arrest and seizure as defined by the concept of the rule of law. These liberties are to be equal by the first principle.

The second principle applies, in the first approximation, to the distribution of income and wealth and to the design of organizations that make use of differences in authority and responsibility. While the distribution of wealth and income need not be equal, it must be to everyone's advantage, and at the same time, positions of authority and responsibility must be accessible to all. One applies the second principle by holding positions open, and then, subject to this constraint, arranges social and economic inequalities so that everyone benefits.

These principles are to be arranged in a serial order with the first principle prior to the second. This ordering means that infringements of the basic equal liberties protected by the first principle cannot be justified, or compensated for, by greater social and economic advantages. These liberties have a central range of application within which they can be limited and compromised only when they conflict with other basic liberties. Since they may be limited when they clash with one another, none of these liberties is absolute; but however they are adjusted to form one system, this system is to be the same for all. It is difficult, and perhaps impossible, to give a complete specification of these liberties independently from the particular circumstances – social, economic, and technological – of a given society. The hypothesis is that the general form of such a list could be devised with sufficient exactness to sustain this conception of justice. Of course, liberties not on the list, for example, the right to own certain kinds of property (e.g., means of production) and freedom of contract as understood by the doctrine of laissez-faire are not basic; and so they are not protected by the priority of the first principle. Finally, in regard to the second principle, the distribution of wealth and income, and positions of authority and responsibility, are to be consistent with both the basic liberties and equality of opportunity.

The two principles are rather specific in their content, and their acceptance rests on certain assumptions that I must eventually try to explain and justify. For the present, it should be observed that these principles are a special case of a more general conception of justice that can be expressed as follows.

All social values – liberty and opportunity, income and wealth, and the social bases of self-respect – are to be distributed equally unless an unequal distribution of any, or all, of these values is to everyone's advantage.

Injustice, then, is simply inequalities that are not to the benefit of all. Of course, this conception is extremely vague and requires interpretation.

As a first step, suppose that the basic structure of society distributes certain primary goods, that is, things that every rational man is presumed to want. These goods normally have a use whatever a person's rational plan of life. For simplicity, assume that the chief primary goods at the disposition of society are rights, liberties, and opportunities, and income and wealth. (Later on in Part Three [of *A Theory of Justice*, eds.] the primary good of self-respect has a central place.) These are the social primary goods. Other primary goods such as health and vigor, intelligence and imagination, are natural goods; although their possession is influenced by the basic structure, they are not so directly under its control. Imagine, then, a hypothetical initial arrangement in which all the social primary goods are equally distributed: everyone has similar rights and duties, and income and wealth are evenly shared. This state of affairs provides a benchmark for judging improvements. If certain inequalities of wealth and differences in authority would make everyone better off than in this hypothetical starting situation, then they accord with the general conception.

Now it is possible, at least theoretically, that by giving up some of their fundamental liberties men are sufficiently compensated by the resulting social and economic gains. The general conception of justice imposes no restrictions on what sort of inequalities are permissible; it only requires that everyone's position be improved. We need not suppose anything so drastic as consenting to a condition of slavery. Imagine instead that people seem willing to forgo certain political rights when the economic returns are significant. It is this kind of exchange which the two principles rule out; being arranged in serial order they do not permit exchanges between basic liberties and economic and social gains except under extenuating circumstances.

For the most part, I shall leave aside the general conception of justice and examine instead the two principles in serial order. The advantage of this procedure is that from the first the matter of priorities is recognized and an effort made to find principles to deal with it. One is led to attend throughout to the conditions under which the absolute weight of liberty with respect to social and economic advantages, as defined by the lexical order of the two principles, would be reasonable. Offhand, this ranking appears extreme and too special a case to be of much interest; but there is more justification for it than would appear at first sight. Or at any rate, so I shall maintain.[8] Furthermore, the distinction between fundamental rights and liberties and economic and social benefits marks a difference among primary social goods that suggests an important division in the social system. Of course, the distinctions drawn and the ordering proposed are at best only approximations. There are surely circumstances in which they fail. But it is essential to depict clearly the main lines of a reasonable conception of justice; and under many conditions anyway, the two principles in serial order may serve well enough.

The fact that the two principles apply to institutions has certain consequences. First of all, the rights and basic liberties referred to by these principles are those which are defined by the public rules of the basic structure. Whether men are free is determined by the rights and duties established by the major institutions of society. Liberty is a certain pattern of social forms. The first principle simply requires that certain sorts of rules, those defining basic liberties, apply to everyone equally and that they allow the most extensive liberty compatible with a like liberty for all. The only reason for circumscribing basic liberties and making them less extensive is that otherwise they would interfere with one another.

Further, when principles mention persons, or require that everyone gain from an inequality, the reference is to representative persons holding the various social positions, or offices established by the basic structure. Thus in applying the second principle I assume that it is possible to assign an expectation of well-being to representative individuals holding these positions. This expectation indicates their life prospects as viewed from their social station. In general, the expectations of representative persons depend upon the distribution of rights and duties throughout the basic structure. Expectations are connected: by raising the prospects of the representative man in one position we presumably increase or decrease the prospects of representative men in other positions. Since it applies to institutional forms, the second principle (or rather the first part of it) refers to the expectations of representative individuals.... [N]either principle applies to distributions of particular goods to particular individuals who may be identified by their proper names. The situation where someone is considering how to allocate certain commodities to needy persons who are known to him is not within the scope of the principles. They are meant to regulate basic institutional arrangements. We must not assume that there is much similarity from the standpoint of justice between an administrative allotment of goods to specific persons and the appropriate design of society. Our common sense intuitions for the former may be a poor guide to the latter.

Now the second principle insists that each person benefit from permissible inequalities in the basic structure. This means that it must be reasonable for each relevant representative man defined by this structure, when he views it as a going concern, to prefer his prospects with the inequality to his prospects without it. One is not allowed to justify differences in income or in positions of authority and responsibility on the ground that the disadvantages of those in one position are outweighed by the greater advantages of those in another. Much less can infringements of liberty be counterbalanced in this way. It is obvious, however, that there are indefinitely many ways in which all may be advantaged when the initial arrangement of equality is taken as a benchmark. How then are we to choose among these possibilities? The principles must be specified so that they yield a determinate conclusion. I now turn to this problem.

V.   Interpretations of the Second Principle

I have already mentioned that since the phrases "everyone's advantage" and "equally open to all" are ambiguous, both parts of the second principle have two natural senses. Because these senses are independent of one another, the principle has four possible meanings. Assuming that the first principle of equal liberty has the same sense throughout, we then have four interpretations of the two principles. These are indicated in the table below.

	"Everyone's advantage"	
"Equally open"	Principle of efficiency	Difference principle
Equality as careers open to talents	System of Natural Liberty	Natural Aristocracy
Equality as equality of fair opportunity	Liberal Equality	Democratic Equality

I shall sketch in turn these three interpretations: the system of natural liberty, liberal equality, and democratic equality. In some respects this sequence is the more intuitive one, but the sequence via the interpretation of natural aristocracy is not without interest and I shall comment on it briefly. In working out justice as fairness, we must decide which interpretation is to be preferred. I shall adopt that of democratic equality, explaining in the next section what this notion means. The argument for its acceptance in the original position does not begin until the next chapter [omitted, eds.].

The first interpretation (in either sequence) I shall refer to as the system of natural liberty. In this rendering the first part of the second principle is understood as the principle of efficiency adjusted so as to apply to institutions or, in this case, to the basic structure of society; and the second part is understood as an open social system in which, to use the traditional phrase, careers are open to talents. I assume in all interpretations that the first principle of equal liberty is satisfied and that the economy is roughly a free market system, although the means of production may or may not be privately owned. The system of natural liberty asserts, then, that a basic structure satisfying the principle of efficiency and in which positions are open to those able and willing to strive for them will lead to a just distribution. Assigning rights and duties in this way is thought to give a scheme which allocates wealth and income, authority and responsibility, in a fair way whatever this allocation turns out to be. The doctrine includes an important element of pure procedural justice which is carried over to the other interpretations.

At this point it is necessary to make a brief digression to explain the principle of efficiency. This principle is simply that of Pareto optimality (as economists refer to it) formulated so as to apply to the basic structure.[9] I shall always use the term "efficiency" instead because this is literally correct and the term "optimality" suggests that the concept is much broader than it is in fact.[10] To be sure, this principle was not originally intended to apply to institutions but to particular configurations of the economic system, for example, to distributions of goods among consumers or to modes of production. The principle holds that a configuration is efficient whenever it is impossible to change it so as to make some persons (at least one) better off without at the same time making other persons (at least one) worse off. Thus a distribution of a stock of commodities among certain individuals is efficient if there exists no redistribution of these goods that improves the circumstances of at least one of these individuals without another being disadvantaged. The organization of production is efficient if there is no way to alter inputs so as to produce more of some commodity without producing less of another. For if we could produce more of one good without having to give up some of another, the larger stock of goods could be used to better the circumstances of some persons without making that of others any worse. These applications of the principle show that it is, indeed, a principle of efficiency. A distribution of goods or a scheme of production is inefficient when there are ways of doing still better for some individuals without doing any worse for others. I shall assume that the parties in the original position accept this principle to judge the efficiency of economic and social arrangements....

Now the principle of efficiency can be applied to the basic structure by reference to the expectations of representative men.[11] Thus we can say that an arrangement of rights and duties in the basic structure is efficient if and only if it is impossible to change the rules, to redefine the scheme of rights and duties, so as to raise the expectations of any representative man (at least one) without at the same time lowering the expectations of some (at least one) other representative man. Of course, these alterations must be consistent with the other principles. That is, in changing the basic structure we are not permitted to violate the principle of equal liberty or the requirement of open positions. What can be altered is the distribution of income and wealth and the way in which those in positions of authority and responsibility can regulate cooperative activities. Consistent with the constraints of liberty and accessibility, the allocation of these primary goods may be adjusted to modify the expectations of representative individuals. An arrangement of the basic structure is efficient when there is no way to change this distribution so as to raise the prospects of some without lowering the prospects of others.

There are, I shall assume, many efficient arrangements of the basic structure. Each of these specifies a division of advantages from social cooperation. The problem is to choose between them, to find a conception of justice that singles out one of these efficient distributions as also just. If we succeed in this, we shall have gone beyond mere efficiency yet in a way compatible with it. Now it is natural to try out the idea that as long as the social system is efficient there is no reason to be concerned with distribution. All efficient arrangements are in this case declared equally just. Of course, this suggestion would be outlandish for the allocation of particular goods to known individuals. No one would suppose that it is a matter of indifference from the standpoint of justice whether any one of a number of men happens to have everything. But the suggestion seems equally unreasonable for the basic structure. Thus it may be that under certain conditions serfdom cannot be significantly reformed without lowering the expectations of some other representative man, say that of landowners, in which case serfdom is efficient. Yet it may also happen under the same conditions that a system of free labor cannot be changed without lowering the expectations of some other representative man, say that of free laborers, so this arrangement is likewise efficient. More generally, whenever a society is relevantly divided into a number of classes, it is possible, let us suppose, to maximize with respect to any one of its representative men. These maxima give at least this many efficient positions, for none of them can be departed from to raise the expectations of others without lowering those of the representative man with respect to whom the maximum is defined. Thus each of these extremes is efficient but they surely cannot be all just.

Now these reflections show only what we knew all along, that is, that the principle of efficiency cannot serve alone as a conception of justice.[12] Therefore it must be supplemented in some way. Now in the system of natural liberty the principle of efficiency is constrained by certain background institutions; when these constraints are satisfied, any resulting efficient distribution is accepted as just. The system of natural liberty selects an efficient distribution roughly as follows. Let us suppose that we know from economic theory that under the standard assumptions defining a competitive market economy, income and wealth will be distributed in an efficient way, and that the particular efficient distribution which results in any period of time is determined by the initial distribution of assets, that is, by the initial distribution of income and wealth, and of natural talents and abilities. With each initial distribution, a definite efficient outcome is arrived at. Thus it turns out that if we are to accept the outcome as just, and not merely as efficient, we must accept the basis upon which over time the initial distribution of assets is determined.

In the system of natural liberty the initial distribution is regulated by the arrangements implicit in the conception of careers open to talents (as earlier defined). These arrangements presuppose a background of equal liberty (as specified by the first principle) and a free market economy. They require a formal equality of opportunity in that all have at least the same legal rights of access to all advantaged social positions. But since there is no effort to preserve an equality, or similarity, of social conditions, except insofar as this is necessary to preserve the requisite background institutions, the initial distribution of assets for any period of time is strongly influenced by natural and social contingencies. The existing distribution of income and wealth, say, is the cumulative effect of prior distributions of natural assets – that is, natural talents and abilities – as these have been developed or left unrealized, and their use favored or disfavored over time by social circumstances and such chance contingencies as accident and good fortune. Intuitively, the most obvious injustice of the system of natural liberty is that it permits distributive shares to be improperly influenced by these factors so arbitrary from a moral point of view.

The liberal interpretation, as I shall refer to it, tries to correct for this by adding to the requirement of careers open to talents the further condition of the principle of fair equality of opportunity. The thought here is that positions are to be not only open in a formal sense, but that all should have a fair chance to attain them. Offhand it is not clear what is meant, but we might say that those with similar abilities and skills should have similar life chances. More specifically, assuming that there is a distribution of natural assets, those who are at the same level of talent and ability, and have the same willingness to use them, should have the same prospects of success regardless of their initial place in the social system. In all sectors of society there should be roughly equal prospects of culture and achievement for everyone similarly motivated and endowed. The expectations of those with the same abilities and aspirations should not be affected by their social class.[13]

The liberal interpretation of the two principles seeks, then, to mitigate the influence of social contingencies and natural fortune on distributive shares. To accomplish this end it is necessary to impose further basic structural conditions on the social system. Free market arrangements must be set within a framework of political and legal institutions which regulates the overall trends of economic events and preserves the social conditions necessary for fair equality of opportunity. The elements of this framework are familiar enough, though it may be worthwhile to recall the importance of preventing excessive accumulations of property and wealth and of maintaining equal opportunities of education for all. Chances to acquire cultural knowledge and skills should not depend upon one's class position, and so the school system, whether public or private, should be designed to even out class barriers.

While the liberal conception seems clearly preferable to the system of natural liberty, intuitively it still appears defective. For one thing, even if it works to perfection in eliminating the influence of social contingencies, it still permits the distribution of wealth and income to be determined by the natural distribution of abilities and talents. Within the limits allowed by the background arrangements, distributive shares are decided by the outcome of the natural lottery; and this outcome is arbitrary from a moral perspective. There is no more reason to permit the distribution of income and wealth to be settled by the distribution of natural assets than by historical and social fortune. Furthermore, the principle of fair opportunity can be only imperfectly carried out, at least as long as some form of the family exists. The extent to which natural capacities develop and reach fruition is affected by all kinds of social conditions and class attitudes. Even the willingness to make an effort, to try, and so to be deserving in the ordinary sense is itself dependent upon happy family and social circumstances. It is impossible in practice to secure equal chances of achievement and culture for those similarly endowed, and therefore we may want to adopt a principle which recognizes this fact and also mitigates the arbitrary effects of the natural lottery itself. That the liberal conception fails to do this encourages one to look for another interpretation of the two principles of justice.

Before turning to the conception of democratic equality, we should note that of natural aristocracy. On this view no attempt is made to regulate social contingencies beyond what is required by formal equality of opportunity, but the advantages of persons with greater natural endowments are to be limited to those that further the good of the poorer sectors of society. The aristocratic ideal is applied to a system that is open, at least from a legal point of view, and the better situation of those favored by it is regarded as just only when less would be had by those below, if less were given to those above.[14] In this way the idea of *noblesse oblige* is carried over to the conception of natural aristocracy.

Now both the liberal conception and that of natural aristocracy are unstable. For once we are troubled by the influence of either social contingencies or natural chance on the determination of distributive shares, we are bound, on reflection, to be bothered by the influence of the other. From a moral standpoint the two seem equally arbitrary. So however we move away from the system of natural liberty, we cannot be satisfied short of the democratic conception. This conception I have yet to explain. And, moreover, none of the preceding remarks are an argument for this conception, since in a contract theory all arguments, strictly speaking, are to be made in terms of what it would be rational to agree to in the original position. But I am concerned here to prepare the way for the favored interpretation of the two principles so that these criteria, especially the second one, will not strike the reader as extreme. Once we try to find a rendering of them which treats everyone equally as a moral person, and which does not weight men's share in the benefits and burdens of social cooperation according to their social fortune or their luck in the natural lottery, the democratic interpretation is the best choice among the four alternatives. With these comments as a preface, I now turn to this conception.

VI. Democratic Equality and the Difference Principle

The democratic interpretation, as the table suggests, is arrived at by combining the principle of fair equality of opportunity with the difference principle. This principle removes the indeterminateness of the principle of efficiency by singling out a particular position from which the social and economic inequalities of the basic structure are to be judged. Assuming the framework of institutions required by equal liberty and fair equality of opportunity, the higher expectations of those better situated are just if and only if they work as part of a scheme which improves the expectations of the least advantaged members of society. The intuitive idea is that the social order is not to establish and secure the more attractive prospects of those better off unless doing so is to the advantage of those less fortunate. (See the discussion of the difference principle that follows.)

The difference principle

Assume that indifference curves now represent distributions that are judged equally just. Then the difference principle is a strongly egalitarian conception in the sense that unless there is a distribution that makes both persons better off (limiting ourselves to the two-person case for simplicity), an equal distribution is to be preferred. The indifference curves take the form depicted in figure 1. These curves are actually made up of vertical and horizontal lines that intersect at right angles at the 45° line (again supposing an interpersonal and cardinal interpretation of the axes). No matter how much either person's situation is improved, there is no gain from the standpoint of the difference principle unless the other gains also.

Suppose that x_1 is the most favored representative man in the basic structure. As his expectations are increased so are the prospects of x_2, the least advantaged man. In figure 2 let the curve OP represent the contribution to x_2's expectations made by the greater expectations of x_1. The point O, the origin,

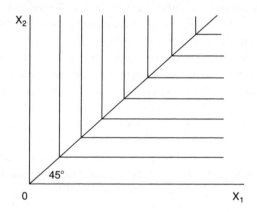

Figure 1

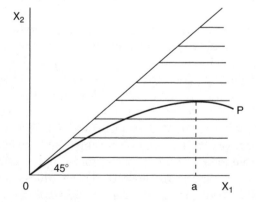

Figure 2

represents the hypothetical state in which all social primary goods are distributed equally. Now the OP curve is always below the 45° line, since x_1 is always better off. Thus the only relevant parts of the indifference curves are those below this line, and for this reason the upper left-hand part of figure 2 is not drawn in. Clearly the difference principle is perfectly satisfied only when the OP curve is just tangent to the highest indifference curve that it touches. In figure 2 this is at the point a.

Note that the contribution curve, the curve OP, rises upward to the right because it is assumed that the social cooperation defined by the basic structure is mutually advantageous. It is no longer a matter of shuffling about a fixed stock of goods. Also, nothing is lost if an accurate interpersonal comparison of benefits is impossible. It suffices that the least favored person can be identified and his rational preference determined.

A view less egalitarian than the difference principle, and perhaps more plausible at first sight, is one in which the indifference lines for just distributions (or for all things considered) are smooth curves convex to the origin, as in figure 3. The indifference curves for social welfare functions are often depicted in this fashion. This shape of the curves expresses the fact that as either person gains relative to the other, further benefits to him become less valuable from a social point of view.

A classical utilitarian, on the other hand, is indifferent as to how a constant sum of benefits is distributed. He appeals to equality only to break ties. If there are but two persons, then assuming an interpersonal cardinal interpretation of the axes, the utilitarian's indifference lines for distributions are straight lines perpendicular to the 45° line. Since, however, x_1 and x_2 are representative men, the gains to them have to be weighted by the number of persons they each represent. Since presumably x_2 represents rather more persons than x_1, the indifference lines become more horizontal, as seen in figure 4. The ratio of the number of advantaged to the number of disadvantaged defines the slope of these straight lines. Drawing the same contribution curve OP as before, we see

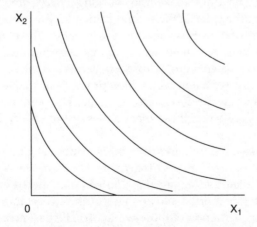

Figure 3

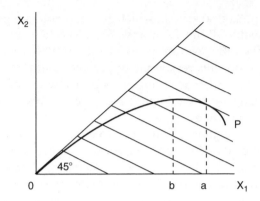

Figure 4

that the best distribution from a utilitarian point of view is reached at the point which is beyond the point b where the OP curve reaches its maximum. Since the difference principle selects the point b and b is always to the left of a, utilitarianism allows, other things equal, larger inequalities.

To illustrate the difference principle, consider the distribution of income among social classes. Let us suppose that the various income groups correlate with representative individuals by reference to whose expectations we can judge the distribution. Now those starting out as members of the entrepreneurial class in property-owning democracy, say, have a better prospect than those who begin in the class of unskilled laborers. It seems likely that this will be true even when the social injustices which now exist are removed. What, then, can possibly justify this kind of initial inequality in life prospects? According to the difference principle, it is justifiable only if the difference in expectation is to the advantage of the representative man who is worse off, in this case the representative unskilled worker. The inequality in expectation is permissible only if lowering it would make the working class even more worse off. Supposedly, given the rider in the second principle concerning open positions, and the principle of liberty generally, the greater expectations allowed to entrepreneurs encourages them to do things which raise the prospects of [the] laboring class. Their better prospects act as incentives so that the economic process is more efficient, innovation proceeds at a faster pace, and so on. I shall not consider how far these things are true. The point is that something of this kind must be argued if these inequalities are to satisfy by the difference principle.

I shall now make a few remarks about this principle. First of all, in applying it, one should distinguish between two cases. The first case is that in which the expectations of the least advantaged are indeed maximized (subject, of course, to the mentioned constraints). No changes in the expectations of those better off can improve the situation of those worst off. The best arrangement obtains, what I shall call a perfectly just scheme. The second case is that in which the expectations of all those better off at least contribute to the welfare of the more unfortunate. That is, if their expectations were decreased, the prospects of the least advantaged would likewise fall. Yet the maximum is not yet achieved. Even higher expectations for the more advantaged would raise the expectations of those in the lowest position. Such a scheme is, I shall say, just throughout, but not the best just arrangement. A scheme is unjust when the higher expectations, one or more of them, are excessive. If these expectations were decreased, the situation of the least favored would be improved. How unjust an arrangement is depends on how excessive the higher expectations are and to what extent they depend upon the violation of the other principles of justice, for example, fair equality of opportunity; but I shall not attempt to measure the degrees of injustice. The point to note here is that while the difference principle is, strictly speaking, a maximizing principle, there is a significant distinction between the cases that fall short of the best arrangement. A society should try to avoid situations where the marginal contributions of those better off are negative, since, other things equal, this seems a greater fault than falling short of the best scheme when these contributions are positive. The even larger difference between classes violates the principle of mutual advantage as well as democratic equality.

A further point is this. We saw that the system of natural liberty and the liberal conception go beyond the principle of efficiency by setting up certain background institutions and leaving the rest to pure procedural justice. The democratic conception holds that while pure procedural justice may be invoked to some extent at least, the way previous interpretations do this still leaves too much to social and natural contingency. But it should be noted that the difference principle is compatible with the principle of efficiency. For when the former is fully satisfied, it is indeed impossible to make any one representative man better off without making another worse off, namely, the least advantaged representative man whose expectations we are to maximize. Thus justice is defined so that it is consistent with efficiency, at least when the two principles are perfectly fulfilled. Of course, if the basic structure is unjust, these principles will authorize changes that may lower the expectations of some of those better off; and therefore the democratic conception is not consistent with the principle of efficiency if this principle is taken to mean that only changes which improve everyone's prospects are allowed. Justice is prior to efficiency and requires some changes that are not efficient in this sense. Consistency obtains only in the sense that a perfectly just scheme is also efficient.

Next, we may consider a certain complication regarding the meaning of the difference principle. It has been taken for granted that if the principle is satisfied, everyone is benefited. One obvious sense in which this is so is that each man's position is improved with respect to the initial arrangement of equality. But it is clear that nothing depends upon being able to identify this initial arrangement; indeed, how well off men are in this situation plays no essential role in applying the difference principle. We simply maximize the expectations of the least favored position subject to the required constraints. As long as doing this is an improvement for everyone, as so far I have assumed it is, the estimated gains from the situation of hypothetical equality are irrelevant, if not largely impossible to ascertain anyway. There may be, however, a further sense in which everyone is advantaged when the difference principle is satisfied, at least if we make certain assumptions. Let us suppose that inequalities in expectations are chain-connected: that is, if an advantage has the effect of raising the expectations of the lowest position, it raises the expectations of all positions in between. For example, if the greater expectations for entrepreneurs benefit the unskilled worker, they also benefit the semi-skilled. Notice that chain connection says nothing about the case where the least advantaged do not gain, so that it does not mean that all effects move together. Assume further that expectations are close-knit: that is, it is impossible to raise or lower the expectation of any representative man without raising or lowering the expectation of every other representative man, especially that of the least advantaged. There is no loose-jointedness, so to speak, in the way expectations hang together. Now with these assumptions there is a sense in which everyone benefits when the difference principle is satisfied. For the representative man who is better off in any two-way comparison gains by the advantages offered him, and the man who is worse off gains from the contributions which these inequalities make. Of course, these conditions may not hold. But in this case those who are better off should not have a veto over the benefits available for the least favored. We are still to maximize the expectations of those most disadvantaged. (See the accompanying discussion of chain connection.)

Chain connection

For simplicity assume that there are three representative men. Let x_1 be the most favored and x_3 the least favored with x_2 in between. Let the expectations of x_1 be marked off along the horizontal axis, the expectations of x_2 and x_3 along the vertical axis. The curves showing the contribution of the most favored to the other groups begin at the origin as the hypothetical position of equality. Moreover, there is a maximum gain permitted to the most favored on the assumption that, even if the difference principle would allow it, there would be unjust effects on the political system and the like excluded by the priority of liberty.

The difference principle selects the point where the curve for x_3 reaches its maximum, for example, the point a in figure 5.

Chain connection means that at any point where the x_3 curve is rising to the right, the x_2 curve is also rising, as in the intervals left of the points a and b in figures 5 and 6. Chain connection says nothing about the case where the x_3 curve is falling to the right, as in the interval to the right of the point a in figure 5. The x_2 curve may be either rising or falling (as indicated by the dashed line x_2'). Chain connection does not hold to the right of b in figure 6.

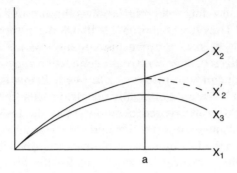

Figure 5

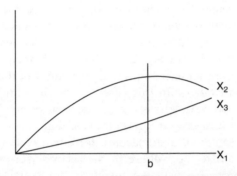

Figure 6

Intervals in which both the x_2 and the x_3 curves are rising define the intervals of positive contributions. Any more to the right increases the average expectation (average utility if utility is measured by expectations) and also satisfies the principle of efficiency as a criterion of change, that is, points to the right improve everyone's situation.

In figure 5 the average expectations may be rising beyond the point a, although the expectations of the least favored are falling. (This depends on the weights of the several groups.) The difference principle excludes this and selects the point a.

Close-knitness means that there are no flat stretches on the curves for x_2 and x_3. At each point both curves are either rising or falling. All the curves illustrated are close-knit.

I shall not examine how likely it is that chain connection and close-knitness hold. The difference principle is not contingent on these relations being satisfied. However, when the contributions of the more favored positions spread generally throughout society and are not confined to particular sectors, it seems plausible that if the least advantaged benefit so do others in between. Moreover, a wide diffusion of benefits is favored by two features of institutions both exemplified by the basic structure: first, they are set up to advance certain fundamental interests which everyone has in common, and second, offices and positions are open. Thus it seems probable that if the authority and powers of legislators and judges, say, improve the situation of the less favored, they improve that of citizens generally. Chain connection may often be true, provided the other principles of justice are fulfilled. If this is so, then we may observe that within the region of positive contributions (the region where the advantages of all those in favored positions raise the prospects of the least fortunate), any movement toward the perfectly just arrangement improves everyone's expectation. Under these circumstances the difference principle has somewhat similar practical consequences for the principles of efficiency and average utility (if utility is measured by primary goods). Of course, if chain connection rarely holds, this similarity is unimportant. But it seems likely that within a just social scheme a general diffusion of benefits often takes place.

There is a further complication. Close-knitness is assumed in order to simplify the statement of the difference principle. It is clearly conceivable, however likely or important in practice, that the least advantaged are not affected one way or the other by some changes in expectations of the best off although these changes benefit others. In this sort of case close-knitness fails, and to cover the situation we can express a more general principle as follows: in a basic structure with n relevant representatives, first maximize the welfare of the worst off representative man; second, for equal welfare of the worst-off representative, maximize the welfare of the second worst-off representative man, and so on until the last case which is, for equal welfare of all the preceding $n-1$ representatives, maximize the welfare of the best-off representative man. We may think of this as the lexical difference principle.[15] I think, however, that in actual cases this principle is unlikely to be relevant, for when the greater potential benefits to the more advantaged are significant, there will surely be some way to improve the situation of the less advantaged as well. The general laws governing the institutions of the basic structure insure that cases requiring the lexical principle will not arise. Thus I shall always use the difference principle in the simpler form, and so the outcome of the last several sections is that the second principle reads as follows:

> Social and economic inequalities are to be arranged so that they are both (a) to the greatest expected benefit of the least advantaged and (b) attached to offices and positions open to all under conditions of fair equality of opportunity.

Finally, a comment about terminology. Economics may wish to refer to the difference principle as the maximin criterion, but I have carefully avoided this name for several reasons. The maximin criterion is generally understood as a rule for choice under great uncertainty (§VII), whereas the difference principle is a principle of justice. It is undesirable to use the same name for two things that are so distinct. The difference principle is a very special criterion: it applies primarily to the basic structure of society via representative individuals whose expectations are to be estimated by an index of primary goods. In addition, calling the difference principle the maximin criterion might wrongly suggest that the main argument for this principle from the original position derives from an assumption of very high risk aversion. There is indeed a relation between the difference principle and such an assumption, but extreme attitudes to risk are not postulated; and in any case, there are many considerations in favor of the difference principle in which the aversion to risk plays no role at all. Thus it is best to use the term "maximin criterion" solely for the rule of choice under uncertainty....

VII.   The Reasoning Leading to the Two Principles of Justice

In this and the next two sections [omitted, eds.] I take up the choice between the two principles of justice and the principle of average utility. Determining the rational preference between these two options is perhaps the central problem in developing the conception of justice as fairness as a viable alternative to the utilitarian tradition. I shall begin in this section by presenting some intuitive remarks favoring the two principles. I shall also discuss briefly the qualitative structure of the argument that needs to be made if the case for these principles is to be conclusive.

Now consider the point of view of anyone in the original position. There is no way for him to win special advantages for himself. Nor, on the other hand, are there grounds for his acquiescing in special disadvantages. Since it is not reasonable for him to expect more than an equal share in the division of social primary goods, and since it is not rational for him to agree to less, the sensible thing is to acknowledge as the first step a principle of justice requiring an equal distribution. Indeed, this principle is so obvious given the symmetry of the parties that it would occur to everyone immediately. Thus the parties start with a principle requiring equal basic liberties for all, as well as fair equality of opportunity and equal division of income and wealth.

But even holding firm to the priority of the basic liberties and fair equality of opportunity, there is no reason why this initial acknowledgement should be final. Society should take into account economic efficiency and the requirements of organization and technology. If there are inequalities in income and wealth, and differences in authority and degrees of responsibility, that work to make everyone better off in comparison with the benchmark of equality, why not permit them? One might think that ideally individuals should want to serve one another. But since the parties are assumed to be mutually disinterested, their acceptance of these economic and institutional inequalities is only the recognition of the relations of opposition in which men stand in the circumstances of justice. They have no grounds for complaining of one another's motives. Thus the parties would agree to these differences only if they would be dejected by the bare knowledge or perception that others are better situated; but I suppose that they decide as if they are not moved by envy. Thus the basic structure should allow these inequalities so long as these improve everyone's situation, including that of the least advantaged, provided that they are consistent with equal liberty and fair opportunity. Because the parties start from an equal division of all social primary goods, those who benefit least have, so to speak, a veto. Thus we arrive at the difference principle. Taking equality as the basis of comparison, those who have gained more must do so on terms that are justifiable to those who have gained the least.

By some such reasoning, then, the parties might arrive at the two principles of justice in serial order. I shall not try to justify this ordering here, but the following remarks may convey the intuitive idea. I assume that the parties view themselves as free persons who have fundamental aims and interests in the name of which they think it legitimate for them to make claims on one another concerning the design of the basic structure of society. The religious interest is a familiar historical example; the interest in the integrity of the person is another. In the original position the parties do not know what particular forms these interests take; but they do assume that they have such interests and that the basic liberties necessary for their protection are guaranteed by the first principle. Since they must secure these interests, they rank the first principle prior to the second. The case for the two principles can be strengthened by spelling out in more detail the notion of a free person. Very roughly the parties regard themselves as having a highest-order interest in how all their other interests, including even their fundamental ones, are shaped and regulated by social institutions. They do not think of themselves as inevitably bound to, or as identical with, the pursuit of any particular complex of fundamental interests that they may have at any given time, although they want the right to advance such interests (provided they are admissible). Rather, free persons conceive of themselves as beings who can revise and alter their final ends and who give first priority to preserving their liberty in these matters. Hence, they not only have final ends that they are in principle free to pursue or to reject, but their original allegiance and continued devotion to these ends are to be formed and affirmed under conditions that are free. Since the two principles secure a social form that maintains these conditions, they would be agreed to rather than the principle of utility. Only by this agreement can the parties be sure that their highest-order interest as free persons is guaranteed.

The priority of liberty means that whenever the basic liberties can be effectively established, a lesser or an unequal liberty cannot be exchanged for an improvement in economic well-being. It is only when social circumstances do not allow the effective establishment of these basic rights that one can concede their limitation; and even then these restrictions can be granted only to the extent that they are necessary to prepare the way for the time when they are no longer justified. The denial of the equal liberties can be defended only when it is essential to change the conditions of civilization so that in due course these liberties can be enjoyed. Thus in adopting the serial order of the two principles, the parties are assuming that the conditions of their society, whatever they are, admit the effective realization of the equal liberties. Or that if they do not, circumstances are nevertheless sufficiently favorable so that the priority of the first principle points out the most urgent changes and identifies the preferred path to the social state in which all the basic liberties can be fully instituted. The complete realization of the two principles in serial order is the long-run tendency of this ordering, at least under reasonably fortunate conditions.

It seems from these remarks that the two principles are at least a plausible conception of justice. The question, though, is how one is to argue for them more systematically. Now there are several things to do. One can work out their consequences for institutions and note their implications for fundamental social policy. In this way they are tested by a comparison with our considered judgments of justice. Part II [of A Theory of Justice, eds.] is devoted to this. But one can also try to find arguments in their favor that are decisive from the standpoint of the original position. In order to see how this might be done, it is useful as a heuristic device to think of the two principles as the maximin solution to the problem of social justice. There is a relation between the two principles and the maximin rule for choice under uncertainty.[16] This is evident from the fact that the two principles are those a person would choose for the design of a society in which his enemy is to assign him his place. The maximin rule tells us to rank alternatives by their worst possible outcomes: we are to adopt the alternative the worst outcome of which is superior to the worst outcomes of the others.[17] The persons in the original position do not, of course, assume that their initial place in society is decided by a malevolent opponent. As I note below, they should not reason from false premises. The veil of ignorance does not violate this idea, since an absence of information is not misinformation. But that the two principles of justice would be chosen if the parties were forced to protect themselves against such a contingency explains the sense in which this conception is the maximin solution. And this analogy suggests that if the original position has been described so that it is rational for the parties to adopt the conservative attitude expressed by this rule, a conclusive argument can indeed be constructed for these principles. Clearly the maximin rule is not, in general, a suitable guide for choices under uncertainty. But it holds only in situations marked by certain special features. My aim, then, is to show that a good case can be made for the two principles based on the fact that the original position has these features to a very high degree.

Now there appear to be three chief features of situations that give plausibility to this unusual rule.[18] First, since the rule takes no account of the likelihoods of the possible circumstances, there must be some reason for sharply discounting estimates of these probabilities. Offhand, the most natural rule of choice would seem to be to compute the expectation of monetary gain for each decision and then to adopt the course of action with the highest prospect. (This expectation is defined as follows: let us suppose that g_{ij} represent the numbers in the gain-and-loss table, where i is the row index and j is the column index; and let p_j, $j = 1, 2, 3$, be the likelihoods of the circumstances, with $\Sigma\, p_j = 1$. expectation for the ith decision is equal to $\Sigma\, p_j g_{ij}$.) Thus it must be, for example, that the situation is one in which a knowledge of likelihoods is impossible, or at best extremely insecure. In this case it is unreasonable not to be skeptical of probabilistic calculations unless there is no other way out, particularly if the decision is a fundamental one that needs to be justified to others.

The second feature that suggests the maximin rule is the following: the person choosing has a conception of the good such that he cares very little, if anything, for what he might gain above the minimum stipend that he can, in fact, be sure of by following the maximin rule. It is not worthwhile for him to take a chance for the sake of a further advantage, especially when it may turn out that he loses much that is important to him. This last provision brings in the third feature, namely, that the rejected alternatives have outcomes that one can hardly accept. The situation involves grave risks. Of course these features work most effectively in combination. The paradigm situation for following the maximin rule is when all three features are realized to the highest degree.

Let us review briefly the nature of the original position with these three special features in mind. To begin with, the veil of ignorance excludes all knowledge of likelihoods. The parties have no basis for determining the probable nature of their society, or their place in it. Thus they have no basis for probability calculations. They must also take into account the fact that their choice of principles should seem reasonable to others, in particular their descendants, whose rights will be deeply affected by it. These considerations are strengthened by the fact that the parties know very little about the possible states of society. Not only are they unable to conjecture the likelihoods of the various possible circumstances, they cannot say much about what the possible circumstances are, much less enumerate them and foresee the outcome of each alternative available. Those deciding are much more in the dark than illustrations by numerical tables suggest. It is for this reason that I have spoken only of a relation to the maximin rule.

Several kinds of arguments for the two principles of justice illustrate the second feature. Thus, if we can maintain that these principles provide a workable theory of social justice, and that they are compatible with reasonable demands of efficiency, then this conception guarantees a satisfactory minimum. There may be, on reflection, little reason for trying to do better. Thus much of the argument, especially in Part Two [of *A Theory of Justice*, eds.], is to show, by their application to some main questions of social justice, that the two principles are a satisfactory conception. These details have a philosophical purpose. Moreover, this line of thought is practically decisive if we can establish the priority of liberty. For this priority implies that the persons in the original position have no desire to try for greater gains at the expense of the basic equal liberties. The minimum assured by the two principles in lexical order is not one that the parties wish to jeopardize for the sake of greater economic and social advantages.

Finally, the third feature holds if we can assume that other conceptions of justice may lead to institutions that the parties would find intolerable. For example, it has sometimes been held that under some conditions the utility principle (in either form) justifies, if not slavery or serfdom, at any rate serious infractions of liberty for the sake of greater social benefits. We need not consider here the truth of this claim. For the moment, this contention is only to illustrate the way in which conceptions of justice may allow for outcomes which the parties may not be able to accept. And having the ready alternative of the two principles of justice which secure a satisfactory minimum, it seems unwise, if not irrational, for them to take a chance that these conditions are not realized.

So much, then, for a brief sketch of the features of situations in which the maximin rule is a useful maxim and of the way in which the arguments for the two principles of justice can be subsumed under them. Thus if the list of traditional views [in *A Theory of Justice*, sect. 21, eds.] represents the possible decisions, these principles would be selected by the rule. The original position exhibits these special features to a sufficiently high degree in view of the fundamental character of the choice of a conception of justice. These remarks about the maximin rule are intended only to clarify the structure of the choice problem in the original position. I shall conclude this section by taking up an objection which is likely to be made against the difference principle and which leads into an important question. The objection is that since we are to maximize (subject to the usual constraints) the prospects of the least advantaged, it seems that the justice of large increases or decreases in the expectations of the more advantaged may depend upon small changes in the prospects of those worst off. To illustrate: the most extreme disparities in wealth and income are allowed provided that they are necessary to raise the expectations of the least fortunate in the slightest degree. But at the same time similar inequalities favoring the more advantaged are forbidden when those in the worst position lose by the least amount. Yet it seems extraordinary that the justice of increasing the expectations of the better placed by a billion dollars, say, should turn on whether the prospects of the least favored increase or decrease by a penny. This objection is analogous to the following familiar difficulty with the maximin rule. Consider the sequence of gain-and-loss tables:

$$
\begin{array}{cc}
0 & n \\
1/n & 1
\end{array}
$$

for all natural numbers n. Even if for some smallish number it is reasonable to select the second row, surely there is another point later in the sequence when it is irrational not to choose the first row contrary to the rule.

Part of the answer is that the difference principle is not intended to apply to such abstract possibilities. As I have said, the problem of social justice is not that of allocating *ad libitum* various amounts of something, whether it be money, or property, or whatever, among given individuals. Nor is there some substance of which expectations are made that can be shuffled from one representative man to another in all possible combinations. The possibilities which the objection envisages cannot arise in real cases; the feasible set is so restricted that they are excluded.[19] The reason for this is that the two principles are tied together as one conception of justice which applies to the basic structure of society as a whole. The operation of the principles of equal liberty and fair equality of opportunity prevents these contingencies from occurring. For we raise the expectations of the more advantaged only in ways required to improve the situation of the worst off. For the greater expectations of the more favored presumably cover the costs of training or answer to organizational requirements, thereby contributing to the general advantage. While nothing guarantees that inequalities will not be significant, there is a persistent tendency for them to be leveled down by the increasing availability of educated talent and ever widening opportunities. The conditions established by the other principles insure that the disparities likely to result will be much less than the differences that men have often tolerated in the past.

We should also observe that the difference principle not only assumes the operation of other principles, but it presupposes as well a certain theory of social institutions. In particular,... it relies on the idea that in a competitive economy (with or without private ownership) with an open class system excessive inequalities will not be the rule. Given the distribution of natural assets and the laws of motivation, great disparities will not long persist. Now the point to stress here is that there is no objection to resting the choice of first principles upon the general facts of economics and psychology. As we have seen, the parties in the original position are assumed to know the general facts about human society. Since this knowledge enters into the premises of their deliberations, their choice of principles is relative to these facts. What is essential, of course, is that these premises be true and sufficiently general. It is often objected, for example, that utilitarianism may allow for slavery and serfdom, and for other infractions of liberty. Whether these institutions are justified is made to depend upon whether actuarial calculations show that they yield a higher balance of happiness. To this the utilitarian replies that the nature of society is such that these calculations are normally against such denials of liberty.

Contract theory agrees, then, with utilitarianism in holding that the fundamental principles of justice quite properly depend upon the natural facts about men in society. This dependence is made explicit by the description of the original position: the decision of the parties is taken in the light of general knowledge. Moreover, the various elements of the original position presuppose many things about the circumstances of human life. Some philosophers have thought that ethical first principles should be independent of all contingent assumptions, that they should take for granted no truths except those of logic and others that follow from these by an analysis of concepts. Moral conceptions should hold for all possible worlds. Now this view makes moral philosophy the study of the ethics of creation: an examination of the reflections an omnipotent deity might entertain in determining which is the best of all possible worlds. Even the general facts of nature are to be chosen. Certainly we have a natural religious interest in the ethics of creation. But it would appear to outrun human comprehension. From the point of view of contract theory it amounts to supposing that the persons in the original position know nothing at all about themselves or their world. How, then, can they possibly make a decision? A problem of choice is well defined only if the alternatives are suitably restricted by natural laws and other constraints, and those deciding already have certain inclinations to choose among them. Without a definite structure of this kind the question posed is indeterminate. For this reason we need have no hesitation in making the choice of the principles of justice presuppose a certain theory of social institutions. Indeed, one cannot avoid assumptions about general facts any more than one can do without a conception of the good on the basis of which the parties rank alternatives. If these assumptions are true and suitably general, everything is in order, for without these elements the whole scheme would be pointless and empty.

It is evident from these remarks that both general facts as well as moral conditions are needed even in the argument for the first principles of justice. (Of course, it has always been obvious that secondary moral rules and particular ethical judgments depend upon factual premises as well as normative principles.) In a contract theory, these moral conditions take the form of a description of the initial contractual situation. It is also clear that there is a division of labor between general facts and moral conditions in arriving at conceptions of justice, and this division can be different from one theory to another. As I have noted before, principles differ in the extent to which they incorporate the desired moral ideal. It is characteristic of utilitarianism that it leaves so much to arguments from general facts. The utilitarian tends to meet objections by holding that the laws of society and of human nature rule out the cases offensive to our considered judgments. Justice as fairness, by contrast, embeds the ideals of justice, as ordinarily understood, more directly into its first principles. This conception relies less on general facts in reaching a match with our judgments of justice. It insures this fit over a wider range of possible cases.

There are two reasons that justify this embedding of ideals into first principles. First of all, and most obviously, the utilitarian's standard assumptions that lead to the wanted consequences may be only probably true, or even doubtfully so. Moreover, their full meaning and application may be highly conjectural. And the same may hold for all the requisite general suppositions that support the principle of utility. From the stand-point of the original position it may be unreasonable to rely upon these hypotheses and therefore far more sensible to embody the ideal more expressly in the principles chosen. Thus it seems that the parties would prefer to secure their liberties straightway rather than have them depend upon what may be uncertain and speculative actuarial calculations. These remarks are further confirmed by the desirability of avoiding complicated theoretical arguments in arriving at a public conception of justice. In comparison with the reasoning for the two principles, the grounds for the utility criterion trespass upon this constraint. But secondly, there is a real advantage in persons' announcing to one another once and for all that even though theoretical computations of utility always happen to favor the equal liberties (assuming that this is indeed the case here), they do not wish that things had been different. Since in justice as fairness moral conceptions are public, the choice of the two principles is, in effect, such an announcement. And the benefits of this collective profession favor these principles even though the utilitarian's assumptions should be true. These matters I shall consider in more detail in connection with publicity and stability.[20] The relevant point here is that while, in general, an ethical theory can certainly invoke natural facts, there may nevertheless be good reasons for embedding convictions of justice more directly into first principles than a theoretically complete grasp of the contingencies of the world may actually require.

Notes

1   *An Enquiry Concerning the Principles of Morals*, sect. III, pt. I, par. 3, ed. L. A. Selby-Bigge, 2nd edn. (Oxford, 1902), p. 184.
2   As the text suggests, I shall regard Locke's *Second Treatise of Government*, Rousseau's *The Social Contract*, and Kant's ethical works beginning with *The Foundations of the Metaphysics of Morals* as definitive of the contract tradition. For all of its greatness, Hobbes's *Leviathan* raises special problems. A general historical survey is provided by J. W. Gough, *The Social Contract*, 2nd edn. (Oxford: Clarendon Press, 1957), and Otto Gierke, *Natural Law and the Theory of Society*, trans. with an introduction by Ernest Barker (Cambridge: The University Press, 1934). A presentation of the contract view as primarily an ethical theory is to be found in G. R. Grice, *The Grounds of Moral Judgment* (Cambridge: The University Press, 1967).
3   Kant is clear that the original agreement is hypothetical. See *The Metaphysics of Morals*, pt. I (*Rechtslehre*), especially §§47, 52; and pt. II of the essay "Concerning the Common Saying: This May Be True in Theory but It Does Not Apply in Practice," in *Kant's Political Writings*, ed. Hans Reiss and trans. by H. B. Nisbet (Cambridge: The University Press, 1970), pp. 73–87. See Georges Vlachos, *La Pensée politique de Kant* (Paris: Presses Universitaires de France, 1962), pp. 326–35; and J. G. Murphy, *Kant: The Philosophy of Right* (London: Macmillan, 1970), pp. 109–12, 133–6, for a further discussion.
4   For the formulation of this intuitive idea I am indebted to Allan Gibbard.
5   The process of mutual adjustment of principles and considered judgments is not peculiar to moral philosophy. See Nelson Goodman, *Fact, Fiction, and Forecast* (Cambridge, Mass.: Harvard University Press, 1955), pp. 65–8, for parallel remarks concerning the justification of the principles of deductive and inductive inference.
6   Henri Poincaré remarks: "Il nous faut une faculté qui nous fasse voir le but de loin, et, cette faculté, c'est l'intuition." *La Valeur de la science* (Paris: Flammarion, 1909), p. 27.
7   Rawls states the final formulation of the two principles in sect. 46 of *A Theory of Justice* and reconsiders the first principle in sect. 39, neither of which is included in this extract [eds.].
8   See *A Theory of Justice*, sect. 82 [eds.].

9   There are expositions of this principle in most any work on price theory or social choice. A perspicuous account is found in T. C. Koopmans, *Three Essays on the State of Economic Science* (New York: McGraw-Hill, 1957), pp. 41–66. See also A. K. Sen, *Collective Choice and Social Welfare* (San Francisco: Holden-Day Inc., 1970), pp. 21f. These works contain everything (and more) that is required for our purposes in this book; and the latter takes up the relevant philosophical questions. The principle of efficiency was introduced by Vilfredo Pareto in his *Manuel d'économie politique* (Paris, 1909), ch. VI, §53, and the appendix, §89. A translation of the relevant passages can be found in A. N. Page, *Utility Theory: A Book of Readings* (New York: John Wiley, 1968), pp. 38f. The related concept of indifference curves goes back to F. Y. Edgeworth, *Mathematical Psychics* (London, 1888), pp. 20–9; also in Page, pp. 160–7.

10 On this point see Koopmans, *Three Essays on the State of Economic Science*, p. 49. Koopmans remarks that a term like "allocative efficiency" would have been a more accurate name.

11 For the application of the Pareto criterion to systems of public rules, see J. M. Buchanan, "The Relevance of Pareto Optimality," *Journal of Conflict Resolution*, vol. 6 (1962), as well as his book with Gordon Tullock, *The Calculus of Consent* (Ann Arbor: The University of Michigan Press, 1962). In applying this and other principles to institutions I follow one of the points of "Two Concepts of Rules," *Philosophical Review*, vol. 64 (1955). Doing this has the advantage, among other things, of constraining the employment of principles by publicity effects.

12 This fact is generally recognized in welfare economics, as when it is said that efficiency is to be balanced against equity. See for example Tibor Scitovsky, *Welfare and Competition* (London: George Allen & Unwin, 1952), pp. 60–9 and I. M. D. Little, *A Critique of Welfare Economics*, 2nd edn. (Oxford: The Clarendon Press, 1957), ch. VI, esp. pp. 112–16. See Sen's remarks on the limitations of the principle of efficiency, *Collective Choice and Social Welfare*, pp. 22, 24–6, 83–6.

13 This definition follows Sidgwick's suggestion in *The Methods of Ethics*, p. 285n. See also R. H. Tawney, *Equality* (London: George Allen & Unwin, 1931), ch. II, sect. ii; and B. A. O. Williams, "The Idea of Equality," in *Philosophy, Politics, and Society*, ed. Peter Laslett and W. G. Runciman (Oxford: Basil Blackwell, 1962), pp. 125f.

14 This formulation of the aristocratic ideal is derived from Santayana's account of aristocracy in ch. IV of *Reason and Society* (New York: Charles Scribner, 1905), pp. 109f. He says, for example, "an aristocratic regimen can only be justified by radiating benefit and by proving that were less given to those above, less would be attained by those beneath them." I am indebted to Robert Rodes for pointing out to me that natural aristocracy is a possible interpretation of the two principles of justice and that an ideal feudal system might also try to fulfill the difference principle.

15 On this point, see Sen, *Collective Choice and Social Welfare*, p. 138n.

16 An accessible discussion of this and other rules of choice under uncertainty can be found in W. J. Baumol, *Economic Theory and Operations Analysis*, 2nd edn. (Englewood Cliffs, NJ: Prentice-Hall Inc., 1965), ch. 24. Baumol gives a geometric interpretation of these rules, including the diagram used in §VI to illustrate the difference principle. See pp. 558–62. See also R. D. Luce and Howard Raiffa, *Games and Decisions* (New York: John Wiley & Sons, Inc., 1957), ch. XIII, for a fuller account.

17   Consider the gain-and-loss table below. It represents the gains and losses for a situation which is not a game of strategy. There is no one playing against the person making the decision; instead he is faced with several possible circumstances which may or may not obtain. Which circumstances happen to exist does not depend upon what the person choosing decides or whether he announces his moves in advance. The numbers in the table are monetary values (in hundreds of dollars) in comparison with some initial situation. The gain (g) depends upon the individual's decision (d) and the circumstances (c). Thus $g = f(d, c)$. Assuming that there are three possible decisions and three possible circumstances, we might have this gain-and-loss table.

		Circumstances	
Decisions	c_1	c_2	c_3
d_1	−7	8	12
d_2	−8	7	14
d_3	5	6	8

The maximin rule requires that we make the third decision. For in this case the worst that can happen is that one gains five hundred dollars, which is better than the worst for the other actions. If we adopt one of these we may lose either eight or seven hundred dollars. Thus, the choice of d_3 maximizes $f(d,c)$ for that value of c, which for a given d, minimizes f. The term "maximin" means the *maximum minimorum*; and the rule directs our attention to the worst that can happen under any proposed course of action, and to decide in the light of that.

18   Here I borrow from William Fellner, *Probability and Profit* (Homewood, Ill.: R. D. Irwin, Inc., 1965), pp. 140–2, where these features are noted.

19   I am indebted to S. A. Marglin for this point.

20   See *A Theory of Justice*, sect. 29 [eds.].

4

An Entitlement Theory

Robert Nozick

The term "distributive justice" is not a neutral one. Hearing the term "distribution," most people presume that some thing or mechanism uses some
principle or criterion to give out a supply of things. Into this process of
distributing shares some error may have crept. So it is an open question, at
least, whether redistribution should take place; whether we should do again
what has already been done once, though poorly. However, we are not in
the position of children who have been given portions of pie by someone who
now makes last minute adjustments to rectify careless cutting. There is no
central distribution, no person or group entitled to control all the resources,
jointly deciding how they are to be doled out. What each person gets, he gets
from others who give to him in exchange for something, or as a gift. In a free
society, diverse persons control different resources, and new holdings arise
out of the voluntary exchanges and actions of persons. There is no more a
distributing or distribution of shares than there is a distributing of mates in
a society in which persons choose whom they shall marry. The total result
is the product of many individual decisions which the different individuals
involved are entitled to make. Some uses of the term "distribution," it is true,
do not imply a previous distributing appropriately judged by some criterion
(for example, "probability distribution"); nevertheless ... it would be best
to use a terminology that clearly is neutral. We shall speak of people's
holdings; a principle of justice in holdings describes (part of) what justice
tells us (requires) about holdings. I shall state first what I take to be the correct
view about justice in holdings, and then turn to the discussion of alternate
views.[1]

Extracts from Robert Nozick, *Anarchy, State, and Utopia* (New York: Basic Books, 1974),
pp. 149–64, 167–82.

I.   The Entitlement Theory

The subject of justice in holdings consists of three major topics. The first is the *original acquisition of holdings*, the appropriation of unheld things. This includes the issues of how unheld things may come to be held, the process, or processes, by which unheld things may come to be held, the things that may come to be held by these processes, the extent of what comes to be held by a particular process, and so on. We shall refer to the complicated truth about this topic, which we shall not formulate here, as the principle of justice in acquisition. The second topic concerns the *transfer of holdings* from one person to another. By what processes may a person transfer holdings to another? How may a person acquire a holding from another who holds it? Under this topic come general descriptions of voluntary exchange, and gift and (on the other hand) fraud, as well as reference to particular conventional details fixed upon in a given society. The complicated truth about this subject (with placeholders for conventional details) we shall call the principle of justice in transfer. (And we shall suppose it also includes principles governing how a person may divest himself of a holding, passing it into an unheld state.)

If the world were wholly just, the following inductive definition would exhaustively cover the subject of justice in holdings.

1   A person who acquires a holding in accordance with the principle of justice in acquisition is entitled to that holding.
2   A person who acquires a holding in accordance with the principle of justice in transfer, from someone else entitled to the holding, is entitled to the holding.
3   No one is entitled to a holding except by (repeated) applications of 1 and 2.

The complete principle of distributive justice would say simply that a distribution is just if everyone is entitled to the holdings they possess under the distribution.

A distribution is just if it arises from another just distribution by legitimate means. The legitimate means of moving from one distribution to another are specified by the principle of justice in transfer. The legitimate first "moves" are specified by the principle of justice in acquisition.[2] Whatever arises from a just situation by just steps is itself just. The means of change specified by the principle of justice in transfer preserve justice. As correct rules of inference are truth-preserving, and any conclusion deduced via repeated application of such rules from only true premises is itself true, so the means of transition from one situation to another specified by the principle of justice in transfer are justice-preserving, and any situation actually arising from repeated transitions in accordance with the principle from a just situation is itself just. The parallel between justice-preserving transformations and truth-preserving transformations illuminates where it fails as well as where it holds. That a conclusion could have been deduced by truth-preserving means from premises that are true suffices to show its truth. That from a just situation a situation *could* have arisen via justice-preserving means does *not* suffice to show its justice. The fact that a thief's victims voluntarily *could* have presented him with gifts does not entitle the thief to his ill-gotten gains. Justice in holdings is historical; it depends upon what actually has happened. We shall return to this point later.

Not all actual situations are generated in accordance with the two principles of justice in holdings: the principle of justice in acquisition and the principle of justice in transfer. Some people steal from others, or defraud them, or enslave them, seizing their product and preventing them from living as they choose, or forcibly exclude others from competing in exchanges. None of these are permissible modes of transition from one situation to another. And some persons acquire holdings by means not sanctioned by the principle of justice in acquisition. The existence of past injustice (previous violations of the first two principles of justice in holdings) raises the third major topic under justice in holdings: the rectification of injustice in holdings. If past injustice has shaped present holdings in various ways, some identifiable and some not, what now, if anything, ought to be done to rectify these injustices? What obligations do the performers of injustice have toward those whose position is worse than it would have been had the injustice not been done? Or, than it would have been had compensation been paid promptly? How, if at all, do things change if the beneficiaries and those made worse off are not the direct parties in the act of injustice, but, for example, their descendants? Is an injustice done to someone whose holding was itself based upon an unrectified injustice? How far back must one go in wiping clean the historical slate of injustices? What may victims of injustice permissibly do in order to rectify the injustices being done to them, including the many injustices done by persons acting through their government? I do not know of a thorough or theoretically sophisticated treatment of such issues.[3] Idealizing greatly, let us suppose theoretical investigation will produce a principle of rectification. This principle uses historical information about previous situations and injustices done in them (as defined by the first two principles of justice and rights against interference), and information about the actual course of events that flowed from these injustices, until the present, and it yields a description (or descriptions) of holdings in the society. The principle of rectification presumably will make use of its best estimate of subjunctive information about what would have occurred (or a probability distribution over what might have occurred, using the expected value) if the injustice had not taken place. If the actual description of holdings turns out not to be one of the descriptions yielded by the principle, then one of the descriptions yielded must be realized.[4]

The general outlines of the theory of justice in holdings are that the holdings of a person are just if he is entitled to them by the principles of justice in acquisition and transfer, or by the principle of rectification of injustice (as specified by the first two principles). If each person's holdings are just, then the total set (distribution) of holdings is just. To turn these general outlines into a specific theory we would have to specify the details of each of the three principles of justice in holdings: the principle of acquisition of holdings, the principle of transfer of holdings, and the principle of rectification of violations of the first two principles. I shall not attempt that task here. (Locke's principle of justice in acquisition is discussed below.)

II.   Historical Principles and End-Result Principles

The general outlines of the entitlement theory illuminate the nature and defects of other conceptions of distributive justice. The entitlement theory of justice in distribution is *historical*; whether a distribution is just depends upon how it came about. In contrast, *current time-slice principles* of justice hold that the justice of a distribution is determined by how things are distributed (who has what) as judged by some *structural* principle(s) of just distribution. A utilitarian who judges between any two distributions by seeing which has the greater sum of utility and, if the sums tie, applies some fixed equality criterion to choose the more equal distribution, would hold a current time-slice principle of justice. As would someone who had a fixed schedule of trade-offs between the sum of happiness and equality. According to a current time-slice principle, all that needs to be looked at, in judging the justice of a distribution, is who ends up with what; in comparing any two distributions one need look only at the matrix presenting the distributions. No further information need be fed into a principle of justice. It is a consequence of such principles of justice that any two structurally identical distributions are equally just. (Two distributions are structurally identical if they present the same profile, but perhaps have different persons occupying the particular slots. My having ten and your having five, and my having five and your having ten are structurally identical distributions.) Welfare economics is the theory of current time-slice principles of justice. The subject is conceived as operating on matrices representing only current information about distribution. This, as well as some of the usual conditions (for example, the choice of distribution is invariant under relabeling of columns), guarantees that welfare economics will be a current time-slice theory, with all of its inadequacies.

Most persons do not accept current time-slice principles as constituting the whole story about distributive shares. They think it relevant in assessing the justice of a situation to consider not only the distribution it embodies, but also how that distribution came about. If some persons are in prison for murder or war crimes, we do not say that to assess the justice of the distribution in the society we must look only at what this person has, and that person has, and that person has,...at the current time. We think it relevant to ask whether someone did something so that he *deserved* to be punished, deserved to have a lower share. Most will agree to the relevance of further information with regard to punishments and penalties. Consider also desired things. One traditional socialist view is that workers are entitled to the product and full fruits of their labor; they have earned it; a distribution is unjust if it does not give the workers what they are entitled to. Such entitlements are based upon some past history. No socialist holding this view would find it comforting to be told that because the actual distribution *A* happens to coincide structurally with the one he desires *D*, *A* therefore is no less just than *D*; it differs only in that the "parasitic" owners of capital receive under *A* what the workers are entitled to under *D*, and the workers receive under *A* what the owners are entitled to under *D*, namely very little. This socialist rightly, in my view, holds onto the notions of earning, producing, entitlement, desert, and so forth, and he rejects current time-slice principles that look only to the structure of the resulting set of holdings. (The set of holdings resulting from what? Isn't it implausible that how holdings are produced and come to exist has no effect at all on who should hold what?) His mistake lies in his view of what entitlements arise out of what sorts of productive processes.

We construe the position we discuss too narrowly by speaking of *current* time-slice principles. Nothing is changed if structural principles operate upon a time sequence of current time-slice profiles and, for example, give someone more now to counterbalance the less he has had earlier. A utilitarian or an egalitarian or any mixture of the two over time will inherit the difficulties of his more myopic comrades. He is not helped by the fact that *some* of the information others consider relevant in assessing a distribution is reflected, unrecoverably, in past matrices. Henceforth, we shall refer to such unhistorical principles of distributive justice, including the current time-slice principles, as *end-result principles* or *end-state principles*.

In contrast to end-result principles of justice, *historical principles* of justice hold that past circumstances or actions of people can create differential entitlements or differential deserts to things. An injustice can be worked by moving from one distribution to another structurally identical one, for the second, in profile the same, may violate people's entitlements or deserts; it may not fit the actual history.

III. Patterning

The entitlement principles of justice in holdings that we have sketched are historical principles of justice. To better understand their precise character, we shall distinguish them from another subclass of the historical principles. Consider, as an example, the principle of distribution according to moral merit. This principle requires that total distributive shares vary directly with moral merit; no person should have a greater share than anyone whose moral merit is greater. (If moral merit could be not merely ordered but measured on an interval or ratio scale, stronger principles could be formulated.) Or consider the principle that results by substituting "usefulness to society" for "moral merit" in the previous principle. Or instead of "distribute according to moral merit," or "distribute according to usefulness to society," we might consider "distribute according to the weighted sum of moral merit, usefulness to society, and need," with the weights of the different dimensions equal. Let us call a principle of distribution *patterned* if it specifies that a distribution is to vary along with some natural dimension, weighted sum of natural dimensions, or lexicographic ordering of natural dimensions. And let us say a distribution is patterned if it accords with some patterned principle. (I speak of natural dimensions, admittedly without a general criterion for them, because for any set of holdings some artificial dimensions can be gimmicked up to vary along with the distribution of the set.) The principle of distribution in accordance with moral merit is a patterned historical principle, which specifies a patterned distribution. "Distribute according to I.Q." is a patterned principle that looks to information not contained in distributional matrices. It is not historical, however, in that it does not look to any past actions creating differential entitlements to evaluate a distribution; it requires only distributional matrices whose columns are labeled by I.Q. scores. The distribution in a society, however, may be composed of such simple patterned distributions, without itself being simply patterned. Different sectors may operate different patterns, or some combination of patterns may operate in different proportions across a society. A distribution composed in this manner, from a small number of patterned distributions, we also shall term "patterned." And we extend the use of "pattern" to include the overall designs put forth by combinations of end-state principles.

Almost every suggested principle of distributive justice is patterned: to each according to his moral merit, or needs, or marginal product, or how hard he tries, or the weighted sum of the foregoing, and so on. The principle of entitlement we have sketched is *not* patterned.[5] There is no one natural dimension or weighted sum or combination of a small number of natural dimensions that yields the distributions generated in accordance with the principle of entitlement. The set of holdings that results when some persons receive their marginal products, others win at gambling, others receive a share of their mate's income, others receive gifts from foundations, others receive interest on loans, others receive gifts from admirers, others receive returns on investment, others make for themselves much of what they have, others find things, and so on, will not be patterned. Heavy strands of patterns will run through it; significant portions of the variance in holdings will be accounted for by pattern-variables. If most people most of the time choose to transfer some of their entitlements to others only in exchange for something from them, then a large part of what many people hold will vary with what they held that others wanted. More details are provided by the theory of marginal productivity. But gifts to relatives, charitable donations, bequests to children, and the like, are not best conceived, in the first instance, in this manner. Ignoring the strands of pattern, let us suppose for the moment that a distribution actually arrived at by the operation of the principle of entitlement is random with respect to any pattern. Though the resulting set of holdings will be unpatterned, it will not be incomprehensible, for it can be seen as arising from the operation of a small number of principles. These principles specify how an initial distribution may arise (the principle of acquisition of holdings) and how distributions may be transformed into others (the principle of transfer of holdings). The process whereby the set of holdings is generated will be intelligible, though the set of holdings itself that results from this process will be unpatterned.

The writings of F. A. Hayek focus less than is usually done upon what patterning distributive justice requires. Hayek argues that we cannot know enough about each person's situation to distribute to each according to his moral merit (but would justice demand we do so if we did have this knowledge?); and he goes on to say, "our objection is against all attempts to impress upon society a deliberately chosen pattern of distribution, whether it be an order of equality or of inequality."[6] However, Hayek concludes that in a free society there will be distribution in accordance with value rather than moral merit; that is, in accordance with the perceived value of a person's actions and services to others. Despite his rejection of a patterned conception of distributive justice, Hayek himself suggests a pattern he thinks justifiable: distribution in accordance with the perceived benefits given to others, leaving room for the complaint that a free society does not realize exactly this pattern. Stating this patterned strand of a free capitalist society more precisely, we get "To each according to how much he benefits others who have the resources for benefiting those who benefit them." This will seem arbitrary unless some acceptable initial set of holdings is specified, or unless it is held that the operation of the system over time washes out any significant effects from the initial set of holdings. As an example of the latter, if almost anyone would have bought a car from Henry Ford, the supposition that it was an arbitrary matter who held the money then (and so bought) would not place Henry Ford's earnings under a cloud. In any event, *his* coming to hold it is not arbitrary. Distribution according to benefits to others *is* a major patterned strand in a free capitalist society, as Hayek correctly points out, but it is only a strand and does not constitute the whole pattern of a system of entitlements (namely, inheritance, gifts for arbitrary reasons, charity, and so on) or a standard that one should insist a society fit. Will people tolerate for long a system yielding distributions that they believe are unpatterned?[7] No doubt people will not long accept a distribution they believe is *unjust*. People want their society to be and to look just. But must the look of justice reside in a resulting pattern rather than in the underlying generating principles? We are in no position to conclude that the inhabitants of a society embodying an entitlement conception of justice in holdings will find it unacceptable. Still, it must be granted that were people's reasons for transferring some of their holdings to others always irrational or arbitrary, we would find this disturbing. (Suppose people always determined what holdings they would transfer, and to whom, by using a random device.) We feel more comfortable upholding the justice of an entitlement system if most of the transfers under it are done for reasons. This does not mean necessarily that all deserve what holdings they receive. It means only that there is a purpose or point to someone's transferring a holding to one person rather than to another; that usually we can see what the transferrer thinks he's gaining, what cause he thinks he's serving, what goals he thinks he's helping to achieve, and so forth. Since in a capitalist society people often transfer holdings to others in accordance with how much they perceive these others benefiting them, the fabric constituted by the individual transactions and transfers is largely reasonable and intelligible.[8] (Gifts to loved ones, bequests to children, charity to the needy also are nonarbitrary components of the fabric.) In stressing the large strand of distribution in accordance with benefit to others, Hayek shows the point of many transfers, and so shows that the system of transfer of entitlements is not just spinning its gears aimlessly. The system of entitlements is defensible when constituted by the individual aims of individual transactions. No overarching aim is needed, no distributional pattern is required.

To think that the task of a theory of distributive justice is to fill in the blank in "to each according to his——" is to be predisposed to search for a pattern; and the separate treatment of "from each according to his——" treats production and distribution as two separate and independent issues. On an entitlement view these are *not* two separate questions. Whoever makes something, having bought or contracted for all other held resources used in the process (transferring some of his holdings for these cooperating factors), is entitled to it. The situation is *not* one of something's getting made, and there being an open question of who is to get it. Things come into the world already attached to people having entitlements over them. From the point of view of the historical entitlement conception of justice in holdings, those who start afresh to complete "to each according to his——" treat objects as if they appeared from nowhere, out of nothing. A complete theory of justice might cover this limit case as well; perhaps here is a use for the usual conceptions of distributive justice.[9]

So entrenched are maxims of the usual form that perhaps we should present the entitlement conception as a competitor. Ignoring acquisition and rectification, we might say:

> From each according to what he chooses to do, to each according to what he makes for himself (perhaps with the contracted aid of others) and what others choose to do for him and choose to give him of what they've been given previously (under this maxim) and haven't yet expended or transferred.

This, the discerning reader will have noticed, has its defects as a slogan. So as a summary and great simplification (and not as a maxim with any independent meaning) we have:

> *From each as they choose, to each as they are chosen.*

IV.   How Liberty Upsets Patterns

It is not clear how those holding alternative conceptions of distributive justice can reject the entitlement conception of justice in holdings. For suppose a distribution favored by one of these non-entitlement conceptions is realized. Let us suppose it is your favorite one and let us call this distribution D_1; perhaps everyone has an equal share, perhaps shares vary in accordance with some dimension you treasure. Now suppose that Wilt Chamberlain is greatly in demand by basketball teams, being a great gate attraction. (Also suppose contracts run only for a year, with players being free agents.) He signs the following sort of contract with a team: In each home game, twenty-five cents from the price of each ticket of admission goes to him. (We ignore the question of whether he is "gouging" the owners, letting them look out for themselves.) The season starts, and people cheerfully attend his team's games; they buy their tickets, each time dropping a separate twenty-five cents of their admission price into a special box with Chamberlain's name on it. They are excited about seeing him play; it is worth the total admission price to them. Let us suppose that in one season one million persons attend his home games, and Wilt Chamberlain winds up with $250,000, a much larger sum than the average income and larger even than anyone else has. Is he entitled to this income? Is this new distribution D_2, unjust? If so, why? There is *no* question about whether each of the people was entitled to the control over the resources they held in D_1; because that was the distribution (your favorite) that (for the purposes of argument) we assumed was acceptable. Each of these persons *chose* to give twenty-five cents of their money to Chamberlain. They could have spent it on going to the movies, or on candy bars, or on copies of *Dissent* magazine, or of *Montly [sic] Review*. But they all, at least one million of them, converged on giving it to Wilt Chamberlain in exchange for watching him play basketball. If D_1 was a just distribution, and people voluntarily moved from it to D_2, transferring parts of their shares they were given under D_1 (what was it for if not to do something with?), isn't D_2 also just? If the people were entitled to dispose of the resources to which they were entitled (under D_1), didn't this include their being entitled to give it to, or exchange it with, Wilt Chamberlain? Can anyone else complain on grounds of justice? Each other person already has his legitimate share under D_1. Under D_1, there is nothing that anyone has that anyone else has a claim of justice against. After someone transfers something to Wilt Chamberlain, third parties *still* have their legitimate shares; *their* shares are not changed. By what process could such a transfer among two persons give rise to a legitimate claim of distributive justice on a portion of what was transferred, by a third party who had no claim of justice on any holding of the others *before* the transfer?[10] To cut off objections irrelevant here, we might imagine the exchanges occurring in a socialist society, after hours. After playing whatever basketball he does in his daily work, or doing whatever other daily work he does, Wilt Chamberlain decides to put in *overtime* to earn additional money. (First his work quota is set; he works time over that.) Or imagine it is a skilled juggler people like to see, who puts on shows after hours.

Why might someone work overtime in a society in which it is assumed their needs are satisfied? Perhaps because they care about things other than needs.

I like to write in books that I read, and to have easy access to books for browsing at odd hours. It would be very pleasant and convenient to have the resources of Widener Library in my back yard. No society, I assume, will provide such resources close to each person who would like them as part of his regular allotment (under D_1). Thus, persons either must do without some extra things that they want, or be allowed to do something extra to get some of these things. On what basis could the inequalities that would eventuate be forbidden? Notice also that small factories would spring up in a socialist society, unless forbidden. I melt down some of my personal possessions (under D_1) and build a machine out of the material. I offer you, and others, a philosophy lecture once a week in exchange for your cranking the handle on my machine, whose products I exchange for yet other things, and so on. (The raw materials used by the machine are given to me by others who possess them under D_1, in exchange for hearing lectures.) Each person might participate to gain things over and above their allotment under D_1. Some persons even might want to leave their job in socialist industry and work full time in this private sector. I shall say something more about these issues in the next chapter [omitted, eds.]. Here I wish merely to note how private property even in means of production would occur in a socialist society that did not forbid people to use as they wished some of the resources they are given under the socialist distribution D_1.[11] The socialist society would have to forbid capitalist acts between consenting adults.

The general point illustrated by the Wilt Chamberlain example and the example of the entrepreneur in a socialist society is that no end-state principle or distributional patterned principle of justice can be continuously realized without continuous interference with people's lives. Any favored pattern would be transformed into one unfavored by the principle, by people choosing to act in various ways; for example, by people exchanging goods and services with other people, or giving things to other people, things the transferrers are entitled to under the favored distributional pattern. To maintain a pattern one must either continually interfere to stop people from transferring resources as they wish to, or continually (or periodically) interfere to take from some persons resources that others for some reason chose to transfer to them. (But if some time limit is to be set on how long people may keep resources others voluntarily transfer to them, why let them keep these resources for *any* period of time? Why not have immediate confiscation?) It might be objected that all persons voluntarily will choose to refrain from actions which would upset the pattern. This presupposes unrealistically (1) that all will most want to maintain the pattern (are those who don't, to be "reeducated" or forced to undergo "self-criticism"?), (2) that each can gather enough information about his own actions and the ongoing activities of others to discover which of his actions will upset the pattern, and (3) that diverse and far-flung persons can coordinate their actions to dovetail into the pattern. Compare the manner in which the market is neutral among persons' desires, as it reflects and transmits widely scattered information via prices, and coordinates persons' activities.

It puts things perhaps a bit too strongly to say that every patterned (or end-state) principle is liable to be thwarted by the voluntary actions of the individual parties transferring some of their shares they receive under the principle. For perhaps some *very* weak patterns are not so thwarted.[12] Any distributional pattern with any egalitarian component is overturnable by the voluntary actions of individual persons over time; as is every patterned condition with sufficient content so as actually to have been proposed as presenting the central core of distributive justice. Still, given the possibility that some weak conditions or patterns may not be unstable in this way, it would be better to formulate an explicit description of the kind of interesting and contentful patterns under discussion, and to prove a theorem about their instability. Since the weaker the patterning, the more likely it is that the entitlement system itself satisfies it, a plausible conjecture is that any patterning either is unstable or is satisfied by the entitlement system. . . .

V. Redistribution and Property Rights

Apparently, patterned principles allow people to choose to expend upon themselves, but not upon others, those resources they are entitled to (or rather, receive) under some favored distributional pattern D_1. For if each of several persons chooses to expend some of his D_1 resources upon one other person, then that other person will receive more than his D_1 share, disturbing the favored distributional pattern. Maintaining a distributional pattern is individualism with a vengeance! Patterned distributional principles do not give people what entitlement principles do, only better distributed. For they do not give the right to choose what to do with what one has; they do not give the right to choose to pursue an end involving (intrinsically, or as a means) the enhancement of another's position. To such views, families are disturbing; for within a family occur transfers that upset the favored distributional pattern. Either families themselves become units to which distribution takes place, the column occupiers (on what rationale?), or loving behavior is forbidden. We should note in passing the ambivalent position of radicals toward the family. Its loving relationships are seen as a model to be emulated and extended across the whole society, at the same time that it is denounced as a suffocating institution to be broken and condemned as a focus of parochial concerns that interfere with achieving radical goals. Need we say that it is not appropriate to enforce across the wider society the relationships of love and care appropriate within a family, relationships which are voluntarily undertaken?[13] Incidentally, love is an interesting instance of another relationship that is historical, in that (like justice) it depends upon what actually occurred. An adult may come to love another because of the other's characteristics; but it is the other person, and not the characteristics, that is loved.[14] The love is not transferrable to someone else with the same characteristics, even to one who "scores" higher for these characteristics. And the love endures through changes of the characteristics that gave rise to it. One loves the particular person one actually encountered. Why love is historical, attaching to persons in this way and not to characteristics, is an interesting and puzzling question.

Proponents of patterned principles of distributive justice focus upon criteria for determining who is to receive holdings; they consider the reasons for which someone should have something, and also the total picture of holdings. Whether or not it is better to give than to receive, proponents of patterned principles ignore giving altogether. In considering the distribution of goods, income, and so forth, their theories are theories of recipient justice; they completely ignore any right a person might have to give something to someone. Even in exchanges where each party is simultaneously giver and recipient, patterned principles of justice focus only upon the recipient role and its supposed rights. Thus discussions tend to focus on whether people (should) have a right to inherit, rather than on whether people (should) have a right to bequeath or on whether persons who have a right to hold also have a right to choose that others hold in their place. I lack a good explanation of why the usual theories of distributive justice are so recipient oriented; ignoring givers and transferrers and their rights is of a piece with ignoring producers and their entitlements. But why is it *all* ignored?

Patterned principles of distributive justice necessitate *re*distributive activities. The likelihood is small that any actual freely-arrived-at set of holdings fits a given pattern; and the likelihood is nil that it will continue to fit the pattern as people exchange and give. From the point of view of an entitlement theory, redistribution is a serious matter indeed, involving, as it does, the violation of people's rights. (An exception is those takings that fall under the principle of the rectification of injustices.) From other points of view, also, it is serious.

Taxation of earnings from labor is on a par with forced labor.[15] Some persons find this claim obviously true: taking the earnings of *n* hours labor is like taking *n* hours from the person; it is like forcing the person to work *n* hours for another's purpose. Others find the claim absurd. But even these, *if* they object to forced labor, would oppose forcing unemployed hippies to work for the benefit of the needy.[16] And they would also object to forcing each person to work five extra hours each week for the benefit of the needy. But a system that takes five hours' wages in taxes does not seem to them like one that forces someone to work five hours, since it offers the person forced a wider range of choice in activities than does taxation in kind with the particular labor specified. (But we can imagine a gradation of systems of forced labor, from one that specifies a particular activity, to one that gives a choice among two activities, to . . . ; and so on up.) Furthermore, people envisage a system with something like a proportional tax on everything above the amount necessary for basic needs. Some think this does not force someone to work extra hours, since there is no fixed number of extra hours he is forced to work, and since he can avoid the tax entirely by earning only enough to cover his basic needs. This is a very uncharacteristic view of forcing for those who *also* think people are forced to do something *whenever* the alternatives they face are considerably worse. However, *neither* view is correct. The fact that others intentionally intervene, in violation of a side constraint against aggression, to threaten force to limit the alternatives, in this case to paying taxes or (presumably the worse alternative) bare subsistence, makes the taxation system one of forced labor and distinguishes it from other cases of limited choices which are not forcings.[17]

The man who chooses to work longer to gain an income more than sufficient for his basic needs prefers some extra goods or services to the leisure and activities he could perform during the possible nonworking hours; whereas the man who chooses not to work the extra time prefers the leisure activities to the extra goods or services he could acquire by working more. Given this, if it would be illegitimate for a tax system to seize some of a man's leisure (forced labor) for the purpose of serving the needy, how can it be legitimate for a tax system to seize some of a man's goods for that purpose? Why should we treat the man whose happiness requires certain material goods or services differently from the man whose preferences and desires make such goods unnecessary for his happiness? Why should the man who prefers seeing a movie (and who has to earn money for a ticket) be open to the required call to aid the needy, while the person who prefers looking at a sunset (and hence need earn no extra money) is not? Indeed, isn't it surprising that redistributionists choose to ignore the man whose pleasures are so easily attainable without extra labor, while adding yet another burden to the poor unfortunate who must work for his pleasures? If anything, one would have expected the reverse. Why is the person with the nonmaterial or nonconsumption desire allowed to proceed unimpeded to his most favored feasible alternative, whereas the man whose pleasures or desires involve material things and who must work for extra money (thereby serving whomever considers his activities valuable enough to pay him) is constrained in what he can realize? Perhaps there is no difference in principle. And perhaps some think the answer concerns merely administrative convenience. (These questions and issues will not disturb those who think that forced labor to serve the needy or to realize some favored end-state pattern is acceptable.) In a fuller discussion we would have (and want) to extend our argument to include interest, entrepreneurial profits, and so on. Those who doubt that this extension can be carried through, and who draw the line here at taxation of income from labor, will have to state rather complicated patterned *historical* principles of distributive justice, since end-state principles would not distinguish *sources* of income in any way. It is enough for now to get away from end-state principles and to make clear how various patterned principles are dependent upon particular views about the sources or the illegitimacy or the lesser legitimacy of profits, interest, and so on; which particular views may well be mistaken.

What sort of right over others does a legally institutionalized end-state pattern give one? The central core of the notion of a property right in X, relative to which other parts of the notion are to be explained, is the right to determine what shall be done with X; the right to choose which of the constrained set of options concerning X shall be realized or attempted.[18] The constraints are set by other principles or laws operating in the society; in our theory, by the Lockean rights people possess (under the minimal state). My property rights in my knife allow me to leave it where I will, but not in your chest. I may choose which of the acceptable options involving the knife is to be realized. This notion of property helps us to understand why earlier theorists spoke of people as having property in themselves and their labor. They viewed each person as having a right to decide what would become of himself and what he would do, and as having a right to reap the benefits of what he did.

This right of selecting the alternative to be realized from the constrained set of alternatives may be held by an *individual* or by a *group* with some procedure for reaching a joint decision; or the right may be passed back and forth, so that one year I decide what's to become of X, and the next year you do (with the alternative of destruction, perhaps, being excluded). Or, during the same time period, some types of decisions about X may be made by me, and others by you. And so on. We lack an adequate, fruitful, analytical apparatus for classifying the *types* of constraints on the set of options among which choices are to be made, and the *types* of ways decision powers can be held, divided, and amalgamated. A *theory* of property would, among other things, contain such a classification of constraints and decision modes, and from a small number of principles would follow a host of interesting statements about the *consequences* and effects of certain combinations of constraints and modes of decision.

When end-result principles of distributive justice are built into the legal structure of a society, they (as do most patterned principles) give each citizen an enforceable claim to some portion of the total social product; that is, to some portion of the sum total of the individually and jointly made products. This total product is produced by individuals laboring, using means of production others have saved to bring into existence, by people organizing production or creating means to produce new things or things in a new way. It is on this batch of individual activities that patterned distributional principles give each individual an enforceable claim. Each person has a claim to the activities and the products of other persons, independently of whether the other persons enter into particular relationships that give rise to these claims, and independently of whether they voluntarily take these claims upon themselves, in charity or in exchange for something.

Whether it is done through taxation on wages or on wages over a certain amount, or through seizure of profits, or through there being a big *social pot* so that it's not clear what's coming from where and what's going where, patterned principles of distributive justice involve appropriating the actions of other persons. Seizing the results of someone's labor is equivalent to seizing hours from him and directing him to carry on various activities. If people force you to do certain work, or unrewarded work, for a certain period of time, they decide what you are to do and what purposes your work is to serve apart from your decisions. This process whereby they take this decision from you makes them a *part-owner* of you; it gives them a property right in you. Just as having such partial control and power of decision, by right, over an animal or inanimate object would be to have a property right in it.

End-state and most patterned principles of distributive justice institute (partial) ownership by others of people and their actions and labor. These principles involve a shift from the classical liberals' notion of self-ownership to a notion of (partial) property rights in *other* people.

Considerations such as these confront end-state and other patterned conceptions of justice with the question of whether the actions necessary to achieve the selected pattern don't themselves violate moral side constraints. Any view holding that there are moral side constraints on actions, that not all moral considerations can be built into end states that are to be achieved ... must face the possibility that some of its goals are not achievable by any morally permissible available means. An entitlement theorist will face such conflicts in a society that deviates from the principles of justice for the generation of holdings, if and only if the only actions available to realize the principles themselves violate some moral constraints. Since deviation from the first two principles of justice (in acquisition and transfer) will involve other persons' direct and aggressive intervention to violate rights, and since moral constraints will not exclude defensive or retributive action in such cases, the entitlement theorist's problem rarely will be pressing. And whatever difficulties he has in applying the principle of rectification to persons who did not themselves violate the first two principles are difficulties in balancing the conflicting considerations so as correctly to formulate the complex principle of rectification itself; he will not violate moral side constraints by applying the principle. Proponents of patterned conceptions of justice, however, often will face head-on clashes (and poignant ones if they cherish each party to the clash) between moral side constraints on how individuals may be treated and their patterned conception of justice that presents an end-state or other pattern that *must* be realized.

May a person emigrate from a nation that has institutionalized some end-state or patterned distributional principle? For some principles (for example, Hayek's) emigration presents no theoretical problem. But for others it is a tricky matter. Consider a nation having a compulsory scheme of minimal social provision to aid the neediest (or one organized so as to maximize the position of the worst-off group); no one may opt out of participating in it. (None may say, "Don't compel me to contribute to others and don't provide for me via this compulsory mechanism if I am in need.") Everyone above a certain level is forced to contribute to aid the needy. But if emigration from the country were allowed, anyone could choose to move to another country that did not have compulsory social provision but otherwise was (as much as possible) identical. In such a case, the person's *only* motive for leaving would be to avoid participating in the compulsory scheme of social provision. And if he does leave, the needy in his initial country will receive no (compelled) help from him. What rationale yields the result that the person be permitted to emigrate, yet forbidden to stay and opt out of the compulsory scheme of social provision? If providing for the needy is of overriding importance, this does militate against allowing internal opting out; but it also speaks against allowing external emigration. (Would it also support, to some extent, the kidnapping of persons living in a place without compulsory social provision, who could be forced to make a contribution to the needy in your community?) Perhaps the crucial component of the position that allows emigration solely to avoid certain arrangements, while not allowing anyone internally to opt out of them, is a concern for fraternal feelings within the country. "We don't want anyone here who doesn't contribute, who doesn't care enough about the others to contribute." That concern, in this case, would have to be tied to the view that forced aiding tends to produce fraternal feelings between the aided and the aider (or perhaps merely to the view that the knowledge that someone or other voluntarily is not aiding produces unfraternal feelings).

VI.   Locke's Theory of Acquisition

... [W]e must introduce an additional bit of complexity into the structure of the entitlement theory. This is best approached by considering Locke's attempt to specify a principle of justice in acquisition. Locke views property rights in an unowned object as originating through someone's mixing his labor with it. This gives rise to many questions. What are the boundaries of what labor is mixed with? If a private astronaut clears a place on Mars, has he mixed his labor with (so that he comes to own) the whole planet, the whole uninhabited universe, or just a particular plot? Which plot does an act bring under ownership? The minimal (possibly disconnected) area such that an act decreases entropy in that area, and not elsewhere? Can virgin land (for the purposes of ecological investigation by high-flying airplane) come under ownership by a Lockean process? Building a fence around a territory presumably would make one the owner of only the fence (and the land immediately underneath it).

Why does mixing one's labor with something make one the owner of it? Perhaps because one owns one's labor, and so one comes to own a previously unowned thing that becomes permeated with what one owns. Ownership seeps over into the rest. But why isn't mixing what I own with what I don't own a way of losing what I own rather than a way of gaining what I don't? If I own a can of tomato juice and spill it in the sea so that its molecules (made radioactive, so I can check this) mingle evenly throughout the sea, do I thereby come to own the sea, or have I foolishly dissipated my tomato juice? Perhaps the idea, instead, is that laboring on something improves it and makes it more valuable; and anyone is entitled to own a thing whose value he has created. (Reinforcing this, perhaps, is the view that laboring is unpleasant. If some people made things effortlessly, as the cartoon characters in *The Yellow Submarine* trail flowers in their wake, would they have lesser claim to their own products whose making didn't *cost* them anything?) Ignore the fact that laboring on something may make it less valuable (spraying pink enamel paint on a piece of driftwood that you have found). Why should one's entitlement extend to the whole object rather than just to the *added value* one's labor has produced? (Such reference to value might also serve to delimit the extent of ownership; for example, substitute "increases the value of" for "decreases entropy in" in the above entropy criterion.) No workable or coherent value-added property scheme has yet been devised, and any such scheme presumably would fall to objections (similar to those) that fell the theory of Henry George.

It will be implausible to view improving an object as giving full ownership to it, if the stock of unowned objects that might be improved is limited. For an object's coming under one person's ownership changes the situation of all others. Whereas previously they were at liberty (in Hohfeld's sense) to use the object, they now no longer are. This change in the situation of others (by removing their liberty to act on a previously unowned object) need not worsen their situation. If I appropriate a grain of sand from Coney Island, no one else may now do as they will with *that* grain of sand. But there are plenty of other grains of sand left for them to do the same with. Or if not grains of sand, then other things. Alternatively, the things I do with the grain of sand I appropriate might improve the position of others, counterbalancing their loss of the liberty to use that grain. The crucial point is whether appropriation of an unowned object worsens the situation of others.

Locke's proviso that there be "enough and as good left in common for others" (sect. 27) is meant to ensure that the situation of others is not worsened. (If this proviso is met is there any motivation for his further condition of nonwaste?) It is often said that this proviso once held but now no longer does. But there appears to be an argument for the conclusion that if the proviso no longer holds, then it cannot ever have held so as to yield permanent and inheritable property rights. Consider the first person Z for whom there is not enough and as good left to appropriate. The last person Y to appropriate left Z without his previous liberty to act on an object, and so worsened Z's situation. So Y's appropriation is not allowed under Locke's proviso. Therefore the next to last person X to appropriate left Y in a worse position, for X's act ended permissible appropriation. Therefore X's appropriation wasn't permissible. But then the appropriator two from last, W, ended permissible appropriation and so, since it worsened X's position, W's appropriation wasn't permissible. And so on back to the first person A to appropriate a permanent property right.

This argument, however, proceeds too quickly. Someone may be made worse off by another's appropriation in two ways: first, by losing the opportunity to improve his situation by a particular appropriation or any one; and second, by no longer being able to use freely (without appropriation) what he previously could. A *stringent* requirement that another not be made worse off by an appropriation would exclude the first way if nothing else counterbalances the diminution in opportunity, as well as the second. A *weaker* requirement would exclude the second way, though not the first. With the weaker requirement, we cannot zip back so quickly from Z to A, as in the above argument; for though person Z can no longer *appropriate*, there may remain some for him to *use* as before. In this case Y's appropriation would not violate the weaker Lockean condition. (With less remaining that people are at liberty to use, users might face more inconvenience, crowding, and so on; in that way the situation of others might be worsened, unless appropriation stopped far short of such a point.) It is arguable that no one legitimately can complain if the weaker provision is satisfied. However, since this is less clear than in the case of the more stringent proviso, Locke may have intended this stringent proviso by "enough and as good" remaining, and perhaps he meant the non-waste condition to delay the end point from which the argument zips back.

Is the situation of persons who are unable to appropriate (there being no more accessible and useful unowned objects) worsened by a system allowing appropriation and permanent property? Here enter the various familiar social considerations favoring private property: it increases the social product by putting means of production in the hands of those who can use them most efficiently (profitably); experimentation is encouraged, because with separate persons controlling resources, there is no one person or small group whom someone with a new idea must convince to try it out; private property enables people to decide on the pattern and types of risks they wish to bear, leading to specialized types of risk bearing; private property protects future persons by leading some to hold back resources from current consumption for future markets; it provides alternate sources of employment for unpopular persons who don't have to convince any one person or small group to hire them, and so on. These considerations enter a Lockean theory to support the claim that appropriation of private property satisfies the intent behind the "enough and as good left over" proviso, *not* as a utilitarian justification of property. They enter to rebut the claim that because the proviso is violated no natural right to private property can arise by a Lockean process. The difficulty in working such an argument to show that the proviso is satisfied is in fixing the appropriate base line for comparison. Lockean appropriation makes people no worse off than they would be *how?*[19] This question of fixing the baseline needs more detailed investigation than we are able to give it here. It would be desirable to have an estimate of the general economic importance of original appropriation in order to see how much leeway there is for differing theories of appropriation and of the location of the baseline. Perhaps this importance can be measured by the percentage of all income that is based upon untransformed raw materials and given resources (rather than upon human actions), mainly rental income representing the unimproved value of land, and the price of raw material *in situ*, and by the percentage of current wealth which represents such income in the past.[20]

We should note that it is not only persons favoring *private* property who need a theory of how property rights legitimately originate. Those believing in collective property, for example those believing that a group of persons living in an area jointly own the territory, or its mineral resources, also must provide a theory of how such property rights arise; they must show why the persons living there have rights to determine what is done with the land and resources there that persons living elsewhere don't have (with regard to the same land and resources).

VII.   The Proviso

Whether or not Locke's particular theory of appropriation can be spelled out so as to handle various difficulties, I assume that any adequate theory of justice in acquisition will contain a proviso similar to the weaker of the ones we have attributed to Locke. A process normally giving rise to a permanent bequeathable property right in a previously unowned thing will not do so if the position of others no longer at liberty to use the thing is thereby worsened. It is important to specify *this* particular mode of worsening the situation of others, for the proviso does not encompass other modes. It does not include the worsening due to more limited opportunities to appropriate (the first way above, corresponding to the more stringent condition), and it does not include how I "worsen" a seller's position if I appropriate materials to make some of what he is selling, and then enter into competition with him. Someone whose appropriation otherwise would violate the proviso still may appropriate provided he compensates the others so that their situation is not thereby worsened; unless he does compensate these others, his appropriation will violate the proviso of the principle of justice in acquisition and will be an illegitimate one.[21] A theory of appropriation incorporating this Lockean proviso will handle correctly the cases (objections to the theory lacking the proviso) where someone appropriates the total supply of something necessary for life.[22]

A theory which includes this proviso in its principle of justice in acquisition must also contain a more complex principle of justice in transfer. Some reflection of the proviso about appropriation constrains later actions. If my appropriating all of a certain substance violates the Lockean proviso, then so does my appropriating some and purchasing all the rest from others who obtained it without otherwise violating the Lockean proviso. If the proviso excludes someone's appropriating all the drinkable water in the world, it also excludes his purchasing it all. (More weakly, and messily, it may exclude his charging certain prices for some of his supply.) This proviso (almost?) never will come into effect; the more someone acquires of a scarce substance which others want, the higher the price of the rest will go, and the more difficult it will become for him to acquire it all. But still, we can imagine, at least, that something like this occurs: someone makes simultaneous secret bids to the separate owners of a substance, each of whom sells assuming he can easily purchase more from the other owners; or some natural catastrophe destroys all of the supply of something except that in one person's possession. The total supply could not be permissibly appropriated by one person at the beginning. His later acquisition of it all does not show that the original appropriation violated the proviso (even by a reverse argument similar to the one above that tried to zip back from Z to A). Rather, it is the combination of the original appropriation *plus* all the later transfers and actions that violates the Lockean proviso.

Each owner's title to his holding includes the historical shadow of the Lockean proviso on appropriation. This excludes his transferring it into an agglomeration that does violate the Lockean proviso and excludes his using it in a way, in coordination with others or independently of them, so as to violate the proviso by making the situation of others worse than their baseline situation. Once it is known that someone's ownership runs afoul of the Lockean proviso, there are stringent limits on what he may do with (what it is difficult any longer unreservedly to call) "his property." Thus a person may not appropriate the only water hole in a desert and charge what he will. Nor may he charge what he will if he possesses one, and unfortunately it happens that all the water holes in the desert dry up, except for his. This unfortunate circumstance, admittedly no fault of his, brings into operation the Lockean proviso and limits his property rights.[23] Similarly, an owner's property right in the only island in an area does not allow him to order a castaway from a shipwreck off his island as a trespasser, for this would violate the Lockean proviso.

Notice that the theory does not say that owners do have these rights, but that the rights are overridden to avoid some catastrophe. (Overridden rights do not disappear; they leave a trace of a sort absent in the cases under discussion.)[24] There is no such external (and *ad hoc?*) overriding. Considerations internal to the theory of property itself, to its theory of acquisition and appropriation, provide the means for handling such cases. The results, however, may be coextensive with some condition about catastrophe, since the baseline for comparison is so low as compared to the productiveness of a society with private appropriation that the question of the Lockean proviso being violated arises only in the case of catastrophe (or a desert-island situation).

The fact that someone owns the total supply of something necessary for others to stay alive does *not* entail that his (or anyone's) appropriation of anything left some people (immediately or later) in a situation worse than the baseline one. A medical researcher who synthesizes a new substance that effectively treats a certain disease and who refuses to sell except on his terms does not worsen the situation of others by depriving them of whatever he has appropriated. The others easily can possess the same materials he appropriated; the researcher's appropriation or purchase of chemicals didn't make those chemicals scarce in a way so as to violate the Lockean proviso. Nor would someone else's purchasing the total supply of the synthesized substance from the medical researcher. The fact that the medical researcher uses easily available chemicals to synthesize the drug no more violates the Lockean proviso than does the fact that the only surgeon able to perform a particular operation eats easily obtainable food in order to stay alive and to have the energy to work. This shows that the Lockean proviso is not an "end-state principle"; it focuses on a particular way that appropriative actions affect others, and not on the structure of the situation that results.[25]

Intermediate between someone who takes all of the public supply and someone who makes the total supply out of easily obtainable substances is someone who appropriates the total supply of something in a way that does not deprive the others of it. For example, someone finds a new substance in an out-of-the-way place. He discovers that it effectively treats a certain disease and appropriates the total supply. He does not worsen the situation of others; if he did not stumble upon the substance no one else would have, and the others would remain without it. However, as time passes, the likelihood increases that others would have come across the substance; upon this fact might be based a limit to his property right in the substance so that others are not below their base-line position; for example, its bequest might be limited. The theme of someone worsening another's situation by depriving him of something he otherwise would possess may also illuminate the example of patents. An inventor's patent does not deprive others of an object which would not exist if not for the inventor. Yet patents would have this effect on others who independently invent the object. Therefore, these independent inventors, upon whom the burden of proving independent discovery may rest, should not be excluded from utilizing their own invention as they wish (including selling it to others). Furthermore, a known inventor drastically lessens the chances of actual independent invention. For persons who know of an invention usually will not try to reinvent it, and the notion of independent discovery here would be murky at best. Yet we may assume that in the absence of the original invention, sometime later someone else would have come up with it. This suggests placing a time limit on patents, as a rough rule of thumb to approximate how long it would have taken, in the absence of knowledge of the invention, for independent discovery.

I believe that the free operation of a market system will not actually run afoul of the Lockean proviso. . . . If this is correct, the proviso will not play a very important role in the activities of protective agencies and will not provide a significant opportunity for future state action. Indeed, were it not for the effects of previous *illegitimate* state action, people would not think the possibility of the proviso's being violated as of more interest than any other logical possibility. (Here I make an empirical historical claim; as does someone who disagrees with this.) This completes our indication of the complication in the entitlement theory introduced by the Lockean proviso.

Notes

1   The reader who has looked ahead and seen that the second part of this chapter [omitted, eds.] discusses Rawls' theory mistakenly may think that every remark or

argument in the first part against alternative theories of justice is meant to apply to, or anticipate, a criticism of Rawls' theory. This is not so; there are other theories also worth criticizing.

2 Applications of the principle of justice in acquisition may also occur as part of the move from one distribution to another. You may find an unheld thing now and appropriate it. Acquisitions also are to be understood as included when, to simplify, I speak only of transitions by transfers.

3 See, however, the useful book by Boris Bittker, *The Case for Black Reparations* (New York: Random House, 1973).

4 If the principle of rectification of violations of the first two principles yields more than one description of holdings, then some choice must be made as to which of these is to be realized. Perhaps the sort of considerations about distributive justice and equality that I argue against play a legitimate role in *this* subsidiary choice. Similarly, there may be room for such considerations in deciding which otherwise arbitrary features a statute will embody, when such features are unavoidable because other considerations do not specify a precise line; yet a line must be drawn.

5 One might try to squeeze a patterned conception of distributive justice into the framework of the entitlement conception, by formulating a gimmicky obligatory "principle of transfer" that would lead to the pattern. For example, the principle that if one has more than the mean income one must transfer everything one holds above the mean to persons below the mean so as to bring them up to (but not over) the mean. We can formulate a criterion for a "principle of transfer" to rule out such obligatory transfers, or we can say that no correct principle of transfer, no principle of transfer in a free society will be like this. The former is probably the better course, though the latter also is true.

Alternatively, one might think to make the entitlement conception instantiate a pattern, by using matrix entries that express the relative strength of a person's entitlements as measured by some real-valued function. But even if the limitation to natural dimensions failed to exclude this function, the resulting edifice would *not* capture our system of entitlements to *particular* things.

6 F. A. Hayek, *The Constitution of Liberty* (Chicago: University of Chicago Press, 1960), p. 87.

7 This question does not imply that they will tolerate any and every patterned distribution. In discussing Hayek's views, Irving Kristol has recently speculated that people will not long tolerate a system that yields distributions patterned in accordance with value rather than merit. ("'When Virtue Loses All Her Loveliness' – Some Reflections on Capitalism and 'The Free Society,'" *The Public Interest*, Fall 1970, pp. 3–15.) Kristol, following some remarks of Hayek's, equates the merit system with justice. Since some case can be made for the external standard of distribution in accordance with benefit to others, we ask about a weaker (and therefore more plausible) hypothesis.

8 We certainly benefit because great economic incentives operate to get others to spend much time and energy to figure out how to serve us by providing things we will want to pay for. It is not mere paradox mongering to wonder whether capitalism should be criticized for most rewarding and hence encouraging, not individualists like Thoreau who go about their own lives, but people who are occupied with serving others and winning them as customers. But to defend capitalism one need not think businessmen are the finest human types. (I do not mean to join here the general maligning of businessmen, either.) Those who think the finest

should acquire the most can try to convince their fellows to transfer resources in accordance with *that* principle.

9   Varying situations continuously from that limit situation to our own would force us to make explicit the underlying rationale of entitlements and to consider whether entitlement considerations lexicographically precede the considerations of the usual theories of distributive justice, so that the *slightest* strand of entitlement outweighs the considerations of the usual theories of distributive justice.

10 Might not a transfer have instrumental effects on a third party, changing his feasible options? (But what if the two parties to the transfer independently had used their holdings in this fashion?) I discuss this question below, but note here that this question concedes the point for distributions of ultimate intrinsic non-instrumental goods (pure utility experiences, so to speak) that are transferrable. It also might be objected that the transfer might make a third party more envious because it worsens his position relative to someone else. I find it incomprehensible how this can be thought to involve a claim of justice....

Here and elsewhere in this chapter, a theory which incorporates elements of pure procedural justice might find what I say acceptable, *if* kept in its proper place; that is, if background institutions exist to ensure the satisfaction of certain conditions on distributive shares. But if these institutions are not themselves the sum or invisible-hand result of people's voluntary (nonaggressive) actions, the constraints they impose require justification. At no point does *our* argument assume any background institutions more extensive than those of the minimal night-watchman state, a state limited to protecting persons against murder, assault, theft, fraud, and so forth.

11 See the selection from John Henry MacKay's novel, *The Anarchists*, reprinted in Leonard Krimmerman and Lewis Perry, eds., *Patterns of Anarchy* (New York: Doubleday Anchor Books, 1966), in which an individualist anarchist presses upon a communist anarchist the following question: "Would you, in the system of society which you call 'free Communism' prevent individuals from exchanging their labor among themselves by means of their own medium of exchange? And further: Would you prevent them from occupying land for the purpose of personal use?" The novel continues: "[the] question was not to be escaped. If he answered 'Yes!' he admitted that society had the right of control over the individual and threw overboard the autonomy of the individual which he had always zealously defended; if on the other hand, he answered 'No!' he admitted the right of private property which he had just denied so emphatically.... Then he answered 'In Anarchy any number of men must have the right of forming a voluntary association, and so realizing their ideas in practice. Nor can I understand how any one could justly be driven from the land and house which he uses and occupies ... every serious man must declare himself: for Socialism, and thereby for force and against liberty, or for Anarchism, and thereby for liberty and against force.'" In contrast, we find Noam Chomsky writing, "Any consistent anarchist must oppose private own-ership of the means of production," "the consistent anarchist then ... will be a socialist ... of a particular sort." Introduction to Daniel Guerin, *Anarchism: From Theory to Practice* (New York: Monthly Review Press, 1970), pp. xiii, xv.

12 Is the patterned principle stable that requires merely that a distribution be Pareto-optimal? One person might give another a gift or bequest that the second could exchange with a third to their mutual benefit. Before the second makes this exchange, there is not Pareto-optimality. Is a stable pattern presented by a principle

choosing that among the Pareto-optimal positions that satisfies some further condition *C*? It may seem that there cannot be a counterexample, for won't any voluntary exchange made away from a situation show that the first situation wasn't Pareto-optimal? (Ignore the implausibility of this last claim for the case of be-quests.) But principles are to be satisfied over time, during which new possibilities arise. A distribution that at one time satisfies the criterion of Pareto-optimality might not do so when some new possibilities arise (Wilt Chamberlain grows up and starts playing basketball); and though people's activities will tend to move then to a new Pareto-optimal position, *this* new one need not satisfy the contentful condition *C*. Continual interference will be needed to insure the continual satisfaction of *C*. (The theoretical possibility of a pattern's being maintained by some invisible-hand process that brings it back to an equilibrium that fits the pattern when deviations occur should be investigated.)

13   One indication of the stringency of Rawls' difference principle, which we attend to in the second part of this chapter [omitted, eds.], is its inappropriateness as a governing principle even within a family of individuals who love one another. Should a family devote its resources to maximizing the position of its least well off and least talented child, holding back the other children or using resources for their education and development only if they will follow a policy through their lifetimes of maximizing the position of their least fortunate sibling? Surely not. How then can this even be considered as the appropriate policy for enforcement in the wider society? (I discuss below what I think would be Rawls' reply: that some principles apply at the macro level which do not apply to micro situations [omitted, eds.].)

14   See Gregory Vlastos, "The Individual as an Object of Love in Plato," in his *Platonic Studies* (Princeton: Princeton University Press, 1973), pp. 3–34.

15   I am unsure as to whether the arguments I present below show that such taxation merely *is* forced labor; so that "is on a par with" means "is one kind of." Or alternatively, whether the arguments emphasize the great similarities between such taxation and forced labor, to show it is plausible and illuminating to view such taxation in the light of forced labor. This latter approach would remind one of how John Wisdom conceives of the claims of metaphysicians.

16   Nothing hangs on the fact that here and elsewhere I speak loosely of *needs*, since I go on, each time, to reject the criterion of justice which includes it. If, however, something did depend upon the notion, one would want to examine it more carefully. For a skeptical view, see Kenneth Minogue, *The Liberal Mind* (New York: Random House, 1963), pp. 103–12.

17   Further details which this statement should include are contained in my essay "Coercion," in *Philosophy, Science, and Method*, ed. S. Morgenbesser, P. Suppes, and M. White (New York: St. Martin, 1969).

18   On the themes in this and the next paragraph, see the writings of Armen Alchian.

19   Compare this with Robert Paul Wolff's "A Refutation of Rawls' Theorem on Justice," *Journal of Philosophy*, March 31, 1966, sect. 2. Wolff's criticism does not apply to Rawls' conception under which the baseline is fixed by the difference principle.

20   I have not seen a precise estimate. David Friedman, *The Machinery of Freedom* (New York: Harper & Row, 1973), pp. xiv, xv, discusses this issue and suggests 5 percent of US national income as an upper limit for the first two factors mentioned. However he does not attempt to estimate the percentage of current wealth which

is based upon such income in the past. (The vague notion of "based upon" merely indicates a topic needing investigation.)

21 Fourier held that since the process of civilization had deprived the members of society of certain liberties (to gather, pasture, engage in the chase), a socially guaranteed minimum provision for persons was justified as compensation for the loss (Alexander Gray, *The Socialist Tradition* (New York: Harper & Row, 1968), p. 188). But this puts the point too strongly. This compensation would be due those persons, if any, for whom the process of civilization was a *net loss*, for whom the benefits of civilization did not counterbalance being deprived of these particular liberties.

22 For example, Rashdall's case of someone who comes upon the only water in the desert several miles ahead of others who also will come to it and appropriates it all. Hastings Rashdall, "The Philosophical Theory of Property," in *Property, its Duties and Rights* (London: Macmillan, 1915).

We should note Ayn Rand's theory of property rights ("Man's Rights" in *The Virtue of Selfishness* (New York: New American Library, 1964), p. 94), wherein these follow from the right to life, since people need physical things to live. But a right to life is not a right to whatever one needs to live; other people may have rights over these other things ... At most, a right to life would be a right to have or strive for whatever one needs to live, provided that having it does not violate anyone else's rights. With regard to material things, the question is whether having it does violate any right of others. (Would appropriation of all unowned things do so? Would appropriating the water hole in Rashdall's example?) Since special considerations (such as the Lockean proviso) may enter with regard to material property, one *first* needs a theory of property rights before one can apply any supposed right to life (as amended above). Therefore the right to life cannot provide the foundation for a theory of property rights.

23 The situation would be different if his water hole didn't dry up, due to special precautions he took to prevent this. Compare our discussion of the case in the text with Hayek, *The Constitution of Liberty*, p. 136; and also with Ronald Hamowy, "Hayek's Concept of Freedom; A Critique," *New Individualist Review*, April 1961, pp. 28–31.

24 I discuss overriding and its moral traces in "Moral Complications and Moral Structures," *Natural Law Forum*, 1968, pp. 1–50.

25 Does the principle of compensation [defended in *Anarchy, State, and Utopia*, ch. 4, eds.] ... introduce patterning considerations? Though it requires compensation for the disadvantages imposed by those seeking security from risks, it is not a patterned principle. For it seeks to remove only those disadvantages which prohibitions inflict on those who might present risks to others, not all disadvantages. It specifies an obligation on those who impose the prohibition, which stems from their own particular acts, to remove a particular complaint those prohibited may make against them.

5

Equality of Resources

Ronald Dworkin

I. The Auction

In Part 1 of this essay we considered the claims of equality of welfare as an interpretation of treating people as equals. In Part 2 we shall consider the competing claims of equality of resources. But we shall be occupied, for the most part, simply in defining a suitable conception of equality of resources, and not in defending it except as such definition provides a defense. I shall assume, for this purpose, that equality of resources is a matter of equality in whatever resources are owned privately by individuals. Equality of political power, including equality of power over publicly or commonly owned resources, is therefore treated as a different issue, reserved for discussion on another occasion. This distinction is, of course, arbitrary on any number of grounds. From the standpoint of any sophisticated economic theory, an individual's command over public resources forms part of his private resources. Someone who has power to influence public decisions about the quality of the air he or she breathes, for example, is richer than someone who does not. So an overall theory of equality must find a means of integrating private resources and political power.

Private ownership, moreover, is not a single, unique relationship between a person and a material resource, but an open-textured relationship many aspects of which must be fixed politically. So the question of what division of resources is an equal division must to some degree include the question of what powers someone who is assigned a resource thereby gains, and that in turn must include the further question of his right to veto whatever changes in

Extracts from Ronald Dworkin, 'What is Equality? Part 2: Equality of Resources' pp. 283–314, from *Philosophy and Public Affairs*, 10:4 (1981), pp. 283–345. The first part of Dworkin's essay, 'What Is Equality? Part 1: Equality of Welfare', appeared in *Philosophy and Public Affairs*, 10:3 (1981), pp. 185–246.

those powers might be threatened through politics. In the present essay, however, I shall for the most part assume that the general dimensions of ownership are sufficiently well understood so that the question of what pattern of private ownership constitutes an equal division of private resources can be discussed independently of these complications.

I argue that an equal division of resources presupposes an economic market of some form, mainly as an analytical device but also, to a certain extent, as an actual political institution. That claim may seem sufficiently paradoxical to justify the following preliminary comments. The idea of a market for goods has figured in political and economic theory, since the eighteenth century, in two rather different ways. It has been celebrated, first, as a device for both defining and achieving certain community-wide goals variously described as prosperity, efficiency, and overall utility. It has been hailed, second, as a necessary condition of individual liberty, the condition under which free men and women may exercise individual initiative and choice so that their fates lie in their own hands. The market, that is, has been defended both through arguments of policy, appealing to the overall, community-wide gains it produces, and arguments of principle that appeal instead to some supposed right to liberty.

But the economic market, whether defended in either or both of these ways, has during this same period come to be regarded as the enemy of equality, largely because the forms of economic market systems developed and enforced in industrial countries have permitted and indeed encouraged vast inequality in property. Both political philosophers and ordinary citizens have therefore pictured equality as the antagonist or victim of the values of efficiency and liberty supposedly served by the market, so that wise and moderate politics consists in striking some balance or trade-off between equality and these other values, either by imposing constraints on the market as an economic environment, or by replacing it, in part or altogether, with a different economic system.

I shall try to suggest, on the contrary, that the idea of an economic market, as a device for setting prices for a vast variety of goods and services, must be at the center of any attractive theoretical development of equality of resources. The main point can be shown most quickly by constructing a reasonably simple exercise in equality of resources, deliberately artificial so as to abstract from problems we shall later have to face. Suppose a number of shipwreck survivors are washed up on a desert island which has abundant resources and no native population, and any likely rescue is many years away. These immigrants accept the principle that no one is antecedently entitled to any of these resources, but that they shall instead be divided equally among them. (They do not yet realize, let us say, that it might be wise to keep some resources as owned in common by any state they might create.) They also accept (at least provisionally) the following test of an equal division of resources, which I shall call the envy test. No division of resources is an equal division if, once the division is complete, any immigrant would prefer someone else's bundle of resources to his own bundle.[1]

Now suppose some one immigrant is elected to achieve the division according to that principle. It is unlikely that he can succeed simply by physically dividing the resources of the island into n identical bundles of resources. The number of each kind of the nondivisible resources, like milking cows, might not be an exact multiple of n, and even in the case of divisible resources, like arable land, some land would be better than others, and some better for one use than another. Suppose, however, that by a great deal of trial and error and care the divider could create n bundles of resources, each of which was somewhat different from the others, but was nevertheless such that he could assign one to each immigrant and no one would in fact envy anyone else's bundle.

The distribution might still fail to satisfy the immigrants as an equal distribution, for a reason that is not caught by the envy test. Suppose (to put the point in a dramatic way) the divider achieved his result by transforming all the available resources into a very large stock of plovers' eggs and pre-phylloxera claret (either by magic or trade with a neighboring island that enters the story only for that reason) and divides this glut into identical bundles of baskets and bottles. Many of the immigrants – let us say all but one – are delighted. But if that one hates plovers' eggs and pre-phylloxera claret he will feel that he has not been treated as an equal in the division of resources. The envy test is met – he does not prefer any one's bundle to his own – but he prefers what he would have had under some fairer treatment of the initially available resources.

A similar, though less dramatic, piece of unfairness might be produced even without magic or bizarre trades. For the combination of resources that composes each bundle the divider creates will favor some tastes over others, compared with different combinations he might have composed. That is, different sets of n bundles might be created by trial and error, each of which would pass the envy test, so that for any such set that the divider chooses, someone will prefer that he had chosen a different set, even though that person would not prefer a different bundle within that set. Trades after the initial distribution may, of course, improve that person's position. But they will be unlikely to bring him to the position he would have had under the set of bundles he would have preferred, because some others will begin with a bundle they prefer to the bundle they would have had in that set, and so will have no reason to trade to that bundle.

So the divider needs a device that will attack two distinct foci of arbitrariness and possible unfairness. The envy test cannot be satisfied by any simple mechanical division of resources. If any more complex division can be found that will satisfy it, many such might be found, so that the choice amongst these would be arbitrary. The same solution will by now have occurred to all readers. The divider needs some form of auction or other market procedure in order to respond to these problems. I shall describe a reasonably straight-forward procedure that would seem acceptable if it could be made to work, though as I shall describe it it will be impossibly expensive of time. Suppose the divider hands each of the immigrants an equal and large number of clamshells, which are sufficiently numerous and in themselves valued by no one, to use as counters in a market of the following sort. Each distinct item on the island (not including the immigrants themselves) is listed as a lot to be sold, unless someone notifies the auctioneer (as the divider has now become) of his or her desire to bid for some part of an item, including part, for example, of some piece of land, in which case that part becomes itself a distinct lot. The auctioneer then proposes a set of prices for each lot and discovers whether that set of prices clears all markets, that is, whether there is only one purchaser at that price and all lots are sold. If not, then the auctioneer adjusts his prices until he reaches a set that does clear the markets.[2] But the process does not stop then, because each of the immigrants remains free to change his bids even when an initially market-clearing set of prices is reached, or even to propose different lots. But let us suppose that in time even this leisurely process comes to an end, everyone declares himself satisfied, and goods are distributed accordingly.[3]

Now the envy test will have been met. No one will envy another's set of purchases because, by hypothesis, he could have purchased that bundle with his clamshells instead of his own bundle. Nor is the choice of sets of bundles arbitrary. Many people will be able to imagine a different set of bundles meeting the no-envy test that might have been established, but the actual set of bundles has the merit that each person played, through his purchases against an initially equal stock of counters, an equal role in determining the set of bundles actually chosen. No one is in the position of the person in our earlier example who found himself with nothing but what he hated. Of course, luck plays a certain role in determining how satisfied anyone is with the outcome, against other possibilities he might envision. If plovers' eggs and old claret were the only resources to auction, then the person who hated these would be as badly off as in our earlier example. He would be unlucky that the immigrants had not washed up on an island with more of what he wanted (though lucky, of course, that it did not have even less). But he could not complain that the division of the actual resources they found was unequal.

He might think himself lucky or unlucky in other ways as well. It would be a matter of luck, for example, how many others shared various of his tastes. If his tastes or ambitions proved relatively popular, this might work in his favor in the auction, if there were economies of scale in the production of what he wanted. Or against him, if what he wanted was scarce. If the immigrants had decided to establish a regime of equality of welfare, instead of equality of resources, then these various pieces of good or bad luck would be shared with others, because distribution would be based, not on any auction of the sort I described, in which luck plays this role, but on a strategy of evening out differences in whatever concept of welfare had been chosen. Equality of resources, however, offers no similar reason for correcting for the contingencies that determine how expensive or frustrating someone's preferences turn out to be.[4]

Under equality of welfare, people are meant to decide what sorts of lives they want independently of information relevant to determining how much their choices will reduce or enhance the ability of others to have what they want.[5] That sort of information becomes relevant only at a second, political level at which administrators then gather all the choices made at the first level to see what distribution will give each of these choices equal success under some concept of welfare taken as the correct dimension of success. Under equality of resources, however, people decide what sorts of lives to pursue against a background of information about the actual cost their choices impose on other people and hence on the total stock of resources that may fairly be used by them. The information left to an independent political level under equality of welfare is therefore brought into the initial level of individual choice under equality of resources. The elements of luck in the auction we have just described are in fact pieces of information of a crucial sort; information that is acquired and used in that process of choice.

So the contingent facts of raw material and the distribution of tastes are not grounds on which someone might challenge a distribution as unequal. They are rather background facts that determine what equality of resources, in these circumstances, is. Under equality of resources, no test for calculating what equality requires can be abstracted from these background facts and used to test them. The market character of the auction is not simply a convenient or ad hoc device for resolving technical problems that arise for equality of resources in very simple exercises like our desert island case. It is an institutionalized form of the process of discovery and adaptation that is at the center of the ethics of that ideal. Equality of resources supposes that the resources devoted to each person's life should be equal. That goal needs a metric. The auction proposes what the envy test in fact assumes, that the true measure of the social resources devoted to the life of one person is fixed by asking how important, in fact, that resource is for others. It insists that the cost, measured in that way, figure in each person's sense of what is rightly his and in each person's judgment of what life he should lead, given that command of justice. Anyone who insists that equality is violated by any particular profile of initial tastes, therefore, must reject equality of resources, and fall back on equality of welfare.

Of course it is sovereign in this argument, and in this connection between the market and equality of resources, that people enter the market on equal terms. The desert island auction would not have avoided envy, and would have no appeal as a solution to the problem of dividing the resources equally, if the immigrants had struggled ashore with different amounts of money in their pocket, which they were free to use in the auction, or if some had stolen clamshells from others. We must not lose sight of that fact, either in the argument that follows or in any reflections on the application of that argument to contemporary economic systems. But neither should we lose sight, in our dismay over the inequities of those systems, of the important theoretical connection between the market and the concept of equality in resources.

There are, of course, other and very different sorts of objection that might be made to the use of an auction, even an equal auction of the sort I described. It might be said, for example, that the fairness of an auction supposes that the preferences people bring to the auction, or form in its course, are authentic – the true preferences of the agent rather than preferences imposed upon him by the economic system itself. Perhaps an auction of any sort, in which one person bids against another, imposes an illegitimate assumption that what is valuable in life is individual ownership of something rather than more cooperative enterprises of the community or some group within it as a whole. Insofar as this (in part mysterious) objection is pertinent here, however, it is an objection against the idea of private ownership over an extensive domain of resources, which is better considered under the title of political equality, not an objection to the claim that a market of some sort must figure in any satisfactory account of what equality in private ownership is.

II. The Project

Since the device of an equal auction seems promising as a technique for achieving an attractive interpretation of equality of resources in a simple context, like the desert island, the question arises whether it will prove useful in developing a more general account of that ideal. We should ask whether the device could be elaborated to provide a scheme for developing or testing equality of resources in a community that has a dynamic economy, with labor, investment, and trade. What structure must an auction take in such an economy – what adjustments or supplements must be made to the production and trade that would follow such an auction – in order that the results continue to satisfy our initial requirement that an equal share of the resources be available to each citizen?

Our interest in this question is three-fold. First, the project provides an important test of the coherence and completeness of the idea of equality of resources. Suppose no auction or pattern of post-auction trade could be described whose results could be accepted as equality in any society much more complex or less artificial than a simple economy of consumption. Or that no auction could produce equality without constraints and restrictions which violate independent principles of justice. This would tend to suggest, at least, that there is no coherent ideal of equality of resources. Or that the ideal is not politically attractive after all.

We might discover, on the contrary, less comprehensive gaps or defects in the idea. Suppose, for example, that the design for the auction we develop does not uniquely determine a particular distribution, even given a stipulated set of initial resources and a stipulated population with fixed interests and ambitions, but is rather capable of producing significantly different outcomes depending on the order of decisions, arbitrary choices about the composition of the initial list of options, or other contingencies. We might conclude that the ideal of equality of resources embraces a variety of different distributions, each of which satisfies the ideal, and that the ideal is therefore partially indeterminate. This would show limitations on the power of the ideal to discriminate between certain distributions, but would not for that reason show that the ideal is either incoherent or practically impotent. So it is worth trying to develop the idea of an equal auction as a test of the theoretical standing and power of the political ideal.

Second, a fully developed description of an equal auction, adequate for a more complex society, might provide a standard for judging actual institutions and distributions in the real world. Of course no complex, organic society would have, in its history, anything remotely comparable to an equal auction. But we can nevertheless ask, for any actual distribution, whether it falls within the class of distributions that might have been produced by such an auction over a defensible description of initial resources. Or, if it is not, how far it differs from or falls short of the closest distribution within this class. The device of the auction might provide, in other words, a standard for judging how far an actual distribution, however it has been achieved, approaches equality of resources at any particular time.

Third, the device might be useful in the design of actual political institutions. Under certain (perhaps very limited) circumstances, when the conditions for an equal auction are at least roughly met, then an actual auction might be the best means of reaching or preserving equality of resources in the real world. This will be true, particularly, when the results of such an auction are antecedently indeterminate in the way just described, so that any result the auction reaches will respect equality of resources even though it is not known, in advance, which result would be reached. In such a case it may be fairer to conduct an actual auction than to choose, through some other political means, one rather than another of the results that an auction might produce. Even in such a case it will rarely be possible or desirable to conduct an actual auction in the design our theoretical investigations recommend. But it may be possible to design an auction surrogate – an economic or political institution having sufficient of the characteristics of a theoretical equal auction so that the arguments of fairness recommending an actual auction were it feasible also recommend the surrogate. The economic markets of many countries can be interpreted, even as they stand, as forms of auctions. (So, too, can many forms of democratic political process.) Once we have developed a satisfactory model of an actual auction (to the extent we can) we can use that model to test these institutions, and reform them to bring them closer to the model.

Nevertheless our project is in the main, within the present essay, entirely theoretical. Our interest is primarily in the design of an ideal, and of a device to picture that ideal and test its coherence, completeness, and appeal. We shall therefore ignore practical difficulties, like problems of gathering information, which do not impeach these theoretical goals, and also make simplifying counterfactual assumptions which do not subvert them. But we should try to notice which simplifications we are making, because they will be of importance, particularly as to the third and most practical application of our projects, at any later stage, at which we consider second-best compromises of our ideal in the real world.

III. Luck and Insurance

If the auction is successful as described, then equality of resources holds for the moment among the immigrants. But perhaps only for the moment, because if they are left alone, once the auction is completed, to produce and trade as they wish, then the envy test will shortly fail. Some may be more skillful than others at producing what others want and will trade to get. Some may like to work, or to work in a way that will produce more to trade, while others like not to work or prefer to work at what will bring them less. Some will stay healthy while others fall sick, or lightning will strike the farms of others but avoid theirs. For any of these and dozens of other reasons some people will prefer the bundle others have in say, five years, to their own.

We must ask whether (or rather how far) such developments are consistent with equality of resources, and I shall begin by considering the character and impact of luck on the immigrants' post-auction fortunes. I shall distinguish, at least for the moment, between two kinds of luck. Option luck is a matter of how deliberate and calculated gambles turn out – whether someone gains or loses through accepting an isolated risk he or she should have anticipated and might have declined. Brute luck is a matter of how risks fall out that are not in that sense deliberate gambles. If I buy a stock on the exchange that rises, then my option luck is good. If I am hit by a falling meteorite whose course could not have been predicted, then my bad luck is brute (even though I could have moved just before it struck if I had any reason to know where it would strike). Obviously the difference between these two forms of luck can be represented as a matter of degree, and we may be uncertain how to describe a particular piece of bad luck. If someone develops cancer in the course of a normal life, and there is no particular decision to which we can point as a gamble risking the disease, then we will say that he has suffered brute bad luck. But if he smoked cigarettes heavily then we may prefer to say that he took an unsuccessful gamble.

Insurance, so far as it is available, provides a link between brute and option luck, because the decision to buy or reject catastrophe insurance is a calculated gamble. Of course, insurance does not erase the distinction. Someone who buys medical insurance and is hit by an unexpected meteorite still suffers brute bad luck, because he is worse off than if he had bought insurance and not needed it. But he has had better option luck than if he had not bought the insurance, because his situation is better in virtue of his not having run the gamble of refusing to insure.

Is it consistent with equality of resources that people should have different income or wealth in virtue of differing option luck? Suppose some of the immigrants plant valuable but risky crops while others play it safer, and that some of the former buy insurance against uncongenial weather while others do not. Skill will play a part in determining which of these various programs succeed, of course, and we shall consider the problems this raises later. But option luck will also play a part. Does its role threaten or invade equality of resources?

Consider, first, the differences in wealth between those who play it safe and those who gamble and succeed. Some people enjoy, while others hate, risks; but this particular difference in personality is comprehended in a more general difference between the kinds of lives that different people wish to lead. The life chosen by someone who gambles contains, as an element, the factor of risk; someone who chooses not to gamble has decided that he prefers a safer life. We have already decided that people should pay the price of the life they have decided to lead, measured in what others give up in order that they can do so. That was the point of the auction as a device to establish initial equality of resources. But the price of a safer life, measured in this way, is precisely forgoing any chance of the gains whose prospect induces others to gamble. So we have no reason to object, against the background of our earlier decisions, to a result in which those who decline to gamble have less than some of those who do not.

But we must also compare the situation of those who gamble and win with that of those who gamble and lose. We cannot say that the latter have chosen a different life and must sacrifice gains accordingly; for they have chosen the same lives as those who won. But we can say that the possibility of loss was part of the life they chose – that it was the fair price of the possibility of gain. For we might have designed our initial auction so that people could purchase (for example) lottery tickets with their clamshells. But the price of those tickets would have been some amount of other resources (fixed by the odds and the gambling preferences of others) that the shells would otherwise have bought, and which will be wholly forgone if the ticket does not win.

The same point can be made by considering the arguments for redistribution from winners to losers after the event. If winners were made to share their winnings with losers, then no one would gamble, as individuals, and the kind of life preferred by both those who in the end win and those who lose would be unavailable. Of course, it is not a good argument, against someone who urges redistribution in order to achieve equality of resources, that redistribution would make some forms of life less attractive or even impossible. For the demands of equality (we assume in this essay) are prior to other desiderata, including variety in the kinds of life available to people. (Equality will in any case make certain kinds of lives – a life of economic and political domination of others, for example – impossible.) In the present case, however, the difference is apparent. For the effect of redistribution from winners to losers in gambles would be to deprive both of lives they prefer, which indicates, not simply that this would produce an unwanted curtailment of available forms of life, but that it would deprive them of an equal voice in the construction of lots to be auctioned, like the man who hated both plovers' eggs and claret but was confronted only with bundles of both. They both want gambles to be in the mix, either originally or as represented by resources with which they can take risks later, and the chance of losing is the correct price, measured on the metric we have been using, of a life that includes gambles with a chance of gain.

We may, of course, have special reasons for forbidding certain forms of gambles. We may have paternalistic reasons for limiting how much any individual may risk, for example. We may also have reasons based in a theory of political equality for forbidding someone to gamble with his freedom or his religious or political rights. The present point is more limited. We have no general reason for forbidding gambles altogether in the bare fact that in the event winners will control more resources than losers, any more than in the fact that winners will have more than those who do not gamble at all. Our initial principle, that equality of resources requires that people pay the true cost of the lives that they lead, warrants rather than condemns these differences.

We may (if we wish) adjust our envy test to record that conclusion. We may say that in computing the extent of someone's resources over his life, for the purpose of asking whether anyone else envies those resources, any resources gained through a successful gamble should be represented by the opportunity to take the gamble at the odds in force, and comparable adjustments made to the resources of those who have lost through gambles. The main point of this artificial construction of the envy test, however, would be to remind us that the argument in favor of allowing differences in option luck to affect income and wealth assumes that everyone has in principle the same gambles available to him. Someone who never had the opportunity to run a similar risk, and would have taken the opportunity had it been available, will still envy some of those who did have it.

Nor does the argument yet confront the case of brute bad luck. If two people lead roughly the same lives, but one goes suddenly blind, then we cannot explain the resulting differences in their incomes either by saying that one took risks that the other chose not to take, or that we could not redistribute without denying both the lives they prefer. For the accident has (we assume) nothing to do with choices in the pertinent sense. It is not necessary to the life either has chosen that he run the risk of going blind without redistribution of funds from the other. This is a fortiori so if one is born blind and the other sighted.

But the possibility of insurance provides, as I suggested, a link between the two kinds of luck. For suppose insurance against blindness is available, in the initial auction, at whatever level of coverage the policy holder chooses to buy. And also suppose that two sighted people have, at the time of the auction, equal chance of suffering an accident that will blind them, and know that they have. Now if one chooses to spend part of his initial resources for such insurance and the other does not, or if one buys more coverage than the other, then this difference will reflect their different opinions about the relative value of different forms or components of their prospective lives. It may reflect the fact that one puts more value on sight than the other. Or, differently, that one would count monetary compensation for the loss of his sight as worthless in the face of such a tragedy while the other, more practical, would fix his mind on the aids and special training that such money might buy. Or simply that one minds or values risk differently from the other, and would, for example, rather try for a brilliant life that would collapse under catastrophe than a life guarded at the cost of resources necessary to make it brilliant.

But in any case the bare idea of equality of resources, apart from any paternalistic additions, would not argue for redistribution from the person who had insured to the person who had not if, horribly, they were both blinded in the same accident. For the availability of insurance would mean that, though they had both had brute bad luck, the difference between them was a matter of option luck, and the arguments we entertained against disturbing the results of option luck under conditions of equal antecedent risk hold here as well. But then the situation cannot be different if the person who decided not to insure is the only one to be blinded. For once again the difference is a difference in option luck against a background of equal opportunity to insure or not. If neither had been blinded, the man who had insured against blindness would have been the loser. His option luck would have been bad – though it seems bizarre to put it this way – because he spent resources that, as things turned out, would have been better spent otherwise. But he would have no claim, in that event, from the man who did not insure and also survived unhurt.

So if the condition just stated were met – if everyone had an equal risk of suffering some catastrophe that would leave him or her handicapped, and everyone knew roughly what the odds were and had ample opportunity to insure – then handicaps would pose no special problem for equality of resources. But of course that condition is not met. Some people are born with handicaps, or develop them before they have either sufficient knowledge or funds to insure on their own behalf. They cannot buy insurance after the event. Even handicaps that develop later in life, against which people do have the opportunity to insure, are not randomly distributed through the population, but follow genetic tracks, so that sophisticated insurers would charge some people higher premiums for the same coverage before the event. Nevertheless the idea of a market in insurance provides a counter-factual guide through which equality of resources might face the problem of handicaps in the real world.

Suppose we can make sense of and even give a rough answer to the following question. If (contrary to fact) everyone had at the appropriate age the same risk of developing physical or mental handicaps in the future (which assumes that no one has developed these yet) but that the total number of handicaps remained what it is, how much insurance coverage against these handicaps would the average member of the community purchase? We might then say that but for (uninsurable) brute luck that has altered these equal odds, the average person would have purchased insurance at that level, and compensate those who do develop handicaps accordingly, out of some fund collected by taxation or other compulsory process but designed to match the fund that would have been provided through premiums if the odds had been equal. Those who develop handicaps will then have more resources at their command than others, but the extent of their extra resources will be fixed by the market decisions that people would supposedly have made if circumstances had been more equal than they are. Of course, this argument does involve the fictitious assumption that everyone who suffers handicaps would have bought the average amount of insurance, and we may wish to refine the argument and the strategy so that that no longer holds.[6] But it does not seem an unreasonable assumption for this purpose as it stands.

Can we answer the counterfactual question with sufficient confidence to develop a program of compensation of that sort? We face a threshold difficulty of some importance. People can decide how much of their resources to devote to insurance against a particular catastrophe only with some idea of the life they hope to lead, because only then can they decide how serious a particular catastrophe would be, how far additional resources would alleviate the tragedy, and so forth. But people who are born with a particular handicap, or develop one in childhood, will of course take that circumstance into account in the plans they make. So in order to decide how much insurance such a person would have bought without the handicap we must decide what sort of life he would have planned in that case. But there may be no answer, even in principle, to that question.

We do not need, however, to make counterfactual judgments that are so personalized as to embarrass us for that reason. Even if people did all have equal risk of all catastrophes, and evaluated the value and importance of insurance differently entirely due to their different ambitions and plans, the insurance market would nevertheless be structured through categories designating the risks against which most people would insure in a general way. After all, risks of most catastrophes are now regarded by the actual insurance market as randomly distributed, and so we might follow actual insurance practice, modified to remove the discriminations insurers make when they know that one group is more likely, perhaps for genetic reasons, to suffer a particular kind of brute bad luck. It would make sense to suppose, for example, that most people would make roughly the same assessment of the value of insurance against general handicaps, such as blindness or the loss of a limb, that affect a wide spectrum of different sorts of lives. (We might look to the actual market to discover the likelihood and the contours of more specialized insurance we might decide to use in more complex schemes, like the insurance of musicians against damage to their hands, and so forth.)

We would, in any case, pay great attention to matters of technology, and be ready to adjust our sums as technology changed. People purchase insurance against catastrophes, for example, against a background of assumptions about the remedial medical technology, or special training, or mechanical aids that are in fact available, and about the cost of these remedies. People would seek insurance at a higher level against blindness, for example, if the increased recovery would enable them to purchase a newly discovered sight-substitute technology, than they would if that increased recovery simply swelled a bank account they could not, in any case, use with much satisfaction.

Of course, any judgments that the officials of a community might make about the structure of the hypothetical insurance market would be speculative and open to a variety of objections. But there is no reason to think, certainly in advance, that a practice of compensating the handicapped on the basis of such speculation would be worse, in principle, than the alternatives, and it would have the merit of aiming in the direction of the theoretical solution most congenial to equality of resources.

We might now remind ourselves of what these alternatives are. I said in Part 1 of this essay that the regime of equality of welfare, contrary to initial impressions, does a poor job of either explaining or guiding our impulse to compensate the severely handicapped with extra resources. It provides, in particular, no upper bound to compensation so long as any further payment would improve the welfare of the wretched; but this is not, as it might seem, generous, because it leaves the standard for actual compensation to the politics of selfishness broken by sympathy, politics that we know will supply less than any defensible hypothetical insurance market would offer.

Consider another approach to the problem of handicaps under equality of resources. Suppose we say that any person's physical and mental powers must count as part of his resources, so that someone who is born handicapped starts with less by way of resources than others have, and should be allowed to catch up, by way of transfer payments, before what remains is auctioned off in any equal market. People's powers are indeed resources, because these are used, together with material resources, in making something valuable out of one's life. Physical powers are resources for that purpose in the way that aspects of one's personality, like one's conception of what is valuable in life, are not. Nevertheless the suggestion, that a design of equality of resources should provide for an initial compensation to alleviate differences in physical or mental resources, is troublesome in a variety of ways. It requires, for example, some standard of "normal" powers to serve as the benchmark for compensation.[7] But whose powers should be taken as normal for this purpose? It suffers, moreover, from the same defect as the parallel recommendation under equality of welfare. In fact, no amount of initial compensation could make someone born blind or mentally incompetent equal in physical or mental resources with someone taken to be "normal" in these ways. So the argument provides no upper bound to initial compensation, but must leave this to a political compromise likely to be less generous, again, than what the hypothetical insurance market would command.

Quite apart from these practical and theoretical inadequacies, the suggestion is troublesome for another reason. Though powers are resources, they should not be considered resources whose ownership is to be determined through politics in accordance with some interpretation of equality of resources. They are not, that is, resources for the theory of equality in exactly the sense in which ordinary material resources are. They cannot be manipulated or transferred, even so far as technology might permit. So in this way it misdescribes the problem of handicaps to say that equality of resources must strive to make people equal in physical and mental constitution so far as this is possible. The problem is, rather, one of determining how far the ownership of independent material resources should be affected by differences that exist in physical and mental powers, and the response of our theory should speak in that vocabulary.

It might be wise (if for no other reason than as a convenient summary of the argument from time to time) to bring our story of the immigrants up to date. By way of supplement to the auction, they now establish a hypothetical insurance market which they effectuate through compulsory insurance at a fixed premium for everyone based on speculations about what the average immigrant would have purchased by way of insurance had the antecedent risk of various handicaps been equal. (We choose for them, that is, one of the simpler possible forms of instituting the hypothetical insurance market. We shall see, when we discuss the problem of skills [omitted, eds.], that they might well choose a more complex scheme of the sort discussed there.)

But now a question arises. Does this decision place too much weight on the distinction between handicaps, which the immigrants treat in this compensatory way, and accidents touching preferences and ambitions (like the accident of what material resources are in fact available, and of how many other people share a particular person's taste)? The latter will also affect welfare, but they are not matters for compensation under our scheme. Would it not now be fair to treat as handicaps eccentric tastes, or tastes that are expensive or impossible to satisfy because of scarcity of some good that might have been common? We might compensate those who have these tastes by supposing that everyone had an equal chance of being in that position and then establishing a hypothetical insurance market against that possibility.

A short answer is available. Someone who is born with a serious handicap faces his life with what we concede to be fewer resources, just on that account, than others do. This justifies compensation, under a scheme devoted to equality of resources, and though the hypothetical insurance market does not right the balance – nothing can – it seeks to remedy one aspect of the resulting unfairness. But we cannot say that the person whose tastes are expensive, for whatever reason, therefore has fewer resources at his command. For we cannot state (without falling back on some version of equality of welfare) what equality in the distribution of tastes and preferences would be. Why is there less equality of resources when someone has an eccentric taste that makes goods cheaper for others, than when he shares a popular taste and so makes goods more expensive for them? The auction, bringing to bear information about the resources that actually exist and the competing preferences actually in play, is the only true measure of whether any particular person commands equal resources. If the auction has in fact been an equal auction, then the man of eccentric tastes has no less than equal material resources, and the argument that justifies a compensatory hypothetical auction in the case of handicaps has no occasion even to begin. It is true that this argument produces a certain view of the distinction between a person and his circumstances, and assigns his tastes and ambitions to his person, and his physical and mental powers to his circumstances. That is the view of a person I sketched in the introductory section, of someone who forms his ambitions with a sense of their cost to others against some presumed initial equality of economic power, and though this is different from the picture assumed by equality of welfare, it is a picture at the center of equality of resources.

In one way, however, my argument might well be thought to overstate the distinction between handicaps and at least certain sorts of what are often considered preferences. Suppose someone finds he has a craving (or obsession or lust or, in the words of an earlier psychology, a "drive") that he wishes he did not have, because it interferes with what he wants to do with his life and offers him frustration or even pain if it is not satisfied. This might indeed be some feature of his physical needs that other people would not consider a handicap at all: for example, a generous appetite for sex. But it is a "preference" (if that is the right word) that he does not want, and it makes perfect sense to say that he would be better off without it. For some people these unwanted tastes include tastes they have (perhaps unwittingly) themselves cultivated, such as a taste for a particular sport or for music of a sort difficult to obtain. They regret that they have these tastes, and believe they would be better off without them, but nevertheless find it painful to ignore them. These tastes are handicaps; though for other people they are rather an essential part of what gives value to their lives.

Now these cases do not present, for particular people, borderline cases between ambitions and handicaps (though no doubt other sorts of borderline cases could be found). The distinction required by equality of resources is the distinction between those beliefs and attitudes that define what a successful life would be like, which the ideal assigns to the person, and those features of body or mind or personality that provide means or impediments to that success, which the ideal assigns to the person's circumstances. Those who see their sexual desires or their taste for opera as unwanted disadvantages will class these features of their body or mind or personality firmly as the latter. These are, for them, handicaps, and are therefore suitable for the regime proposed for handicaps generally. We may imagine that everyone has an equal chance of acquiring such a craving by accident. (Of course, for each person the content of a craving that would have that consequence would be different. We are supposing here, not the risk of any particular craving, but the risk of whatever craving would interfere with set goals in that way.) We may then ask – with as much or as little intelligibility as in the case of blindness – whether people generally would purchase insurance against that risk, and if so at what premium and what level of coverage. It seems unlikely that many people would purchase such insurance, at the rates of premium likely to govern if they sought it, except in the case of cravings so severe and disabling as to fall under the category of mental disease. But that is a different matter.

The important point, presently, is that the idea of an insurance market is available here, because we can imagine people who have such a craving not having it, without thereby imagining them to have a different conception of what they want from life than what in fact they do want. So the idea of the imaginary insurance auction provides at once a device for identifying cravings and distinguishing them from positive features of personality, and also for bringing these cravings within the general regime designed for handicaps.

IV.   Labor and Wages

Equality of resources, once established by the auction, and corrected to provide for handicaps, would be disturbed by production and trade. If one of the immigrants, for example, was specially proficient at producing tomatoes, he might trade his surplus for more than anyone else could acquire, in which case others would begin to envy his bundle of resources. Suppose we wished to create a society in which the division of resources would be continuously equal, in spite of different kinds and degrees of production and trade. Can we adapt our auction so as to produce such a society?

We should begin by considering a different sequence after which people would envy each other's resources, and the division might be thought no longer to be equal. Suppose all the immigrants are in fact sufficiently equal in talent at the few modes of production that the resources allow so that each could produce roughly the same goods from the same set of resources. Nevertheless they wish to lead their lives in different ways, and they in fact acquire different bundles of resources in the initial auction and use them differently thereafter. Adrian chooses resources and works them with the single-minded ambition of producing as much of what others value as possible; and so, at the end of a year, his total stock of goods is larger than anyone else's. Each of the other immigrants would now prefer Adrian's stock to his own; but by hypothesis none of them would have been willing to lead his life so as to produce them. If we look for envy at particular points in time, then each envies Adrian's resources at the end of the year, and the division is therefore not equal. But if we look at envy differently, as a matter of resources over an entire life, and we include a person's occupation as part of the bundle of his goods, then no one envies Adrian's bundle, and the distribution cannot be said to be unequal on that account.

Surely we should take the second, synoptic, point of view. Our final aim is that an equal share of resources should be devoted to the lives of each person, and we have chosen the auction as the right way to measure the value of what is made available to a person, through his decision, for that purpose. If Bruce chooses to acquire land for use as a tennis court, then the question is raised how much his account should be charged, in the reckoning whether an equal share has been put to his use, in virtue of that choice, and it is right that his account should be charged the amount that others would have been willing to pay had the land been devoted to their purposes instead. The appeal of the auction, as a device for picturing equality of resources, is precisely that it enforces that metric. But this scheme will fail, and the device disappoint us, unless Adrian is able to bid a price for the same land that reflects his intention to work rather than play on it and so to acquire whatever gain would prompt him to make that decision. For unless this is permitted, those who want tomatoes and would pay Adrian his price for them will not be able to bid indirectly, through Adrian's decision, against Bruce, who will then secure his tennis court at a price that, because it is too low, defeats equality of resources. This is not, I should add, an argument from efficiency as distinct from fairness; but rather an argument that in the circumstances described, in which talents are equal, efficiency simply is fairness, at least as fairness is conceived under equality of resources. If Adrian is willing to spend his life at drudgery, in return for the profit he will make at prices that others will pay for what he produces, then the land on which he would drudge should not be used for a tennis court instead, unless its value as a tennis court is greater as measured by someone's willingness to invade an initially equal stock of abstract resources.

Now this is to look at the matter entirely from the standpoint of those who want Adrian's tomatoes, a standpoint that treats Adrian only as a means. But we reach the same conclusion if we look at the matter from his point of view as well. If someone chooses to have something inexpensive in his life, under a regime of equality of resources, then he will have more left over for the rest of what he wants. Someone who accepts Algerian wine may use it to wash down plovers' eggs. But a decision to produce one thing rather than another with land, or to use the land for leisure rather than production, is also the choice of something for one's life, and this may be inexpensive as well. Suppose Adrian is desperate for plovers' eggs but would rather work hard at tilling his land than settle for less than champagne. The total may be no more expensive, measured in terms of what his decisions cost others, than a life of leisure and grape juice. If he earns enough by working hard, or by working at work that no one else wants to do, to satisfy all his expensive tastes, then his choice for his own life costs the rest of the community no more than if his tastes were simpler and his industry less. So we have no more reason to deny him hard work and high consumption than less work and frugality. The choice should be indifferent under equality of resources, so long as no one envies the total package of work plus consumption that he chooses. So long as no one envies, that is, his life as a whole. Of course, Adrian might actually enjoy his hard work, so that he makes no sacrifice. He prefers working hard to anything else. But this cannot provide any argument, under equality of resources, that he should gain less in money or other goods by his work than if he hated every minute of it, any more than it argues against charging someone a low price for lettuce, which he actually prefers to truffles.

So we must apply the envy test diachronically: it requires that no one envy the bundle of occupation and resources at the disposal of anyone else over time, though someone may envy another's bundle at any particular time. It would therefore violate equality of resources if the community were to redistribute Adrian's wealth, say, at the end of each year. If everyone had equal talents (as we have been assuming just now), the initial auction would produce continuing equality of resources even though bank-account wealth became more and more unequal as years passed.

Is that unlikely condition – that everyone has equal talent – absolutely necessary to that conclusion? Would the auction produce continuing equality of resources if (as in the real world) talents for production differed sharply from person to person? Now the envy test would fail, even interpreted diachronically. Claude (who likes farming but has a black thumb) would not bid enough for farming land to take that land from Adrian. Or, if he did, he would have to settle for less in the rest of his life. But he would then envy the package of Adrian's occupation and wealth. If we interpret occupation in a manner sensitive to the joys of craft, then Adrian's occupation, which must then be described as skillful, craftsmanlike farming, is simply unavailable to Claude. If we interpret occupation in a more census-like fashion, then Claude may undertake Adrian's occupation, but he cannot have the further resources that Adrian has along with it. So if we continue to insist that the envy test is a necessary condition of equality of resources, then our initial auction will not insure continuing equality, in the real world of unequal talents for production.

But it may now be objected that we should not insist on the envy test at this point, even in principle, for the following reason. We are moving too close to a requirement that people must not envy each other, which is different from the requirement that they must not envy each other's bundles of resources. People may envy each other for a variety of reasons: some are physically more attractive, some more easily satisfied with their condition, some better liked by others, some more intelligent or able in different ways, and so on. Of course, under a regime of equality of welfare each of these differences would be taken into account, and transfers made to erase their welfare consequences so far as possible or feasible. But the point of equality of resources is fundamentally different: it is that people should have the same external resources at their command to make of them what, given these various features and talents, they can. That point is satisfied by an initial auction, but since people are different it is neither necessary nor desirable that resources should remain equal thereafter, and quite impossible that all envy should be eliminated by political distribution. If one person, by dint of superior effort or talent, uses his equal share to create more than another, he is entitled to profit thereby, because his gain is not made at the expense of someone else who does less with his share. We recognized that, just now, when we conceded that superior industry should be rewarded, so that Adrian, who worked hard, should be allowed to keep the rewards of his effort.

Now this objection harbors many mistakes, but they all come to this: it confuses equality of resources with the fundamentally different idea sometimes called equality of opportunity. It is not true, in the first place, that someone who does more with his initial share does not, in so doing, lessen the value of what others have. If Adrian were not so successful at agriculture, then Claude's own efforts would be rewarded more, because people would buy his inferior produce having no better alternative. If Adrian were not so successful and hence so rich he would not be able to pay so much for wine, and Claude, with his smaller fortune, would be able to buy more at a cheaper price. These are simply the most obvious consequences of the fact that the immigrants form one economy, after the initial auction, rather than a set of distinct economies. Of course these consequences also follow from the situation we discussed a moment ago. If Adrian and Bruce have the same talents, but Adrian chooses to work harder or differently and acquires more money, then this may also decrease the value of Claude's share to him. The difference between these two circumstances, if there is one, lies elsewhere; but it is important to reject the claim, instinct in some arguments for equality of opportunity, that if people start with equal shares the prosperity of one does no damage to the other.

Nor is it true that if we aim at a result in which those with less talent do not envy the circumstances of those with more talent we have destroyed the distinction between envying others and envying what they have. For Adrian has two things that Claude would prefer to have which belong to Adrian's circumstances rather than his person. The desires and needs of other people provide Adrian but not Claude with a satisfying occupation, and Adrian has more money than Claude can have. Perhaps nothing can be done, by way of political structure or distribution, to erase these differences and remove the envy entirely. We cannot, for example, alter the tastes of other people by electrical means so as to make them value what Claude can produce more and what Adrian can produce less. But this provides no argument against other schemes, like schemes of education that would allow Claude to find satisfaction in his work or of taxation that would redistribute some of Adrian's wealth to him, and we could fairly describe these schemes as aiming to remove Claude's envy of what Adrian has rather than of what Adrian is.

Important as these points are, it is more important still to identify and correct another mistake that the present objection makes. It misunderstands our earlier conclusion, that when talents are roughly equal the auction provides continuing equality of resources, and so misses the important distinction between that case and the present argument. The objection supposes that we reached that conclusion because we accept, as the basis of equality of resources, what we might call the starting-gate theory of fairness: that if people start in the same circumstances, and do not cheat or steal from one another, then it is fair that people keep what they gain through their own skill. But the starting-gate theory of fairness is very far from equality of resources. Indeed it is hardly a coherent political theory at all.

The starting-gate theory holds that justice requires equal initial resources. But it also holds that justice requires laissez-faire thereafter, in accordance, presumably, with some version of the Lockean theory that people acquire property by mixing their labor with goods or something of that sort. But these two principles cannot live comfortably together. Equality can have no greater force in justifying initial equal holdings when the immigrants land – against the competing view that all property should be available for Lockean acquisition at that time – than later in justifying redistributions when wealth becomes unequal because people's productive talents are different. The same point may be put the other way around. The theory of Lockean acquisition (or whatever other theory of justice in acquisition is supposed to justify the laissez-faire component in a starting-gate theory) can have no less force in governing the initial distribution than it has in justifying title through talent and effort later. If the theory is sound later, then why does it not command a Lockean process of acquisition in the first instance, rather than an equal distribution of all there is? The moment when the immigrants first land is, after all, an arbitrary point in their lives at which to locate any one-shot requirement that they each have an equal share of any available resources. If that requirement holds then, it must also hold on the tenth anniversary of that date, which is, in the words of the banal and important cliché, the first day in the rest of their lives. So if justice requires an equal auction when they land, it must require a fresh, equal auction from time to time thereafter; and if justice requires laissez-faire thereafter, it must require it when they land.

Suppose someone replies that there is an important difference between the initial distribution of resources and any later redistribution. When the immigrants land, no one owns any of the resources, and the principle of equality therefore dictates equal initial shares. But later, after the initial resources have been auctioned, they are each owned in some way by someone, so that the principle of equality is superceded by respect for people's rights in property or something of that sort. This reply begs the question straightway. For we are considering precisely the question whether a system of ownership should be established in the first instance that has that consequence, or, rather, whether a different system of ownership should be chosen that explicitly makes any acquisition subject to schemes of redistribution later. If the latter sort of system is chosen, at the outset, then no one can later complain that redistribution is ruled out by his property rights alone. I do not mean that no theory of justice can consistently distinguish between justice in initial acquisition and justice in transfer on the ground that anyone may do what he wants with property that is already his. Nozick's theory, for example, does just that. This is consistent, because his theory of justice in initial acquisition purports to justify a system of property rights which have that consequence: justice in transfer, that is, flows from the rights the theory of acquisition claims are acquired in acquiring property. But the theory of initial acquisition on which the starting-gate theory relies, which is equality of resources, does not even purport to justify a characterization of property that necessarily includes absolute control without limit of time thereafter.

So the starting-gate theory, that the immigrants should start off equal in resources but grow prosperous or lean through their own efforts thereafter, is an indefensible combination of very different theories of justice. Something like that combination makes sense in games, such as Monopoly, whose point is to allow luck and skill to play a highly circumscribed and, in the last analysis, arbitrary, role; but it cannot hold together a political theory. Our own principle, that if people of equal talent choose different lives it is unfair to redistribute halfway through those lives, makes no appeal to the starting-gate theory at all. It is based on the very different idea that the equality in question is equality of resources devoted to whole lives. This principle offers a clear answer to the question that embarrasses the present objection. Our theory does not suppose that an equal division of resources is appropriate at one moment in someone's life but not at any other. It argues only that resources available to him at any moment must be a function of resources available or consumed by him at others, so that the explanation of why someone has less money now may be that he has consumed expensive leisure earlier. Nothing like that explanation is available to explain why Claude, who has worked as hard and in the same way as Adrian, should have less in virtue of the fact that he is less skillful.

So we must reject the starting-gate theory, and recognize that the requirements of equality (in the real world at least) pull in opposite directions. On the one hand we must, on pain of violating equality, allow the distribution of resources at any particular moment to be (as we might say) ambition-sensitive. It must, that is, reflect the cost or benefit to others of the choices people make so that, for example, those who choose to invest rather than consume, or to consume less expensively rather than more, or to work in more rather than less profitable ways, must be permitted to retain the gains that flow from these decisions in an equal auction followed by free trade. But on the other hand, we must not allow the distribution of resources at any moment to be endowment-sensitive, that is, to be affected by differences in ability of the sort that produce income differences in a laissez-faire economy among people with the same ambitions. Can we devise some formula that offers a practical, or even a theoretical, compromise between these two, apparently competing, requirements?

We might mention, but only to dismiss, one possible response. Suppose we allow our initial auction to include, as resources to be auctioned, the labor of the immigrants themselves, so that each immigrant can bid for the right to control part or all of his own or other people's labor. Special skills would accrue to the benefit, not of the laborer himself, but of the community as a whole, like any other valuable resource the immigrants found when they landed. Except in unusual cases, since people begin with equal resources for bidding, each agent would bid enough to secure his own labor. But the result would be that each would have to spend his life in close to the commercially most profitable manner he could, or, at least if he is talented, suffer some very serious deprivation if he did not. For since Adrian, for example, is able to produce prodigious income from farming, others would be willing to bid a large amount to have the right to his labor and the vegetables thereof, and if he outbids them, but chooses to write indifferent poetry instead of farming full time, he will have spent a large part of his initial endowment on a right that will bring him little financial benefit. This is indeed the slavery of the talented.

We cannot permit this, but it is worth pausing to ask what grounds we have for barring it. Shall we say that since a person owns his own mind and body, he owns the talents that are only capacities thereof, and therefore owns the fruits of those talents? This is, of course, a series of nonsequiturs. It is also a familiar argument in favor of the laissez-faire labor market we have decided is a violation of equality of resources when people are unequal in talent. But we could not accept it in any case, because it uses the idea of pre-political entitlement based on something other than equality, and that is inconsistent with the premise of the scheme of equality of resources we have developed.

So we must look elsewhere for the ground of our objection to taking people's labor as a resource for the auction. We need not, in fact, look very far; for the principle that people should not be penalized for talent is simply part of the same principle we relied on in rejecting the apparently opposite idea, that people should be allowed to retain the benefits of superior talent. The envy test forbids both of these results. If Adrian is treated as owning whatever his talents enable him to produce, then Claude envies the package of resources, including occupation, that Adrian has over his life considered as a whole. But if Adrian is required to purchase leisure time or the right to a less productive occupation at the cost of other resources, then Adrian will envy Claude's package. If equality of resources is understood to include some plausible version of the envy test, as a necessary condition of an equal distribution, then the role of talent must be neutralized in a way that no simple addition to the stock of goods to be auctioned can accomplish.

We should turn, therefore, to a more familiar idea: the periodic redistribution of resources through some form of income tax.[8] We want to develop a scheme of redistribution, so far as we are able, that will neutralize the effects of differential talents, yet preserve the consequences of one person choosing an occupation, in response to his sense of what he wants to do with his life, that is more expensive for the community than the choice another makes. An income tax is a plausible device for this purpose because it leaves intact the possibility of choosing a life in which sacrifices are constantly made and discipline steadily imposed for the sake of financial success and the further resources it brings, though of course it neither endorses nor condemns that choice. But it also recognizes the role of genetic luck in such a life. The accommodation it makes is a compromise; but it is a compromise of two requirements of equality, in the face of both practical and conceptual uncertainty how to satisfy these requirements, not a compromise of equality for the sake of some independent value such as efficiency.

But of course the appeal of a tax depends on our ability to fix rates of taxation that will make that compromise accurately. It might be helpful, in that aim, if we were able to find some way of identifying, in any person's wealth at any particular time, the component traceable to differential talents as distinguished from differential ambitions. We might then try to devise a tax that would recapture, for redistribution, just this component. But we cannot hope to identify such a component, even given perfect information about people's personalities. For we will be thwarted by the reciprocal influence that talents and ambitions exercise on each other. Talents are nurtured and developed, not discovered full-blown, and people choose which talents to develop in response to their beliefs about what sort of person it is best to be. But people also wish to develop and use the talents they have, not simply because they prefer a life of relative success, but because the exercise of talent is enjoyable and perhaps also out of a sense that an unused talent is a waste. Someone with a good eye or a skilled hand conceives a picture of what would make his life valuable that someone more clumsy would not.

So we cannot hope to fix the rates of our income tax so as to redistribute exactly that part of each person's income that is attributable to his talent as distinguished from his ambitions. Talents and ambitions are too closely inter-twined. Can we do better by proceeding on a slightly different tack? Can we aim to fix rates so as to leave each person with the income he would have had if, counterfactually, talents for production had all been equal? No, because it is impossible to say, in any relevant way, what sort of world that would be. We should have to decide what sort and level of talent everyone would have equally, and then what income people exploiting those talents to different degrees of effort would reach. Should we stipulate that in that world everyone would have the talents that the most talented people in the real world now have? Do we mean, by "the most talented people," the people who are able to earn the most money in the actual world if they work single-mindedly for money? But in a world in which everyone could hit a high inside pitch, or play sexy roles in films, with equal authority, there would probably be no baseball or films; in any case no one would be paid much for exercising such talents. Nor would any other description of the talents everyone would be supposed to have in equal degree be any more help.

But though this crude counterfactual exercise must fail, it suggests a more promising exercise. Let us review our situation. We want to find some way to distinguish fair from unfair differences in wealth generated by differences in occupation. Unfair differences are those traceable to genetic luck, to talents that make some people prosperous but are denied to others who would exploit them to the full if they had them. But if this is right, then the problem of differential talents is in certain ways like the problem of handicaps we have already considered.

Notes

1   D. Foley, "Resource Allocation and the Public Sector," *Yale Economic Essays* 7 (Spring 1967); H. Varian, "Equity, Energy and Efficiency," *Journal of Economic Theory* (Sept. 1974), 63–91.

2   I mean to describe a Walrasian auction in which all productive resources are sold. I do not assume that the immigrants enter into complete forward contingent claims contracts, but only that markets will remain open and will clear in a Walrasian fashion once the auction of productive resources is completed. I make all the assumptions about production and preferences made in G. Debreu, *Theory of Value* (New Haven: Yale University Press, 1959). In fact the auction I describe here will become more complex in virtue of a tax scheme discussed later.

3   The process does not guarantee that the auction will come to an end in this way, because there may be various equilibria. I am supposing that people will come to understand that they cannot do better by further runs of the auction, and will for practical reasons settle on one equilibrium. If I am wrong, then this fact provides one of the aspects of incompleteness I describe in the next section.

4   See, however, the discussion of handicaps below, which recognizes that certain kinds of preferences, which people wish they did not have, may call for compensation as handicaps.

5   See Part I of this essay (*Philosophy & Public Affairs* 10, no. 3 [Summer 1981]) for a discussion of whether equality of welfare can be modified so as to make an exception here for "expensive tastes" deliberately cultivated. I argue that it cannot.

6   The averaging assumption is a simplifying assumption only, made to provide a result in the absence of the detailed (and perhaps, for reasons described in the text, indeterminate) information that would enable us to decide how much each handicapped person would have purchased in the hypothetical market. If we had such full information, so that we could tailor compensation to what a particular individual in fact would have bought, the accuracy of the program would be improved. But in the absence of such information averaging is second best, or in any case better than nothing.

7   The hypothetical insurance approach does not require any stipulation of "normal" powers, because it allows the hypothetical market to determine which infirmities are compensable.

8   Notice that our analysis of the problem that differential talents presents to equality of resources calls for an income tax, rather than either a wealth or a consumption tax. If people begin with equal resources, then we wish to tax to adjust for different skills so far as these produce different income, because it is only in that way that they threaten equality of resources. Someone's decision to spend rather than save what he has earned is precisely the kind of decision whose impact should be determined by the market uncorrected for tax under this analysis. Of course, there might be technical or other reasons why a society dedicated to equality of welfare would introduce taxes other than income taxes. Such a society might want to encourage savings, for example. But these taxes would not be responses to the problem now under consideration. Should unearned (investment) income be taxed under the present argument? I assume that unearned income reflects skill in investment as well as preferences for later consumption, in which case that argument would extend to taxing such income. Since I am not considering, in this essay, the problem of later generations, I do not consider inheritance or estate taxes at all.

6

Against Equality of Resources: Relocating Dworkin's Cut

G. A. Cohen

I

Ronald Dworkin denies that equality of welfare provides the right reading of the egalitarian aim, and I agree with him about that.[1] But I do not share his view that the demise of equality of welfare should prompt egalitarians to embrace equality of resources instead. Part of my reason for disagreeing with Dworkin on that score is my belief, to be defended in a moment, that one of his major objections to equality of welfare can be met by a revised form of that principle. The revised welfare principle, unlike equality of welfare, permits and indeed enjoins departures from welfare equality when they reflect choices of relevant agents, as opposed to deficient *opportunity* for welfare. If a person's welfare is low because he freely risked a welfare loss in gambling for a welfare gain, then, under the opportunity form of the principle, he has no claim to compensation. Nor does a person who frittered away welfare opportunities which others seized. Nor, to take a different kind of example, does a person who chose to forgo welfare out of devotion to an ideal which (expressly, or merely as it happened) required self-denial.

The revised principle can be called equality of opportunity for welfare.[2] It is not a principle that I shall endorse. Equality of opportunity for welfare is a better reading of egalitarianism than equality of welfare itself is, but it is not as good as what currently strikes me as the right reading of egalitarianism, namely, that its purpose is to eliminate *involuntary disadvantage*, by which I (stipulatively) mean disadvantage for which the sufferer cannot be held responsible, since it does not appropriately reflect choices that he has made or is making or would make. Equality of opportunity for welfare eliminates involuntary welfare deficiencies, and welfare deficiencies are forms of

Extracts from G. A. Cohen, 'On the Currency of Egalitarian Justice' pp. 916–34 (section IV), from *Ethics*, 99 (1989), pp. 906–44.

disadvantage. Hence the principle I endorse responds to inequalities in people's welfare opportunities. But, as will be illustrated below, advantage is a broader notion than welfare. Anything which enhances my welfare is *pro tanto* to my advantage, but the converse is not true. And disadvantage is correspondingly broader than welfare deficiency, so the view I favor, which can be called *equal opportunity for advantage*, or, preferably, equal *access* to advantage, corrects for inequalities to which equal opportunity for welfare is insensitive.

Why is "equal *access* to advantage" a better name for the view than "equal *opportunity* for advantage" is? We would not normally regard meager personal capacity as detracting from opportunity. Your opportunities are the same whether you are strong and clever or weak and stupid: if you are weak and stupid, you may not use them well – but that implies that you have them. But shortfalls on the side of personal capacity nevertheless engage egalitarian concern, and they do so because they detract from access to valuable things, even if they do not diminish the opportunity to get them. Hence my preference for "access,"[3] but I still require this possibly unnatural stipulation: I shall treat anything which a person actually has as something to which he has access.[4]

Some of Dworkin's counter-examples to equality of welfare fail to challenge equality of opportunity for welfare, and they fail, a fortiori, to challenge the wider disadvantage principle. The Dworkin examples I here have in mind, which are to do with expensive tastes, not only do not challenge equality of opportunity for welfare: one can say the stronger thing that they bring its claims to the fore as a candidate reading of the egalitarian aim. But other counter-examples to equality of welfare presented by Dworkin necessitate movement beyond equality of opportunity for welfare to the broader conception of equality of access to advantage. One sort of counter-example that has that effect concerns handicaps, in the literal sense of the word, and I shall be presenting a handicap counter-example to equality of opportunity for welfare at the beginning of the next section.

In my view, however, equality of resources is subject to objections which are just as strong as those which defeat equality of welfare (and equality of opportunity for welfare). I shall now defend that conclusion, by describing the case of a doubly unfortunate person. I believe that egalitarians will be moved to compensate him for both of his misfortunes, but the fact that the first calls for egalitarian compensation challenges equality of welfare and the fact that the second does challenges equality of resources.

II

My unfortunate person's legs are paralyzed. To get around, he needs an expensive wheelchair. Egalitarians will be disposed to recommend that he be given one. And they will be so disposed before they have asked about the welfare level to which the man's paralysis reduces him. When compensating for disability, egalitarians do not immediately distinguish between the different amounts of misery induced by similar disabilities in people who have different (dis)utility functions. They propose compensation for the disability *as such*, and not, or not only, for its deleterious welfare effects. Insofar as we can distinguish compensation for resource deficiency from compensation for welfare deficiency, the first appears to enjoy independent egalitarian favor.

The egalitarian response to disability seems to defeat not only equality of welfare but also equality of opportunity for welfare. Tiny Tim is not only *actually* happy, by any standard. He is also, because of his fortunate disposition, blessed with abundant *opportunity* for happiness: he need not do much to get a lot of it. But egalitarians would not on that account strike him off the list of free wheelchair receivers. They do not think that wheelchair distribution should be controlled exclusively by the welfare opportunity requirements of those who need them. Lame people need them to be adequately resourced, whether or not they also need them to be, or to be capable of being, happy.

Note that I do not say that, whatever other demands they face, egalitarians will always service people like Tiny Tim. One could imagine him surrounded by curably miserable sound-limbed people whose welfare was so low that their requirements were judged to precede his. The essential point is that his abundant happiness is not as such decisive against compensating him for his disability.

In face of (what I say are) the intuitive phenomena, the only way of sustaining the view that equality of welfare is the right reading of the egalitarian aim is to claim that egalitarians propose assistance for disability without gathering welfare information because of a general correlation between disability and illfare which it is impossible or too costly to confirm in individual cases. Like Sen and Dworkin, I find that defense unpersuasive, and I consequently conclude that the egalitarian response to disability defeats equality of welfare.[5] And, as I argued, it also defeats equality of opportunity for welfare, since the response to disability is shaped by something other than the different costs in lost opportunity for welfare which disability causes in different people.

I have not completed my description of the man's misfortune. There is also something wrong with his arms. He is not less able to move them than most people are: I shall even assume, to make my point more vivid, that he is especially good at moving them. But there is, nevertheless, something seriously wrong with them, and it is this: after he moves them, he suffers severe pain in his arm muscles.

In the terms of a distinction which I once had occasion to make in a different context, it is not *difficult* for the man to move his arms, but it is very *costly* for him to do so.[6] What I call 'difficulty' and 'cost' are two widely conflated but importantly distinct ways in which it can be *hard* for a person to do something. (It is costly, but not difficult, for me to supply you with a check for £500, or for me to tell you some secret the revelation of which will damage me. It is extremely difficult for me to transport you to Heathrow on the back of my bicycle, but it is not costly, since I love that kind of challenge, and I have nothing else to do today. At the far end of the difficulty continuum lies the *impossible*, but it is the *unbearable* which occupies that position in the case of costliness.)[7]

Now there is an expensive medicine which, taken regularly, suppresses the pain that otherwise follows the man's arm movement, and this medicine is so expensive that it has no adverse side effects. Egalitarians would, I am sure, favor supplying our man with the medicine, even if it costs what a wheelchair does. But providing the medicine cannot be represented as compensating for a resource incapacity. The man's capacity to move his arms is, *in the relevant sense*, better (so I stipulated) than that of most people.

"In the relevant sense" does a lot of work here, so let me explain it. Someone might insist, and I do not have to deny, that there is *a* sense in which a typical normal person has a capacity which this man lacks. I need not deny that he lacks the capacity to move his arms without pain, or, if you prefer, to move his arms without pain without taking medicine. I can even agree that it is his lack of *that* capacity which is the egalitarian ground for compensating him. *But compensating for a lack of capacity which needs to be described in that way for the ground of the compensation to be revealed cannot be represented as compensating for incapacity when that is opposed to compensating for welfare opportunity deficiency.* A would-be resource egalitarian who said, "Compensation is in order here because the man lacks the resource of being able to avoid pain" would be invoking the idea of equality of opportunity for welfare even if he would be using resourcist language to describe it.

My example was medically fanciful, but a medically more ordinary example makes the same point, though you have to exercise slightly sharper perception to see it. It was fanciful in the foregoing case that the pain should wholly succeed and not also accompany the pain-inducing movement. Think now of a more ordinary case, in which arthritic pain accompanies movement, and suppose, what is likely, that the movement is not only painful but, consequently and/or otherwise, *also* difficult. That difficulty introduces a resource deficiency into the case, but the example nevertheless stands as a challenge to equality of resources. For it seems not coherently egalitarian to cater only to the difficulty of moving and not independently to the pain which moving occasions. So there is an irreducible welfare aspect in the case for egalitarian compensation in real-life disability examples.

Or just think of poor people in Britain who suffer discomfort in the winter cold. The egalitarian case for helping them with their electricity bills is partly founded on that discomfort itself. It does not rest entirely on the disenablement which the cold, both through discomfort and independently, also causes.

People vary in the amount of discomfort which given low temperatures cause them, and, consequently, in the volume of resources which they need to alleviate their discomfort. Some people need costly heavy sweaters and a great deal of fuel to achieve an average level of thermal well-being. With respect to warmth, they have what Dworkin calls *expensive tastes*: they need unusually large doses of resources to achieve an ordinary level of welfare. They are losers under Dworkin's equality of resources, because, as we shall see, it sets itself against compensation for expensive tastes.

The two grounds of egalitarian compensation which apply in the case of the disabled man have something in common. The man's straightforward inability to move his legs and his liability to pain when moving his arms are both disadvantages for which (I tacitly assumed) he cannot be held responsible, and, I suggest, that is why an egalitarian would compensate him for them. Both aspects of his plight represent unavoidable disadvantages, which he was unable to forestall and which he cannot now rectify. On my understanding of egalitarianism, it does not enjoin redress of or compensation for disadvantage as such. It attends, rather, to "involuntary" disadvantage, which is the sort that does not reflect the subject's choice. People's advantages are unjustly unequal (or unjustly equal) when the inequality (or equality) reflects unequal access to advantage, as opposed to patterns of choice against a background of equality of access. Severe actual disadvantage is a fairly reliable sign of inequality of access to advantage, but the prescribed equality is not of advantage per se but of access, all things considered, to it.

When deciding whether or not justice (as opposed to charity) requires redistribution, the egalitarian asks if someone with a disadvantage could have avoided it or could now overcome it.[8] If he could have avoided it, he has no claim to compensation, from an egalitarian point of view. If he could not have avoided it but could now overcome it, then he can ask that his effort to overcome it be subsidized, but, unless it costs more to overcome it than to compensate for it without overcoming it, he cannot expect society to compensate for his disadvantage.

I affirm equality of access to advantage, whatever advantage is rightly considered to be, but I cannot say, in a pleasingly systematic way, exactly what should count as an advantage, partly because I have not thought hard enough about this question, which is surely one of the deepest in normative philosophy.[9] What does appear clear is that resource deficiencies and welfare deficiencies are distinct types of disadvantage and that each of them covers pretty distinct subtypes: poverty and physical weakness are very different kinds of resource limitation, and despondency and failure to achieve aims are very different kinds of illfare. Whatever the boundaries and types of welfare may be,[10] lack of pain is surely a form of it, and lack of disability, considered just as such, is not, if there is to be a contrast between equality of resources and equality of welfare. Those two classificatory judgments are reasonably uncontentious, and they are the ones I need to sustain the criticism of Dworkin which arises from reflection on the case of involuntary pain.

(I warned at the outset that my positive proposal would be crude. One thing that makes it so and makes me wish that it will be superseded is the unlovely heterogeneity of the components of the vector of advantage. One hopes that there is a currency more fundamental than either resources or welfare in which the various egalitarian responses which motivated my proposal can be expressed. But I certainly have not discovered it, so, at least for now, I stay with the appearances, which contradict welfare, resources, and opportunity for welfare readings of the egalitarian demand, and which point, in the first instance, to the theory [or semitheory: it is perhaps too close to the intuitive phenomena to merit the name "theory"] I have affirmed.)

III

Whatever number of dimensions the space of disadvantage may have, egalitarianism, on my reading, cuts through each of its dimensions, judging certain inequalities of advantage as acceptable and others as not, its touchstone being a set of questions about the responsibility or lack of it of the disadvantaged agent.

In Ronald Dworkin's different reading of egalitarianism, people are to be compensated for shortfalls in their powers, that is, their material resources and mental and physical capacities, but not for shortfalls traceable to their tastes and preferences. What they get should reflect differences in what they want and seek, but not in their *ability* to get things.

Dworkin's "cut" contrasts with mine in two ways. First, it calls for compensation for resource deficiencies only, and not also for pain and other illfare considered as such. "There is no place in [Dworkin's] theory . . . for comparisons of the welfare levels of different people," nor, I infer, for catering to people whose pains do not diminish their capacity, since that service reflects a judgment about how their welfare, in one relevant sense, compares with that of others.[11] My cut awards redress for both resource and welfare disadvantages, but, in Dworkin's theory, there is not even "some small room for equality of welfare," alongside other considerations.[12]

So, for purposes of egalitarian intervention, Dworkin-style, only one dimension of disadvantage is recognized. And the second difference between our cuts is that, within that single resource dimension, Dworkin does not put absence of responsibility in the foreground as a necessary condition of just compensation.

I say that the question of responsibility is not *foregrounded* in Dworkin's presentation, because I shall argue that, insofar as he succeeds in making his cut plausible, it is by obscuring both of the differences between it and the different cut that I have recommended. I shall also argue that the grounding idea of Dworkin's egalitarianism is that no one should suffer because of bad brute luck and that, since the relevant opposite of an unlucky fate is a fate traceable to its victim's control, my cut is more faithful to Dworkin's grounding idea than the one he ostensibly favors is.

For Dworkin, it is not choice but preference which excuses what would otherwise be an unjustly unequal distribution. He proposes compensation for power deficiencies, but not for expensive tastes,[13] whereas I believe that we should compensate for disadvantage beyond a person's control, as such, and that we should not, accordingly, draw a line between unfortunate resource endowment and unfortunate utility function.[14] A person with *wantonly* expensive tastes has no claim on us, but neither does a person whose powers are feeble because he recklessly failed to develop them. There is no moral difference, from an egalitarian point of view, between a person who irresponsibly acquires (or blamelessly chooses to develop) an expensive taste and a person who irresponsibly loses (or blamelessly chooses to consume) a valuable resource. The right cut is between responsibility and bad luck, not between preferences and resources.

The difference between those two cuts will have policy significance in the case of those expensive tastes which cannot be represented as reflecting choice. There will be no policy difference with respect to Dworkin's leading example of a person with expensive tastes. I refer to Louis, who requires ancient claret and plovers' eggs in order to reach an ordinary level of welfare. I treat Louis in practice the way Dworkin does, because, as Dworkin describes him, he did not just get stuck with his taste: he schooled himself into it. But, while Dworkin and I both refuse Louis's request for a special allowance, we ground our refusals differently. Dworkin says: sorry, Louis, we egalitarians do not finance expensive tastes; whereas I say: sorry Louis, we egalitarians do not finance expensive tastes which people choose to develop.

Now consider a case of expensive taste where there will be a policy difference. Paul loves photography, while Fred loves fishing.[15] Prices are such that Fred pursues his pastime with ease while Paul cannot afford to. Paul's life is a lot less pleasant as a result: it might even be true that it has less meaning than Fred's does. I think the egalitarian thing to do is to subsidize Paul's photography. But Dworkin cannot think that. His envy test for equality of resources is satisfied: Paul can afford to go fishing as readily as Fred can. Paul's problem is that he hates fishing and, so I am permissibly assuming, could not have helped hating it – it does not suit his natural inclinations. He has a genuinely involuntary expensive taste, and I think that a commitment to equality implies that he should be helped in the way that people like Paul are indeed helped by subsidized community leisure facilities. As this example suggests, there is between Dworkin's account of egalitarian justice and mine the difference that my account mandates less market pricing than his does.

I distinguish among expensive tastes according to whether or not their bearer can reasonably be held responsible for them. There are those which he could not have helped forming and/or could not now unform, and then there are those for which, by contrast, he can be held responsible, because he could have forestalled them and/or because he could now unlearn them. Notice that I do not say that a person who deliberately develops an expensive taste deserves criticism. I say no such severe thing because there are all kinds of reasons why a person might want to develop an expensive taste, and it is each person's business whether he does so or not. But it is also nobody else's business to pick up the tab for him if he does. Egalitarians have good reason not to minister to deliberately cultivated expensive tastes, and equality of welfare must, therefore, be rejected. But we should not embrace equality of resources instead, since that doctrine wrongly refuses compensation for involuntary expensive tastes, and it does not refuse compensation for voluntary ones for the right reason.

In Dworkin's view, only the principle of equality of resources can explain why Louis's expensive tastes should not be indulged by egalitarians. But his long discussion of Louis rejects the most obvious reason the egalitarian has for denying Louis the resources needed to service his taste: that he "sets out deliberately to cultivate" it.[16] It is crucial that, as Dworkin acknowledges, "Louis has a choice": the taste is not instilled in him by a process which circumvents his volition.[17]

Instead of foregrounding the fact of Louis's choice, Dworkin asserts that he can be denied extra resources only if we think that, were Louis to demand them, he would be asking for more than his fair share of resources, where "fair share" is defined in welfare-independent terms. For Dworkin, it requires great "ingenuity" to "produce some explanation or interpretation of the argument in question – that Louis does not deserve more resources just because he has chosen a more expensive life – which does not use the idea of fair shares or any similar ideas."[18]

Now, it is certainly, because trivially, true that if we think that Louis should be denied the resources he demands, then we must believe that he would have more than his fair share if we gave them to him. But we could use equality of opportunity for welfare to define fair shares here: we could say that shares are fair when they equalize welfare opportunities. It is therefore false, and it scarcely takes ingenuity to show it, that only if we move toward equality of resources, toward fair shares in Dworkin's special sense, can we explain egalitarianism's lack of sympathy for Louis.

I conclude that while it is indeed true that "expensive tastes are embarrassing for the theory that equality means equality of welfare precisely because we believe that equality...condemns rather than recommends compensating for deliberately cultivated expensive tastes," the proposal that equality means equality of opportunity for welfare[19] glides by the Louis counter-example.[20]

IV

While a proponent of equality of opportunity for welfare can readily deal with Louis, the case of Jude is much harder for him to handle.[21] I shall argue that Jude's case reflects credit on equality of access to advantage, by comparison with both equality of resources and equality of opportunity for welfare.

Jude has what might be called *cheap expensive tastes*. They are cheap in that he needs fewer resources to attain the same welfare level as others. But they are expensive in that he could have achieved that welfare level with fewer resources still, had he not cultivated tastes more expensive than those with which he began. Jude began with very modest desires, but then he read

Hemingway and cultivated a desire to watch bullfights, and, once he had it, he needed more money than before to achieve an average level of welfare, though still less than what others needed.

A believer in equality of opportunity for welfare has to keep Jude poor, since he did not have to become a bullfight-lover (it is reasonable to suppose that he could have suppressed, at no great cost, his desire to cultivate that taste). A believer in Dworkin-style equality of resources ignores Jude's tastes, and their history, and finds no reason, in anything said so far, to grant him less income than anyone else. I reject both views. Pace equality of opportunity for welfare, I see no manifest injustice in Jude's getting the funds he needs to travel to Spain. He then still has fewer resources than others, and only the same welfare, so equality of access to advantage cannot say, on that basis, that he is overpaid. But, pace equality of resources, it seems not unreasonable to expect Jude to accept some deduction from the normal resource stipend because of his fortunate high ability to get welfare out of resources. Unlike either Dworkin's theory or Arneson's, mine explains why both gross underresourcing and gross "underwelfaring" (despite, respectively, a decent welfare level and a decent resource bundle) look wrong.[22]

V

There are some expensive tastes which Dworkin regards as "obsessions" or "cravings" and which he is prepared to assimilate to resource deficiency, for the purposes of distributive justice. This kind of taste is one that its bearer "wishes he did not have, because it interferes with what he wants to do with his life and offers him frustration or even pain if it is not satisfied."[23] Dworkin concludes that "these tastes are handicaps," and, since equality of resources redistributes for handicap, it will presumably do so (within the bounds of practicality) in the case of tastes which meet the quoted description.

Now, Dworkin's description of them assigns (at least) two features to "handicap" tastes, and he fails to say which feature makes them handicaps, or, equivalently, endows their owner with a claim to compensation. Is the crucial feature of the taste the fact that the person wishes he did not have it? Or is it his reason for wishing he did not have it, namely, that, among other things, it threatens to cause him frustration and pain?[24]

The latter proposal is unavailable to Dworkin. An involuntary liability to frustration and pain does indeed command compensation, but, as I urged in Section II above, that thought reflects egalitarian sensitivity to people's welfare, rather than to their resources position. Since Dworkin defends intervention in response to handicaps but not in response to shortfalls in welfare, he is not entitled to classify a taste as a handicap *because* it causes pain.

But perhaps the crucial feature of the tastes we are considering is that the individual whose tastes they are "wishes he did not have" them. He disidentifies with them, so that – we can attribute this thought to Dworkin – they are

not inalienable aspects of his person (see Sect. VI below), but more like unfortunate environing circumstances. They form no part of his *ambition*, in the special
sense in which Dworkin uses that word, and that is why equality of resources
can regard them as handicaps. I believe that this is indeed Dworkin's position,
that the following regimented statement of it is not unfair: tastes are (subsidy-
warranting) handicaps if and only if they represent obsessions, which they do if
and only if the individual whose tastes they are disidentifies with them.

I have four comments on the thesis that it is the individual's alienation from
his taste which makes it an obsession and therefore allows us to regard it as a
handicap.

1. Some people in the grip of cravings are too unreflective to form
the second-order preference-repudiating preference by reference to which
Dworkin justifies the "handicap" epithet. But it would seem unfair to deny
to them the assistance to be extended to others, just because of their deficient
reflectiveness. So the disidentification criterion does not cover all compen-
sation-worthy cravings.

2. Not all tastes which hamper the individual's life and therefore raise a
case for compensation qualify either as obsessions or as tastes whose bearers,
even if highly reflective, would repudiate. Paul (see Sect. III above) might not
want not to want to take pictures, and a person whose unhappy taste is "for
music of a sort difficult to obtain" might well not disidentify with his desire for
that music.[25] He has *a* reason to regret his musical preference, since it causes
him frustration, but that is not a conclusive reason for wishing he did not have
it. What he most likely regrets is not (as Dworkin stipulates) his musical
preference as such, but the impossibility or expense of satisfying it. His taste
is involuntary and unfortunate, but it is probably not an "obsession" or
"craving": addiction is not the right model here.

A typical unrich bearer of an expensive musical taste would regard it as a
piece of bad luck *not that he has the taste itself but that it happens to be expensive* (I
emphasize those words because, simple as the distinction they formulate may
be, it is one that undermines a lot of Dworkin's rhetoric about expensive tastes).
He might say that in a perfect world he would have chosen to have his actual
musical taste, but he would also have chosen that it not be expensive. He can
take responsibility for the taste, for his personality being that way, while
reasonably denying responsibility for needing a lot of resources to satisfy it.

3. By contrast with the more representative person described above,
Dworkin's music craver prefers not to have his unfortunate preference yet,
by hypothesis, persists in having it. That rather suggests that he cannot help
having it, and that in turn raises the suspicion that it is its unchosen and
uncontrolled, rather than its dispreferred, character, which renders compensation for it appropriate. Would not Dworkin's attitude to the music craver be
less solicitous if he learned that he had been warned not to cultivate his
particular musical interest by a sapient teacher who knew it would cause
frustration?

4. Suppose that there was no such warning, that our unfortunate contracted his expensive taste innocently, and that we now offer him, gratis, an inexpensive unrepugnant therapy which would school him out of it. If he agrees to the free therapy, then, so I believe, the ideal of equality says that he should get it, regardless of whether he says farewell to his taste with unmixed relief or, instead, with a regret which reflects some degree of identification. This suggests that identification and disidentification matter for egalitarian justice only if and insofar as they indicate presence and absence of choice.[26]

VI

The foregoing reflection brings me to the claim which I ventured in Section III, to wit, that, insofar as we find Dworkin's cut plausible, it is because we are apt to suppose that it separates presence and absence of choice. Choice is in the background, doing a good deal of unacknowledged work. Here is a passage which supports this allegation: "It is true that [my] argument produces a certain view of the distinction between a person and his circumstances, and assigns his tastes and ambitions to his person, and his physical and mental powers to his circumstances. That is the view of the person I sketched in the introductory section, of someone who *forms* his ambitions with a sense of their cost to others against some presumed initial equality of economic power, and though this is different from the picture assumed by equality of welfare, it is a picture at the center of equality of resources."[27]

This passage offers two characterizations of "tastes and ambitions" in putative justification of placing them outside the ambit of redistributive compensation. The first says that, by contrast with mental and physical powers, they belong to the person rather than to his circumstances. But, in the usual senses of those words, that classification cannot be sustained. Using language in the ordinary way, my mental powers are as integral to what I am as my tastes and ambitions are. The person/circumstances distinction must therefore be a technical one, which means that there must be another way of expressing it, and a possible different way emerges in the second sentence of the passage. That different way has to do with the suggestion that people *form* their preferences but not, presumably, their powers. But there are difficulties with this suggestion.

The first is that it proposes a false alignment. People certainly form some of their ambitions, but they arguably do not form all of them, and they certainly do not form all of their tastes, which are also supposed to belong to the person.[28] Dworkin emphasizes that people "decide what sort of lives to pursue," but they do not decide what in all pertinent respects their utility functions will be: pace Dworkin, they are extensively unable to "decide what sorts of lives they *want*."[29] So being "formed" by the person cannot be a necessary condition of being part of the person, if tastes and ambitions make up the person.

It confirms my claim that Dworkin's cut looks plausible because it seems to separate presence and absence of choice that he uses the two phrases "decide what sort of life to pursue" and "decide what sort of life one wants" interchangeably, thus assimilating two very different kinds of process, only the first of which straightforwardly embodies choice, in the general case. Elsewhere, and similarly, "the choice between expensive and less expensive *tastes*" is put on the same level as "choosing a more [or a less] expensive *life*."[30] And we are also told, in another place, that, when "people choose plans or schemes for their lives," "their choices define a set of [resultant] preferences."[31] That formulation sweeps away the (often unchosen)[32] preferences which lie in the determining background of choice. A person in possession of his faculties always chooses (within the constraints he faces) what career to pursue, but he does not always choose what career to prefer, and the latter fact may reasonably restrict his responsibility for choosing to pursue an expensive one.

Being "formed" is not only not a necessary condition of belonging to what Dworkin calls the person: it is also not a sufficient one. For mental and physical powers fall outside the person, in his circumstances, and some of those powers are, unquestionably, formed. On either side of the preference/circumstance line people both find things and form things. Hence appeal to formedness does not show that distributive justice should ignore variations in preference and taste.

If, moreover, the false alignment (formed/not formed = person/circumstances) indeed worked, it would, surely, constitute a reduction of the person/circumstances distinction to the distinction between what is and what is not subject to choice. To repeat one of my main claims: it is only because Dworkin's preference/resource distinction *looks* alignable with the one it cannot in the end match that it commands appeal.

The idea that we *form* our ambitions is absent from a different formulation of the person/circumstances distinction, which comes soon after the one we have just studied: "The distinction required by equality of resources is the distinction between those beliefs and attitudes that define what a successful life would be like, which the ideal assigns to the person, and those features of body or mind or personality that provide means or impediments to that success, which the ideal assigns to the person's circumstances."[33] This proposal has different implications from the one (see above) which counterposes *tastes and ambitions* to circumstances, since not all ambitions, and few tastes, are informed by beliefs and attitudes: plenty of tastes and ambitions arise without being drawn forth by any sort of doxastic pull.[34] But I shall here set aside the problem of discrepancy between the "belief" cut and the "preference" one, in order to assess the belief cut in its own terms, in the light of Dworkin's larger purposes.

Within those purposes, the person/circumstances distinction is meant to be not only exclusive but (relevantly) exhaustive: we do not have to review anything beyond people's persons and circumstances to know how to treat them from an egalitarian point of view.[35] But, if that is so, then where are we to place the life-enhancing feature of cheerfulness, from the point of view of egalitarian justice? Cheerfulness raises two difficulties, one small and one big.

First, the small difficulty. Cheerfulness is not something that "defines what a successful life would be like." It should therefore count as a circumstance. But circumstances are elsewhere characterized as powers and incapacities, and cheerfulness is neither of those. It is not a power but a fortunate disposition which, for given inputs, generates higher than ordinary utility outputs. It is not something a person *exercises* when pursuing his goals, even if it tends often to improve his pursuit of them. Since it does the latter, the fact that it is not, strictly, a power is perhaps not a very important point. But there is another point which is certainly important.

The important point is that the value of cheerfulness is not merely, or mainly, that it raises the probability of a person's achieving what, by his lights, is "a successful life." Cheerfulness is a marvelous thing quite apart from that, and one different thing that it does is diminish the sadness of failure. It is a welfare-enhancer independently of being a goal-promoter. This makes it difficult for Dworkin to compensate cheerless people fully for their gloominess. But then there is an inconsistency between the criterion for determining what lies outside the person and the principle that disadvantages not deriving from the character of the person require compensation. Cheerlessness lies outside the person, but it is difficult to see how Dworkin can award appropriate compensation for it.

When I discussed gloominess with Dworkin he suggested that it was a borderline case with respect to the person/circumstances dichotomy and that the best way to cope with it would be to ask whether an individual would have insured against turning out to be gloomy, and to compensate him for his gloom if we think that the answer is "yes."

I think that the insurance device does have some appeal as a method of deciding whether or not to compensate for gloom. But its appeal seems to me to have nothing to do with the person/circumstances distinction: the individual who chooses to, or not to, insure against gloom is not thereby making *that* distinction. And if we suppose that he is indeed making it, then another problem arises. For in Dworkin's main use of the insurance device the individual *knows* what belongs to his person when he decides whether or not to insure: Dworkin's veil of ignorance is, in that important way, thinner than Rawls's.[36] But an individual who decides not to insure against gloominess remains, *ex hypothesi*, ignorant of whether or not he is gloomy.

The insurance device seems, then, unable to solve Dworkin's gloom problem. It is, nevertheless, independently attractive, especially when the veil of ignorance is indeed thickened, and that, I opine, is because it seems to sort out a big difference that really matters for egalitarian justice: between disadvantages that are and disadvantages that are not due to bad brute luck.[37] It is in the essential nature of insurance that luck is what we insure against, and genuine choice contrasts with luck. So anyone who, like Dworkin, is strongly drawn to the insurance test should consider accepting the choice/luck cut and giving up the attempt to defend the different cut of preferences/resources.

VII

In my view, a large part of the fundamental egalitarian aim is to extinguish the influence of brute luck on distribution. Brute luck is an enemy of just equality, and, since effects of genuine choice contrast with brute luck, genuine choice excuses otherwise unacceptable inequalities.

Curiously enough, Dworkin advocates something very like the foregoing point of view in sketchy statements in "Why Liberals Should Care about Equality," but he is not faithful to it in "What Is Equality?" He says, in "Why Liberals Should Care about Equality," that we should attend to "which aspects of any person's economic position flow from his choices and which from advantages and disadvantages that were not matters of choice."[38] That is the compelling core idea, but it is misrendered in the cut between preferences and resources. Elsewhere in "Why Liberals Should Care about Equality," Dworkin also comes close to adopting genuine-choice/*luck* as the basic distinction. He says that the liberal "accepts two principles":

> The first requires that people have, at any point in their lives, different amounts of wealth insofar as the genuine choices they have made have been more or less expensive or beneficial to the community, measured by what other people want for their lives. The market seems indispensable to this principle. The second requires that people not have different amounts of wealth just because they have different inherent capacities to produce what others want, or are differently favored by chance. This means that market allocations must be corrected in order to bring some people closer to the share of resources they would have had but for these various differences of initial advantage, luck and inherent capacity.[39]

I say that Dworkin comes close to the basic distinction I favor here, but he does not quite get there, partly because luck (or chance) appears in his text as only one element in a set of unjust distributors, others being differences in initial advantage and in inherent capacity. And I find Dworkin's disjunctions of unjust distributors strange. For anyone who thinks that initial advantage and inherent capacity are unjust distributors thinks so because he believes that they make a person's fate depend too much on sheer luck: the taxa in Dworkin's disjunctions belong to different levels, and one of them subsumes the others.

Now, once we see the central role that luck should play in a broadly Dworkinian theory of distributive justice, Dworkin's own propensity to compensate for resource misfortune but not for utility function misfortune comes to seem entirely groundless. For people can be unlucky not only in their unchosen resource endowments but also in their unchosen liabilities to pain and suffering and in their unchosen expensive preferences. A willingness to compensate for deficiencies in productive capacity but not in capacity to draw welfare from consumption consequently leads to absurd contrasts.

Consider lucky Adrian and unlucky Claude.[40] "The desires and needs of other people" mean that unlike Claude, Adrian can pursue "a satisfying [gainful] occupation." People are happy to buy what Adrian, but not Claude, can enjoy producing, and that, for Dworkin, gives Claude a claim to redress quite separate from the one arising from the income difference between him and Adrian. But now suppose that, with respect to their leisure preferences, Adrian is like fisherman Fred, and Claude is like would-be photographer Paul,[41] and that the reason why fishing is cheap and photography is expensive is that many want to fish and few want to take pictures, so that economies of scale are realized in the production of fishing, but not of photographic, equipment. It would follow that "the desires and needs of other people" mean that, unlike Claude, Adrian can pursue "a satisfying [leisure] occupation." Yet Dworkin will not redistribute for that luck-derived discrepancy, since it lies in the domain of consumption and not that of production.[42] But that is not a good basis for redistributive reluctance. It is quite absurd to regard Adrian's opportunity to pursue a satisfying profession as an enviable "circumstance," justifying redistribution,[43] without extending the same treatment to his opportunity for satisfying leisure.[44]

We must eschew Dworkin's preferences/resources distinction in favor of a wider access-oriented egalitarianism. We can agree with him that "it is perhaps the final evil of a genuinely unequal distribution of resources that some people have reason for regret just in the fact that they have been cheated of the chances others have had to make something valuable of their lives."[45] But equalizing those chances requires a discriminating attention to what is and is not chosen, not to what belongs to preference as opposed to endowment. In a brilliant exposition of how Dworkin's theory corrects deficiencies in Rawls's, Will Kymlicka remarks that "it is unjust if people are disadvantaged by inequalities of their circumstances, but it is equally unjust for me to demand that someone else pay for the costs of my choices."[46] That expresses Dworkin's fundamental insight very well, but a proper insistence on the centrality of choice leads to a different development of the insight from Dworkin's own. Dworkin has, in effect, performed for egalitarianism the considerable service of incorporating within it the most powerful idea in the arsenal of the anti-egalitarian right: the idea of choice and responsibility.[47] But that supreme effect of his contribution needs to be rendered more explicit.

Someone might say that to make choice central to distributive justice lands political philosophy in the morass of the free will problem. The distinction between preferences and resources is not metaphysically deep, but it is, by contrast, awesomely difficult to identify what represents *genuine* choice. Replacing Dworkin's cut by the one I have recommended subordinates political philosophy to metaphysical questions that may be impossible to answer.

To that expression of anxiety I have one unreassuring and one reassuring thing to say. The unreassuring thing is that we may indeed be up to our necks in the free will problem, but that is just tough luck. It is not a reason for not following the argument where it goes.

Now for the reassuring point. We are not looking for an absolute distinction between presence and absence of genuine choice. The amount of genuineness that there is in a choice is a matter of degree,[48] and egalitarian redress is indicated to the *extent* that a disadvantage does not reflect genuine choice. That extent is a function of several things, and there is no aspect of a person's situation which is wholly due to genuine choice.

Let me illustrate this point. One of the things that affects how genuine a choice was is the amount of relevant information that the chooser had. But we do not have to ask, Exactly what sort and amount of information must a person have to count as having genuinely chosen his fate? All that we need say, from the point of view of egalitarian justice, is: the more relevant information he had, the less cause for complaint he now has.

It seems to me that this plausible nuancing approach reduces the dependence of political philosophy on the metaphysics of mind.[49]

Notes

1   Explaining how he understands welfare, Cohen writes: "Of the many readings of 'welfare' alive (if not well) in economics and philosophy, I am interested in two: welfare as enjoyment, or, more broadly, as a desirable or agreeable state of consciousness, which I shall call *hedonic welfare*, and welfare as *preference satisfaction*, where preferences order states of the world, and where a person's preference is satisfied if a state of the world that he prefers obtains, whether or not he knows that it does and, a fortiori, whatever hedonic welfare he does or does not get as a result of its obtaining. A person's hedonic welfare increases as he gets more enjoyment, and his preference satisfaction increases as more of his preferences, or his stronger preferences, are fulfilled. Note that one way to achieve more preference satisfaction is to cultivate, if you can, preferences that are easier to satisfy than those which you currently have. It will sometimes be necessary to say which of those two ideas I mean by 'welfare,' but not always. For very often the debates on which I comment have a similar shape under either interpretation of welfare, so that I shall have each in mind (by which I do not mean some amalgam of the two) at once. Unless I indicate otherwise, my contentions are meant to hold under either of the two readings of welfare...". [eds.]

2   For a clear articulation and persuasive defense of it, in its preference satisfaction interpretation, see Arneson's "Equality and Equality of Opportunity for Welfare," *Philosophical Studies* 55 (1989), pp. 77–93.

3   For analogous reasons, Arneson would have been better advised to call his theory "equality of access to welfare."

4   I am not entirely happy with the word 'advantage' in the title of the view I am espousing; I use the word only because I have been unable to find a better one. Its infelicity relates to the fact that it is so frequently used to denote competitive advantage, advantage, that is, *over* somebody else. But here 'advantage' must be

understood shorn of that implication, which it does not always have. Something can add to someone's advantage without him, as a result, being better placed, or less worse placed, than somebody else, and the word will here be used in that noncompetitive sense.

5   Dworkin, "Equality of Welfare," *Philosophy and Public Affairs* 10:3 (1981) pp. 241–2, following Sen, "Equality of What?", in *Tanner Lectures on Human Values*, ed. S. McMurrin (Salt Lake City: University of Utah Press, 1980), pp. 217–18. Sen is surely right that it is his deficient capability as such which explains the claim to assistance of a contented crippled person who requires expensive prosthesis and who is not particularly poor. Compare Sen, "Well-Being, Agency and Freedom," *Journal of Philosophy* 82 (1985), pp. 195–7.

6   G. A. Cohen, *Karl Marx's Theory of History* (Oxford: Oxford University Press, 1978), p. 238.

7   A man otherwise like the one I described might find it difficult to move his arms for the psychological reason that he could not face the thought of what would follow their movement. But my man is psychologically robust: he can easily move his arms, though he often (coolly) decides not to on occasions when other people would move theirs.

8   The answers to those questions will not always be as simple as the sample answers that follow, but they are always the right questions to ask.

9   Another matter about which I cannot say anything systematic is the problem of how to compare the net advantage positions of different people. The right place to begin would be with Amartya Sen's perspicacious discussion of the (at least) structurally analogous problem of how to order different capability-sets (see his *Commodities and Capabilities* [Amsterdam: North Holland, 1985], ch. 5). (I say "[at least] structurally analogous" because it may turn out to be the same problem.)

10   Dworkin's "Equality of Welfare" is a masterful exposé of ambiguities in the concept of welfare, even if it does not prove that egalitarian justice should ignore welfare comparisons.

11   The quoted material is from Dworkin, "Equality of Resources," *Philosophy and Public Affairs* 10:4 (1981), p. 335.

12   Dworkin, "Equality of Welfare," p. 240.

13   On the hedonic conception of welfare, X's taste is *pro tanto* more expensive than Y's if more resources are needed to raise X to a given level of enjoyment. On the preference satisfaction conception of welfare, levels of preference satisfaction replace levels of enjoyment in the characterization of what makes a taste expensive. The discussion below of expensive tastes may be interpreted along either hedonic or preference lines.

14   An unfortunate utility function could itself be regarded as a resource deficiency, but not by someone concerned to contrast equality of resources and equality of welfare.

15   I thank Alice Knight for this example.

16   Dworkin, "Equality of Welfare," p. 229.

17   The quoted material is from ibid., p. 237.

18   Ibid., p. 239.

19   Which must, on other grounds, be broadened into equality of access to advantage (see Sects. II and IV). The quoted material is from Dworkin, "Equality of Welfare," p. 235.

20 Equality of opportunity for welfare and, a fortiori, equality of access to advantage, also supply what seems to me to be an adequate response to a complicated argument which Dworkin thinks contributes a great deal to this drive to subvert equality of welfare in favor of equality of resources. The argument first appears in the context of Dworkin's exploration of the hypothesis that equality of welfare be understood as equality of overall success – that hypothesis surfaces after the supposed wreckage of several previous ones. The argument has two premises, each of which I find hard to assess, but neither of which I shall here contest. The first premise is that "equality of overall success cannot be stated as an attractive ideal at all without making the idea of reasonable regret central" (ibid., p. 217): equality of overall success will seem defensible only if it promises to make people "equal in what they have reasonably to regret" (ibid., pp. 217, 218). And the second premise is that the idea of reasonable regret "requires an independent theory of fair shares of social resources . . . which would contradict equality of overall success" (ibid., p. 217). But if both premises are true, so that such a theory is indeed required, why can it not be a theory which says that shares are fair when they induce equality of opportunity for welfare, or equality of access to advantage? I do not find anything in Dworkin's dense ratiocination which appears to rule that out. It follows that the supposed self-destruction of equality of welfare on the altar of reasonable regret is much less of an argument for equality of resources than Dworkin appears to think it is. (For criticism of Dworkin's second premise, see James Griffin, "Modern Utilitarianism," *Revue Internationale de Philosophie* 36 [1982], 365–6; and for an argument that the idea of overall success should never have been floated in the first place, see sect. 4 of Richard Arneson's "Liberalism, Distributive Subjectivism and Equal Opportunity for Welfare" [Department of Philosophy, University of California, San Diego, 1987, typescript].)

21 Dworkin, "Equality of Welfare," pp. 239–40.

22 I do not feel comfortable about this victory, since, in achieving it, I exploit to the hilt a feature of my theory which I regard as suspect: the heterogeneity of its conception of advantage (see latter part of Sect. II above).

23 Dworkin, "Equality of Resources," p. 302 [p. 124 in this volume, eds.].

24 This is one of several key places at which there is reason to regret that, in expounding his views, Dworkin abjures the device of canonical statement. Other cases in point are passages quoted at Sect. VI below (on choosing tastes and choosing pursuits) and passages quoted at Sects. VI and VII, which give three materially different renderings of Dworkin's "master cut."

25 The quote comes from Dworkin, "Equality of Resources," p. 302 [p. 124 in this volume, eds.].

26 For an amendment to that suggestion, see Sect. VA [of "On the Currency of Egalitarian Justice"], where, inter alia, I comment on the case, which is not addressed above, of a person who would refuse the offer of therapy because of his musical convictions.

27 Dworkin, "Equality of Resources," p. 302 [p. 124 in this volume, eds.], my emphasis. The word 'produces' in the first sentence of the passage should, Dworkin confirms, be 'presupposes': note the contrast with the picture "assumed" by equality of welfare. (But the question whether Dworkin has argued for, as opposed to from, his distinction does not matter here.) Dworkin does not describe the different picture which he thinks is assumed by equality of welfare. If it is a picture

of the person as passive and unchoosing, that would help to justify my immanent critique of his view. For that picture, see Rawls, "Social Unity and Primary Goods," in *Utilitarianism and Beyond*, ed. Amartya Sen and Bernard Williams (Cambridge: Cambridge University Press, 1982), p. 169.

28   Dworkin does not actually say in the passage under scrutiny that people form their *tastes*: "tastes and ambitions" have shrunk to "ambitions" by the time that we get to the motif of self-formation. But unless Dworkin claims that tastes, too, are in general formed, on what basis is he here assigning them to a person's person?

29   The quotes are from Dworkin, "Equality of Resources," p. 288 [p. 114 in this volume, eds.], my emphasis.

30   Ronald Dworkin, "Liberalism," in his *A Matter of Principle* (Oxford: Oxford University Press, 1985), p. 193, my emphases.

31   Dworkin, "Equality of Welfare," p. 206. I introduce "resultant" to forestall the misinterpretation that Dworkin means that the choices *reflect* preferences.

32   "Many of a person's desires are indeed voluntary, since they derive simply from his own decisions. Someone typically acquires the desire to see a certain movie, for example, just by making up his mind what movie to see. Desires of this sort are not aroused in us; they are formed or constructed by acts of will that we ourselves perform, often quite apart from any emotional or affective state. However, there are also occasions when what a person wants is not up to him at all, but is rather a matter of feelings or inclinations that arise and persist independently of any choice of his own" (Harry Frankfurt, *The Importance of What We Care About* [Cambridge: Cambridge University Press, 1988], p. 107).

33   Dworkin, "Equality of Resources," p. 303 [p. 124 in this volume, eds.].

34   Frankfurt's sensitive distinction (see n. 32 above) between desires which do and desires which do not reflect decisions could be matched by a similar one between those which do and those which do not display attitude and commitment.

35   At an Oxford seminar on economic justice of February 22, 1988, Dworkin was explicitly exhaustive. He spoke of his proposal requiring "a sharp distinction between personality (equals attachments, projects, etc.) and circumstances (equals everything else, the material with and against which people labour to achieve what their personality favours)."

36   Dworkin's main use of the insurance device is to deal with handicaps and talents: see "Equality of Resources," sects. 3, 5, and 6 and see p. 296 [pp. 119–20 in this volume, eds.], and esp. p. 345 for the particular point that Dworkin insurers know what they think "is valuable in life."

37   If it is relevant that, given the chance, a person might have insured against cheerlessness, why is it not relevant that he might have insured against ending up with tastes that happen to be expensive? Compare L. Alexander and M. Schwarzchild, "Liberalism, Neutrality, and Equality of Welfare versus Equality of Resources," *Philosophy and Public Affairs* 16 (1987), 99 ff.

38   Ronald Dworkin, "Why Liberals Should Care about Equality," in *A Matter of Principle*, p. 208. ("What Is Equality?" is the joint title of "Equality of Welfare" and "Equality of Resources.")

39   Dworkin, "Why Liberals Should Care about Equality," p. 207.

40   Dworkin, "Equality of Resources," p. 308 [p. 128 in this volume, eds.].

41   See Sect. III above.

42 Dworkin's refusal to redistribute for the discrepancy is explicit at "Equality of Resources," p. 288 [pp. 113–14 in this volume, eds.].

43 Ibid., p. 308 [p. 128 in this volume, eds.].

44 The foregoing criticism depends on Dworkin's classification (ibid., p. 304) of a satisfying occupation as, so described, a resource. In his 1988 Oxford University B.Phil. thesis on "Justice and Alienation," Michael Otsuka argues that that was a superficial error on Dworkin's part. But I do not think that Dworkin can declassify occupation as a resource – and thereby escape my argument in the text – except at the severe cost of losing his argument against throwing people's powers to produce into his island auction, since that argument rests on the idea that, with people's powers to produce up for auction, the talented would end up envying the package of occupation and income enjoyed by the ungifted (see Dworkin, "Equality of Resources," pp. 311–12) [pp. 130–1 in this volume, eds.].

45 Dworkin, "Equality of Welfare," p. 219.

46 His 1987 Princeton lecture notes on Contemporary Political Philosophy, section on Rawls, subsection called "Subsidizing People's Choices" (Philosophy Department, University of Toronto, 1987, typescript), p. 5.

47 It is an idea much less deniable than the different idea of self-ownership, which is also central to right-wing thought. See the closing pages of G. A. Cohen, "Are Freedom and Equality Compatible?," in *Alternatives to Capitalism*, ed. Jon Elster and Karl O. Moene (Cambridge: Cambridge University Press, 1989).

48 This point corresponds to Dworkin's point that there is a continuum between brute and option luck (see "Equality of Resources," p. 293 [p. 117 in this volume, eds.]).

49 Thomas Scanlon's recent Tanner Lectures on "The Significance of Choice" [<http://www.tannerlectures.utah.edu/rstu.html>, eds.] present a liberatingly nonmetaphysical approach to choice in the context of, among other things, distributive justice. I have not yet had the time to determine to what extent what he offers can be used to improve the statement of a broadly Dworkinian theory of distributive justice.

Against Luck Egalitarianism: What Is the Point of Equality?

Elizabeth S. Anderson

If much recent academic work defending equality had been secretly penned by conservatives, could the results be any more embarrassing for egalitarians? Consider how much of this work leaves itself open to classic and devastating conservative criticisms. Ronald Dworkin defines equality as an "envy-free" distribution of resources.[1] This feeds the suspicion that the motive behind egalitarian policies is mere envy. Philippe Van Parijs argues that equality in conjunction with liberal neutrality among conceptions of the good requires the state to support lazy, able-bodied surfers who are unwilling to work.[2] This invites the charge that egalitarians support irresponsibility and encourage the slothful to be parasitic on the productive. Richard Arneson claims that equality requires that, under certain conditions, the state subsidize extremely costly religious ceremonies that its citizens feel bound to perform.[3] G. A. Cohen tells us that equality requires that we compensate people for being temperamentally gloomy, or for being so incurably bored by inexpensive hobbies that they can only get fulfilling recreation from expensive diversions.[4] These proposals bolster the objection that egalitarians are oblivious to the proper limits of state power and permit coercion of others for merely private ends. Van Parijs suggests that to fairly implement the equal right to get married, when male partners are scarce, every woman should be given an equal tradable share in the pool of eligible bachelors and have to bid for whole partnership rights, thus implementing a transfer of wealth from successful brides to compensate the losers in love.[5] This supports the objection that egalitarianism, in its determination to correct perceived unfairness everywhere, invades our privacy and burdens the personal ties of love and affection that lie at the core of family life.

Those on the left have no less reason than conservatives and libertarians to be disturbed by recent trends in academic egalitarian thought. First, consider

Extracts from Elizabeth S. Anderson, 'What Is the Point of Equality?', from *Ethics*, 109 (1999), pp. 287–326 and 336–7 (abridged by the author).

those whom recent academic egalitarians have singled out for special attention: beach bums, the lazy and irresponsible, people who can't manage to entertain themselves with simple pleasures, religious fanatics. Thomas Nagel[6] and Gerald Cohen give us somewhat more sympathetic but also pitiable characters in taking stupid, talentless, and bitter people to be exemplary beneficiaries of egalitarian concern. What has happened to the concerns of the politically oppressed? What about inequalities of race, gender, class, and caste? Where are the victims of nationalist genocide, slavery, and ethnic subordination?

Second, the agendas defined by much recent egalitarian theorizing are too narrowly focused on the distribution of divisible, privately appropriated goods, such as income and resources, or privately enjoyed goods, such as welfare. This neglects the much broader agendas of actual egalitarian political movements. For example, gay and lesbian people seek the freedom to appear in public as who they are, without shame or fear of violence, the right to get married and enjoy benefits of marriage, to adopt and retain custody of children. The disabled have drawn attention to the ways the configuration of public spaces has excluded and marginalized them, and campaigned against demeaning stereotypes that cast them as stupid, incompetent, and pathetic. Thus, with respect to both the targets of egalitarian concern and their agendas, recent egalitarian writing seems strangely detached from existing egalitarian political movements.

What has gone wrong here? I shall argue that these problems stem from a flawed understanding of the point of equality. Recent egalitarian writing has come to be dominated by the view that the fundamental aim of equality is to compensate people for undeserved bad luck – being born with poor native endowments, bad parents, and disagreeable personalities, suffering from accidents and illness, and so forth. I shall argue that in focusing on correcting a supposed cosmic injustice, recent egalitarian writing has lost sight of the distinctively political aims of egalitarianism. The proper negative aim of egalitarian justice is not to eliminate the impact of brute luck from human affairs, but to end oppression, which by definition is socially imposed. Its proper positive aim is not to ensure that everyone gets what they morally deserve, but to create a community in which people stand in relations of equality to others.

In this article, I will compare the implications of these two conceptions of the point of equality. The first conception, which takes the fundamental injustice to be the natural inequality in the distribution of luck, can be called "luck egalitarianism" or "equality of fortune." I shall argue that equality of fortune fails the most fundamental test any egalitarian theory must meet: that its principles express equal respect and concern for all citizens. It fails this test in three ways. First, it excludes some citizens from enjoying the social conditions of freedom on the spurious ground that it's their fault for losing them. It escapes this problem only at the cost of paternalism. Second, equality of fortune makes the basis for citizens' claims on one another the fact that some are inferior to others in the worth of their lives, talents, and personal qualities. Thus, its principles express contemptuous pity for those the state stamps as sadly inferior and uphold envy as a basis for distributing goods from the lucky to the unfortunate. Such principles stigmatize the unfortunate and disrespect the fortunate by failing to show how envy can obligate them. Third, equality of fortune, in attempting to ensure that people take responsibility for their choices, makes demeaning and intrusive judgments of people's capacities to exercise responsibility and effectively dictates to them the appropriate uses of their freedom.

The theory I shall defend can be called "democratic equality." In seeking the construction of a community of equals, democratic equality integrates principles of distribution with the expressive demands of equal respect. Democratic equality guarantees all law-abiding citizens effective access to the social conditions of their freedom at all times. It justifies the distributions required to secure this guarantee by appealing to the obligations of citizens in a democratic state. In such a state, citizens make claims on one another in virtue of their equality, not their inferiority, to others. Because the fundamental aim of citizens in constructing a state is to secure everyone's freedom, democratic equality's principles of distribution neither presume to tell people how to use their opportunities nor attempt to judge how responsible people are for choices that lead to unfortunate outcomes. Instead, it avoids bankruptcy at the hands of the imprudent by limiting the range of goods provided collectively and expecting individuals to take personal responsibility for the other goods in their possession.

I.   Justice as Equality of Fortune

The following passage by Richard Arneson aptly describes the conception of justice I aim to criticize: "The concern of distributive justice is to compensate individuals for misfortune. Some people are blessed with good luck, some are cursed with bad luck, and it is the responsibility of society – all of us regarded collectively – to alter the distribution of goods and evils that arises from the jumble of lotteries that constitutes human life as we know it...Distributive justice stipulates that the lucky should transfer some or all of their gains due to luck to the unlucky."[7] This conception of justice can be traced to the work of John Rawls,[8] and has been (I believe mistakenly) attributed to him. Equality of fortune is now one of the dominant theoretical positions among egalitarians, as evidenced by the roster of theorists who endorse it, including Richard Arneson, Gerald Cohen, Ronald Dworkin, Thomas Nagel, Eric Rakowski, and John Roemer.[9] Philippe Van Parijs also incorporates this principle into his theory of equality of resources or assets. Luck egalitarianism relies on two moral premises: that people should be compensated for undeserved misfortunes and that the compensation should come only from that part of others' good fortune that is undeserved.

Part of the appeal of equality of fortune comes from its apparently humanitarian impulse. When decent people see others suffer for no good reason – say, children dying from starvation – they tend to regard it as a matter of obligation that the more fortunate come to their aid. Part of its appeal comes from the force of the obviously correct claim that no one deserves their genetic endowments or other accidents of birth, such as who their parents are or where they were born. This seems to weaken claims of those blessed by their genes or social circumstances to retain all of the advantages that typically flow from such good fortune. Besides these intrinsic sources of appeal, proponents of equality of fortune have tried to build support for egalitarianism by responding to many of the formidable objections that conservatives and libertarians have made against egalitarians of the past. . . .

Luck egalitarians have been most responsive to criticisms of equality based on ideals of desert, responsibility, and markets. Critics of equality object that egalitarians take goods away from the deserving.[10] Proponents of equality of fortune reply that they take from the fortunate only that portion of their advantages that everyone acknowledges is undeserved. On the receiving side, the critics protest that egalitarianism undermines personal responsibility by guaranteeing outcomes independent of people's personal choices.[11] In response, luck egalitarians have moved from an equality of outcome to an equality of opportunity conception of justice: they ask only that people start off with equal opportunities to achieve welfare or access to advantage, or that they start off with an equal share of resources.[12] But they accept the justice of whatever inequalities result from adults' voluntary choices. All place great stress on the distinction between the outcomes for which an individual is responsible – that is, those that result from her voluntary choices – and the outcomes for which she is not responsible – good or bad outcomes that occur independent of her choice or of what she could have reasonably foreseen. Luck egalitarians dub this the distinction between "option luck" and "brute luck."[13]

The resulting theories of equality of fortune thus share a common core: a hybrid of capitalism and the welfare state. For the outcomes for which individuals are held responsible, luck egalitarians prescribe rugged individualism: let the distribution of goods be governed by capitalist markets and other voluntary agreements.[14] This reliance on markets responds to the objection that egalitarianism does not appreciate the virtues of markets as efficient allocative mechanisms and as spaces for the exercise of freedom.[15] For the outcomes determined by brute luck, equality of fortune prescribes that all good fortune be equally shared and that all risks be pooled. . . . Luck egalitarians thus view the welfare state as a giant insurance company that insures its citizens against all forms of bad brute luck. Taxes for redistributive purposes are the moral equivalent of insurance premiums against bad luck. Welfare payments compensate people against losses traceable to bad brute luck, just like insurance policies do.

Ronald Dworkin has articulated this insurance analogy most elaborately.[16] He argues that justice demands that the state compensate each individual for whatever brute risks they would have insured themselves against, on the assumption that all were equally likely to suffer from the risk. The state steps in to provide social insurance when private insurance for a risk is not available to all on equal and affordable terms. Where such private insurance is available, brute luck is automatically converted into option luck, for society can hold individuals responsible for purchasing insurance on their own behalf.[17] . . .

Luck egalitarians disagree with one another primarily over the space in which they advocate equality. Should egalitarians seek equality of resources or assets (Dworkin, Rakowski, Roemer), real freedom – that is, legal rights plus the means to achieve one's ends (Van Parijs), equal opportunity for welfare (Arneson), or equal access to advantage – a mixed bag of internal capabilities, opportunities for welfare, and resources (Cohen, Nagel)? This looks like a wide diversity of views, but the central disagreement among them separates luck egalitarians into two camps: one which accepts equality of welfare as a legitimate (if not the only) object of egalitarian concern (Arneson, Cohen, Roemer, probably Nagel), and one which only equalizes resources (Dworkin, Rakowski, Van Parijs). All parties accept an analysis of an individual's welfare in terms of the satisfaction of her informed preferences. The role of individual preferences in equality of fortune shall be a central object of my critique, so it pays to consider these differences.

Should egalitarians care whether people have equal opportunities for welfare, or only that their share of resources be equal? Resource egalitarians object to taking welfare as an equalisandum because of the problem of expensive tastes.[18] Some people – spoiled brats, snobs, sybarites – have preferences that are expensive to satisfy. It takes a lot more resources to satisfy them to the same degree that a modest, self-controlled person can be satisfied. If equalizing welfare or opportunities for welfare were the object of equality, then the satisfaction of self-controlled people would be held hostage to the self-indulgent. This seems unfair. Resource egalitarians argue, therefore, that people should be entitled to equal resources, but be held responsible for developing their tastes so that they can live satisfactorily within their means.

Against this view, those who believe welfare is a legitimate space of egalitarian concern . . . argue that resource egalitarians unfairly hold people responsible for all of their preferences and for the costs of satisfying them. Although some preferences are voluntarily cultivated by individuals, many others are shaped by genetic and environmental influences beyond their control and are highly resistant to deliberate change. Moreover, an individual may not be responsible for the fact that satisfying them is so expensive. For example, an unforeseeable event may cause a dramatic shortage of a once abundant means of satisfying some taste, and thereby escalate its price. Welfarists argue that it is unfair, and inconsistent with the basic premise of luck egalitarianism, to hold people responsible for their involuntary, or involuntarily expensive, tastes.[19] . . .

[This] defense is open to the following reply by resource egalitarians. Justice demands that the claims that people are entitled to make on others should be sensitive not only to the benefits expected on the part of the claimants but to the burdens these claims place on others. These burdens are measured by the opportunity costs of the resources devoted to meeting them, which are a function of the preferences of others for the same resources. For egalitarian purposes, the value of a bundle of external resources should thus be determined not by how much welfare the owner can get from it, but by the price it would fetch in a perfectly competitive market if everyone could bid for it and all enjoyed the same monetary assets.[20]

The importance of this reply is that it shows how even resource egalitarians give subjective preferences a central role to play in the measurement of equality. For the value of resources is measured by the market prices they would command in a hypothetical auction, and these prices are a function of everyone's subjective preferences for those resources. Everyone is said to have an equal bundle of resources when the distribution of resources is envy-free: no one prefers someone else's bundle of resources to their own.... The difference between resource egalitarians and welfare egalitarians thus does not consist in whether the measure of equality is based on subjective preferences. They differ only in that for welfare egalitarians, the claims a person makes are dependent on her tastes, whereas for resource egalitarians, they are a function of everyone's tastes....

In the next two sections, I shall present a series of cases in which luck egalitarianism generates injustice. Not every version of equality of fortune is vulnerable to each counterexample; but each version is vulnerable to one or more counterexamples in each section.

II. The Victims of Bad Option Luck

The state, says Ronald Dworkin, should treat each of its citizens with equal respect and concern.[21] Virtually all egalitarians accept this formula, but rarely have they analyzed it. Instead, they invoke the formula, then propose their favored principle of egalitarian distribution as an interpretation of it, without providing an argument proving that their principle really does express equal respect and concern for all citizens. In this section, I will argue that the reasons luck egalitarians offer for refusing to come to the aid of the victims of bad option luck express a failure to treat these unfortunates with equal respect and concern...

Luck egalitarians say that, assuming everyone had equal opportunity to run a particular risk, any outcomes due to voluntary choices whose consequences could reasonably be foreseen by the agent should be born or enjoyed by the agent. The inequalities they generate neither give rise to redistributive claims on others if the outcome is bad, nor are subject to redistributive taxation if the outcome is good.[22] This, at least, is the doctrine in its hard-line form. Let us start with Rakowski's version of equality of fortune, since his sticks most closely to the hard line.

Consider an uninsured driver who negligently makes an illegal turn that causes an accident with another car. Witnesses call the police, reporting who is at fault; the police transmit this information to emergency medical technicians. When they arrive at the scene and find that the driver at fault is uninsured, they leave him to die by the side of the road. According to Rakowski's doctrine, this action is just, for they have no obligation to give him emergency care.... Call this the problem of *abandonment of negligent victims.*

If the faulty driver survives, but is disabled as a result, society has no obligation to accommodate his disability. Arneson joins Rakowski on this point.[23] It follows that the post office must let the guide dogs of the congenitally blind guide their owners through the building, but it can with justice turn away the guide dogs of faulty drivers who lost their sight in a car accident.... Call this the problem of *discrimination among the disabled.*

Luck egalitarians abandon even prudent people to their fates when the risks they run turn sour. "If a citizen of a large and geographically diverse nation like the United States builds his house in a flood plain, or near the San Andreas fault, or in the heart of tornado country, then the risk of flood, earthquake, or crushing winds is one he chooses to bear, since those risks could be all but eliminated by living elsewhere."[24] We must not forget the threat of hurricanes devastating the Gulf and East Coasts....[25] Rakowski's view effectively limits disaster relief to only those citizens who reside in certain portions of the country. Call this the problem of *geographical discrimination among citizens.*

Consider next the case of workers in dangerous occupations. Police officers, firefighters, members of the armed forces, farmers, fishers, and miners suffer from significantly higher than average risks of injury and death at work. But these are "exemplary instances of option luck" and hence can generate no claims to publicly subsidized medical care or aid to dependents if an accident occurs.[26] ... Call this the problem of *occupational discrimination.*

Dependent caretakers and their children face special problems under equality of fortune. Many people who care for dependents – children, the ill and infirm – command no market wage for discharging their obligations to those who cannot take care of themselves, and lack the time and flexibility to earn a decent wage. For this reason, dependent caretakers, who are almost all women, tend to be either financially dependent on a wage earner, dependent on welfare payments, or extremely poor. Women's financial dependence on a male wage earner results in their systematic vulnerability to exploitation, violence, and domination.[27] But Rakowski's doctrine implies that this poverty and resulting subordination is by choice and therefore generates no claims of justice on others. It is a "lifestyle," perhaps taken up from deep conviction but precisely for that reason not something that can be pursued at the expense of those who don't share their "zeal" or "belief" that one owes duties of care to family members.[28] If women don't want to be subject to such poverty and vulnerability, they shouldn't choose to have children.

Nor do children have any claim to assistance from anyone but their parents. From the point of view of everyone else, they are an unwelcome intrusion, who would reduce the fair shares of natural resources to which the first comers are entitled were they allowed to lay a claim to such shares independently of their claim to their parents' shares. "It is...unjust to declare...that because two people decide to have a child...*everyone* is required to share their resources with the new arrival, and to the same extent as its parents. With what right can two people force all the rest, through deliberate behavior rather than bad brute luck, to settle for less than their fair shares after resources have been divided justly?"[29] The desire to procreate is just another expensive taste, which resource egalitarians need not subsidize.

Rakowski's view is, certainly, on the harsh end among luck egalitarians. Most luck egalitarians would consider the time at which a person enters society as irrelevant to their claim to their fair share of the bounties of nature. Children are not responsible either for their parents' lack of wealth or for their parents' decision to reproduce. Thus it is a matter of bad brute luck, requiring compensation, if their parents lack the means to give them their fair share. But the women who devote themselves to caring for children are another story. Since women are not on average less talented than men, but choose to develop and exercise talents that command little or no market wage, it is not clear whether luck egalitarians have any basis for remedying the injustices that attend their dependence on male wage earners. Call this the problem of *vulnerability of dependent caretakers*.

On Rakowski's hard-line version of equality of fortune, once people risk and lose their fair share of natural wealth, they have no claims against others to stop their free fall into misery and destitution. Equality of fortune imposes no constraints on the structure of opportunities generated by free markets. Nothing would prevent people, even those whose gambles were prudent but who suffered from bad option luck, from subjection to debt peonage, sweatshops, or other forms of exploitation. The inequalities and suffering permitted by this view are unlimited. Call these the problems of *exploitation* and the *lack of a safety net*.

Rakowski could insist that private or public insurance be made available to all to prevent such conditions. Then it would be the fault of individuals who failed to purchase such insurance that they were so destitute and vulnerable to exploitation. But justice does not permit the exploitation or abandonment of anyone, even the imprudent. Moreover, a person's failure to keep up with all of the insurance payments needed to protect herself against innumerable catastrophes need not reflect imprudence. If her option luck is particularly bad, she may not be able to pay for all that insurance and still provide for her family's basic needs. Under these conditions, it is perfectly rational, and indeed morally obligatory, to serve the family's urgent needs over its speculative needs – for example, to drop some insurance in order to pay for food. Call this the problem of the *abandonment of the prudent*.

Rakowski's version of equality of fortune treats the victims of bad option luck most harshly....Do other luck egalitarians do a better job than Rakowski in shielding the victims of bad option luck from the worst fates? Dworkin's theory offers no better protection than Rakowski's against predatory practices in the free market, once people have lost their fair share of resources through bad option luck. Nor would it help dependent caretakers, or people who are disabled as a result of choices they made.

Van Parijs would guarantee everyone the maximum unconditional basic income that could be sustained in a society. If this income were significant, it would certainly help dependent caretakers, the disabled and involuntarily unemployed, and anyone else down on their luck.[30] However, Van Parijs concedes that the size of this income might be very low, even zero.[31] The chief difficulty with his proposal is that his basic income would be awarded to all unconditionally, regardless of whether they were able or performing socially useful work. Lazy, able-bodied surfers would be just as entitled to that income as dependent caretakers or the disabled. In order to offer an incentive for people to work and thereby provide the tax revenue to fund a basic income, there would have to be a substantial gap between the basic income and the wage provided by the lowest paid unskilled job. Such a low basic income might be satisfactory to footloose beach bums, who might be happy camping on the beach. But it would hardly be enough for struggling parents, the involuntarily unemployed, or the disabled, who have special expenses. Were the guaranteed basic income tied to a requirement that able-bodied people engage in socially useful work, it could be raised to a much higher level. Van Parijs's proposal effectively indulges the tastes of the lazy and irresponsible at the expense of others who need assistance.[32]

Arneson proposes that everyone be guaranteed equal opportunity for welfare. Upon reaching adulthood, everyone should face a range of choices such that the sum of expected utilities for each equally accessible life history is equal to the sum of utilities that any other person faces in their possible life histories. Once these opportunities are guaranteed, people's fates are determined by their choices and option luck.[33] Like Dworkin's and Rakowski's theories, Arneson's theory guarantees equality, indeed even a minimally decent life, only *ex ante*, before one has made any adult choices. This is small comfort to the person who led a cautious and prudent life, but still fell victim to extremely bad option luck.[34] ... In addition, we have seen that Arneson would not require accommodation of people who are disabled by their own fault. Dependent caretakers also would not get much help from Arneson. As Roemer says, explaining Arneson's and Cohen's position, "Society should not compensate people for their choice of [a more altruistic, self-sacrificing] path because it owes people no compensation on account of their moral views."[35] People who want to avoid the vulnerabilities that attend dependent caretaking must therefore decide to care only for themselves. This is egalitarianism for egoists alone. One wonders how children and the infirm are to be cared for, with a system that offers so little protection to their caretakers against poverty and domination.

Cohen's and Roemer's theories are the only ones to question the structure of opportunities generated by markets in response to people's choices. Cohen argues that equality demands equality of access to advantage, and defines advantage to include not just welfare but freedom from exploitation or subjection to unfair bargains.[36] Roemer's version of market socialism, in which households would share equally in the returns to capital through a universal grant, would also prevent the worst outcomes generated by laissez faire capitalism, such as debt peonage and sweatshop labor. However, as theorists from the marxist tradition, they focus on the exploitation of wage laborers to the exclusion of non-wage-earning dependent caretakers.[37]

What do luck egalitarians say in response to these problems? None recognize the sexist implications of assimilating the performance of moral obligations to care for dependents to the class of voluntarily expensive tastes. Most are sensitive to the fact that an egalitarian view that guarantees equality only *ex ante*, before adults start making choices for themselves, and makes no provision for people after that, will in fact generate substantial inequalities in people's fates as they lead their lives, to the point where the worst off will often be extremely badly off. They assume that the prudent will prevent such fates by taking advantage of the availability of private (or, where needed, public) insurance. All agree, then, that the chief difficulty for luck egalitarians is how to insure against the wretchedness of the imprudent.

Arneson has considered this problem most deeply within the terms of luck egalitarianism. He argues that it is sometimes unfair to hold people responsible for the degree to which they are responsible agents. The capacities needed for responsible choice – foresight, perseverance, calculative ability, strength of will, self-confidence – are partly a function of genetic endowments and partly of the good fortune of having decent parents. Thus, the imprudent are entitled to special paternalistic protection by society against their poor choices. This might involve, for example, mandatory contributions to a pension plan to provide for old age.[38] The other luck egalitarians agree that pure equality of fortune might have to be modified by a significant dose of paternalistic intervention, to save the imprudent from the worst consequences of their choices. However, in their view, *only* paternalistic reasons can justify making mandatory the various universal social insurance programs characteristic of modern welfare states: social security, health and disability insurance, disaster relief, and so forth. *Only* paternalistic reasons justify meting out individuals' basic income grant on a monthly basis, rather than in a lump sum upon coming of age.[39] Call this the problem of *paternalism*.

Let us pause to consider whether these policies express respect for citizens. Luck egalitarians tell the victims of very bad option luck that, having chosen to run their risks, they deserve their misfortune, so society need not secure them against destitution and exploitation. Yet a society that permits its members to sink to such depths, due to entirely reasonable (and, for dependent caretakers, even obligatory) choices, hardly treats them with respect. ... Luck egalitarians do entertain modifications of their harsh system, but only on paternalistic grounds. ... It is hard to see how citizens could be expected to accept such reasoning and still retain their self-respect.

Against these objections, one might argue as follows.[40] First, given their concern that no one suffer undeserved misfortune, luck egalitarians ought to be able to argue that some outcomes are so awful that no one deserves to suffer them, not even the imprudent. Negligent drivers don't deserve to die from a denial of health care. Second, paternalism can be an honest and compelling rationale for legislation. For example, it is no great insult for a state to pass laws requiring the use of seat belts, so long as the law is democratically passed. Self-respecting people can endorse some paternalistic laws as simply protecting themselves from their own thoughtlessness.

I accept the spirit of these arguments. But they suggest desiderata for egalitarian theory that move us away from equality of fortune. The first argument points to the need to distinguish between goods that society guarantees to all citizens and goods that may be entirely lost without generating any claims to compensation. This is not simply a matter of defining minimum guaranteed aggregate levels of welfare or property endowments. A negligent driver might suffer far more from the death of her son in a car accident she caused than from denial of rehabilitative surgery to her injured leg. Society owes her no compensation for the worse suffering, even if it brings her below some threshold of welfare, but ought not to deprive her of health care, even if she would not drop below that level without it. Egalitarians must try to secure certain *kinds* of goods for people. This thought goes against the spirit of equality of fortune, which aims for comprehensive indemnification of people against undeserved losses of all kinds within the general space of equality they specify (welfare or resources). . . .

The second argument raises the question of how to justify liberty-limiting laws that aim to provide benefits to those whose liberty is limited. Seat belt laws are fine, but represent an insignificant case, because the liberty they limit is trifling. When the liberty being limited is significant, as in the case of mandatory participation in a social insurance scheme, citizens are owed a more dignified explanation than that Big Brother knows better than they do where their interests lie. It is a desideratum of egalitarian theory that it be capable of supplying such an explanation.

III.   The Victims of Bad Brute Luck

Consider now the victims of bad brute luck: those born with serious genetic or congenital handicaps, or who become significantly disabled due to childhood neglect, illness, or accidents for which they cannot be held responsible. Luck egalitarians assimilate to this category those who have little native talent and those whose talents do not command much market value. Van Parijs would also include in this group anyone who is dissatisfied with their other native endowments, whether of nonpecuniary talents, beauty and other physical features, or of agreeable personality traits.[41] Cohen and Arneson would add, also, those people who have involuntarily expensive tastes or chronically depressed psychic states.[42] Equality of fortune says that such victims of bad brute luck are entitled to compensation for their defective internal assets and internal states.

Where luck egalitarians tend to be either harsh or paternalistic toward the victims of bad option luck, they seem compassionate toward the victims of bad brute luck. . . . I shall argue here that the appearance of humanitarianism is belied by the doctrine of equality of fortune in two ways. First, its rules for determining who shall be included among the blamelessly worst off fail to express concern for everyone who is worst off. Second, the reasons it offers for granting aid to the worst off are deeply disrespectful of those to whom the aid is directed.

When is a deficit in internal assets so bad as to require compensation? . . . Dworkin argues that the people who should be compensated for defects in internal assets are those who would have purchased insurance against their having the defect if they were behind a veil of ignorance and did not know whether they would have that defect. It follows, uncharitably, that people who have an extremely rare but severe disability could be ineligible for special aid just because the chances of anyone suffering from it were so minute that it was *ex ante* rational for people not to purchase insurance against it. . . . In addition, Dworkin's proposal would treat two people with the same disability differently, depending on their tastes.[43] A risk-averse blind person could be entitled to aid denied to a risk-loving blind person, on the grounds that the latter probably would not have insured against being blind, given the probabilities. These are further cases of discrimination among the disabled.

Dworkin's criterion of compensable disability, since it depends on people's individualized preferences for insurance, also falls prey to the problem of *expensive tastes.*[44] Suppose a vain person would get hysterical over the prospect of being genetically determined to have a hooked nose. A person's anxiety over this prospect might be enough to make it rational for her to take out insurance for plastic surgery before knowing how her nose would turn out. It is hard to see how such a preference could create an obligation on the part of society to pay for her plastic surgery. Moreover, many people don't see hooked noses as such a bad thing, and many of these people have hooked noses: they would rightly feel insulted if society treating having a hooked nose as such a grievous defect that it was entitled to compensation. . . .

A similar problem afflicts welfarist egalitarian theories such as Arneson's. Cohen objects that in Arneson's view, if Tiny Tim would still be happy without his wheelchair and sullen Scrooge would be consoled by having the money it costs, then Tim should have to give up his wheelchair to Scrooge.[45] The trouble is that these theories, in relying on subjective evaluations, and in aggregating over different dimensions of well-being, allow private satisfactions to count as making up for publicly imposed disadvantages. If people find happiness in their lives despite being oppressed by others, this hardly justifies continuing the oppression. Similarly, would it be all right to compensate for natural inequalities, such as being born ugly, by means of social advantages, such as getting preferential hiring over the beautiful?[46] Call this the problem of *using private (dis)satisfaction to justify public oppression.* It suggests a further desideratum of egalitarian theory, that the form of remedy it supplies match the type of injustice it addresses....

Consider now those whom equality of fortune singles out as the exemplary beneficiaries of aid. Consider Thomas Nagel's view: "When racial and sexual injustice have been reduced, we shall still be left with the great injustice of the smart and the dumb, who are so differently rewarded for comparable effort.... Perhaps someone will discover a way to reduce the socially produced inequalities (especially the economic ones) between the intelligent and the unintelligent, the talented and the untalented, or even the beautiful and the ugly."[47] What do luck egalitarians have to say to those cursed by such defects in their internal assets? Suppose their compensation checks arrived in the mail along with a letter signed by the State Equality Board explaining the reasons for their compensation. Imagine what these letters would say.

> To the disabled: Your defective native endowments or current disabilities, alas, make your life less worth living than the lives of normal people. To compensate for this misfortune, we, the able ones, will give you extra resources, enough to make the worth of living your life good enough that at least *one* person out there thinks it is comparable to someone else's life.
>
> To the stupid and untalented: Unfortunately, other people don't value what little you have to offer in the system of production. Your talents are too meager to command much market value. Because of the misfortune that you were born so poorly endowed with talents, we productive ones will make it up to you: we'll let you share in the bounty of what we have produced with our vastly superior and highly valued abilities.
>
> To the ugly and socially awkward: How sad that you are so repulsive to people around you that no one wants to be your friend or lifetime companion. We won't make it up to you by being your friend or your marriage partner – we have our own freedom of association to exercise – but you can console yourself in your miserable loneliness by consuming these material goods that we, the beautiful and charming ones, will provide. And who knows? Maybe you won't be such a loser in love once potential dates see how rich you are.

Could a self-respecting citizen fail to be insulted by such messages? How dare the state pass judgment on its citizens' worth as workers and lovers! Furthermore, to require citizens to display evidence of personal inferiority in order to get aid from the state is to reduce them to groveling for support. Nor is it the state's business to pass judgment on the worth of the qualities of citizens that they exercise or display in their private affairs. Even if everyone thought that A was so ugly or socially unappealing that they preferred socially attractive B's personal qualities, it is none of the state's business to attach an official stamp of recognition on such private judgments. If it is humiliating to be widely regarded by one's associates as a social clod, think how much more degrading it would be for the state to raise such private judgments to the status of publicly recognized opinions, accepted as true for purposes of administering justice. Equality of fortune *disparages the internally disadvantaged* and *raises private disdain to the status of officially recognized truth....*

Equality of fortune bases its distributive principles on considerations that can only express *pity* for its supposed beneficiaries. Look back at the reasons offered for distributing extra resources to the handicapped and those low in talent or personal appeal: in each case, it is some relative deficiency or defect in their persons or their lives. People lay claim to the resources of egalitarian redistribution in virtue of their inferiority to others, not in virtue of their equality to others. Pity is incompatible with respecting the dignity of others. To base rewards on considerations of pity is to fail to follow principles of distributive justice that express equal respect for all citizens. Luck egalitarianism therefore violates the fundamental expressive requirement of any sound egalitarian theory.[48]

One might argue that the concern expressed by equality of fortune is simple humanitarian compassion, not contemptuous pity. We must be clear about the difference. Compassion is based on an awareness of suffering, an intrinsic condition of a person. Pity, by contrast, is aroused by a comparison of the observer's condition with the condition of the object of pity. Its characteristic judgment is not "she is badly off" but "she is worse off than me." When the conditions being compared are internal states in which people take pride, pity's thought is "she is sadly inferior to me." Compassion and pity can both move a person to act benevolently, but only pity is condescending....

If pity is the attitude the more fortunate express toward the less fortunate when they adopt luck egalitarianism as their principle of action, what is the attitude the less fortunate express toward the more fortunate when they make claims in accordance with the theory? The resourcist luck egalitarians are explicit on this point: it is envy. Their criterion of an equal distribution of resources is an envy-free distribution: one which is such that no one wants anyone else's bundle of resources.[49] The two attitudes are well-suited to each other: the most generous attitude the envied could appropriately have toward the envious is pity. While this makes equality of fortune emotionally consistent, it hardly justifies the theory. Envy's thought is "I want what you have." It is hard to see how such wants can generate *obligations* on the part of the envied. To even offer one's own envy as a reason to the envied to satisfy one's desire is profoundly disrespectful.

Luck egalitarianism thus fails to express concern for those excluded from aid, and fails to express respect for those included among its beneficiaries as well as for those expected to pay for its benefits. It fails the most fundamental tests any egalitarian theory must meet.

IV. The Ills of Luck Egalitarianism: A Diagnosis

We have seen that equality of fortune underwrites a hybrid institutional scheme: free markets, to govern the distribution of goods attributable to factors for which individuals are responsible, and the welfare state, to govern the distribution of goods attributable to factors beyond the individual's control. Equality of fortune can thus be seen as an attempt to combine the best of capitalism and socialism. Its free market aspects promote efficiency, freedom of choice, "consumers' sovereignty," and individual responsibility. Its socialist aspects give everyone a fair start in life and protect the innocent against bad brute luck. . . .

But the counterintuitive judgments that luck egalitarians pass on the cases discussed above suggest a more dismal judgment: equality of fortune appears to give us some of the worst aspects of capitalism and socialism. . . .

How could luck egalitarians go so wrong? Consider first the ways equality of fortune invites problems in the ways it relies on market decisions. It offers a very inadequate safety net for the victims of bad option luck. This reflects the fact that equality of fortune is essentially a "starting-gate theory": as long as people enjoy fair shares at the start of life, it does not much concern itself with the suffering and subjection generated by people's voluntary agreements in free markets.[50] The fact that these evils are the product of voluntary choices hardly justifies them: free choice within a set of options does not justify the set of options itself. In focusing on correcting the supposed injustices of nature, luck egalitarians have forgotten that the primary subject of justice is the institutional arrangements that generate people's opportunities over time. . . .

Now consider the ways luck egalitarianism invites problems in the ways it relies on socialist principles. Equality of fortune tells us that no one should suffer from undeserved misfortune. To implement its principles, the state must make judgments of moral desert or responsibility in assigning outcomes to brute or option luck. To determine whether a smoker who picked up the habit while a soldier shall get state-funded medical treatment for lung cancer, other people must judge whether he should have shown stronger resolve against smoking, given the social pressures he faced from peers and advertisers while serving in the army, the anxiety-reducing benefits of smoking in the highly stressful situation of combat, the opportunities he was offered to overcome his habit after the war, and so forth.[51]

F. A. Hayek has identified the central problem with such merit-based systems of reward: in order to lay a claim to some important benefit, people are forced to obey other people's judgments of what uses they should have made of their opportunities, rather than following their own judgments.[52] Such a system requires the state to make grossly intrusive, moralizing judgments of individuals' choices. Equality of fortune thus *interferes with citizens' privacy and liberty*. Furthermore, as Arneson and Roemer make clear, such judgments require the state to determine how much responsibility each citizen was capable of exercising in each case. But it is disrespectful for the state to pass judgment on how much people are responsible for their expensive tastes or their imprudent choices.[53] . . .

In promoting such an unhappy combination of capitalist and socialist institutions, equality of fortune succeeds not in establishing a society of equals, but only in reproducing the stigmatizing regime of the Poor Laws, in which citizens lay claim to aid from the state only on condition that they accept inferior status. Poor Law thinking pervades the reasoning of luck egalitarians. This is most evident in their distinction between the deserving and the undeserving disadvantaged – between those who are not responsible for their misfortune and those who are. Like the Poor Law regime, it abandons those disadvantaged through their own choices to their miserable fates, and defines the deserving disadvantaged in terms of their innate inferiority of talent, intelligence, ability, or social appeal.

Moreover, in classifying those who devote the bulk of their energies to caring for dependents with those who have a voluntarily expensive taste for charity, equality of fortune *assumes atomistic egoism and self-sufficiency as the norm for human beings*. It promises equality only to those who tend only to their own self-interest, who avoid entering into relationships with others that might generate obligations to engage in dependent caretaking, and who therefore can manage to take care of themselves though their own wage earning, without having to depend on market-generated income provided by anyone else. But such a norm for human beings cannot be universalized. Long periods of dependency on others' caretaking are a normal and inevitable part of everyone's life cycle. It is therefore an indispensable condition of the continuation of human society that many adults devote a great deal of their time to such caretaking, however poorly such work may be remunerated in the market. And this, in turn, entails some dependency of caretakers on income generated by others. Equality of fortune, in representing the dependency of caretakers as voluntary deviance from a falsely universalized androcentric norm, ends up justifying the subordination of women to male wage earners and the stigmatization of dependent caretaking relative to self-sufficient wage earning. A more perfect reproduction of Poor Law thinking, including its sexism and its conflation of responsible work with market wage-earning, could hardly be imagined.[54]

V.   What Is the Point of Equality?

There must be a better way to conceive of the point of equality. To do so, it is helpful to recall how egalitarian political movements have historically conceived of their aims. What have been the inegalitarian systems that they have opposed? Inegalitarianism asserted the justice or necessity of basing social order on a hierarchy of human beings, ranked according to intrinsic worth. Inequality referred not so much to distributions of goods as to relations between superior and inferior persons. Those of superior rank were thought entitled to inflict violence on inferiors, to exclude or segregate them from social life, to treat them with contempt, to force them to obey, work without reciprocation, and abandon their own cultures. These are what Iris Young has identified as the faces of oppression: marginalization, status hierarchy, domination, exploitation, and cultural imperialism.[55] Such unequal social relations generate, and were thought to justify, inequalities in the distribution of freedoms, resources, and welfare. This is the core of inegalitarian ideologies of racism, sexism, nationalism, caste, class, and eugenics.

Egalitarian political movements oppose such hierarchies. They assert the equal moral worth of persons. This assertion does not mean that all have equal virtue or talent. Negatively, the claim repudiates distinctions of moral worth based on birth or social identity – on family membership, inherited social status, race, ethnicity, gender, or genes. There are no natural slaves, plebeians, or aristocrats. Positively, the claim asserts that all competent adults are equally moral agents: everyone equally has the power to develop and exercise moral responsibility, to cooperate with others according to principles of justice, to shape and fulfill a conception of their good.[56]

Egalitarians base claims to social and political equality on the fact of universal moral equality. These claims also have a negative and a positive aspect. Negatively, egalitarians seek to abolish oppression – that is, forms of social relationship by which some people dominate, exploit, marginalize, demean, and inflict violence upon others. Diversities in socially ascribed identities, distinct roles in the division of labor, or differences in personal traits, whether these be neutral biological and psychological differences, valuable talents and virtues, or unfortunate disabilities and infirmities, never justify the unequal social relations listed above. Nothing can justify treating people in these ways, except just punishment for crimes and defense against violence. Positively, egalitarians seek a social order in which persons stand in relations of equality. They seek to live together in a democratic community, as opposed to a hierarchical one. Democracy is here understood as collective self-determination by means of open discussion among equals, in accordance with rules acceptable to all. To stand as an equal before others in discussion means that one is entitled to participate, that others recognize an obligation to listen respectfully and respond to one's arguments, that no one need bow and scrape before others or represent themselves as inferior to others as a condition of having their claim heard.[57]

Contrast this democratic conception of equality with equality of fortune. First, democratic equality aims to abolish socially created oppression. Equality of fortune aims to correct what it takes to be injustices generated by the natural order. Second, democratic equality is what I shall call a relational theory of equality: it views equality as a social relationship. Equality of fortune is a distributive theory of equality: it conceives of equality as a pattern of distribution. Thus, equality of fortune regards two people as equal so long as they enjoy equal amounts of some distributable good – income, resources, opportunities for welfare, and so forth. Social relationships are largely seen as instrumental to generating such patterns of distribution. By contrast, democratic equality regards two people as equal when each accepts the obligation to justify their actions by principles acceptable to the other, and in which they take mutual consultation, reciprocation, and recognition for granted. Certain patterns in the distribution of goods may be instrumental to securing such relationships, follow from them, or even be constitutive of them. But democratic egalitarians are fundamentally concerned with the relationships within which goods are distributed, not only with the distribution of goods themselves. This implies, third, that democratic equality is sensitive to the need to integrate the demands of equal recognition with those of equal distribution.[58] Goods must be distributed according to principles and processes that express respect for all. People must not be required to grovel or demean themselves before others as a condition of laying claim to their share of goods. The basis for people's claims to distributed goods is that they are equals, not inferiors, to others.

This gives us a rough conception of equality. How do we derive principles of justice from it? Our investigation of equality of fortune has not been completely fruitless: from its failures, we have gleaned some desiderata for egalitarian principles. First, such principles must identify certain goods to which all citizens must have effective access over the course of their whole lives. Some goods are more important from an egalitarian point of view than others, within whatever space of equality is identified as of particular concern for egalitarians. And starting-gate theories, or any other principles that allow law-abiding citizens to lose access to adequate levels of these goods, are unacceptable. Second, egalitarians should be able to justify such guarantees of lifetime accessibility without resorting to paternalism. Third, egalitarian principles should offer remedies that match the type of injustice being corrected. Private satisfactions cannot make up for public oppression. Fourth, egalitarian principles should uphold the responsibility of individuals for their own lives without passing demeaning and intrusive judgments on their capacities for exercising responsibility or on how well they have used their freedoms. Finally, such principles should be possible objects of collective willing. They should be capable of supplying sufficient reasons for citizens acting together to collectively guarantee the particular goods of concern to egalitarians.

Let us take up the last desideratum first. The determination of what can or must be collectively willed has been the traditional task of social contract theory. In liberal democratic versions of social contract theory, the fundamental aim of the state is to secure the liberty of its members. Since the democratic state is nothing more than citizens acting collectively, it follows that the fundamental obligation of citizens to one another is to secure the social conditions of everyone's freedom.[59] Because libertarians also embrace this formula, it might be thought to lead to inegalitarian implications. Instead of repudiating this formula, democratic equality interprets it. It claims that the social condition of living a free life is that one stand in relations of equality with others.

This claim might seem paradoxical, given the prevailing view that represents equality and freedom as conflicting ideals. We can see how it is true by considering the oppressive relationships that social equality negates. Equals are not subject to arbitrary violence or physical coercion by others.

Choice unconstrained by arbitrary physical coercion is one of the fundamental conditions of freedom. Equals are not marginalized by others. They are therefore free to participate in politics and the major institutions of civil society. Equals are not dominated by others; they do not live at the mercy of others' wills. This means that they govern their lives by their own wills, which is freedom. Equals are not exploited by others. This means they are free to secure the fair value of their labor. Equals are not subject to cultural imperialism: they are free to practice their own culture, subject to the constraint of respecting everyone else. To live in an egalitarian community, then, is to be free from oppression to participate in and enjoy the goods of society, and to participate in democratic self-government.

Egalitarians thus differ from libertarians in advocating a more expansive understanding of the social conditions of freedom. Importantly, they view private relations of domination, even those entered into by consent or contract, as violations of individual freedom. Libertarians tend to identify freedom with formal, negative freedom: enjoying the legal right to do what one wants without having to ask anyone else's permission and without interference from others. This definition of freedom neglects the importance of having the means to do what one wants. In addition, the definition implicitly assumes that, given the material means and internal capacity to do what one wants, the absence of interference from others is all one needs to do what one wants. This ignores the fact that most of the things people want to do require participation in social activities, and hence communication and interaction with others. One cannot do these things if others make one an outcast. A libertarian might argue that freedom of association entails the right of people to refuse to associate with others on any grounds. Yet, a society embodying such an unconditional right hardly needs physical coercion to force others to obey the wishes of those with the power to exclude others from participation in social life. The same point applies to a society in which property is so unequally distributed that some adults live in abject dependence on others, and so live at the mercy of others. Societies that permit the creation of outcasts and subordinate classes can be as repressive as any despotic regime.

VI.   Equality in the Space of Freedom: A Capabilities Approach

Amartya Sen has proposed a better way to understand freedom. Consider the states of being and doing that constitute a person's well-being: a person can be healthy, well-nourished, physically fit, literate, an active participant in community life, mobile, happy, respected, confident, and so forth. A person may also care about other states of being and doing that reflect her autonomous ends: she may want to be outgoing, to raise children, practice medicine, play soccer, make love, and so forth. Call such states *functionings*. A person's *capabilities* consist of the sets of functionings she can achieve, given the personal, material, and social resources available to her. Capabilities measure not actually achieved functionings, but a person's freedom to achieve valued functionings. A person enjoys more freedom the greater the range of effectively accessible, significantly different opportunities she has for functioning or leading her life in ways she values most.[60] We can understand the egalitarian aim to secure for everyone the social conditions of their freedom in terms of capabilities. Following Sen, I say that egalitarians should seek equality for all in the space of capabilities.

Sen's capability egalitarianism leaves open a large question, however. *Which* capabilities does society have an obligation to equalize? Some people care about playing cards well, others about enjoying luxury vacations in Tahiti.... Surely there are limits to which capabilities citizens are obligated to provide one another. We should heed our first desideratum, to identify particular goods within the space of equality that are of special egalitarian concern.

Reflection on the negative and positive aims of egalitarianism helps us meet this requirement. Negatively, people are entitled to whatever capabilities are necessary to enable them to avoid or escape entanglement in oppressive social relationships. Positively, they are entitled to the capabilities necessary for functioning as an equal citizen in a democratic state. While the negative and positive aims of egalitarianism overlap to a large extent, they are not identical. If functioning as an equal citizen were all that egalitarians cared about, they could not object to forced clitoridectomy, by which men control women's sexuality in private relations. But egalitarians also aim at abolishing private relations of domination, and therefore support the functionings needed for individual sexual autonomy. If having the capabilities needed to avoid oppression were all that mattered, then egalitarians would not oppose discrimination among the relatively privileged – for example, the glass ceiling for female executives. But egalitarians also aim at enabling all citizens to stand as equals to one another in civil society, and this requires that careers be open to talents.

Democratic equality thus aims for equality across a wide range of capabilities. But it does not support comprehensive equality in the space of capabilities. Being a poor card player does not make one oppressed.... Nor is being a good card player necessary for functioning as a citizen. Society therefore has no obligation to provide free card lessons to citizens. Democratic equality satisfies the first desideratum of egalitarian theory.

Consider further the capabilities that democratic equality does guarantee to citizens. Let us focus on the capabilities necessary for functioning as an equal citizen. Citizenship involves functioning not only as a political agent – voting, engaging in political speech, petitioning government, and so forth – but participating as an equal in civil society. Civil society is the sphere of social life that is open to the general public and is not part of the state bureaucracy, in charge of the administration of laws. Its institutions include public streets and parks, public accommodations such as restaurants, shops, theaters, buses and airlines, communications systems such as broadcasting, telephones, and the Internet, public libraries, hospitals, schools, and so forth. Enterprises engaged in production for the market are also part of civil society, because they sell their products to any customer and draw their employees from the general public. One of the important achievements of the civil rights movement was to vindicate an understanding of citizenship that includes the right to participate as an equal in civil society as well as in government affairs. A group that is excluded from or segregated within the institutions of civil society, or subject to discrimination on the basis of ascribed social identities by institutions in civil society, has been relegated to second-class citizenship, even if its members enjoy all of their political rights.

So, to be capable of functioning as an equal citizen involves not just the ability to effectively exercise specifically political rights, but also to participate in the various activities of civil society more broadly, including participation in the economy. And functioning in these ways presupposes functioning as a human being. Consider, then, three aspects of individual functioning: as a human being, as a participant in a system of cooperative production, and as a citizen of a democratic state. To be capable of functioning as a human being requires effective access to the means of sustaining one's biological existence – food, shelter, clothing, medical care – and access to the basic conditions of human agency – knowledge of one's circumstances and options, the ability to deliberate about means and ends, the psychological conditions of autonomy, including the self-confidence to think and judge for oneself, freedom of thought and movement. To be capable of functioning as an equal participant in a system of cooperative production requires effective access to the means of production, access to the education needed to develop one's talents, freedom of occupational choice, the right to make contracts and enter into cooperative agreements with others, the right to receive fair value for one's labor, and recognition by others of one's productive contributions. To be capable of functioning as a citizen requires rights to political participation, such as freedom of speech and the franchise, and also effective access to the goods and relationships of civil society. This entails freedom of association, access to public spaces such as roads, parks, and public accommodations including public transportation, the postal service, and telecommunications. This also entails the social conditions of being accepted by others, such as the ability to appear in public without shame, and not being ascribed outcast status. The freedom to form relationships in civil society also requires effective access to private spaces, since many such relationships can only function when protected from the scrutiny and intrusions of others. Homelessness – that is, having only public dwelling – is a condition of profound unfreedom.

Three points should be made about the structure of egalitarian guarantees in the space of freedom or capabilities. First, democratic equality guarantees not actual levels of functioning, but effective access to those levels. Individuals are free to choose to function at a lower level than they are guaranteed. For example, they might choose to join a religious group that discourages political participation. Moreover, democratic equality can make access to certain functionings – those requiring an income – conditional upon working for them, provided that citizens have effective access to those conditions – they are physically capable of performing the work, doing so is consistent with their other duties, they can find a job, and so forth. Effective access to a level of functioning means that people can achieve that functioning by deploying means already at their disposal, not that the functioning is unconditionally guaranteed without any effort on their own part. Thus, democratic equality is consistent with constructing the incentive systems needed for a modern economy to support the production needed to support egalitarian guarantees in the first place.

Second, democratic equality guarantees not effective access to equal levels of functioning but effective access to levels of functioning sufficient to stand as an equal in society. For some functionings, equal citizenship requires equal levels. For example, each citizen is entitled to the same number of votes in an election as everyone else. But for other functionings, standing as an equal does not require equal levels of functioning. To be capable of standing as an equal in civil society requires literacy. But in the U.S. context, it does not require literacy in any language other than English, nor the ability to interpret obscure works of literary theory. Democratic equality does not object if not everyone knows a foreign language, and only a few have a Ph.D.-level training in literature....

Third, democratic equality guarantees effective access to a package of capabilities sufficient for standing as an equal over the course of an entire life. It is not a starting-gate theory, in which people could lose their access to equal standing through bad option luck. Access to the egalitarian capabilities is also market-inalienable: contracts whereby individuals irrevocably transfer their fundamental freedoms to others are null and void.[61] The rationale for establishing such inalienable rights might seem difficult to grasp from the point of view of the rights holder. Why shouldn't she be free to trade some of her egalitarian-guaranteed freedoms for other goods that she prefers? Isn't it paternalistic to deny her the freedom to trade?

We can avoid this thought by considering the point of view of the obligation holder. The counterpart to an individual's inalienable right to the social conditions of her freedom is the unconditional obligation of others to respect her dignity or moral equality. Kant would put the point as follows: every individual has a worth or dignity that is not conditional upon anyone's desires or preferences, not even the individual's own desires. This implies that there are some things one may never do to other people, such as to enslave them, even if one has their permission or consent. Contracts into slavery or servitude are therefore invalid. In basing inalienable rights on what others are obligated to do rather than on the rights bearer's own subjective interests, democratic equality satisfies the second desideratum of egalitarian theory: to justify lifetime guarantees without resorting to paternalism.

One advantage of the capabilities approach to equality is that it allows us to analyze injustices in regard to other matters besides the distribution of resources and other divisible goods. One's capabilities are a function not just of one's fixed personal traits and divisible resources, but of one's mutable traits, social relations and norms, and the structure of opportunities, public goods, and public spaces. Egalitarian political movements have never lost sight of the whole range of targets of egalitarian assessment. For example, feminists work to overcome the internal obstacles to choice – self-abnegation, lack of confidence, and low self-esteem – that women often face from internalizing norms of femininity. Gays and lesbians seek the ability to publicly reveal their identities without shame or fear, which requires significant changes in social relations of contempt and hostility, and changes in norms of gender and sexuality. The disabled aim to reconfigure public spaces to make them accessible and adapt work situations to their needs, so that they can participate in productive activity. No mere redistribution of divisible resources can secure the freedoms these groups seek.

Of course, democratic equality is also concerned with the distribution of divisible resources. It requires that everyone have effective access to enough resources to avoid being oppressed by others and to function as an equal in civil society. What counts as "enough" varies with cultural norms, the natural environment, and individual circumstance. For example, cultural norms and climate influence what kind of clothing one needs to be able to appear in public without shame and with adequate protection from the elements. Individual circumstances, such as disabilities, influence how much resources one needs to function as an equal. People without use of their legs may need more resources – wheelchairs, specially adapted vans – to achieve mobility comparable to that of ambulatory persons.... What citizens ultimately owe one another is the social conditions of the freedoms people need to function as equal citizens. Because of differences in their internal capacities and social situations, people are not equally able to convert resources into capabilities for functioning. They are therefore entitled to different amounts of resources so they can enjoy freedom as equals....

VII.   Participation as an Equal in a System of Cooperative Production

So far we have considered what citizens are obligated to provide one another. But how are such things to be produced, and by what means and principles shall they be distributed? In stressing the concept of obligation, democratic equality heads off the thought that in an egalitarian society everyone somehow could have a right to receive goods without anyone having an obligation to produce them. Democratic equality seeks equality in the capability or effective freedom to achieve functionings that are part of citizenship, broadly construed. For those capable of working and with access to jobs, the actual achievement of these functionings is, in the normal case, conditional on participating in the productive system.... Most able-bodied citizens, then, will get access to the divisible resources they need to function by earning a wage or some equivalent compensation due to them on account of their filling some role in the division of labor.

In deciding principles for a just division of labor and a just division of the fruits of that labor, workers are to regard the economy as a system of cooperative, joint production.[62]... By "joint production," I mean that people regard every product of the economy as jointly produced by everyone working together. From the point of view of justice, the attempt, independent of moral principles, to credit specific bits of output to specific bits of input by specific individuals represents an arbitrary cut in the causal web that in fact makes everyone's productive contribution dependent on what everyone else is doing.... In regarding the division of labor as a comprehensive system of joint production, workers and consumers regard themselves as collectively commissioning everyone else to perform their chosen role in the economy. In performing their role in an efficient division of labor, each worker is regarded as an agent for the people who consume their products and for the other workers who, in being thereby relieved from performing that role, become free to devote their talents to more productive activities.

In regarding the economy as a cooperative venture, workers accept the demand of what G. A. Cohen has defined as the principle of interpersonal justification:[63] any consideration offered as a reason for a policy must serve to justify that policy when uttered by anyone to anyone else who participates in the economy as a worker or a consumer. The principles that govern the division of labor and the assignment of particular benefits to the performance of roles in the division of labor must be acceptable to everyone in this sense. To see how interpersonal justification works within the context of the economy considered as a system of cooperative, joint production, consider three of the cases equality of fortune gets wrong: disability compensation for workers in dangerous occupations, federal disaster relief, and dependent caretakers with their children.

Rakowski argues that workers who choose particularly dangerous occupations, such as farming, fishing, mining, forestry, firefighting, and policing, have no claims to medical care, rehabilitation, or compensation if they are injured on the job.[64] Since they engage in these occupations by choice, any bad fortune they suffer on the job is a form of option luck, the consequences of which must be born by the worker alone. Cohen's test invites us to consider how persuasive this argument is, when uttered to the disabled workers by the consumers who eat the food, use the metal and wood, and enjoy the protection from fire and crime that these workers provide. These consumers are not free to disclaim all responsibility for the bad luck that befalls workers in dangerous occupations. For they commissioned these workers to perform those dangerous tasks on their own behalf. The workers were acting as agents for the consumers of their labor. It cannot be just to designate a work role in the division of labor that entails such risks and then assign a package of benefits to performance in the role that fails, given the risks, to secure the social conditions of freedom to those who occupy the role. The principle "let us be served by occupations so inadequately compensated that those in them shall lack the means necessary to secure their freedom, given the risks and conditions of their work" cannot survive the test of interpersonal justification.

Similar reflections apply to those who choose to live and work in areas prone to particularly severe natural disasters, such as residents near the San Andreas fault. Rakowski argues that such residents should be excluded from federal disaster relief because they live there by choice.[65] But they live there because other citizens have, through their demand for California products, commissioned them to exploit the natural resources in California. To deny them federal disaster relief is to invoke the rejected principle above. Economists may object that, on balance, it may not be efficient to continue production in a particular region, and that disaster relief, in subsidizing the costs of living in disaster-prone regions, perpetuates a costly error. However, if, on balance, citizens decide that a region should be designated uninhabitable, because the costs of relief are too high, the proper response is not to leave its residents in the lurch but to designate their relief toward helping them relocate. Citizens are not to be deprived of basic capabilities on account of where they live.[66]

The case of non-wage-earning dependent caretakers and children might seem to fall outside the purview of society as system of cooperation. But this is to confuse the economy with the market sector.[67] Non-wage-earning dependent caretakers contribute to production in at least three ways. First, most engage in household production – cleaning, cooking, and so forth – which services, if not performed, would have to be hired out. Second, they raise the future workers of the economy and help rehabilitate the sick and injured ones so they can return to work. Third, in discharging the obligations everyone has to dependents, considered as human beings, and the obligations all family members have toward their dependent kin, they relieve others of such responsibility and thereby free them to participate in the market economy. Fathers would not be so productive in the market if the non-wage-earning or part-time working mothers of their children did not relieve them of so much of their responsibility to engage in direct caretaking.[68] The principle "let us assign others to discharge our caretaking obligations to dependents, and attach such meager benefits to performance in this role that these caretakers live at our mercy" cannot survive interpersonal justification, either. Dependent caretakers are entitled to enough of a share of their partner's income that they are not vulnerable to domination and exploitation within the relationship. This principle supports Okin's proposal that pay-checks be split between husband and wife.[69] If this is not sufficient to eliminate caretakers' vulnerability in domestic partnership, a case can be made for socializing some of the costs of dependent care through a child-care (or elder-care) subsidy, as is common in western Europe. Ultimately, full equality may not be achievable simply through the redistribution of material resources. Equality may require a change in social norms, by which men as well as women would be expected to share in caretaking responsibilities.[70] . . .

The conception of society as a system of cooperation provides a safety net through which even the imprudent are never forced to fall. It provides that no role in the productive system shall be assigned such inadequate benefits that, given the risks and requirements of the job, people could be deprived of the social conditions of their freedom because they have fulfilled its requirements. Society may not define work roles that amount to peonage or servitude, nor, if it can avoid it, pay them so little that an able-bodied person working full time would still lack basic capabilities.[71]...Democratic equality also favors a qualified entitlement to work on the part of willing, able-bodied adults. Unemployment insurance is a poor substitute for work, given the central importance of participation in productive activity to living life as an equal in civil society....

It is instructive to consider what democratic equality says to those with low talents. Equality of fortune would offer compensation to those with low talents, precisely because their innate inferiority makes their labor so relatively worthless to others, as judged by the market. Democratic equality calls into question the very idea that inferior native endowments have much to do with observed income inequalities in capitalist economies. The biggest fortunes are made not by those who work but by those who own the means of production. Even among wage workers, most of the differences are due to the fact that society has invested far more in developing some people's talents than others and that it puts very unequal amounts of capital at the disposal of each worker. Productivity attaches mainly to work roles, not to individuals. Democratic equality deals with these facts by stressing the importance of educating the less advantaged and by offering firms incentives to increase the productivity of low-wage jobs through capital investment.

Moreover, in regarding society as a system of cooperation, democratic equality has a less demeaning rationale than equality of fortune for state interventions designed to raise the wages of low-wage workers. Society need not try to make the impossible and insulting judgment of whether low-wage workers are there by choice or by the fact that their meagre native endowments prevent them from getting better work. Instead, it focuses on appreciation for the roles that low-wage workers fill. In performing routine, low-skill tasks, these workers free other people to make more productive uses of their talents. Those occupying more productive roles owe much of their productivity to the fact that those occupying less productive roles have freed them from the need to spend their time on low-skill tasks....Such reflections express appreciation for the ways that everyone benefits from the diversity of talents and roles in society....and thereby help motivate a conception of reciprocity that would squeeze the gap between the highest-and lowest-paid workers.

Would democratic equality support a wage-squeezing policy as demanding as Rawls's difference principle? This would forbid all income inequalities that do not improve the incomes of the worst off.[72]...Democratic equality would urge a less demanding form of reciprocity. Once all citizens enjoy a decent set of freedoms, sufficient for functioning as an equal in society, income inequalities beyond that point do not seem so troubling in themselves. The degree of acceptable income inequality would depend in part on how easy it was to convert income into status inequality – differences in the social bases of self-respect, influence over elections, and the like. The stronger the barriers against commodifying social status, political influence, and the like, the more acceptable are significant income inequalities.[73] The moral status of free market allocations is strengthened the more carefully defined is the domain in which these allocations have free rein. . . .

VIII.   Democratic Equality and the Obligations of Citizens

Democratic equality refocuses egalitarian theorizing in several ways. It conceives of justice as a matter of obligations that are not defined by the satisfaction of subjective preferences. This ensures that people's rights do not depend on arbitrary variations in individual tastes and that people may not claim rights without accepting corresponding obligations to others. Democratic equality applies judgments of justice to human arrangements, not to the natural order. This helps us see that people, not nature, are responsible for turning the natural diversity of human beings into oppressive hierarchies. It locates unjust deficiencies in the social order rather than in people's innate endowments. Instead of lamenting the human diversity of talents and trying to make up for what is represented as innate deficiencies in talent, democratic equality offers a way of conceiving and harnessing human diversity so that it benefits everyone and is recognized as doing so. Democratic equality conceives of equality as a relationship among people rather than merely as a pattern in the distribution of divisible goods. This helps us see how egalitarians can take other features of society besides the distribution of goods, such as social norms, as subject to critical scrutiny. It lets us see how injustices may be better remedied by changing social norms and the structure of public goods than by redistributing resources. And it allows us to integrate the demands of equal distribution and equal respect, ensuring that the principles by which we distribute goods, however equal resulting patterns may be, do not in fact express contemptuous pity for the beneficiaries of egalitarian concern. Democratic equality thus offers a superior way to understand the expressive demands of justice – the demand to act only on principles that express respect for everyone. Finally, in refocusing academic egalitarian theorizing, democratic equality holds out the promise of reestablishing connections with actually existing egalitarian movements. It is not a moral accident that beach bums and people who find themselves slaves to their expensive hobbies are not organizing to make claims of justice on behalf of their lifestyles. Nor is it irrelevant that the disabled are repudiating forms of charity that appeal to pity for their condition and are struggling for respect from others, not just handouts. Democratic equality helps articulate the demands of genuine egalitarian movements in a framework that offers some hope of broader appeal.

Notes

I thank Louise Antony, Stephen Everson, Allan Gibbard, Mark Hansen, Don Herzog, David Hills, Louis Loeb, Martha Nussbaum, David Velleman, and audience participants at the University of North Carolina and the University of Chicago, where I delivered earlier versions of this article. Special thanks go to Amy Gutmann, for her penetrating comments at the thirty-first annual Philosophy Colloquium at Chapel Hill, N. C.

1 Ronald Dworkin, "What Is Equality? II. Equality of Resources," *Philosophy and Public Affairs* 10 (1981), 283–345, p. 285 [p. 112 in this volume, eds.].
2 Philippe Van Parijs, "Why Surfers Should Be Fed: The Liberal Case for an Unconditional Basic Income," *Philosophy and Public Affairs* 20 (1991), 101–31.
3 Richard Arneson, "Equality and Equality of Opportunity for Welfare," in *Equality: Selected Readings*, ed. Louis Pojman and Robert Westmoreland (New York: Oxford University Press, 1997), p. 231.
4 G. A. Cohen, "On the Currency of Egalitarian Justice," *Ethics* 99 (1989), 906–44, pp. 922–3, 930–1 [pp. 139–41, 145–7 in this volume, eds.].
5 Philippe Van Parijs, *Real Freedom for All* (Oxford: Clarendon, 1995), p. 127.
6 Thomas Nagel, "The Policy of Preference," in his *Mortal Questions* (Cambridge: Cambridge University Press, 1979), pp. 91–105.
7 Richard Arneson, "Rawls, Responsibility, and Distributive Justice," in *Justice, Political Liberalism, and Utilitarianism: Themes from Harsanyi*, ed. Maurice Salles and John A. Weymark (Cambridge: Cambridge University Press, in press).
8 John Rawls, *A Theory of Justice* (Cambridge, Mass.: Harvard University Press, 1971), pp. 100–4.
9 Thomas Nagel, *Equality and Partiality* (New York: Oxford University Press, 1991), p. 71; Eric Rakowski, *Equal Justice* (New York: Oxford University Press, 1991); John Roemer, "A Pragmatic Theory of Responsibility for the Egalitarian Planner," in his *Egalitarian Perspectives* (Cambridge: Cambridge University Press, 1994), pp. 179–80.
10 P. T. Bauer, *Equality, the Third World, and Economic Delusion* (Cambridge, Mass.: Harvard University Press, 1981).
11 Lawrence Mead, *Beyond Entitlement: The Social Obligations of Citizenship* (New York: Free Press, 1986).
12 Arneson, "Equality and Equality of Opportunity for Welfare," p. 235.
13 Dworkin, "Equality of Resources," p. 293 [p. 117 in this volume, eds.].
14 Cohen is the only prominent luck egalitarian to regard society's reliance on capitalist markets as an unfortunate if, in the foreseeable future, necessary compromise with justice, rather than as a vital instrument of just allocation. See Cohen, "Incentives, Inequality, and Community," in *Equal Freedom*, ed. Stephen Darwall (Ann Arbor: University of Michigan Press, 1995), p. 395. John Roemer, *Egalitarian Perspectives*, supports a complex version of market socialism on distributive grounds, but these grounds do not appear sufficient to demonstrate the superiority of market socialism to, say, Van Parijs's version of capitalism.
15 See Hayek, *The Constitution of Liberty* (Chicago: University of Chicago Press, 1960).
16 Dworkin, "Equality of Resources."
17 Rakowski, pp. 80–1.

18   Ronald Dworkin, "What Is Equality? I. Equality of Welfare," *Philosophy and Public Affairs* 10 (1981), 228–40.

19   Arneson, "Equality and Equality of Opportunity for Welfare," pp. 230–1; Cohen, "On the Currency of Egalitarian Justice," pp. 922–3 [pp. 139–41 in this volume, eds.].

20   Dworkin, "Equality of Resources," pp. 285–9.

21   Ronald Dworkin, *Taking Rights Seriously* (Cambridge, Mass.: Harvard University Press, 1977), pp. 272–3.

22   Rakowski, pp. 74–5.

23   Arneson, "Liberalism, Distributive Subjectivism, and Equal Opportunity for Welfare," *Philosophy and Public Affairs* 19 (1990), p. 187.

24   Rakowski, p. 79.

25   Rakowski allows that, in areas that suffer from no more than average risk of natural disaster, "any losses resulting from whatever risk was a necessary concomitant to the ownership of property essential to live a moderately satisfying life" would be fully compensable, "as instances of bad brute luck." But once private insurance becomes available, brute luck converts to option luck and uninsured parties are on their own again (p. 80).

26   Ibid., p. 79.

27   Susan Moller Okin, *Justice, Gender, and the Family* (New York: Basic, 1989), pp. 134–69.

28   Rakowski, p. 109.

29   Ibid., p. 153.

30   Van Parijs, "Why Surfers Should Be Fed," p. 131.

31   Van Parijs, *Real Freedom for All*, p. 76.

32   Brian M. Barry, "Equality, Yes, Basic Income, No," in *Arguing for Basic Income*, ed. Philippe Van Parijs (New York: Verso, 1992), p. 138.

33   Arneson, "Equality and Equality of Opportunity for Welfare."

34   John Roemer, *Theories of Distributive Justice* (Cambridge, Mass.: Harvard University Press, 1996), p. 270.

35   Ibid.

36   Cohen, "On the Currency of Egalitarian Justice," p. 908.

37   John Roemer, "The Morality and Efficiency of Market Socialism," *Ethics* 102 (1992), 448–64.

38   Arneson, "Equality and Equality of Opportunity for Welfare," p. 239.

39   Van Parijs, *Real Freedom for All*, p. 47; Richard Arneson, "Is Socialism Dead? A Comment on Market Socialism and Basic Income Capitalism," *Ethics* 102 (1992), 485–511, p. 510.

40   Amy Gutmann made these points in her public comments on an earlier version of this article, delivered at the thirty-first annual Philosophy Colloquium at Chapel Hill, NC.

41   Van Parijs, *Real Freedom for All*, p. 68.

42   Arneson, "Liberalism, Distributive Subjectivism, and Equal Opportunity for Welfare"; Cohen, "On the Currency of Egalitarian Justice," pp. 930–1 [pp. 145–7 in this volume, eds.].

43   Van Parijs, *Real Freedom for All*, p. 70.

44   Ibid.

45   Cohen, "On the Currency of Egalitarian Justice," pp. 917–18 [pp. 135–6 in this volume, eds.].

46 Thomas Pogge, "Three Problems with Contractarian-Consequentialist Ways of Assessing Social Institutions," in *The Just Society*, ed. Ellen Frankel Paul, Fred Miller, Jr., and Jeffrey Paul (Cambridge: Cambridge University Press, 1995), pp. 247–8.

47 Nagel, "The Policy of Preference," p. 105.

48 This is a concern with what attitudes the theory expresses, not with the consequences of expressing those attitudes. Self-respecting citizens would reject a society based on principles that treat them as inferiors, even if the principles are kept secret. Government house utilitarianism is thus no solution. Nor is it a satisfactory defense of equality of fortune to recommend that society adopt more generous distributive policies than the theory requires so as to avoid insulting people. The question is not whether to deviate from what justice requires so as to avoid bad consequences. It is whether a theory of justice based on contemptuous pity for its supposed beneficiaries satisfies the egalitarian requirement that justice must be founded on equal respect for persons.

49 Dworkin, "Equality of Resources," p. 285 [p. 112 in this volume, eds.]; Rakowski, pp. 65–6; Van Parijs, *Real Freedom for All*, p. 51.

50 Dworkin denies that his is a "starting-gate theory," but only because he would allocate compensation for unequal talents over the course of a lifetime ("Equality of Resources," pp. 309–11 [pp. 128–30 in this volume, eds.]).

51 What if someone runs a health risk that only increases her already significant chance of illness? Let scientific studies apportion the risks of illness due to involuntary causes (e.g., faulty genes) and voluntary causes (e.g. eating a fatty diet), and discount the resources contributed to care for the ill by the proportion to which their risk was one they ran voluntarily (Rakowski, p. 75). Roemer accepts this logic, but insists that people's responsibility for their conditions should be discounted by unchosen sociological as well as genetic influences. Thus, if two people with lung cancer smoke the median number of years for their sociological type (determined by sex, race, class, occupation, parents' smoking habits, etc.), then they are entitled, other things equal, to equal indemnification against the costs of their cancer, even if one smoked for eight years and the other for twenty-five years (Roemer, "A Pragmatic Theory of Responsibility for the Egalitarian Planner," p. 183). His intuition is that people who exercise comparable degrees of responsibility, adjusted to make up for the different social influences on their behavior, should be entitled to equal degrees of compensation against the costs of their behavior. Roemer does not consider the expressive implications of the state assuming that different classes of citizens should be held to different standards of responsible behavior.

52 Hayek, pp. 95–7.

53 Christine Korsgaard, "Commentary on G. A. Cohen and Amartya Sen," in *The Quality of Life*, ed. Martha Nussbaum and Amartya Sen (Oxford: Clarendon, 1993), p. 61.

54 Iris Marion Young, "Mothers, Citizenship, and Independence: A Critique of Pure Family Values," *Ethics* 105 (1995), 535–56, makes a similar critique, unconnected to luck egalitarianism, of contemporary welfare reform movements. Van Parijs's version of luck egalitarianism might seem to escape from Poor Law thinking because it promises an unconditional income to everyone, regardless of whether they work for a wage. However, as noted above, even his view implicitly takes the tastes of the egoistic adult without caretaking responsibilities as the norm. For the gap between the minimum wage and the unconditional income will be set by

184   *Elizabeth S. Anderson*

the incentives needed to bring the marginal footloose egoist into the labor market. The fate of non-wage-earning dependent caretakers will thus depend on the labor/leisure trade-offs of beach bums, rather than on their own needs. The more attached to leisure the beach bum is, the lower must the unconditional income be.

55 Iris Marion Young, *Justice and the Politics of Difference* (Princeton, NJ: Princeton University Press, 1990).

56 John Rawls, "Kantian Constructivism in Moral Theory," *Journal of Philosophy* 77 (1980), 515–72, p. 525. The use of "equally" to modify "moral agents" might seem otiose: why not just say that all competent adults are moral agents? Egalitarians deny a hierarchy of types of moral agency – e.g., any theory that says there is a lower type of human only able to follow moral commands issued by others and a higher type able to issue or discover moral commands for themselves.

57 Elizabeth Anderson, "The Democratic University: The Role of Justice in the Production of Knowledge," *Social Philosophy and Policy* 12 (1995), 186–219. Does this requirement mean that we must always listen patiently to those who have proven themselves to be stupid, cranky, or dishonest? No. It means (1) that everyone must be granted the initial benefit of the doubt, (2) a person can be ignored or excluded from discussion only on demonstrated grounds of communicative incompetence or unwillingness to engage in fair discussion, and (3) reasonable opportunities must be available to the excluded to demonstrate their communicative competence and thereby win back a place in the conversation.

58 Nancy Fraser, "From Redistribution to Recognition? Dilemmas of Justice in a "Postsocialist" Age," in her *Justice Interruptus* (New York: Routledge, 1997), pp. 11–39; Axel Honneth, *The Struggle for Recognition*, trans. Joel Anderson (Cambridge: Polity Press, 1995).

59 Korsgaard.

60 Amartya Sen, *Inequality Reexamined* (Cambridge, Mass.: Harvard University Press, 1992), pp. 39–42, 49.

61 Margaret Radin, "Market Inalienability," *Harvard Law Review* 100 (1987), 1849–1937. A person might have to forfeit some of her market inalienable freedoms, however, if she is convicted of a serious crime.

62 I shift from talk of "citizens" to talk of "workers" in part because the moral implications of regarding the economy as a system of cooperative production cross international boundaries. As the economy becomes global, we are all implicated in an international division of labor subject to assessment from an egalitarian point of view. We have obligations not only to the citizens of our country but to our fellow workers, who are now found in virtually every part of the globe. We also have global humanitarian obligations to everyone, considered simply as human beings – to relieve famine and disease, avoid fomenting or facilitating aggressive warfare, and the like. Alas, I do not have the space to consider the international implications of democratic equality.

63 Cohen, "Incentives, Inequality, and Community," in *Equal Freedom*, ed. Stephen Darwall (Ann Arbor: University of Michigan Press, 1995), p. 348.

64 Rakowski, p. 79.

65 Ibid.

66 What about rich people who build their vacation homes in disaster-prone areas? They haven't been commissioned by others to live there, nor does it seem fair to force taxpayers to insure their luxurious estates. Democratic equality cannot allow

even unproductive citizens to lose everything, but it does not indemnify them against all their losses either. It only guarantees sufficient relief to get them back on their feet, not to shod them in luxurious footwear. If even this relief seems too expensive, an egalitarian state can forbid people from inhabiting disaster-prone areas, or tax people who do to cover the excess costs of disaster relief. What it may not do is let them live there at their own risk and then abandon them in their hour of need. Such action treats even the imprudent with impermissible contempt.

67 Marilyn Waring, *If Women Counted* (San Francisco: HarperCollins, 1990).
68 Joan Williams, "Is Coverture Dead?" *Georgetown Law Journal* 82 (1994), 2227–90, p. 2227.
69 Okin, pp. 180–2 [pp. 210–12 in this volume, eds.].
70 Nancy Fraser, "After the Family Wage: A Postindustrial Thought Experiment," in her *Justice Interruptus*, pp. 41–66.
71 It might be thought that poor societies cannot afford even basic capabilities for all workers. However, Sen's studies of the standard of living in India and China show that even extremely poor societies can supply an impressive set of basic capabilities – decent nutrition, health, literacy, and the like – to all of their members, if they apply themselves to the task. See, e.g., Amartya Sen, *Commodities and Capabilities* (Amsterdam: North-Holland, 1985).
72 Rawls, *A Theory of Justice*, pp. 75–8 [pp. 67–70 in this volume, eds.].
73 Michael Walzer, *Spheres of Justice* (New York: Basic, 1983); Mickey Kaus, *The End of Equality* (New York: Basic, 1992).

8

The Concept of Desert

David Miller

I

When people make claims about justice, or social justice, they very often do so using the language of desert. They say it is unfair when a woman is not given the promotion or the pay rise that she deserves, and if a law or an institution regularly fails to treat people as they deserve – for instance by working in favour of people with the 'right' connections or the 'right' skin colour – it will be condemned as socially unjust. The centrality of desert as a criterion of distributive justice is confirmed when popular conceptions of justice are explored empirically.[1] Political philosophers, by contrast, have generally been far more sceptical in recent years. They have been unwilling to accept popular conceptions of desert and justice at face value, preferring instead either to abandon the concept of desert altogether, or to put forward revisionist accounts of that concept, whose effect is to give it a less prominent role in thinking about social justice.

This scepticism about desert stems from a number of different sources. One is the thought that, rather than being an independent principle of justice, desert is actually *parasitic* upon justice. In other words, rather than establishing first what people deserve, and then deriving from this claims about justice requires them to have, we in fact do the opposite, whether we realise it or not: we begin with principles that define a just distribution of resources, and then we identify what each person deserves as whatever he or she would receive under that distribution. This idea can be found in the work of John Rawls, and has recently been developed further by Samuel Scheffler.[2]

A different source of scepticism about desert is the thought that conventional desert judgements involve crediting people for things that, in reality,

David Miller, 'The Concept of Desert', abridged and revised by the author from chapter 7 in his *Principles of Social Justice* (Cambridge, MA: Harvard University Press, 1999).

they can claim no credit for. We talk about clever children deserving to go to university, skilful tennis players deserving to win championships, successful entrepreneurs deserving to make large profits, and so on, but in each case we are talking about qualities or achievements for which the individuals in question can, at most, take partial credit. Much more is due to good genes, a fortunate family background, lucky breaks early in someone's career. Appealing to desert, according to these critics, becomes a way of sanctifying what is in fact largely a morally arbitrary distribution of society's resources.

In this chapter I cannot hope to lay to rest all the reasons one might have for scepticism about desert. My aim is more specific. First I try to explain as precisely as possible what we actually mean when we say that someone deserves something. Then I consider how far desert claims are undermined by the presence of different kinds of luck. Next I look at the particular issue of natural talents: can people deserve on the basis of performances that require special talents to accomplish? Finally I ask how *determinate* desert judgements can be. How far can they guide us in deciding what a just distribution of resources looks like? Overall, I want to show that the concept of desert is in better shape, and of more use to us, than many recent philosophers have thought.

II

Let me then begin with the notion of desert itself.[3] Consider the wide range of cases in which we make judgements to the effect that a person deserves some benefit by virtue of some performance or attribute. I propose to distinguish *primary* desert judgements, which fall within the core of the concept, *secondary* desert judgements, which still invoke the concept but are parasitic on primary judgements, and *sham* desert judgements, which use the language of desert but are really appeals to some other ethical idea.

When primary desert judgements are made, some agent A is said to deserve some benefit B on the basis of an activity or performance P. A is most often an individual but may also be a collective such as a football team. B is something generally considered beneficial to its recipient: a prize, a reward, income, a promotion, an honour, praise, recognition, and so on. P may be a single act or a course of activity extending over time. The important thing is that P should be in the relevant sense A's performance; that is, A should be responsible for P. This rules out a number of possibilities. One is the case in which A is coerced or manipulated into performing P – for example, under hypnosis I accomplish some dangerous task that I would normally be too scared to perform.[4] Another is the case where A performs P inadvertently: he intends to perform Q but because of circumstances beyond his control he ends up performing P. Yet another is the case in which A's performing P is some kind of fluke; although he intends to perform P, the fact that he succeeds is very largely a matter of luck. For example, suppose that I am a very poor archer but manage to persuade the local archery club to let me take part in its annual tournament. By sheer good luck I send three arrows into the gold, something I could not repeat in a million attempts. I could not on this basis deserve the trophy that is presented to me.[5]

To deserve B on the basis of P, I must intend to perform P and the performance of P must be sufficiently within my control. But although *intention* is in this way relevant to desert, *motive* may very often not be. It is a characteristic mistake of philosophers writing on this topic to suppose that deserving agents must have moral motives for their performances – that to deserve on the basis of P, one must have performed P out of a sense of duty, or in order to confer benefits on others.[6] Clearly there is a *kind* of desert of which this is true, namely moral desert; people who display virtuous qualities when they act deserve praise and moral commendation, and possibly though not necessarily certain kinds of honour. But generally speaking desert depends on the performance itself and not on the motive that lies behind it. The athlete whose performance in the marathon is such that she deserves to win may be motivated to run by ambition, greed, or simply the wish to prove something to herself. The junior lawyer who deserves a pay rise for hard work and long hours may equally be driven by a desire for income or status. Admittedly, having the wrong motive does sometimes appear to reduce a person's deserts, even where the desert in question is not moral desert. But this may be because it reveals something about the quality of the performance itself. Thus if someone carries out a hazardous rescue, but then discloses that he only did it in the hope of being rewarded by his grateful victim, we may revise downwards our estimate of what he deserves, but perhaps this is because we think that someone who did it for *that* reason isn't likely to have found the rescue as scaring as we had supposed. In other cases revealing a bad moral character may generate negative desert, which has to be set against the positive desert of the performance itself. (Many Westerns have central characters who perform good and courageous deeds for what appear to be cynical reasons, leaving the heroine in a dilemma at the end, not knowing what to think of her champion; if desert required a moral motive there would be no such dilemma.)

What of the performance itself? P must be something that is positively appraised or valued by the surrounding community, but once again this need not amount to a *moral* evaluation. The grounds of the evaluation will differ greatly from case to case. The author who deserves to win the Booker Prize does so because he has written a book that is excellent by literary standards. The employee who deserves the biggest slice of the firm's profits is the one who has done most to raise its productive output. The girl who deserves the highest examination grades is the one who has achieved the best mastery of the various subjects. No doubt in the background there often stands some idea of social utility: we appraise literary excellence, productivity and academic achievement positively because we think that the exercise of these qualities enriches our lives in one way or another, but it does not seem to me essential to the idea of desert itself that this should be so. Although athletics competitions may create social benefits (as entertaining spectacles, for instance), the performances that form the basis of athletes' deserts, such as running down a track very fast, have no social utility in themselves. And to take a case where the performance is in fact socially harmful, there seems nothing incoherent or bizarre in saying that the man who masterminded the bank raid deserves a larger share of the loot than the guy who merely drove the getaway car.

The concept of desert does not itself settle the basis on which people come to deserve advantages of various kinds. It imposes certain requirements – principally, as we have seen, that the performance which composes the basis should be in the right way the *agent's* performance, and that this performance should be positively appraised – but the concrete content comes from elsewhere.[7] This raises the question of whether desert is merely a conventional idea: is it merely being used to signal the benefits and advantages that are customarily attached to performances of various kinds? For the moment I simply want to distinguish claims about desert itself from more substantive claims about the kinds of performance that *ought* to constitute bases of desert.

Finally, we must explore the connection between the performance and the benefit that is said to be deserved. It is implicit in the idea of desert that it is good or desirable for A, who has performed P, to have B; the world is in a better state when he has B than when he does not have it. Furthermore, in most cases some or all of us have reason to ensure that A gets B. The exceptions are cases in which there is nothing we can do to produce this outcome or in which attempting to do so would violate some other requirement of justice. Thus we might say of a scientist who has worked hard at a problem for many years, 'He really deserves to make a breakthrough', but in this case there is nothing we can do to bring about the result. Or we might say of an athlete, 'She deserves to win the gold', but it would be wrong for that reason to try to tip the race in her favour, since we are bound by norms of fairness and impartiality to treat all competitors equally. But these cases are unusual and perhaps marginal. Usually desert gives us a reason to assign B to A, either by direct action or else by changing our practices or institutions so that A is likely to end up with B.

This reason is a basic reason. The performance has taken place, and A's being put in a position to enjoy B is the fitting or appropriate response on our part to that fact. Many people find this relationship a mysterious one, and therefore seek to translate desert judgements into another form in which they do not have the implication that A's doing P at one moment simply *is* a reason for his being given B at some later moment. For instance, it may be said that giving B to A serves as an incentive for A and others like him to perform P in future; or it may be said that A's performing P shows the strength of his ambition to achieve B, so that by giving him B we are satisfying a strongly felt desire. But although it is often the case that requiting desert also achieves aims such as these, the suggested translations do not capture what we mean by desert. Desert belongs together with 'reactive attitudes' like gratitude and resentment within what Peter Strawson has called the 'participant' perspective on human life, in which we regard others as freely choosing agents like ourselves, and respond to their actions accordingly.[8] If we switch, as we sometimes must, to the 'objective' perspective, regarding others as creatures to be trained, managed, and cared for, either in their interest or in ours, we should drop all talk of desert rather than trying to invent a surrogate meaning for it.

Thus far I have been trying to elucidate the meaning of what I earlier called 'primary' desert judgements, and it will not have escaped the reader's attention that some parts at least of our thinking about desert do not seem to fit into the framework I have proposed. In particular, we sometimes say that people deserve things on the basis of personal qualities rather than performances: we say the ablest candidate deserves the scholarship, that the applicant who has the greatest capacity to perform the job deserves to be offered it, that (in advance of the race) the fastest runner deserves to win it. Here past performance may yield evidence that the person in question does have the qualities that we attribute to her, but the basis for desert seems to be the quality itself rather than the performance. It is sometimes suggested that we should mark this contrast by talking of *merit* rather than desert in these cases.

'Merit is often understood in the same sense as desert, but it is useful to distinguish the two, using merit to refer to the personal qualities a man may possess, and desert to refer to the deeds he has done.'[9]

Although this distinction is a useful one, I propose that merit judgements of this kind are best understood as secondary desert judgements deriving their moral force from others that are primary. Roughly speaking, when we say that a person deserves some benefit on the basis of a quality, we are anticipating a future performance in which that quality is displayed. When we identify A as the fastest runner and say that he deserves to win, we mean that we expect him to turn in a performance when the race takes place such that he will deserve to win.[10] Of course for unforeseen reasons the race may not take place, and even when it does there are a number of factors that may interfere with A's performance that would not lead us to revise our original judgment, so we are not offering a prediction, but something like a *ceteris paribus* judgement. The same applies to the scholarship case, in which the person who deserves it is the person who, other things being equal, will subsequently perform at the highest level, and, as I try to show elsewhere,[11] to the case of deserving a job.

If a judgement of merit cannot be linked in this way to an anticipated performance, then we do not have desert in its proper meaning. Thus when we say, to take a well-worn case, that Miss Australia deserves to win the Miss World contest because we think she's the best-looking contestant, we are simply assessing her according to the criteria used in this contest; we are saying that she fits the criteria best. The judgement involved is really no different from the judgement we might make about the finest dahlia in the annual flower show. It is what I call a 'sham desert' judgement. Sham desert judgements are those in which 'A deserves B' means no more than 'It is right or fitting for A to be given B' without the grounds for the judgement being performance-based desert as identified above. These include cases where the 'deserving' A is not a human agent ('Horses deserve to spend their last years in comfort'), cases in which we think A is entitled to some benefit under the rules ('They changed the closing date without telling anyone, so Smith deserves to have his application considered'), cases in which we think A needs or can make good use of B ('All patients deserve access to the best available medical care') and cases in which we just think that enjoying B is appropriate to the occasion ('After that piece of good news we all deserve a drink'). In all these cases we could replace 'deserves' with 'should have' and absolutely nothing would be lost, whereas in the case of genuine desert judgements 'deserves' supplies the *ground* for 'should have'. We appeal to desert to explain why somebody should be given or allowed to enjoy a benefit, and it is implicit here that there might be reasons of other kinds to which we are *not* appealing.

III

I now turn briefly to the relationship between desert and *luck*. To what extent can we say that people are deserving when we know that their performances have been affected by different kinds of luck? By luck here I mean random events outside of the agent's control. Luck affects performance in two ways. On the one hand, the performance itself – what the agent actually achieves – may depend to a greater or lesser extent on his luck. I gave the example earlier of a poor archer who shoots three lucky arrows and wins the competition. I shall label luck of this kind 'integral luck'. On the other hand, luck may determine whether someone has the opportunity to perform in the first place. The car carrying the athlete to the meeting may break down so that she has no chance to run. One soldier may be given an opportunity to show courage in battle, while another never gets within range of the enemy. Luck of this kind can be called 'circumstantial luck'.

Integral luck does appear to nullify desert. In other words, when we assess someone's performance in order to judge what he or she deserves, we try to factor out the effects of both good and bad luck. The athlete whose performance is affected by bad luck, such as being tripped by another competitor, may still deserve to win the race. Conversely, the entrepreneur who decides to manufacture a product which turns out unexpectedly to be a runaway success doesn't deserve all his gains – though here it will be much harder to separate genuine luck from an inspired hunch.[12]

It is a somewhat different story with circumstantial luck. It may be luck that a young scientist gets a job in a particular laboratory, but if he then does a pathbreaking piece of research, he may well deserve a Nobel Prize. The performance is entirely his, but it was to some extent a matter of luck that he was in a position to execute it. Equally it may be a matter of luck that I am walking by at the moment when a child falls into the river, but if I plunge in and rescue her then I deserve gratitude and reward in proportion to the difficulty and danger of my action. How can this be? Consider the position of a second person who claims to be equally deserving on the grounds that she, too, would have done the research or carried out the rescue if she had only been given the chance. Why would we reject her claims as unjustified?

Two reasons seem to count here. The first is epistemic: we can never really know what she might have done if luck had been on her side. Even if we know on other grounds that she is a good scientist, we can't tell whether she would have had the particular insight needed to crack the problem that the Nobel winner has cracked. Even if she can demonstrate that she has rescued other children in similar circumstances, we can't be sure that when the moment actually came she would have braced herself and jumped into the swirling river.

Even in cases where we can be relatively certain that Jones would have done what Smith actually did if his circumstantial luck had been better, however, we are still reluctant to say that Jones deserves what Smith does, and this is because our notion of desert tracks actual performance rather than hypothetical performance.[13] As noted, when integral luck plays a part, we adjust our estimate of the performance to eliminate its effects, so that the person who finishes third in the race may deserve to have won it if his coming third is due to bad luck. But the athlete who never makes it to the race track, and so does not put in a performance at all, cannot deserve to win. We feel sympathy for her, of course, and we may think that she is the victim of unfairness if her failure to appear stems from causes that the race authorities ought to have eliminated, but the unfairness does not consist in her failing to receive the medal she deserves.

Do differences in circumstantial luck have *any* effect on how much one person deserves compared with others? Whether they do depends on at least two factors. First, the benefit that is deserved may to a greater or lesser extent be competitive as between possible claimants. There can only be one Nobel Prize for chemistry in any given year, whereas there is no limit to the amount of gratitude that can be shown towards acts of kindness or courage. In the first case people who are lucky deservedly gain at the expense of the unlucky, and this may lead us to qualify our judgements somewhat. To the extent that we are convinced that several other scientists might easily have made the discovery that led to the award of the Nobel Prize had they been in a position to do so, we will see the actual winner as less deserving. He's still pretty deserving of course – not many could have solved that problem – but he's not much more deserving than several others who in the nature of the case are excluded from receiving Nobel prizes. In contrast, the rescuer who gets a case of champagne from the grateful parents of the salvaged child isn't standing in the way of some other rescuer being rewarded on some other occasion.

Second, to the extent that the impact of luck is itself under human control, a decision to allow greater scope to luck will reduce desert. Suppose, for example, that we decided to allocate jobs by lottery. Those who ended up in these jobs would still be more or less deserving than others – one would work

hard and skilfully, another would shirk, and so forth – but the random allocation would cast a shadow over these judgements. Many could legitimately
claim that it was only their bad luck in the draw that prevented them exercising their talents for science or music productively. How can Smith deserve
more than me for the work he is doing when I would have done as well or
better if given the chance? Desert is strengthened when opportunities to
become deserving themselves depend on the initiative and choice of individuals, and are not artificially distributed by some other human agency.

Integral luck nullifies desert, I have argued – we have to factor it out when
judging what people deserve on the basis of their performances – and circumstantial luck may lead us to qualify our judgements about the deserts of those
who are its beneficiaries. But if we want to keep the notion of desert and use it
to make practical judgements, we cannot compensate completely for luck of
the second kind. It is luck that I was born in the time and place that I was, with
the range of opportunities that my society provides. I become deserving by
taking these opportunities and producing intentional performances of an
appropriately valuable kind. Judgements about my deserts are not affected
by the fact that other people in different physical and social circumstances may
have very different sets of opportunities. Circumstantial luck always lies in the
background of human performances, and only when it intrudes in a fairly clear
and direct way on what different people achieve relative to one another do we
allow it to modify our judgements of desert.

IV

The performances on which everyday judgements of desert are based may
depend not only on people's circumstantial luck, but also on their natural
talents – the capacities and abilities with which they are genetically endowed.
These, too, can be regarded as a form of luck. No one has any control over their
natural endowments, though he can, of course, decide which of these endowments to develop and exercise. Ought we therefore to discount natural talents
when estimating desert, factoring out of people's performances whatever
depends on natural talent? Many philosophers have thought so.[14]

If followed through consistently, this suggestion, I shall argue, would sabo-
tage the whole notion of desert rather than, as its proponents believe, refining
its moral quality. Note, first, that according to the concept of desert being
defended here, people can deserve benefits only on the basis of intentional
performances, so though the performance may depend on natural talent – as in
the case of the athletic examples I have been using – it also requires choice and
effort. The desert is based on the *performance*, not the talent that may be its
necessary condition. Where there is not even an anticipated performance, as
there is in the case of secondary desert judgements, there can be no desert. It
follows that people cannot deserve anything merely for *having*, as opposed to
exercising, talents. Whenever people are judged meritorious on the basis of

native endowments alone – as in the beauty contest case – we only have sham desert judgements.

Second, even those who want to say that having a talent is merely luck would, I think, concede that luck of this sort has a less negative impact on desert than other kinds either of integral or of circumstantial luck.[15] Consider two mountaineers setting out to scale Everest; one succeeds, the other fails. What does each deserve? The second had bad luck in the form of adverse weather and a rope that unexpectedly broke; she was also physically weaker than the first. It would be very odd to treat these as equivalent kinds of luck. We would want to factor out the weather and the broken rope as far as we were able, because these were external to the second climber's performance, the skill and determination she showed. Perhaps on this basis she deserved to reach the top, to have her achievement commemorated in some way. But her physical strength was integral to her performance; indeed it was partly what made it *her* performance as opposed to anyone else's. So to discount it, and to say that what she deserved was what she would have achieved had she been stronger, would be decidedly strange.

Conceding these points, the critic of talent-dependent desert may still argue that one person can only deserve more than another, in the morally relevant sense of desert, on the basis of those aspects of his performance that are under his voluntary control. Let us begin to think through the implications of this principle. Consider a performance that depends on natural talent, such as climbing Everest or playing a Beethoven concerto at concert level. In cases like this the performer must (a) have chosen and worked to turn a natural ability like manual dexterity into a developed talent like musical skill; and (b) have decided to deploy the talent so as to produce the performance – to spend his evening playing a concerto rather than watching television. These choices and exertions are presumably what the critic would want to count as *genuine* desert bases. But now observe that these voluntary acts take place against the background of unchosen factors: on the one hand the performer's native talents, on the other his tastes and preferences (insofar as these are not themselves subject to choice). The person who decides that she wants to become a mountaineer does so on the basis of what she knows about her physical capacities, and also on the basis of her liking for being out in the open air. Of course tastes and preferences can to some extent be cultivated; but they are usually cultivated on the basis of other existing tastes and capacities.[16]

My point is that a greater or lesser element of contingency enters into even those elements of performance that the purist about desert would want to allow in as possible bases. If we say that the concert pianist deserves applause, not for his performance as such, since this depends in part on his natural talents, but for what is left over when the effect of natural talent is removed – the choice and effort involved in raising himself to this level – then we immediately have to recognize that his making those choices and efforts itself depends on contingencies that are not under his control. He did not choose to be born dexterous and with a good musical ear. Other people have not been confronted with the same range of options as this person.

If, in the light of this argument, our critic decides to retreat still further in his search for a desert basis that is not affected by contingencies outside of the agent's control, he is likely to end up saying, with Kant, that the only possible basis is the good will – deciding for moral reasons to try to act in this way rather than that. If Kant is right, moral reasons are completely independent of preferences, and since all that matters is the will to act and not the outcome, the agent's natural talents as well as his external circumstances become irrelevant to his desert.[17] I happen to think that Kant is wrong, but the main point to note here is that desert shrinks to within a tiny fraction of its normal range.[18] We can no longer talk about athletes deserving medals, workers deserving wages, soldiers deserving military honours, parents deserving their children's gratitude, and so on. All we are left to talk about is people deserving moral praise or blame for deciding to act rightly or wrongly.

We therefore stand at a parting of the ways. Do we want to continue using a concept of desert that is able to guide us in making our distributive decisions, as individuals or as a political community, or should we remove it from the armoury of social justice and use it only to make individual moral appraisals?[19] We may, of course, decide that the concept is so fraught with difficulties that we should dispense with it altogether, as Rawls and utilitarians like Sidgwick effectively recommend.[20] But if we decide that we want to keep the concept in a form that captures most of the desert judgements people actually make, then we cannot hope to find a basis for desert that is untouched by contingency. What we need instead is the idea of an agent and a performance, where the performance is intended and controlled by the agent, but makes use of qualities and characteristics that are integral to him or her – natural tastes and abilities among them.[21] We want to factor out luck proper – features of the environment like the fraying rope that makes the agent's performance turn out differently from what she might reasonably have expected – but if we try to eliminate contingency of every kind we find that our judgements are directed at a radically thinned-down idea of the human agent. Instead of assessing the deserts of flesh-and-blood actors who make a visible impact on the world, we find ourselves at best judging the qualities of Kantian noumenal wills.

V

What role can judgements of desert play in our thinking about social justice? How far can we use them to specify a determinate allocation of social resources? To answer these questions, it is helpful to separate desert judgements into different categories, according to their level of determinacy. I shall distinguish four such categories, beginning with the least determinate.

In the first category are judgements to the effect that certain benefits are *not* deserved because they have been allocated by criteria that have nothing to do with desert – for instance when hiring decisions are affected by the race, sex, or religious affiliation of the job applicants. Such judgements seem relatively unproblematic. In order to make them, we do not have to assume very much about the grounds of desert itself (e.g. in virtue of which capacities or performances people deserve to be hired for jobs). All we need to know is that race, sex or religious affiliation *cannot* be such grounds. And they guide our thinking about social justice when we condemn practices that discriminate between people on irrelevant grounds like social background or sex.

In the second category are claims that when two people are equally deserving, it is unjust if one receives more benefit than the other. Claims of this kind are often made in support of uniform treatment – e.g. if workers in one part of the company are being paid more than workers in another part for doing jobs that are essentially similar in nature. On a wider scale 'comparable worth' legislation is guided by the same ideal.[22] These claims require identification of the relevant desert basis, and judgements to the effect that two individuals or two groups have performed equally by that standard, but they do not require us to say how much *absolutely* any given individual or group deserves – say what absolute level of income a particular job should command. These claims, too, feature frequently in debates about social justice.

In the third category we find more ambitious comparative claims to the effect that there is a disproportion between what group A is receiving by virtue of P and what group A' is receiving by virtue of P'. Examples here would be the claim that nurses are grossly underpaid in comparison to doctors, or the claim that it is unfair if equivalent honours are given to civil servants simply for doing their jobs as to private citizens who have performed supererogatory acts of public service. These claims require us first to make comparative judgements about the deserts of different groups of individuals, and then to make judgements about what, comparatively, would be suitable requital. Such judgements may be more or less precise. In many cases all that is required is an ordinal ranking. If we have to allocate prizes, we have to judge who has written the best book, for instance, perhaps also who should get second prize, but we aren't required to say that the winner has performed 10% better than the runner-up; similarly if we have to allocate a limited number of college places among a pool of applicants. In other cases what we are doing is essentially grading performances, placing them in a number of bands. When implementing a system of military honours, for instance, we have to be able to say that this action displayed the highest form of courage and deserves the Victoria Cross; that action was courageous but less so and deserves the DSO. Where cardinal judgements do have to be made, we are most confident when performances can be judged along a single dimension: we are reasonably happy about attaching numbers to performances in academic tests ('Smith deserves a 65 for that essay, but Jones doesn't deserve more than 58 for his'), far less happy about estimating the worth of different and unrelated jobs, say, where several possible standards of value may conflict (How much is the work of a university teacher worth? It may contribute to knowledge, but how much does it contribute to GDP?)

When used in this way our concept of desert constrains the set of just social distributions without fully determining how different groups should be treated comparatively to one another. If one society pays its doctors five times as much as its manual workers, while another society pays them only three times as much, we cannot say simply by appealing to desert that one of them is more just than the other. The judgements that we can justifiably make are not sufficiently determinate (they are however determinate enough for us to say that a society that pays its doctors *less* than its manual workers is virtually certain to be unjust).[23]

Finally we come to non-comparative judgements of desert: judgements to the effect that people who have performed P deserve some identifiable benefit B without reference to what others have done or are getting. Such judgements, I believe, play at best a marginal role in our thinking about social justice. They are more important in two other contexts. One is in discussions of punishment.[24] When we say that no one deserves to be hanged for stealing a sheep, we are not saying merely that this penalty is disproportionate to others, but that there is an absolute lack of fit between the wrong committed and the proposed penalty. The other is in the sphere of personal relations. Good deeds may deserve gratitude, where the amount of gratitude it is appropriate to feel and express is not dependent on what has been shown to others on similar occasions. And Feinberg has drawn attention to the justice of judgements, where the unfairness of the judgement that A's book is secondrate and derivative does not depend on the judgements passed on the works of others.[25] But if we are thinking about desert of property, positions, prizes, honours, income and so forth, then our judgements are at best judgements about what A deserves in comparison to others.[26]

To sum up, I have argued that we have a coherent concept of desert that is sufficiently independent of our existing institutions for it to serve as a critical weapon in the armoury of social justice. A just society is, in considerable part, a society whose institutions are arranged so that people get the benefits they deserve, and many legitimate complaints about existing societies appeal to this principle. But considerations of desert do not fully determine these institutional arrangements. They do not, for instance, tell us whether we should award prizes for athletic prowess or literary merit at all; nor do they tell us precisely how wide the dispersion of incomes should be. I have tried to steer a course between the view that desert is merely a formal principle that comes into play once we have decided what institutions to establish and the view that it tells us how everything in a society should be distributed. Because it is not wholly determinate, desert leaves room for other principles of justice to operate, as well as contrasting values such as efficiency and social equality.[27] A society can give people what they deserve, but also set resources aside to cater for needs, and be guided in economic matters in part by considerations of efficiency. This is a welcome result.

Notes

1   See the evidence cited in *Principles of Social Justice*, ch. 4.
2   J. Rawls, *A Theory of Justice* (Cambridge, Mass.: Harvard University Press, 1971), sect. 48; S. Scheffler, *Boundaries and Allegiances: Problems of Justice and Responsibility in Liberal Thought* (Oxford: Oxford University Press, 2001), ch. 10.
3   Since my underlying interest is in distributive justice as opposed to the justice of punishment, I shall examine what it means to deserve benefits without asking how far the analysis can be extended to desert of harms. My method is to attempt to identify the core idea that lies behind everyday judgements of desert, and then to see how far this idea can survive the various critical attacks that philosophers have launched against it. At the same time I appeal to these judgements in order to set aside various restrictive or revisionary accounts of desert found in the philosophical literature.
4   In cases of coercion some desert may persist, since the coerced agent may, for instance, still have choices to make, albeit from a restricted range of options, or may be able to display a greater or lesser degree of skill in carrying out the task she is coerced into performing. It remains true that if one is coerced into doing X one's deserts are typically less extensive than if one does X freely.
5   Although under the rules of the competition I am obviously entitled to receive it. I explore the relationship between desert and entitlement more fully in the longer version of this chapter, *Principles of Social Justice*, ch. 7.
6   Among these is Rawls, who formulates the desert principle as 'Justice is happiness according to virtue' (*Theory of Justice*, p. 310) and then proceeds to criticize it on this interpretation. I have discussed Rawls's critique of desert briefly in *Market, State, and Community: Theoretical Foundations of Market Socialism* (Oxford: Clarendon Press, 1989), pp. 158–9, and in *Principles of Social Justice*, pp. 138–41. Hayek is another who assumes that desert must be moral desert; I discuss his views in *Principles of Social Justice*, ch. 9.
7   This argument is well made in J. Lamont, 'The Concept of Desert in Distributive Justice', *Philosophical Quarterly*, 44 (1994), 45–64.
8   P. Strawson, 'Freedom and Resentment', in G. Watson (ed.), *Free Will* (Oxford: Oxford University Press, 1982). The connection between desert and a view of human beings as free agents is also stressed in J. Lucas, *On Justice* (Oxford: Clarendon Press, 1980), ch. 11. 'If we deny people their deserts, we are not really treating them as persons because we are taking them for granted. They are not in our eyes autonomous agents who had it in their power to act or not to act, but merely natural phenomena which we have been manipulating at our will' (p. 202).
9   Lucas, *On Justice*, p. 166. See also J. Lucas, *Responsibility* (Oxford: Clarendon Press, 1993), pp. 124–6.
10   Notice, however, that statements such as 'A deserves to win the 1500 metres' may have different meanings and invoke different desert-bases in different contexts. The desert at issue can be based on past performance: 'Jones has trained far harder than the other competitors; though he's not likely to, he really deserves to win this race'. It can be based on present performance viewed retrospectively: 'Smith deserved to win; it wasn't his fault that he got badly boxed in on the last bend'. Finally, as indicated in the text, it can be based on anticipated future

performance: 'Brown is the outstanding athlete in the field; he really deserves to win'.

11   *Principles of Social Justice*, ch. 8.

12   It is not clear to me whether the factoring out goes all the way, or whether a residue is left in the sense that the actual performance still counts for something despite its elements of contingency. In the case in which someone does something harmful, it seems that there is a residue. To use an example of Nagel's, we think that a negligent lorry driver who kills a child deserves more blame and punishment than an equally negligent driver who is lucky enough not to have a child cross his path (T. Nagel, 'Moral Luck', in *Mortal Questions* (Cambridge: Cambridge University Press, 1991)). This can be explained partly on epistemic grounds: we know that the first driver was acting dangerously, whereas we can't be certain in the second case that some countervailing factor might not have eliminated the negligence (for example, that a driver who drove too fast by normal standards didn't have exceptionally good reflexes). (See N. Richards, 'Luck and Desert', *Mind*, 95 (1986), 198–209, for an explanation along these lines.) My view, however, is that the epistemic explanation doesn't account for everything, and that desert in such cases irreducibly depends, in part, on the actual nature or consequences of the actor's performance; I am less sure, though, whether this is also true when we are considering desert of prizes and other advantages.

13   As Nagel puts it, 'we judge people for what they actually do or fail to do, not just for what they would have done if circumstances had been different' ('Moral Luck', p. 34).

14   These include Rawls, *Theory of Justice*, sects. 17 and 48; J. Rachels, 'What People Deserve', in J. Arthur and W. H. Shaw (eds.), *Justice and Economic Distribution* (Englewood Cliffs, NJ: Prentice-Hall, 1978); W. Sadurski, *Giving Desert its Due: Social Justice and Legal Theory* (Dordrecht: D. Reidel, 1985), ch. 5; T. Campbell, *Justice* (London: Macmillan, 1988), esp. ch. 6.

15   In an interesting discussion of the causes of social inequality, Nagel gives reasons that inequalities deriving from differences in talent are commonly regarded as less unjust than inequalities arising from discrimination or from inherited class differences. See T. Nagel, *Equality and Partiality* (New York: Oxford University Press, 1991), ch. 10.

16   On this point see A. T. Kronman, 'Talent Pooling', in J. R. Pennock and J. W. Chapman (eds.), *Nomos 23: Human Rights* (New York: New York University Press, 1981).

17   See the discussion of Kant in Nagel, 'Moral Luck'. The original source is I. Kant, *Foundations of the Metaphysics of Morals* (Indianapolis: Bobbs-Merrill, 1959), First Section.

18   Wrong about the nature of morality. But one might also ask, more specifically, whether he is correct in supposing that a person's capacity to will rightly is unaffected by contingent facts about him such as his preferences and natural capacities.

19   I present this as a stark choice, though there may be intermediate possibilities: for instance, it is sometimes argued that because of worries about desert we should not allow people's incomes to depend on differences in their economic performance, though we might permit such differences to be recognized in other ways – by tokens of esteem, for instance. (See, for instance, G. Marshall, A. Swift and

S. Roberts, *Against the Odds? Social Class and Social Justice in Industrial Societies* (Oxford: Clarendon Press, 1997), p. 166.) I am not, however, convinced that this is a cogent proposal. Although there may be other grounds for preferring tokens to cash as a way of recognizing desert (considerations of need, for instance), if it is wrong in principle to reward people for their talent-dependent performances, then *any* form of reward, material or immaterial, is wrong. Conversely, if people do deserve differently on this basis, I cannot see what argument would rule out financial rewards as an appropriate form of requital.

20   According to Rawls, 'desert is understood as entitlement acquired under fair conditions' (J. Rawls, *Justice as Fairness; A Restatement* (Cambridge, Mass.: Harvard University Press, 1990), p. 64). According to Sidgwick, 'the only tenable Determinist interpretation of desert is, in my opinion, the Utilitarian: according to which, when a man is said to deserve reward for any services to society, the meaning is that it is expedient to reward him, in order that he and others may be induced to render similar services by the expectation of similar rewards' (H. Sidgwick, *The Methods of Ethics*, 7th edn. (London: Macmillan, 1963), p. 284). Note that both Rawls and Sidgwick are happy to continue using the *words* 'desert' and 'deserves' so long as their meaning is transformed as each of them proposes.

21   As Sher puts this point, we need the idea of a self with its constitutive preferences and abilities. 'No being that did not stand in some suitably intimate relation to its preferences, values, skills, talents and abilities could choose and act in the full sense.' (G. Sher, *Desert* (Princeton: Princeton University Press, 1987), p. 159.)

22   This is legislation aimed primarily at eliminating the gap between men's and women's levels of pay by applying the principle of equal pay for work of equal value, regardless of whether the work is traditionally done by men or by women.

23   Can we imagine a society in which manual work is genuinely valued more highly than medical practice? Hypothetically we can, but it is interesting to find that in the Soviet Union, which in its heyday went to great lengths to glorify manual labour, the occupation of doctor was still ranked considerably above that of manual worker. See A. Inkeles, *The Soviet Citizen: Daily Life in a Totalitarian Society* (Cambridge, Mass.: Harvard University Press, 1959), pp. 76–80, for evidence to this effect.

24   See J. Feinberg, 'Noncomparative Justice', *Philosophical Review*, 83 (1974), 297–338.

25   Ibid.

26   I have explored the comparative and non-comparative aspects of desert judgements in much greater detail in 'Comparative and Non-Comparative Desert', in S. Olsaretti (ed.), *Desert and Justice* (Oxford: Oxford University Press, 2003). In this article I also examine further the role played by judgements of desert in our thinking about social justice.

27   For discussion of how desert and social equality may be reconciled, see my articles 'Complex Equality', in D. Miller and M. Walzer (eds.), *Pluralism, Justice and Equality* (Oxford: Oxford University Press, 1995), and 'Equality and Market Socialism', in P. Bardhan and J. Roemer (eds.), *Market Socialism: the Current Debate* (New York: Oxford University Press, 1993).

Part III

Issues

9

The Family: Gender and Justice

Susan Moller Okin

I. Introduction

We as a society pride ourselves on our democratic values. We don't believe people should be constrained by innate differences from being able to achieve desired positions of influence or to improve their well-being; equality of opportunity is our professed aim.... Yet substantial inequalities between the sexes still exist in our society. In economic terms, full-time working women (after some very recent improvement) earn on average 71 percent of the earnings of full-time working men. One-half of poor and three-fifths of chronically poor households with dependent children are maintained by a single female parent. The poverty rate for elderly women is nearly twice that for elderly men.[1] On the political front, two out of a hundred U.S. senators are women, one out of nine justices seems to be considered sufficient female representation on the Supreme Court, and the number of men chosen in each congressional election far exceeds the number of women elected in the entire history of the country. Underlying and intertwined with all these inequalities is the unequal distribution of the unpaid labor of the family.

An equal sharing between the sexes of family responsibilities, especially child care, is "the great revolution that has not happened."[2] Women, including mothers of young children, are, of course, working outside the household far more than their mothers did. And the small proportion of women who reach high-level positions in politics, business, and the professions command a vastly disproportionate amount of space in the media, compared with the millions of women who work at low-paying, dead-end jobs, the millions who do part-time work with its lack of benefits, and the millions of others who stay home performing for no pay what is frequently not even acknowledged as

Extracts from Susan Moller Okin, *Justice, Gender, and the Family* (New York: Basic Books, 1989), pp. 3–6, 89, 103–5, 170–2, 173, 175–7, 180–2, 183–6, 187 (notes), 197 (notes).

work. Certainly, the fact that women are doing more paid work does not imply that they are more equal. It is often said that we are living in a postfeminist era. This claim, due in part to the distorted emphasis on women who have "made it," is false, no matter which of its meanings is intended. It is certainly not true that feminism has been vanquished, and equally untrue that it is no longer needed because its aims have been fulfilled. Until there is justice within the family, women will not be able to gain equality in politics, at work, or in any other sphere.

The typical current practices of family life, structured to a large extent by gender, are not just. Both the expectation and the experience of the division of labor by sex make women vulnerable. As I shall show, a cycle of power relations and decisions pervades both family and workplace, each reinforcing the inequalities between the sexes that already exist within the other. Not only women, but children of both sexes, too, are often made vulnerable by gender-structured marriage. One-quarter of children in the United States now live in families with only one parent – in almost 90 percent of cases, the mother. Contrary to common perceptions – in which the situation of never-married mothers looms largest – 65 percent of single-parent families are a result of marital separation or divorce.[3] Recent research in a number of states has shown that, in the average case, the standard of living of divorced women and the children who live with them plummets after divorce, whereas the economic situation of divorced men tends to be better than when they were married.

A central source of injustice for women these days is that the law, most noticeably in the event of divorce, treats more or less as equals those whom custom, workplace discrimination, and the still conventional division of labor within the family have made very unequal. Central to this socially created in-equality are two commonly made but inconsistent presumptions: that women are primarily responsible for the rearing of children; and that serious and committed members of the work force (regardless of class) do not have pri-mary responsibility, or even shared responsibility, for the rearing of children. The old assumption of the workplace, still implicit, is that workers have wives at home. It is built not only into the structure and expectations of the work-place but into other crucial social institutions, such as schools, which make no attempt to take account, in their scheduled hours or vacations, of the fact that parents are likely to hold jobs.

Now, of course, many wage workers do not have wives at home. Often, they *are* wives and mothers, or single, separated, or divorced mothers of small children. But neither the family nor the workplace has taken much account of this fact. Employed wives still do by far the greatest proportion of unpaid family work, such as child care and housework. Women are far more likely to take time out of the workplace or to work part-time because of family responsi-bilities than are their husbands or male partners. And they are much more likely to move because of their husbands' employment needs or opportunities than their own. All these tendencies, which are due to a number of factors, including the sex segregation and discrimination of the workplace itself, tend to be cyclical in their effects: wives advance more slowly than their husbands at work and thus gain less seniority, and the discrepancy between their wages increases over time. Then, because both the power structure of the family and what is regarded as consensual "rational" family decision making reflect the fact that the husband usually earns more, it will become even less likely as time goes on that the unpaid work of the family will be shared between the spouses. Thus the cycle of inequality is perpetuated. Often hidden from view within a marriage, it is in the increasingly likely event of marital breakdown that the socially constructed inequality of married women is at its most visible.

This is what I mean when I say that gender-structured marriage *makes* women vulnerable. These are not matters of natural necessity, as some people would believe. Surely nothing in our natures dictates that men should not be equal participants in the rearing of their children. Nothing in the nature of work makes it impossible to adjust it to the fact that people are parents as well as workers. That these things have not happened is part of the historically, socially constructed differentiation between the sexes that feminists have come to call *gender*. We live in a society that has over the years regarded the innate characteristic of sex as one of the clearest legitimizers of different rights and restrictions, both formal and informal. While the legal sanctions that uphold male dominance have begun to be eroded in the past century, and more rapidly in the last twenty years, the heavy weight of tradition, combined with the effects of socialization, still works powerfully to reinforce sex roles that are commonly regarded as of unequal prestige and worth. The sexual division of labor has not only been a fundamental part of the marriage contract, but so deeply influences us in our formative years that feminists of both sexes who try to reject it can find themselves struggling against it with varying degrees of ambivalence. Based on this linchpin, "gender" – by which I mean *the deeply entrenched institutionalization of sexual difference* – still permeates our society....

II. Justice as Fairness and Gender

...Now, I turn to Rawls's theory of justice as fairness, to examine...what it *implies*, on the subjects of gender, women, and the family....I shall argue [that] a consistent and wholehearted application of Rawls's liberal principles of justice can lead us to challenge fundamentally the gender system of our society....

The critical impact of a feminist application of Rawls's theory comes chiefly from his second principle, which requires that inequalities be both "to the greatest benefit of the least advantaged" and "attached to offices and positions open to all."[4] This means that if any roles or positions analogous to our current sex roles – including those of husband and wife, mother and father – were to survive the demands of the first requirement, the second requirement would prohibit any linkage between these roles and sex. Gender, with its ascriptive designation of positions and expectations of behavior in accordance with the inborn characteristic of sex, could no longer form a legitimate part of the social structure, whether inside or outside the family. Three illustrations will help to link this conclusion with specific major requirements that Rawls makes of a just or well-ordered society.

First, after the basic political liberties, one of the most essential liberties is "the important liberty of free choice of occupation."[5] It is not difficult to see that this liberty is compromised by the assumption and customary expectation, central to our gender system, that women take far greater responsibility for housework and child care, whether or not they also work for wages outside the home. In fact, both the assignment of these responsibilities to women – resulting in their asymmetric economic dependence on men – and the related responsibility of husbands to support their wives compromise the liberty of choice of occupation of both sexes. But the customary roles of the two sexes inhibit women's choices over the course of a lifetime far more severely than those of men; it is far easier in practice to switch from being a wage worker to occupying a domestic role than to do the reverse. While Rawls has no objection to some aspects of the division of labor, he asserts that, in a well-ordered society, "no one need be servilely dependent on others and made to choose between monotonous and routine occupations which are deadening to human thought and sensibility" and that work will be "meaningful for all."[6] These conditions are far more likely to be met in a society that does not assign family responsibilities in a way that makes women into a marginal sector of the paid work force and renders likely their economic dependence upon men. Rawls's principles of justice, then, would seem to require a radical rethinking not only of the division of labor within families but also of all the nonfamily institutions that assume it.

Second, the abolition of gender seems essential for the fulfillment of Rawls's criterion for political justice. For he argues that not only would equal formal political liberties be espoused by those in the original position, but that any inequalities in the *worth* of these liberties (for example, the effects on them of factors like poverty and ignorance) must be justified by the difference principle. Indeed, "the constitutional process should preserve the equal representation of the original position to the degree that this is practicable."[7] While Rawls discusses this requirement in the context of class differences, stating that those who devote themselves to politics should be "drawn more or less equally from all sectors of society,"[8] it is just as clearly and importantly applicable to sex differences. The equal political representation of women and men, especially if they are parents, is clearly inconsistent with our gender system. The paltry number of women in high political office is an obvious indication of this. Since 1789, over 10,000 men have served in the United States House of Representatives, but only 107 women; some 1,140 men have been senators, compared with 15 women. Only one recent appointee, Sandra Day O'Connor, has ever served on the Supreme Court. These levels of representation of any other class constituting more than a majority of the population would surely be perceived as a sign that something is grievously wrong with the political system. But as British politician Shirley Williams recently said, until there is "a revolution in shared responsibilities for the family, in child care and in child rearing," there will not be "more than a very small number of women . . . opting for a job as demanding as politics."[9]

Finally, Rawls argues that the rational moral persons in the original position would place a great deal of emphasis on the securing of self-respect or self-esteem. They "would wish to avoid at almost any cost the social conditions that undermine self-respect," which is "perhaps the most important" of all the primary goods.[10] In the interests of this primary value, if those in the original position did not know whether they were to be men or women, they would surely be concerned to establish a thoroughgoing social and economic equality between the sexes that would protect either sex from the need to pander to or servilely provide for the pleasures of the other. They would emphasize the importance of girls' and boys' growing up with an equal sense of respect for themselves and equal expectations of self-definition and development. They would be highly motivated, too, to find a means of regulating pornography that did not seriously compromise freedom of speech. In general, they would be unlikely to tolerate basic social institutions that asymmetrically either forced or gave strong incentives to members of one sex to serve as sex objects for the other.

There is, then, implicit in Rawls's theory of justice a potential critique of gender-structured social institutions, which can be developed by taking seriously the fact that those formulating the principles of justice do not know their sex. . . .

III.   Addressing Gender Injustice

. . . In spite of all the rhetoric about equality between the sexes, the traditional or quasi-traditional division of family labor still prevails. Women are made vulnerable by constructing their lives around the expectation that they will be primary parents; they become more vulnerable within marriages in which they fulfill this expectation, whether or not they also work for wages; and they are most vulnerable in the event of separation or divorce, when they usually take over responsibility for children without adequate support from their ex-husbands. Since approximately half of all marriages end in divorce, about half of our children are likely to experience its dislocations, often made far more traumatic by the socioeconomic consequences of both gender-structured marriage and divorce settlements that fail to take account of it.[11] I have suggested that, for very important reasons, the family *needs* to be a just institution. . . . How can we address this injustice? . . .

I shall argue here that any just and fair solution to the urgent problem of women's and children's vulnerability must encourage and facilitate the equal sharing by men and women of paid and unpaid work, of productive and reproductive labor. We must work toward a future in which all will be likely to choose this mode of life. A just future would be one without gender. In its social structures and practices, one's sex would have no more relevance than one's eye color or the length of one's toes. No assumptions would be made about "male" and "female" roles; childbearing would be so conceptually separated from child rearing and other family responsibilities that it would be a cause for surprise, and no little concern, if men and women were not equally responsible for domestic life or if children were to spend much more time with one parent than the other. It would be a future in which men and women participated in more or less equal numbers in every sphere of life, from infant care to different kinds of paid work to high-level politics. Thus it would no longer be the case that having no experience of raising children would be the practical prerequisite for attaining positions of the greatest social influence. Decisions about abortion and rape, about divorce settlements and sexual harassment, or about any other crucial social issues would not be made, as they often are now, by legislatures and benches of judges overwhelmingly populated by men whose power is in large part due to their advantaged position in the gender structure. If we are to be at all true to our democratic ideals, moving away from gender is essential. Obviously, the attainment of such a social world requires major changes in a multitude of institutions and social settings outside the home, as well as within it.

Such changes will not happen overnight. Moreover, any present solution to the vulnerability of women and children that is just and respects individual freedom must take into account that most people currently live in ways that are greatly affected by gender, and most still favor many aspects of current, gendered practices. Sociological studies confirm what most of us already infer from our own personal and professional acquaintances: there are no currently shared meanings in this country about the extent to which differences between the sexes are innate or environmental, about the appropriate roles of men and women, and about which family forms and divisions of labor are most benefi-cial for partners, parents, and children. There are those, at one extreme, for whom the different roles of the two sexes, especially as parents, are deeply held tenets of religious belief. At the other end of the spectrum are those of us for whom the sooner all social differentiation between the sexes vanishes, the better it will be for all of us. And there are a thousand varieties of view in between. Public policies must respect people's views and choices. But they must do so only insofar as it can be ensured that these choices do not result, as they now do, in the vulnerability of women and children. Special protections must be built into our laws and public policies to ensure that, for those who choose it, the division of labor between the sexes does not result in injustice. In the face of these difficulties – balancing freedom and the effects of past choices against the needs of justice – I do not pretend to have arrived at any complete or fully satisfactory answers. But I shall attempt to suggest some social reforms, including changes in public policies and reforms of family law that may help us work toward a solution to the injustices of gender. . . . There are many directions that public policy can and should take in order to make relations between men and women more just....

First, public policies and laws should generally assume no social differentiation of the sexes. Shared parental responsibility for child care would be both assumed and facilitated. Few people outside of feminist circles seem willing to acknowledge that society does not have to choose between a system of female parenting that renders women and children seriously vulnerable and a system of total reliance on day care provided outside the home. While high-quality day care, subsidized so as to be equally available to all children, certainly constitutes an important part of the response that society should make in order to provide justice for women and children, it is only one part.[12] If we start out with the reasonable assumption that women and men are equally parents of their children, and have equal responsibility for both the unpaid effort that goes into caring for them and their economic support, then we must rethink the demands of work life throughout the period in which a worker of either sex is a parent of a small child. We can no longer cling to the by now largely mythical assumption that every worker has "someone else" at home to raise "his" children.

The facilitation and encouragement of equally shared parenting would require substantial changes.[13] It would mean major changes in the workplace, all of which could be provided on an entirely (and not falsely) gender-neutral basis. Employers must be required by law not only completely to eradicate sex discrimination, including sexual harassment. They should also be required to make positive provision for the fact that most workers, for differing lengths of time in their working lives, are also parents, and are sometimes required to nurture other family members, such as their own aging parents. Because children are borne by women but can (and, I contend, should) be raised by both parents equally, policies relating to pregnancy and birth should be quite distinct from those relating to parenting. Pregnancy and childbirth, to whatever varying extent they require leave from work, should be regarded as temporarily disabling conditions like any others, and employers should be mandated to provide leave for all such conditions.[14] Of course, pregnancy and childbirth are far *more* than simply "disabling conditions," but they should be treated as such for leave purposes, in part because their disabling effects vary from one woman to another. It seems unfair to mandate, say, eight or more weeks of leave for a condition that disables many women for less time and some for much longer, while *not* mandating leave for illnesses or other disabling conditions. Surely a society as rich as ours can afford to do both.

Parental leave during the postbirth months must be available to mothers and fathers on the same terms, to facilitate shared parenting; they might take sequential leaves or each might take half-time leave. All workers should have the right, without prejudice to their jobs, seniority, benefits, and so on, to work less than full-time during the first year of a child's life, and to work flexible or somewhat reduced hours at least until the child reaches the age of seven. Correspondingly greater flexibility of hours must be provided for the parents of a child with any health problem or disabling condition. The professions whose greatest demands (such as tenure in academia or the partnership hurdle in law) coincide with the peak period of child rearing must restructure their demands or provide considerable flexibility for those of their workers who are also participating parents. Large-scale employers should also be required to provide high-quality on-site day care for children from infancy up to school age. And to ensure equal quality of day care for all young children, *direct government subsidies* (not tax credits, which benefit the better-off) should make up the difference between the cost of high-quality day care and what less well paid parents could reasonably be expected to pay.

There are a number of things that schools, too, must do to promote the minimization of gender. As Amy Gutmann has recently noted, in their present authority structures (84 percent of elementary school teachers are female, while 99 percent of school superintendents are male), "schools do not simply reflect, they perpetuate the social reality of gender preferences when they educate children in a system in which men rule women and women rule children." She argues that, since such sex stereotyping is "a formidable obstacle" to children's rational deliberation about the lives they wish to lead, sex should be regarded as a relevant qualification in the hiring of both teachers and administrators, until these proportions have become much more equal.[15]

An equally important role of our schools must be to ensure in the course of children's education that they become fully aware of the politics of gender. This does not only mean ensuring that women's experience and women's writing are included in the curriculum, although this in itself is undoubtedly important.[16] Its political significance has become obvious from the amount of protest that it has provoked. Children need also to be taught about the present inequalities, ambiguities, and uncertainties of marriage, the facts of workplace discrimination and segregation, and the likely consequences of making life choices based on assumptions about gender. They should be discouraged from thinking about their futures as *determined* by the sex to which they happen to belong. For many children, of course, personal experience has already "brought home" the devastating effects of the traditional division of labor between the sexes. But they do not necessarily come away from this experience with positive ideas about how to structure their own future family lives differently. As Anita Shreve has recently suggested, "the old home-economics courses that used to teach girls how to cook and sew might give way to the new home economics: teaching girls *and boys* how to combine working and parenting."[17] Finally, schools should be required to provide high-quality after-school programs, where children can play safely, do their homework, or participate in creative activities. . . .

IV.   Protecting the Vulnerable

The pluralism of beliefs and modes of life is fundamental to our society, and the genderless society I have just outlined would certainly not be agreed upon by all as desirable. Thus when we think about constructing relations between the sexes that could be agreed upon in the original position, and are therefore just from all points of view, we must also design institutions and practices acceptable to those with more traditional beliefs about the characteristics of men and women, and the appropriate division of labor between them. It is essential, if men and women are to be allowed to so divide their labor, as they must be if we are to respect the current pluralism of beliefs, that society protect the vulnerable. Without such protection, the marriage contract seriously exacerbates the initial inequalities of those who entered into it, and too many women and children live perilously close to economic disaster and serious social dislocation; too many also live with violence or the continual threat of it. It should be noted here that the rights and obligations that the law would need to promote and mandate in order to protect the vulnerable need not – and should not – be designated in accordance with sex, but in terms of different functions or roles performed. There are only a minute percentage of "househusbands" in this country, and a very small number of men whose work lives take second priority after their wives'. But they can quite readily be protected by the same institutional structures that can protect traditional and quasi-traditional wives, so long as these are designed without reference to sex.

Gender-structured marriage, then, needs to be regarded as a currently necessary institution (because still chosen by some) but one that is socially problematic. It should be subjected to a number of legal requirements, at least when there are children.[18] Most important, there is no need for the division of labor between the sexes to involve the economic dependence, either complete or partial, of one partner on the other. Such dependence can be avoided if both partners have *equal legal entitlement* to all earnings coming into the household. The clearest and simplest way of doing this would be to have employers make out wage checks equally divided between the earner and the partner who provides all or most of his or her unpaid domestic services. In many cases, of course, this would not change the way couples actually manage their finances; it would simply codify what they already agree on – that the household income is rightly shared, because in a real sense jointly earned. Such couples recognize the fact that the wage-earning spouse is no more supporting the homemaking and child-rearing spouse than the latter is supporting the former; the form of support each offers the family is simply different. Such couples might well take both checks, deposit them in a joint account, and really share the income, just as they now do with the earnings that come into the household.

In the case of some couples, however, altering the entitlement of spouses to the earned income of the household as I have suggested *would* make a significant difference. It would make a difference in cases where the earning or higher-earning partner now directly exploits this power, by refusing to make significant spending decisions jointly, by failing to share the income, or by psychologically or physically abusing the nonearning or low-earning partner, reinforced by the notion that she (almost always the wife) has little option but to put up with such abuse or to take herself and her children into a state of destitution. It would make a difference, too, in cases where the higher-earning partner indirectly exploits this earning power in order to perpetuate the existing division of labor in the family. In such instances considerable changes in the balance of power would be likely to result from the legal and societal recognition that the partner who does most of the domestic work of the family contributes to its well-being just as much, and therefore rightly *earns* just as much, as the partner who does most of the workplace work.

What I am suggesting is *not* that the wage-working partner pay the home-making partner for services rendered. I do not mean to introduce the cash nexus into a personal relationship where it is inappropriate. I have simply suggested that since both partners in a traditional or quasi-traditional marriage work, there is no reason why only one of them should get paid, or why one should be paid far more than the other. The equal splitting of wages would constitute public recognition of the fact that the currently unpaid labor of families is just as important as the paid labor. If we do *not* believe this, then we should insist on the complete and equal sharing of both paid and unpaid labor, as occurs in the genderless model of marriage and parenting described earlier. It is only if we *do* believe it that society can justly allow couples to distribute the two types of labor so unevenly....

V.   Conclusion

I have suggested two basic models of family rights and responsibilities, both of which are currently needed because this is a time of great transition for men and women and great disagreement about gender. Families in which roles and responsibilities are equally shared regardless of sex are far more in accord with principles of justice than are typical families today. So are families in which those who undertake more traditional domestic roles are protected from the risks they presently incur. In either case, justice as a whole will benefit from the changes. Of the two, however, I claim that the genderless family is more just, in the three important respects that I spelled out at the beginning of this book: it is more just to women; it is more conducive to equal opportunity both for women and for children of both sexes; and it creates a more favorable environment for the rearing of citizens of a just society. Thus, while protecting those whom gender now makes vulnerable, we must also put our best efforts into promoting the elimination of gender.

The increased justice to women that would result from moving away from gender is readily apparent. Standards for just social institutions could no longer take for granted and exclude from considerations of justice much of what women now do, since men would share in it equally. Such central components of justice as what counts as productive labor, and what count as needs and deserts, would be greatly affected by this change. Standards of justice would become *humanist*, as they have never been before. One of the most important effects of this would be to change radically the situation of women as citizens. With egalitarian families, and with institutions such as workplaces and schools designed to accommodate the needs of parents and children, rather than being based as they now are on the traditional assumption that "someone else" is at home, mothers would not be virtually excluded from positions of influence in politics and the workplace. They would be represented at every level in approximately equal numbers with men.

In a genderless society, children too would benefit. They would not suffer in the ways that they do now because of the injustices done to women. It is undeniable that the family in which each of us grows up has a deeply formative influence on us – on the kind of persons we want to be as well as the kind of persons we are.[19] This is one of the reasons why one *cannot* reasonably leave the family out of "the basic structure of society," to which the principles of justice are to apply. Equality of opportunity to become what we want to be would be enhanced in two important ways by the development of families without gender and by the public policies necessary to support their development. First, the growing gap between the economic well-being of children in single-parent and those in two-parent families would be reduced. Children in single-parent families would benefit significantly if fathers were held equally responsible for supporting their children, whether married to their mothers or not; if more mothers had sustained labor force attachment; if high-quality day care were subsidized; and if the workplace were designed to accommodate parenting. These children would be far less likely to spend their formative years in conditions of poverty, with one parent struggling to fulfill the functions of two. Their life chances would be significantly enhanced.

Second, children of both sexes in gender-free families would have (as some already have) much more opportunity for self-development free from sex-role expectations and sex-typed personalities than most do now. Girls and boys who grow up in highly traditional families, in which sex difference is regarded as a determinant of everything from roles, responsibilities, and privileges to acceptable dress, speech, and modes of behavior, clearly have far less freedom to develop into whatever kind of person they want to be than do those who are raised without such constraints. It is too early for us to know a lot about the developmental outcomes and life choices of children who are equally parented by mothers and fathers, since the practice is still so recent and so rare. Persuasive theories such as Chodorow's, however, would lead us to expect much less differentiation between the sexes to result from truly shared parenting. Even now, in most cases without men's equal fathering, both the daughters and the sons of wage-working mothers have been found to have a more positive view of women and less rigid views of sex roles; the daughters (like their mothers) tend to have greater self-esteem and a more positive view of themselves as workers, and the sons, to expect equality and shared roles in their own future marriages.[20] We might well expect that with mothers in the labor force *and* with fathers as equal parents, children's attitudes and psychologies will become even less correlated with their sex. In a very crucial sense, their opportunities to become the persons they want to be will be enlarged.

Finally, it seems undeniable that the enhancement of justice that accompanies the disappearance of gender will make the family a much better place for children to develop a sense of justice. We can no longer deny the importance of the fact that families are where we first learn, by example and by how we are treated, not only how people do relate to each other but also how they *should*. How would families not built on gender be better schools of moral development? First, the example of co-equal parents with shared roles, combining love with justice, would provide a far better example of human relations for children than the domination and dependence that often occur in traditional marriage. The fairness of the distribution of labor, the equal respect, and the *inter*dependence of his or her parents would surely be a powerful first example to a child in a family with equally shared roles. Second, as I have argued, having a sense of justice requires that we be able to empathize, to abstract from our own situation and to think about moral and political issues from the points of view of others. We cannot come to either just principles or just specific decisions by thinking, as it were, as if we were nobody, or thinking from nowhere; we must, therefore, learn to think from the point of view of others, including others who are different from ourselves.

To the extent that gender is de-emphasized in our nurturing practices, this capacity would seem to be enhanced, for two reasons. First, if female primary parenting leads, as it seems to, to less distinct ego boundaries and greater capacity for empathy in female children, and to a greater tendency to self-definition and abstraction in males, then might we not expect to find the two capacities better combined in children of both sexes who are reared by parents of both sexes? Second, the experience of *being* nurturers, throughout a significant portion of our lives, also seems likely to result in an increase in empathy, and in the combination of personal moral capacities, fusing feelings with reason, that just citizens need.[21]

For those whose response to what I have argued here is the practical objection that it is unrealistic and will cost too much, I have some answers and some questions. Some of what I have suggested would not cost anything, in terms of public spending, though it would redistribute the costs and other responsibilities of rearing children more evenly between men and women. Some policies I have endorsed, such as adequate public support for children whose fathers cannot contribute, may cost more than present policies, but may not, depending on how well they work.[22] Some, such as subsidized high-quality day care, would be expensive in themselves, but also might soon be offset by other savings, since they would enable those who would otherwise be full-time child carers to be at least part-time workers.

All in all, it seems highly unlikely that the *long-term* costs of such programs – even if we count only monetary costs, not costs in human terms – would outweigh the long-term benefits. In many cases, the cycle of poverty could be broken – and children enabled to escape from, or to avoid falling into, it – through a much better early start in life.[23] But even if my suggestions would cost, and cost a lot, we have to ask: How much do we care about the injustices of gender? How much do we care that women who have spent the better part of their lives nurturing others can be discarded like used goods? How ashamed are we that one-quarter of our children, in one of the richest countries in the world, live in poverty? How much do we care that those who raise children, *because* of this choice, have restricted opportunities to develop the rest of their potential, and very little influence on society's values and direction? How much do we care that the family, our most intimate social grouping, is often a school of day-to-day injustice? How much do we *want* the just families that will produce the kind of citizens we need if we are ever to achieve a just society?

Notes

1   U.S. Department of Labor, *Employment and Earnings: July 1987* (Washington, D.C.: Government Printing Office, 1987); Ruth Sidel, *Women and Children Last: The Plight of Poor Women in Affluent America* (New York: Viking, 1986), pp. xvi, 158. See also David T. Ellwood, *Poor Support: Poverty in the American Family* (New York: Basic Books, 1988), pp. 84–5, on the chronicity of poverty in single-parent households. . . .
2   Shirley Williams, in Williams and Elizabeth Holtzman, "Women in the Political World: Observations," *Daedalus* 116, no. 4 (Fall 1987): 30.
3   Twenty-three percent of single parents have never been married and 12 percent are widowed (U.S. Bureau of the Census, Current Population Reports, *Household and Family Characteristics: March 1987* [Washington, D.C.: Government Printing Office, 1987], p. 79). In 1987, 6.8 percent of children under eighteen were living with a never-married parent ("Study Shows Growing Gap Between Rich and Poor," *New York Times*, March 23, 1989, p. A24). The proportions for the total population are very different from those for black families, of whom in 1984 half of those with adult members under thirty-five years of age were maintained by single, female parents, three-quarters of whom were never married (Frank Levy, *Dollars and Dreams: The Changing American Income Distribution* [New York: Russell Sage, 1987], p. 156).
4   Rawls, *A Theory of Justice* (Cambridge, MA: Harvard University Press, 1971), p. 302.
5   Ibid., p. 274.
6   Ibid., p. 529.
7   Ibid., p. 222; see also pp. 202–5, 221–8.
8   Ibid., p. 228.
9   Williams and Holtzman, "Women in the Political World: Observations." The statistics cited here are also from this article. Despite superficial appearances, the situation is no different in Great Britain. As of 1987, 41 out of the 630 members of the British House of Commons were women, and Margaret Thatcher is far more of an anomaly among British prime ministers than the few reigning queens have been among British monarchs.
10   Rawls, *Theory*, pp. 440, 396; see also pp. 178–9.

11   Okin cites the evidence for these claims in ch. 7 of *Justice, Gender, and the Family* [eds.].

12   It seems reasonable to conclude that the effects of day care on children are probably just as variable as the effects of parenting – that is to say, very widely variable depending on the quality of the day care and of the parenting. There is no doubt that good out-of-home day care is expensive – approximately $100 per full-time week in 1987, even though child-care workers are now paid only about two-thirds as much per hour as other comparably educated women workers (Victor Fuchs, *Women's Quest for Economic Equality* [Cambridge: Harvard University Press, 1988], pp. 137–8). However, it is undoubtedly easier to control its quality than that of informal "family day care." In my view, based in part on my experience of the excellent day-care center that our children attended for a total of seven years, good-quality day care must have small-scale "home rooms" and a high staff-to-child ratio, and should pay staff better than most centers now do. For balanced studies of the effects of day care on a poor population, see Sally Provence, Audrey Naylor, and June Patterson, *The Challenge of Daycare* (New Haven: Yale University Press, 1977); and, most recently, Lisbeth B. Schorr (with Daniel Schorr), *Within Our Reach – Breaking the Cycle of Disadvantage* (New York: Anchor Press, Doubleday, 1988), ch. 8.

13   Much of what I suggest here is not new; it has formed part of the feminist agenda for several decades, and I first made some of the suggestions I develop here in the concluding chapter of *Women in Western Political Thought* (Princeton: Princeton University Press, 1979). Three recent books that address some of the policies discussed here are Fuchs, *Women's Quest*, ch. 7; Philip Green, *Retrieving Democracy: In Search of Civic Equality* (Totowa, N.J.: Rowman and Allanheld, 1985), pp. 96–108; and Anita Shreve, *Remaking Motherhood: How Working Mothers Are Shaping Our Children's Future* (New York: Fawcett Columbine, 1987), pp. 173–8. In Fuchs's chapter he carefully analyzes the potential economic and social effects of alternative policies to improve women's economic status, and concludes that "child-centered policies" such as parental leave and subsidized day care are likely to have more of a positive impact on women's economic position than "labor market policies" such as antidiscrimination, comparable pay for comparable worth, and affirmative action have had and are likely to have. Some potentially very effective policies, such as on-site day care and flexible and/or reduced working hours for parents of young or "special needs" children, seem to fall within both of his categories.

14   The dilemma faced by feminists in the recent California case *Guerra v. California Federal Savings and Loan Association*, 107 S. Ct. 683 (1987) was due to the fact that state law mandated leave for pregnancy and birth that it did *not* mandate for other disabling conditions. Thus to defend the law seemed to open up the dangers of discrimination that the earlier protection of women in the workplace had resulted in. (For a discussion of this general issue of equality versus difference, see, for example, Wendy W. Williams, "The Equality Crisis: Some Reflections on Culture, Courts, and Feminism," *Women's Rights Law Reporter* 7, no. 3 [1982].) The Supreme Court upheld the California law on the grounds that it treated workers equally in terms of their rights to become parents.

15   Amy Gutmann, *Democratic Education* (Princeton: Princeton University Press, 1987), pp. 112–15; quotation from pp. 113–14. See also Elisabeth Hansot and David Tyack,

"Gender in American Public Schools: Thinking Institutionally," *Signs* 13, no. 4 (1988).

16   A classic text on this subject is Dale Spender, eds., *Men's Studies Modified: The Impact of Feminism on the Academic Disciplines* (Oxford: Pergamon Press, 1981).

17   Shreve, *Remaking Motherhood*, p. 237.

18   I see no reason why what I propose here should be restricted to couples who are legally married. It should apply equally to "common law" relationships that produce children, and in which a division of labor is practiced. Mary Ann Glendon has set out a "children first" approach to divorce (Glendon, *Abortion and Divorce in Western Law* [Cambridge, MA: Harvard University Press, 1987], pp. 94 ff.); here I extend the same idea to ongoing marriage, where the arrival of a child is most often the point at which the wife becomes economically dependent.

19   Here I paraphrase Rawls's wording in explaining why the basic structure of society is basic. "The Basic Structure as Subject," *American Philosophical Quarterly* 14, no. 2 (1977): 160 [For a revised version, see Rawls, *Political Liberalism*, Lecture VII, esp. sect. 5, eds.].

20   Shreve, *Remaking Motherhood*, chs. 3–7.

21   See, for example, Sara Ruddick, "Maternal Thinking," *Feminist Studies* 6, no. 2 (1980); Diane Ehrensaft, "When Women and Men Mother," in *Mothering: Essays in Feminist Theory*, ed. Joyce Trebilcot (Totowa, NJ: Rowman and Allanheld, 1984); Judith Kegan Gardiner, "Self Psychology as Feminist Theory," *Signs* 12, no. 4 (1987), esp. 778–80.

22   David Ellwood estimates that "if most absent fathers contributed the given percentages, the program would actually save money" (*Poor Support: Poverty in the American Family* (New York: Basic Books, 1988), p. 169).

23   Schorr's *Within Our Reach* documents the ways in which the cycle of disadvantage can be effectively broken, even for those in the poorest circumstances.

10

The Market: On the Site of Distributive Justice

G. A. Cohen

I

In this paper I defend a claim which can be expressed in the words of a now familiar slogan: the personal is political. That slogan, as it stands, is vague, but I shall mean something reasonably precise by it here, to wit, that principles of distributive justice, principles, that is, about the just distribution of benefits and burdens in society, apply, wherever else they do, to people's legally unconstrained choices. Those principles, so I claim, apply to the choices that people make *within* the legally coercive structures to which, so everyone would agree, principles of justice (also) apply. In speaking of the choices that people make *within* coercive structures, I do not include the choice whether or not to comply with the rules of such structures (to which choice, once again, so everyone would agree, principles of justice [also] apply), but the choices left open by those rules because neither enjoined nor forbidden by them.

The slogan that I have appropriated here is widely used by feminists.[1] More importantly, however, the idea itself, which I have here used the slogan to formulate, and which I have tried to explicate above, is a feminist idea. Notice, however, that, in briefly explaining the idea that I shall defend, I have not mentioned relations between men and women in particular, or the issue of sexism. We can distinguish between the substance and the form of the feminist critique of standard ideas about justice, and it is the form of it which is of prime concern to me here,[2] even though I also endorse its substance.

The substance of the feminist critique is that standard liberal theory of justice, and the theory of Rawls in particular, unjustifiably ignore an unjust division of labor, and unjust power relations, within families (whose legal structure *may* show no sexism at all). That is the key point of the feminist

G. A. Cohen, 'Where the Action Is: On the Site of Distributive Justice', from *Philosophy and Public Affairs*, 26 (1997), pp. 3–30.

critique, from a political point of view. But the (often merely implicit) form of the feminist critique, which we get when we abstract from its gender-centered content, is that choices not regulated by the law fall within the primary purview of justice, and that is the key lesson of the critique, from a theoretical point of view.

In defending the claim that the personal is political, the view that I oppose is the Rawlsian one that principles of justice apply only to what Rawls calls the "basic structure" of society. Feminists have noticed that Rawls wobbles, across the course of his writings, on the matter of whether or not the family belongs to the basic structure and is therefore, in his view, a site at which principles of justice apply. I shall argue that Rawls's wobble on this matter is not a case of mere indecision, which could readily be resolved in favor of inclusion of the family within the basic structure: that is the view of Susan Okin,[3] and, in my opinion, she is wrong about that. I shall show (in Section V below) that Rawls cannot admit the family into the basic structure of society without abandoning his insistence that it is to the basic structure only that principles of distributive justice apply. In supposing that he could include family relations, Okin shows failure to grasp the *form* of the feminist critique of Rawls.

II

I reach the conclusion announced above at the end of a trail of argument that runs as follows. Here, in Section II, I restate a criticism that I have made elsewhere of John Rawls's application of his difference principle,[4] to wit, that he does not apply it in censure of the self-seeking choices of high-flying marketeers, which induce an inequality that, so I claim, is harmful to the badly off. In Section III, I present an objection to my criticism of Rawls. The objection says that the difference principle is, by stipulation and design, a principle that applies only to social institutions (to those, in particular, which compose the basic structure of society), and, therefore, not one that applies to the choices, such as those of self-seeking high fliers, that people make *within* such institutions. Sections IV and V offer independent replies to that *basic structure objection*. I show, in Section IV, that the objection is inconsistent with many statements by Rawls about the role of principles of justice in a just society. I then allow that the discordant statements may be dropped from the Rawlsian canon, and, in Section V, I reply afresh to the basic structure objection, by showing that no defensible account of what the basic structure *is* allows Rawls to insist that the principles which apply to it do not apply to choices within it. I conclude that my original criticism of Rawls rests vindicated, against the particular objection in issue here. (Section VI comments on the implications of my position for the moral blamability of individuals whose choices violate principles of justice. The Endnote explores the distinction between coercive and noncoercive institutions, which plays a key role in the argument of Section V).

My criticism of Rawls is of his application of the difference principle. That principle says, in one of its formulations,[5] that inequalities are just if and only if they are necessary to make the worst off people in society better off than they would otherwise be. I have no quarrel here with the difference principle itself,[6] but I disagree sharply with Rawls on the matter of *which* inequalities pass the test for justifying inequality that it sets and, therefore, about how *much* inequality passes that test. In my view, there is hardly any serious inequality that satisfies the requirement set by the difference principle, when it is conceived, as Rawls himself proposes to conceive it,[7] as regulating the affairs of a society whose members themselves accept that principle. If I am right, affirmation of the difference principle implies that justice requires (virtually) unqualified equality itself, as opposed to the "deep inequalities" in initial life chances with which Rawls thinks justice to be consistent.[8]

It is commonly thought, for example by Rawls, that the difference principle licenses an argument for inequality which centers on the device of material incentives. The idea is that talented people will produce more than they otherwise would if, and only if, they are paid more than an ordinary wage, and some of the extra which they will then produce can be recruited on behalf of the worst off.[9] The inequality consequent on differential material incentives is said to be justified within the terms of the difference principle, for, so it is said, that inequality benefits the worst off people: the inequality is necessary for them to be positioned as well as they are, however paltry their position may nevertheless be.

Now, before I mount my criticism of this argument, a *caveat* is necessary with respect to the terms in which it is expressed. The argument focuses on a *choice* enjoyed by well-placed people who command a high salary in a market economy: they can choose to work more or less hard, and also to work at this occupation rather than that one, and for this employer rather than that one, in accordance with how well they are remunerated. These well-placed people, in the foregoing standard presentation of the argument, are designated as "the talented," and, for reasons to be given presently, I shall so designate them throughout my criticism of the argument. Even so, these fortunate people need not be thought to be talented, in any sense of that word which implies something more than a capacity for high market earnings, for the argument to possess whatever force it has. All that need be true of them is that *they are so positioned that, happily, for them, they do command a high salary and they can vary their productivity according to exactly how high it is*. But, as far as the incentives argument is concerned, their happy position could be due to circumstances that are entirely accidental, relative to whatever kind of natural or even socially induced endowment they posses. One need not think that the average dishwasher's endowment of strength, flair, ingenuity, and so forth falls below that of the average chief executive to accept the argument's message. One no doubt does need to think some such thing to agree with the different argument which justifies rewards to well-placed people in whole or in part as a fair return to exercise of unusual ability, but Rawls's theory is built around his rejection of such desert considerations. Nor are the enhanced rewards justified because extra contribution warrants extra reward on grounds of proper reciprocity. They are justified purely because they elicit more productive performance.

I nevertheless persist in designating the relevant individuals as "the talented," because to object that they are not actually especially talented *anyway* is to enter an empirical claim which is both contentious and, in context, misleading, since it would give the impression that it should matter to our assessment of the incentives argument whether or not well-placed people merit the contestable designation. The particular criticism of the incentives argument that I shall develop is best understood in its specificity when the apparently concessive word "talented" is used: it does not indicate a concession on the factual question of how top people in a market society get to be where they are. My use of the argument's own terms shows the strength of my critique of it: that critique stands even if we make generous assumptions about how well-placed people secured their powerful market positions. It is, moreover, especially appropriate to make such assumptions here, since the Rawlsian difference principle is lexically secondary to his principle that fair equality of opportunity has been enforced with respect to the attainment of desired positions: if anything ensures that those who occupy them possess superior creative endowment, that does. (Which is not to say that it indeed ensures that: it is consistent with fair equality of opportunity that what principally distinguishes top people is superior cunning and/or prodigious aggressivity, and nothing more admirable.)

Now, for the following reasons, I believe that the incentives argument for inequality represents a distorted application of the difference principle, even though it is its most familiar and perhaps even its most persuasive application. Either the relevant talented people themselves affirm the difference principle or they do not. That is: either they themselves believe that inequalities are unjust if they are not necessary to make the badly off better off, or they do not believe that to be a dictate of justice. If they do not believe it, then their society is not just in the appropriate Rawlsian sense, for a society is just, according to Rawls, only if its members themselves affirm and uphold the correct principles of justice. The difference principle might be appealed to in justification of a government's toleration, or promotion, of inequality in a society in which the talented do not themselves accept it, but it then justifies a public policy of inequality in a society some members of which – the talented – do not share community with the rest:[10] their behavior is then taken as fixed or parametric, a datum vis-à-vis a principle applied to it from without, rather than as itself answerable to that principle. That is not how principles of justice operate in a just society, as Rawls specifies that concept: within his terms, one may distinguish between a just society and a just government, one, that is, which applies just principles to a society whose members may not themselves accept those principles.

So we turn to the second and only remaining possibility, which is that the talented people do affirm the difference principle, that, as Rawls says, they apply the principles of justice *in their daily life* and achieve a sense of their own justice in doing so.[11] But they can then be asked why, in the light of their own belief in the principle, they require more pay than the untalented get, for work that may indeed demand special talent, but which is not specially unpleasant (for no such consideration enters the Rawlsian justification of incentives-derived inequality). The talented can be asked whether the extra they get is *necessary* to enhance the position of the worst off, which is the only thing, according to the difference principle, that could justify it. Is it necessary *tout court*, that is, independently of human will, so that, with all the will in the world, removal of inequality would make everyone worse off? Or is it necessary only insofar as the talented would *decide* to produce less than they now do, or not to take up posts where they are in special demand, if inequality were removed (by, for example, income taxation which redistributes to fully egalitarian effect[12])?

Talented people who affirm the difference principle would find those questions hard to handle. For they could not claim, *in self-justification*, at the bar of the difference principle, that their high rewards are necessary to enhance the position of the worst off, since, in the standard case,[13] it is they themselves who *make* those rewards necessary, through their own unwillingness to work for ordinary rewards as productively as they do for exceptionally high ones, an unwillingness which ensures that the untalented get less than they otherwise would. Those rewards are, therefore, necessary only because the choices of talented people are not appropriately informed by the difference principle.

Apart, then, from the very special cases in which the talented literally *could* not, as opposed to the normal case where they (merely) would not, perform as productively as they do without superior remuneration, the difference principle can justify inequality only in a society where not everyone accepts that very principle. It therefore cannot justify inequality in the appropriate Rawlsian way.

Now, this conclusion about what it means to accept and implement the difference principle implies that the justice of a society is not exclusively a function of its legislative structure, of its legally imperative rules, but also of the choices people make within those rules. The standard (and, in my view, misguided) Rawlsian application of the difference principle can be modeled as follows. There is a market economy all agents in which seek to maximize their own gains, and there is a Rawlsian state that selects a tax function on income that maximizes the income return to the worst off people, within the constraint that, because of the self-seeking motivation of the talented, a fully equalizing taxation system would make everyone worse off than one which is less than fully equalizing. But this double-minded modeling of the implementation of the difference principle, with citizens inspired by justice endorsing a state policy which plays a tax game against (some of) them in their manifestation as self-seeking economic agents, is wholly out of accord with the (sound) Rawlsian requirement on a just society that its citizens themselves willingly submit to the standard of justice embodied in the difference principle. A society that is just within the terms of the difference principle, so we may conclude, requires not simply just coercive *rules*, but also an *ethos* of justice that informs individual choices. In the absence of such an ethos, inequalities will obtain that are not necessary to enhance the condition of the worst off: the required ethos promotes a distribution more just than what the rules of the economic game by themselves can secure.

To be sure, one might imagine, in the abstract, a set of coercive rules so finely tuned that universally self-interested choices within them would raise the worst off to as high a position as any other pattern of choices would produce. Where coercive rules had and were known to have such a character, agents could choose self-interestedly in confidence that the results of their choices would satisfy an appropriately uncompromising interpretation of the difference principle. In that (imaginary) case, the only ethos necessary for difference principle justice would be willing obedience to the relevant rules, an ethos which Rawls expressly requires. But the vast economics literature on incentive-compatibility teaches that rules of the contemplated perfect kind cannot be designed. Accordingly, as things actually are, the required ethos must, as I have argued, guide choice within the rules, and not merely direct agents to obey them. (I should emphasize that this is not so because it is *in general* true that the point of the rules governing an activity must be aimed at when agents pursue that activity in good faith: every competitive sport represents a counterexample to that generalization. But my argument for the conclusion stated above did not rest on that false generalization.)

III

There is an objection which friends of Rawls's *Theory of Justice* would press against my argument in criticism of his application of the difference principle. The objection is that my focus on the posture of talented producers in daily economic life is inappropriate, since their behavior occurs within, and does not determine, *the basic structure* of society, and it is only to the latter that the difference principle applies.[14] Whatever people's choices within it may be, the basic structure is just provided that it satisfies the two principles of justice. To be sure, so Rawls acknowledges, people's choices can themselves be assessed as just or unjust, from a number of points of view. Thus, for example, appointment to a given job of candidate A rather than candidate B might be judged unjust, even though it occurs within the rules of a just basic structure.[15] But injustice in such a choice is not the sort of injustice that the Rawlsian principles are designed to condemn. For, *ex hypothesi*, that choice occurs within an established basic structure: it therefore cannot affect the justice of the basic structure itself, which is what, according to Rawls, the two principles govern. Nor, similarly, should the choices with respect to work and remuneration that talented people make be submitted for judgment at the bar of the difference principle. So to judge those choices is to apply that principle at the wrong point. The difference principle is a "principle of justice for institutions."[16] It governs the choice of institutions, not the choices made within them. The development of the second horn of the dilemma argument at pp. 221–2 above misconstrues the Rawlsian requirement that citizens in a just society uphold the principles that make it just: by virtue of the stipulated scope of the difference principle, talented people do count as faithfully upholding it, as long as they conform to the prevailing economic rules *because* that principle requires those rules.

Call that "the basic structure objection." Now, before I develop it further, and then reply to it, I want to point out that there is an important ambiguity in the concept of the basic structure, as that is wielded by Rawlsians. The ambiguity turns on whether the Rawlsian basic structure includes only coercive aspects of the social order or, also, conventions and usages that are deeply entrenched but not legally or literally coercive. I shall return to that ambiguity in Section V below, and I shall show that it shipwrecks not only the basic structure objection but also the whole approach to justice that Rawls has taught so many to pursue. But, for the time being, I shall ignore the fatal ambiguity, and I shall take the phrase "basic structure," as it appears in the basic structure objection, as denoting *some* sort of structure, be it legally coercive or not, but whose key feature, for the purposes of the objection, is that it is indeed a structure, that is, a framework of rules within which choices are made, as opposed to a set of choices and/or actions.[17] Accordingly, my Rawlsian critic would say, whatever structure, precisely, the basic structure is, the objection stands that my criticism of the incentives argument misapplies principles devised for a structure to individual choices and actions.

In further clarification of the polemical position, let me make a background point about the difference between Rawls and me with respect to the site or sites at which principles of justice apply. My own fundamental concern is neither the basic structure of society, in any sense, nor people's individual choices, but the pattern of benefits and burdens in society: that is neither a structure in which choice occurs nor a set of choices, but the upshot of structure and choices alike. My concern is *distributive justice*, by which I uneccentrically mean justice (and its lack) in the distribution of benefits and burdens to individuals. My root belief is that there is injustice in distribution when inequality of goods reflects not such things as differences in the arduousness of different people's labors, or people's different preferences and choices with respect to income and leisure, but myriad forms of lucky and unlucky circumstance. Such differences of advantage are a function of the structure *and* of people's choices within it, so I am concerned, secondarily, with *both* of those.

Now Rawls could say that his concern, too, is distributive justice, in the specified sense, but that, for him, distributive justice obtains just in case the allocation of benefits and burdens in society results from actions which display full conformity with the rules of a just basic structure.[18] When full compliance with the rules of a just basic structure obtains, it follows, on

Rawls's view, that there is no scope for (further) personal justice and injustice which affects *distributive* justice, whether it be by enhancing it or by reducing it. There is, Rawls would, of course, readily agree, scope, within a just structure, for distribution-affecting meanness and generosity,[19] but generosity, though it would alter the distribution, and might make it more equal than it would otherwise be, could not make it more *just* than it would otherwise be, for it would then be doing the impossible, to wit, enhancing the justice of what is already established as a (perfectly) just distribution by virtue merely of the just structure in conformity with which it is produced. But, as I have indicated, I believe that there is scope for relevant (relevant, that is, because it affects justice in distribution) personal justice and injustice *within* a just structure, and, indeed, that it is not possible to achieve distributive justice by purely structural means.

In discussion of my claim (see p. 223 above) that social justice requires a social *ethos* that inspires uncoerced equality-supporting choice, Ronald Dworkin suggested[20] that a Rawlsian government might be thought to be charged with a duty, under the difference principle, of promoting such an ethos. Dworkin's suggestion was intended to support Rawls, against me, by diminishing the difference between Rawls's position and my own, and thereby reducing the reach of my criticism of him. I do not know what Rawls's response to Dworkin's proposal would be, but one thing is clear: Rawls could not say that, to the extent that the indicated policy failed, society would, as a result, be less just than if the policy had been more successful. Accordingly, if Dworkin is right that Rawlsian justice requires government to promote an ethos friendly to equality, it could not be for the sake of making society more distributively just that it was doing so, *even* though it would be for the sake of making its distribution more *equal*. The following threefold conjunction, which is an inescapable consequence of Rawls's position, on Dworkin's not unnatural interpretation of it, is strikingly incongruous: (1) the difference principle is an egalitarian principle of distributive justice; (2) it imposes on government a duty to promote an egalitarian ethos; (3) it is not for the sake of enhancing distributive justice in society that it is required to promote that ethos. Dworkin's attempt to reduce the distance between Rawls's position and my own threatens to render the former incoherent.

Now, before I mount my two replies to the basic structure objection, a brief conceptual digression is required, in clarification of the relationship between a just *society*, in Rawls's (and my own) understanding of that idea (see p. 221 above) and a just *distribution*, in my (non-Rawlsian) understanding of that different idea (see pp. 224–5). A just society, here, is one whose citizens affirm and act upon the correct principles of justice, but justice in distribution, as here defined, consists in a certain egalitarian profile of rewards. It follows that, as a matter of logical possibility, a just distribution might obtain in a society that is not itself just.

To illustrate this possibility, imagine a society whose ethos, though not inspired by a belief in equality, nevertheless induces an equal distribution.

An example of such an ethos would be an intense Protestant ethic, which is indifferent to equality (on earth) as such, but whose stress on self-denial, hard work, and investment of assets surplus to needs somehow (despite the asceticism in it) makes the worst off as well off as is possible. Such an ethos achieves difference principle justice in distribution, but agents informed by it would not be motivated by the difference principle, and they could not, therefore, themselves be accounted just, within the terms of that principle. Under the specifications that were introduced here, this Protestant society would not be just, despite the fact that it displays a just distribution. We might say of the society that it is accidentally, but not constitutively, just. But, whatever phrasings we may prefer, the important thing is to distinguish "society" and "distribution" as candidate subjects of the predicate "just." (And it bears mentioning that, in contemporary practice, an ethos that achieves difference principle equality would almost certainly have to be equality-inspired: the accident of a non-equality-inspired ethos producing the right result is, at least in modern times, highly unlikely. The Protestantism described here is utterly fantastic, at least for our day.)

Less arresting is the opposite case, in which people strive to govern their behavior by (what are in fact) just principles, but ignorance, or the obduracy of wholly external circumstance, or collective action problems, or self-defeating-ness of the kinds studied by Derek Parfit,[21] or something else which I have not thought of, frustrates their intention, so that the distribution remains unjust. It would perhaps be peculiar to call such a society *just*, and neither Rawls nor I need do so: justice in citizens was put, above, as a *necessary* condition of a just society.

However we resolve the secondary, and largely verbal, complications raised in this digression, the point will stand[22] that an ethos informing choice within just rules is necessary in a society that is committed to the difference principle. My argument for that conclusion did not rely on aspects of my conception of justice which distinguish it from Rawls's, but on our shared conception of what a just society is. The fact that distributive justice, as I conceive it, causally requires an ethos (be it merely equality-promoting, such as our imaginary Protestantism, or also equality-inspired) that goes beyond conformity to just rules, was not a premise in my argument against Rawls. The argument of Section II turned essentially on my understanding of Rawls's well-considered requirement that the citizens of a just society are themselves just. The basic structure objection challenges that understanding.

IV

I now present a preliminary reply to the basic structure objection. It is preliminary in that it precedes my interrogation, in Section V, of what the phrase "basic structure" denotes, and also in that, by contrast with the fundamental reply that will follow that interrogation, there is a certain way out for Rawls, in face of the preliminary reply. That way out is not costless for him, but it does exist.

Although Rawls says often enough that the two principles of justice govern only justice in basic structure, he also says three things that tell against that restriction. This means that, in each case, he must either uphold the restriction and repudiate the comment in question, or maintain the comment and drop the restriction.[23]

First, Rawls says that, when the difference principle is satisfied, society displays *fraternity*, in a particularly strong sense: its citizens do not want

> to have greater advantages unless this is to the benefit of others who are less well off.... Members of a family commonly do not wish to gain unless they can do so in ways that further the interests of the rest. Now wanting to act on the difference principle has precisely this consequence.[24]

But fraternity of that strong kind is not realized when all the justice delivered by that principle comes from the basic structure, and, therefore, whatever people's motivations may be. Wanting not "to gain unless they can do so in ways that further the interests of the rest" is incompatible with the self-interested motivation of market maximizers, which the difference principle, in its purely structural interpretation, does not condemn.[25]

Second, Rawls says that the worst off in a society governed by the difference principle can bear their inferior position with dignity, since they know that no improvement of it is possible, that they would lose under any less unequal dispensation. Yet that is false, if justice relates to structure alone, since it might then be necessary for the worst off to occupy their relatively low place only because the choices of the better off tend strongly against equality. Why should the fact that no purely structurally induced improvement in their position is possible suffice to guarantee the dignity of the worst off, when their position might be very inferior indeed, because of unlimited self-seekingness in the economic choices of well-placed people?[26] Suppose, for example, that, as many politicians claim, raising rates of income taxation with a view to enhancing benefits for the badly off would be counterproductive, since the higher rates would induce severe disincentive effects on the productivity of the better off. Would awareness of that truth contribute to a sense of dignity on the part of the badly off?

Third, Rawls says that people in a just society act with a sense of justice *from* the principles of justice in their daily lives: they strive to apply those principles in their own choices. And they do so because they

> have a desire to express their nature as free and equal moral persons, and this they do most adequately by acting *from* the principles that they would acknowledge in the original position. When all strive to comply with these principles and each succeeds, then individually and collectively their nature as moral persons is most fully realized, and with it their individual and collective good.[27]

But why do they have to act *from* the principles of justice, and "apply" them "as their circumstances require"[28] if just behavior consists in choosing as one pleases within, and without disturbing, a structure designed to effect an implementation of those principles? And how can they, without a redolence of hypocrisy, celebrate the full realization of their natures as moral persons, when they know that they are out for the most that they can get in the market?

Now, as I said, these inconsistencies are not decisive against Rawls. For, in each case, he could stand pat on his restriction of justice to basic structure, and give up, or weaken, the remark that produces the inconsistency. And that is indeed what he is disposed to do at least with respect to the third inconsistency that I have noted. He said[29] that *A Theory of Justice* erred by in some respects treating the two principles as defining a *comprehensive* conception of justice:[30] he would, accordingly, now drop the high-pitched homily which constitutes the text to footnote 27. But this accommodation carries a cost: it means that the ideals of dignity, fraternity, and full realization of people's moral natures can no longer be said to be delivered by Rawlsian justice.[31]

V

I now provide a more fundamental reply to the basic structure objection. It is more fundamental in that it shows, decisively, that justice requires an ethos governing daily choice that goes beyond one of obedience to just rules,[32] on grounds which do not, as the preliminary reply did, exploit things that Rawls says in apparent contradiction of his stipulation that justice applies to the basic structure of society alone. The fundamental reply interrogates, and refutes, that stipulation itself.

A major fault line in the Rawlsian architectonic not only wrecks the basic structure objection but also produces a dilemma for Rawls's view of the subject[33] of justice from which I can imagine no way out. The fault line exposes itself when we ask the apparently simple question: what (exactly) *is* the basic structure? For there is a fatal ambiguity in Rawls's specification of the basic structure, and an associated discrepancy between his criterion for what justice judges and his desire to exclude the effects of structure-consistent personal choice from the purview of its judgment.

The basic structure, the primary subject of justice, is always said by Rawls to be a set of institutions, and, so he infers, the principles of justice do not judge the actions of people within (just) institutions whose rules they observe. But it is seriously unclear *which* institutions are supposed to qualify as part of the basic structure. Sometimes it appears that coercive (in the legal sense) institutions exhaust it, or, better, that institutions belong to it only insofar as they are (legally) coercive.[34] In this widespread interpretation of what Rawls intends by the "basic structure" of a society, that structure is legible in the provisions of its constitution, in such specific legislation as may be required to implement those provisions, and in further legislation and policy which are of central importance but which resist formulation in the constitution itself.[35] The basic structure, in this first understanding of it, is, so one might say, the *broad coercive outline* of society, which determines in a relatively fixed and general way what people may and must do, in advance of legislation that is optional, relative to the principles of justice, and irrespective of the constraints and opportunities created and destroyed by the choices that people make within the given basic structure, so understood.

Yet it is quite unclear that the basic structure is *always* thus defined, in exclusively coercive terms, within the Rawlsian texts. For Rawls often says that the basic structure consists of the *major* social institutions, and he does not put a particular accent on coercion when he announces *that* specification of the basic structure.[36] In this second reading of what it is, institutions belong to the basic structure whose structuring can depend far less on law than on convention, usage, and expectation: a signal example is the family, which Rawls sometimes includes in the basic structure and sometimes does not.[37] But once the line is crossed, from coercive ordering to the non-coercive ordering of society by rules and conventions of accepted practice, then the ambit of justice can no longer exclude chosen behavior, since the usages which constitute informal structure (think, again, of the family) are bound up with the customary actions of people.

"Bound up with" is vague, so let me explain how I mean it, here. One can certainly speak of the structure of the family, and it is not identical with the choices that people customarily make within it; but it is nevertheless impossible to claim that the principles of justice which apply to family structure do not apply to day-to-day choices within it. For consider the following contrast. The *coercive* structure arises independently of people's quotidian choices: it is formed by those specialized choices which legislate the law of the land. By contrast, the non-coercive structure of the family has the character it does only because of the choices that its members routinely make. The constraints and pressures that sustain the non-coercive structure reside in the dispositions of agents which are actualized as and when those agents choose to act in a constraining or pressuring way. With respect to coercive structure, one may fairly readily distinguish the choices which institute and sustain a structure from the choices that occur within it.[38] But with respect to informal structure, that distinction, though conceptually intelligible, collapses extensionally: when A chooses to conform to the prevailing usages, the pressure on B to do so is reinforced, and no such pressure exists, the very usages themselves do not exist, in the absence of conformity to them.

Now, since that is so, since behavior is *constitutive* of *non*-coercive structure, it follows that the only way of protecting the basic structure objection against my claim that the difference principle condemns maximizing economic behavior (and, more generally, of protecting the restriction of justice to the basic structure against the insistence that the personal, too, is political) is by holding fast to a purely coercive specification of the basic structure. But that way out is not open to Rawls, because of a further characterization that he offers of the basic structure: this is where the discrepancy adverted to in the second paragraph of this section appears. For Rawls says that "the basic structure is the primary subject of justice because its effects are so profound and present from the start."[39] Nor is that further characterization of the basic structure optional: it is needed to explain why it *is* primary, as far as justice is concerned. Yet it is false that only the *coercive* structure causes profound effects, as the example of the family once again reminds us.[40] Accordingly, if Rawls retreats to coercive structure, he contradicts his own criterion for what justice judges, and he lands himself with an arbitrarily narrow definition of his subject matter. So he must let other structure in, and that means, as we have seen, letting chosen behavior in. What is more, even if behavior were not, as I claim it is, constitutive of non-coercive structure, it will come in by direct appeal to the profundity-of-effect criterion for what justice governs. So, for example, we need not decide whether or not a regular practice of favoring sons over daughters in the matter of providing higher education forms part of the *structure* of the family to condemn it as unjust, under that criterion.[41]

Given, then, his stated rationale[42] for exclusive focus on the basic structure – and what *other* rationale could there be for calling it the *primary* subject of justice? – Rawls is in a dilemma. For he must either admit application of the principles of justice to (legally optional) social practices, and, indeed, to patterns of personal choice that are not legally prescribed, *both* because they are the substance of those practices, *and* because they are similarly profound in effect, in which case the restriction of justice to structure, in any sense, collapses; or, if he restricts his concern to the coercive structure only, then he saddles himself with a purely arbitrary delineation of his subject matter. I now illustrate this dilemma by reference to the two contexts that have figured most in this paper: the family, and the market economy.

Family structure is fateful for the benefits and burdens that redound to different people, and, in particular, to people of different sexes, where "family structure" includes the socially constructed expectations which lie on husband and wife. And such expectations are sexist and unjust if, for example, they direct the woman in a family where both spouses work outside the home to carry a greater burden of domestic tasks. Yet such expectations need not be supported by the law for them to possess informal coercive force: sexist family structure is consistent with sex-neutral family law. Here, then, is a circumstance, outwith the basic structure, as that would be coercively defined, which profoundly affects people's life-chances, *through the choices people make in response to the stated expectations, which are, in turn, sustained by those choices.*[43] Yet Rawls must say, on pain of giving up the basic structure objection, that (legally uncoerced) family structure and behavior have no implications for justice in the sense of "justice" in which the basic structure has implications for justice, since they are not a consequence of the formal coercive order. But that implication of the stated position is perfectly incredible: no such differentiating sense is available.

John Stuart Mill taught us to recognize that informal social pressure can restrict liberty as much as formal coercive law does. And the family example shows that informal pressure is as relevant to distributive justice as it is to liberty. One reason why the rules of the basic structure, when it is coercively defined, do not by themselves determine the justice of the distributive upshot is that, by virtue of circumstances that are relevantly independent of coercive rules, some people have much more power than others to determine what happens *within* those rules.

The second illustration of discrepancy between what coercive structure commands and what profoundly affects the distribution of benefits and burdens is my own point about incentives. Maximinizing legislation,[44] and, hence, a coercive basic structure that is just as far as the difference principle is concerned, are consistent with a maximizing ethos across society which, under many conditions, will produce severe inequalities and a meager level of provision for the worst off, yet both have to be declared just by Rawls, if he stays with a coercive conception of what justice judges. And that implication is, surely, perfectly incredible.

Rawls cannot deny the difference between the coercively defined basic structure and that which produces major distributive consequences: the coercively defined basic structure is only an instance of the latter. Yet he must, to retain his position on justice and personal choice, restrict the ambit of justice to what a coercive basic structure produces. But, so I have (by implication) asked: why should we *care* so disproportionately about the coercive basic structure, when the major reason for caring about it, its impact on people's lives, is *also* a reason for caring about informal structure and patterns of personal choice? To the extent that we care about coercive structure because it is fateful with regard to benefits and burdens, we must care equally about the ethi that sustain gender inequality, and inegalitarian incentives. And the similarity of our reasons for caring about these matters will make it lame to say: ah, but only the caring about coercive structure is a caring about *justice*, in a certain distinguishable sense. That thought is, I submit, incapable of coherent elaboration.

My response to the basic structure objection is now fully laid out, but before proceeding, in the sections that remain, to matters arising, it will be useful to rehearse, in compressed form, the arguments that were presented in Sections II through V.

My original criticism of the incentives argument ran, in brief, as follows:

(1) Citizens in a just society adhere to its principles of justice.

But

(2) They do not adhere to the difference principle if they are acquisitive maximizers in daily life.

∴ (3) In a society that is governed by the difference principle, citizens lack the acquisitiveness that the incentives argument attributes to them.

The basic structure objection to that criticism is of this form:

    (4)   The principles of justice govern only the basic structure of a just society.

∴ (5)   Citizens in a just society may adhere to the difference principle what-
          ever their choices may be within the structure it determines, and, in
          particular, even if their economic choices are entirely acquisitive.

∴ (6)   Proposition (2) lacks justification.

My preliminary reply to the basic structure objection says:

    (7)   Proposition (5) is inconsistent with many Rawlsian statements about the
          relationship between citizens and principles of justice in a just society.

And my fundamental reply to the basic structure objection says:

    (8)   Proposition (4) is unsustainable.

VI

So the personal is indeed political: personal choices to which the writ of the law
is indifferent are fateful for social justice.

But that raises a huge question, with respect to *blame*. The injustice in
distribution that reflects personal choices within a just coercive structure can
plainly not be blamed on that structure itself, nor, therefore, on whoever
legislated that structure. Must it, then, be blamed, in our two examples, on
men[45] and on acquisitive people, respectively?

I shall presently address, and answer, that question about blame, but, before
I do so, I wish to explain why I could remain silent in the face of it, why, that is,
my argument in criticism of Rawls's restricted application of the principles of
justice requires no judgment about blaming individual choosers. The conclusion
of my argument is that the principles of justice apply not only to coercive rules
but also to the pattern in people's (legally) uncoerced choices. Now, if we judge a
certain set of rules to be just or unjust, we need not add, as pendant to that
judgment, that those who legislated the rules in question should be praised or
blamed for what they did.[46] And something analogous applies when we come to
see that the ambit of justice covers the pattern of choices in a society. We can
believe whatever we are inclined to do about how responsible and/or culpable
people are for their choices, and that includes believing that they are not responsible and/or culpable for them at all, while holding that on which I insist: that
the pattern in such choices is relevant to how just or unjust a society is.

That said, I return to the question of how blamable individuals are. It would
be inappropriate to answer it, here, by first declaring my position, if, indeed, I
have one, on the philosophical problem of the freedom of the will. Instead,
I shall answer the question about blame on the prephilosophical assumptions
which inform our ordinary judgments about when, and how much, blame is
appropriate. On such assumptions, we should avoid two opposite mistakes
about how culpable chauvinistic men and self-seeking high fliers are. One is

the mistake of saying: there is no ground for blaming these people *as individuals*, for they simply participate in an accepted social practice, however tawdry or awful that practice may be. That is a mistake, since people do have choices: it is, indeed, *only* their choices that reproduce social practices; and some, moreover, choose *against* the grain of nurture, habit, and self-interest. But one also must not say: look how each of these people shamefully decides to behave so badly. That, too, is unbalanced, since, although there exists personal choice, there is heavy social conditioning behind it and there can be heavy costs in deviating from the prescribed and/or permitted ways. If we care about social justice, we have to look at four things: the coercive structure, other structures, the social ethos, and the choices of individuals, and judgment on the last of those must be informed by awareness of the power of the others. So, for example, a properly sensitive appreciation of these matters allows one to hold that an acquisitive ethos is profoundly unjust in its effects, without holding that those who are gripped by it are commensurately unjust. It is essential to apply principles of justice to dominant patterns in social behavior – that, as it were, is where the action is – but it doesn't follow that we should have a persecuting attitude to the people who emit that behavior. We might have good reason to exonerate the perpetrators of injustice, but we should not deny, or apologize for, the injustice itself.[47]

On an extreme view, which I do not accept but need not reject, a typical husband in a thoroughly sexist society, one, that is, in which families in their overwhelming majority display an unjust division of domestic labor, is literally incapable of revising his behavior, or capable of revising it only at the cost of cracking up, to nobody's benefit. But even if that is true of typical husbands, we know it to be false of husbands in general. It is a plain empirical fact that some husbands are capable of revising their behavior, since some husbands have done so, in response to feminist criticism. These husbands, we could say, were moral pioneers. They made a path which becomes easier and easier to follow as more and more people follow it, until social pressures are so altered that it becomes harder to stick to sexist ways than to abandon them. That is a central way in which a social ethos changes. Or, for another example, consider the recent rise in ecological consciousness. At first, only people that appear to be freaky because they do so bother to save and recycle their paper, plastic, and so forth. Then, more do that, and, finally, it becomes not only difficult not to do it but easy to do it. It is pretty easy to discharge burdens that have become part of the normal round of everybody's life. Expectations determine behavior, behavior determines expectations, which determine behavior, and so on.

Are there circumstances in which a similar incremental process could occur with respect to economic behavior? I do not know. But I do know that universal maximizing is by no means a necessary feature of a market economy. For all that much of its industry was state-owned, the United Kingdom from 1945 to 1951 had a market economy. But salary differentials were nothing like as great as they were to become, or as they were then in the United States. Yet, so I hazard, when British executives making five times what their workers did met American counterparts making fifteen times what their (anyhow better paid) workers did, many of the British executives would *not* have felt: *we* should press for more. For there was a social ethos of reconstruction after war, an ethos of common project, that restrained desire for personal gain. It is not for a philosopher to delimit the conditions under which such, and even more egalitarian ethi, can prevail. But a philosopher can say that a maximizing ethos is not a necessary feature of society, even of market society, and that, to the extent that such an ethos prevails, satisfaction of the difference principle is prejudiced.

In 1988, the ratio of top executive salaries to production worker wages was 6.5 to 1 in West Germany and 17.5 to 1 in the United States.[48] Since it is not plausible to think that Germany's lesser inequality was a disincentive to productivity, since it is plausible to think that an ethos that was relatively friendly to equality[49] protected German productivity in the face of relatively modest material incentives, we can conclude that the said ethos caused the worst paid to be better paid than they would have been under a different culture of reward. It follows, on my view of things, that the difference principle was better realized in Germany in 1988 than it would have been if its culture of reward had been more similar to that of the United States. But Rawls cannot say that, since the smaller inequality that benefited the less well off in Germany was not a matter of law but of ethos. I think that Rawls's inability to regard Germany as having done comparatively well with respect to the difference principle is a grave defect in his conception of the site of distributive justice.

Endnote on Coercive and Other Structure

The legally coercive structure of society functions in two ways. It *prevents* people from doing things by erecting insurmountable barriers (fences, police lines, prison walls, etc.), and it *deters* people from doing things by ensuring that certain forms of unprevented behavior carry an (appreciable risk of) penalty.[50] The second (deterrent) aspect of coercive structure may be described counterfactually, in terms of what would or might happen to someone who elects the forbidden behavior: knowledge of the relevant counterfactual truths motivates the complying citizen's choices.

Not much pure prevention goes on within the informal structure of society: not none, but not much. (Locking an errant teenager in her room would represent an instance of pure prevention, which, if predictable for determinate behavior, would count as part of a society's informal structure: it would be a rule in accordance with which that society operates.) That being set aside, informal structure manifests itself in predictable sanctions such as criticism, disapproval, anger, refusal of future cooperation, ostracism, beating (of, for example, wives who refuse sexual service) and so on.

Finally, to complete this conceptual review, the ethos of a society is the set of sentiments and attitudes in virtue of which its normal practices, and informal pressures, are what they are.

Now, the pressures that sustain the informal structure lack force save insofar as there is a normal practice of compliance with the rules they enforce. That is especially true of that great majority of those pressures (beating does not belong to that majority) which carry a moral coloring: criticism and disapproval are ineffective when they come from the mouths of those who ask others not to do what they do themselves. To be sure, that is not a conceptual truth, but a social-psychological one. Even so, it enables us to say that what people ordinarily do supports and partly constitutes (again, not conceptually, but in effect) the informal structure of society, in such a way that it makes no sense to pass judgments of justice on that structure while withholding such judgment from the behavior that supports and constitutes it: that point is crucial to the anti-Rawlsian inference at p. 229 above.[51] Informal structure is not a behavioral pattern, but a set of rules, yet the two are so closely related that, so one might say, they are *merely* categorially different. Accordingly, so I argued, to include (as one must) informal structure within the basic structure is to countenance behavior, too, as a primary subject of judgments of justice.

Now, two truths about legally coercive structure might be thought to cast doubt on the contrast I drew between it and informal structure in Section V above. First, although the legally coercive structure of society is indeed discernible in the ordinances of its constitution and law, those ordinances count as delineating it only on condition that they enjoy a broad measure of compliance.[52] And, second, legally coercive structure achieves its intended social effect only in and through the actions which constitute compliance with its rules. To be more accurate, those propositions are true provided that we exclude from consideration "1984" states in which centralized brute force prevails against nonconformity even, if necessary, at the cost of half the population being in jail. But it is appropriate to ignore 1984 scenarios here.[53]

In light of those truths, it might be objected that the dilemma that I posed for Rawls (see p. 230 above), and by means of which I sought to defeat his claim that justice judges structure *as opposed to* the actions of agents, was critically misframed. For I said, against that claim, that the required opposition between structure and actions works for coercive structure only, with respect to which a relevantly strong distinction can be drawn between structure-sustaining and structure-conforming action, but that coercive structure could not reasonably be thought to exhaust the structure falling within the purview of justice: accordingly, so I concluded, justice must also judge everyday actions.

The truths rehearsed two paragraphs back challenge my articulation of the distinction between coercive structure and action within it. They thereby also challenge the contrast that I drew between two relationships, that between coercive structure and action, and that between informal structure and action.

This problem needs more thought than I have to date spent on it. For the moment I shall say this: even if coercive structure counts as such only if appropriate compliance obtains, that structure may nevertheless be *identified* with a set of laws which are not themselves patterns of behavior. And one can distinguish sharply between behavior forbidden and directed by those laws, and behavior that is optional under them, however systematic and widespread it may be. By contrast, the identity of informal structure is less separable from practice: no distinction is sustainable between widespread practices which manifest or represent informal structure and widespread practices which do not.

If the would-be saving contrast which I there essay is an unrealistic idealization, then the distinction, vis-à-vis action, between coercive and informal structure, may be more blurred than I have been disposed to allow. Yet that would not be because informal structure is more separable from action than I claimed, but because coercive structure is less separable from it. Therefore, even if the dilemma constructed on p. 230 was for the stated reasons misframed, the upshot would hardly be congenial to Rawls's position, that justice judges structure rather than actions, but, if anything, congenial to my own rejection of it, if not, indeed, to the terms in which some of the argument for that rejection was cast.

Notes

For comments that influenced the final version of this paper, I thank Gerald Barnes, Diemut Bubeck, Joshua Cohen, Margaret Gilbert, Susan Hurley, John McMurtry, Derek Parfit, Thomas Pogge, John Roemer, Amelie Rorty, Hillel Steiner, Andrew Williams, Erik Wright, and Arnold Zuboff.

1   But it was, apparently, used by Christian liberation theologians before it was used by feminists: see Denys Turner, "Religion: Illusions and Liberation," in Terrel Carver, ed., *The Cambridge Companion to Marx* (Cambridge: Cambridge University Press, 1991), p. 334.

2   Or, more precisely, that which *distinguishes* its form. (Insofar as the feminist critique targets government legislation and policy, there is nothing distinctive about its form.)

3   Okin is singularly alive to Rawls's ambivalence about admitting or excluding the family from the basic structure: see, e.g. her "*Political Liberalism*, Justice and Gender," *Ethics* 105, no. 1 (Oct. 1994), 23–4, and, more generally, her *Justice, Gender and the Family* (New York: Basic Books, 1989), chapter 5. But, so far as I can tell, she is unaware of the wider consequences, for Rawls's view of justice in general, of the set of ambiguities of which this one is an instance.

4   See "Incentives, Inequality, and Community," in Grethe Peterson, ed., *The Tanner Lectures on Human Values*, vol. 13 (Salt Lake City: University of Utah Press, 1992), and "The Pareto Argument for Inequality," *Social Philosophy and Policy*, 12 (Winter 1995). These articles are henceforth referred to as "Incentives" and "Pareto," respectively.

5   See "Incentives," p. 266, n. 6, for four possible formulations of the difference principle, all of which, arguably, find support in *A Theory of Justice* (Cambridge, MA: Harvard University Press, 1971). The argument of the present paper is, I believe, robust across those variant formulations of the principle.

6 I do have some reservations about the principle, but they are irrelevant to this paper. I agree, for example, with Ronald Dworkin's criticism of the "ambition-insensitivity" of the difference principle: see his "What Is Equality? Part 2: Equality of Resources," *Philosophy & Public Affairs*, 10, no. 4 (Fall 1981), 343.

7 "Proposes to conceive it": I use that somewhat precious phrase because part of the present criticism of Rawls is that he does not succeed in so conceiving it – he does not, that is, recognize the implications of so conceiving it.

8 *A Theory of Justice*, p. 7 [p. 49 in this volume, eds.].

9 This is just the crudest causal story connecting superior payment to the better off with benefit to the worst off. I adopt it here for simplicity of exposition.

10 They do not, more precisely, share *justificatory community* with the rest, in the sense of the italicized phrase that I specified at p. 282 of "Incentives."

11 "Citizens in everyday life affirm and act from the first principles of justice." They act "from these principles as their sense of justice dictates" and thereby "their nature as moral persons is most fully realized." (Quotations drawn from, respectively, "Kantian Constructivism in Moral Theory," *The Journal of Philosophy*, 77, no. 9 (Sept. 1980), 521, 528, and *A Theory of Justice*, p. 528.)

12 That way of achieving equality preserves the information function of the market while extinguishing its motivational function: see Joseph Carens, *Equality, Moral Incentives, and the Market* (Chicago: University of Chicago Press, 1981).

13 See "Incentives," p. 298 *et circa*, for precisely what I mean by "the standard case."

14 For a typical statement of this restriction, see, John Rawls, *Political Liberalism* (New York: Columbia University Press 1993), pp. 282–3.

15 See the first sentence of Sect. 2 of *A Theory of Justice* ("The Subject of Justice"): "Many different kinds of things are said to be just and unjust: not only laws, institutions, and social systems, but also particular actions of many kinds, including decisions, judgments, and imputations" (ibid., p. 7) [p. 49 in this volume, eds.]. But Rawls excludes examples such as the one given in the text above from his purview, because "our topic . . . is that of social justice. For us the primary subject of justice is the basic structure of society" (ibid.).

16 *A Theory of Justice*, p. 303.

17 The contrast between structure and action is further explained, though also, as it were, put in its place, in the Endnote to this article.

18 *A Theory of Justice*, pp. 274–5: "The principles of justice apply to the basic structure. . . . The social system is to be designed so that the resulting distribution is just however things turn out." Cf. ibid., p. 545: " . . . the distribution of material means is left to take care of itself in accordance with the idea of pure procedural justice."

19 This is a different point from the one made at p. 223 above, to wit, that there is scope within a just structure for justice and injustice in choice in a "nonprimary" sense of "justice."

20 At a seminar in Oxford, in Hilary Term of 1994.

21 See his *Reasons and Persons* (Oxford: Oxford University Press, 1984), chapter 4.

22 If, that is, my argument survives the basic structure objection, to which I reply in Sects. IV and V.

23 Because of these tensions in Rawls, people have resisted my incentives critique of him in two opposite ways. Those convinced that his primary concern is the basic structure object in the fashion set out in Sect. III. But others do not realize how important that commitment is to him: they accept my (as I see it, anti-Rawlsian)

view that the difference principle should condemn incentives, but they believe that Rawls would also accept it, since they think his commitment to that principle is relevantly uncompromising. They therefore do not regard what I say about incentives as a *criticism* of Rawls.

Those who respond in that second fashion seem not to realize that Rawls's liberalism is jeopardized if he takes the route that they think open to him. He then becomes a radical egalitarian socialist, whose outlook is very different from that of a liberal who holds that "deep inequalities" are "inevitable in the basic structure of any society" (*A Theory of Justice*, p. 7) [p. 49 in this volume, eds.].

24   *A Theory of Justice*, p. 105.
25   See, further, "Incentives," pp. 321–2, "Pareto," pp. 178–9.
26   See, further, "Incentives," pp. 320–1.
27   *A Theory of Justice*, p. 528, my emphasis. See, further, note 11 above, and "Incentives," pp. 316–20.
28   John Rawls, "Justice as Fairness: A Briefer Restatement," Harvard University, 1989, typescript, p. 154.
29   In reply to a lecture that I gave at Harvard in March of 1993.
30   That is, as (part of) a complete moral theory, as opposed to a purely political one: see, for explication of that distinction, *Political Liberalism, passim*, and, in particular, pp. xv–xvii.
31   See "Incentives," p. 322.
32   Though not necessarily an ethos embodying the very principles that the rules formulate: see the last four paragraphs of Sect. III above. Justice will be shown to require an ethos, and the basic structure objection will thereby be refuted, but it will be a contingent question whether the ethos required by justice can be read off the content of the just rules themselves. Still, as I suggested at p. 226, the answer to that question is almost certainly "Yes."
33   That is, the subject matter that principles of justice judge. I follow Rawls's usage here (e.g. in the title of Lecture VII of *Political Liberalism*: "The Basic Structure as Subject"; and cf. n. 15 above).
34   Henceforth, unless I indicate otherwise, I shall use "coercive," "coercion," etc. to mean "legally coercive," etc.
35   Thus, the difference principle, though pursued through (coercively sustained) state policy, cannot, so Rawls thinks, be aptly inscribed in a society's constitution: see *Political Liberalism*, pp. 227–30.
36   Consider, for example, the passage at pp. 7–8 [pp. 49–50 in this volume, eds.] of *A Theory of Justice* in which the concept of the basic structure is introduced:

> Our topic . . . is that of social justice. For us the primary subject of justice is the basic structure of society, or more exactly, the way in which the major social institutions distribute fundamental rights and duties and determine the division of advantages from social cooperation. By major institutions I understand the political constitution and the principal economic and social arrangements. Thus the legal protection of freedom of thought and liberty of conscience, competitive markets, private property in the means of production, and the monogamous family are examples of major social institutions. . . . I shall not consider the justice of institutions and social practices generally. . . . [The two principles of justice] may not work for the rules and

practices of private associations or for those of less comprehensive social groups. They may be irrelevant for the various informal conventions and customs of everyday life; they may not elucidate the justice, or perhaps better, the fairness of voluntary cooperative arrangements or procedures for making contractual agreements.

I cannot tell, from those statements, what is to be included in, and what excluded from, the basic structure, nor, more particularly, whether coercion is the touchstone of inclusion. Take, for example, the case of the monogamous family. Is it simply its "legal protection" that is a major social institution, in line with a coercive definition of the basic structure (if not, perhaps, with the syntax of the relevant sentence)? Or is the monogamous family itself part of that structure? And, in that case, are its typical usages part of it? They certainly constitute a "principal social arrangement," yet they may also count as "practices of private associations or ... of less comprehensive social groups," and they are heavily informed by the "conventions and customs of everyday life."

Puzzlement with respect to the bounds of the basic structure is not relieved by examination of the relevant pages of *Political Liberalism*, to wit, 11, 68, 201–2, 229, 258, 268, 271–2, 282–3, and 301. Some formulations on those pages lean toward a coercive specification of the basic structure. Others do not.

37 See the final paragraph of Sect. I of this paper.

38 For more on structure and choice, see the Endnote to this article. Among other things, I there entertain a doubt about the strength of the distinction drawn in the above sentence, but, as I indicate, if that doubt is sound, then my case against Rawls is not weakened.

39 *A Theory of Justice*, p. 7 [p. 49 in this volume, eds.].

40 Or consider access to that primary good which Rawls calls "the social basis of selfrespect." While the law may play a large role in securing that good to people vulnerable to racism, legally unregulable racist attitudes also have an enormous negative impact on how much of that primary good they get.

But are the profound effects of the family, or of racism, "present from the start" (see the text to n. 39)? I am not sure how to answer that question, because I am unclear about the intended import, here, of the quoted phrase. Rawls probably means "present from the start of each person's life": the surrounding text at *Theory*, p. 7 [p. 49 in this volume, eds.] supports this interpretation. If so, the family, and racial attitudes, certainly qualify. If not, then I do not know how to construe the phrase. But what matters, surely, is the asserted profundity of effect, not whether it is "present from the start," whatever may be the sense which attaches, here, to that phrase.

41 Note that one can condemn the said practice without condemning those who engage in it. For there might be a collective action problem here, which weighs heavily on poor families in particular. If, in addition to discrimination in education, there is discrimination in employment, then a poor family might sacrifice a great deal through choosing evenhandedly across the sexes with whatever resources it can devote to its children's education. This illustrates the important distinction between condemning injustice and condemning the people whose actions perpetuate it: see, further, Sect. VI below.

42 See the text to n. 39 above.

43   Hugo Adam Bedau noticed that the family falls outside the basic structure, under the coercive specification of it often favored by Rawls, though he did not notice the connection between non-coercive structure and choice that I emphasize in the above sentence: see his "Social Justice and Social Institutions," *Midwest Studies in Philosophy*, 3 (1978), 171.

44   That is, legislation which maximizes the size of the primary goods bundle held by the worst off people, given whatever is correctly expected to be the pattern in the choices made by economic agents.

45   We can here set aside the fact that women often subscribe to, and inculcate, male-dominative practices.

46   We can distinguish between how unjust past practices (e.g. slavery) were and how unjust those who protected and benefited from those unjust practices were. Most of us (rightly) do not condemn Lincoln for his (conditional) willingness to tolerate slavery as strongly as we would a statesman who did the same in 1997, but the institution of slavery itself was as unjust in Lincoln's time as it would be today.

   What made slavery unjust in, say, Greece, is exactly what would make slavery (with, of course, the very same rules of subordination) unjust today, to wit, the content of its rules. But sound judgments about the justice and injustice of people are much more contextual: they must take into account the institutions under which they live, the prevailing level of intellectual and moral development, collective action problems such as the one delineated in n. 41 above, and so forth. The morally best slaveholder might deserve admiration. The morally best form of slavery would not.

47   See the preceding note.

48   See Lawrence Mishel and David M. Frankel, *The State of Working America, 1990–1991* (Armonk, NY: M. E. Sharpe, 1991), p. 122.

49   That ethos need not have been an egalitarian one. For present purposes, it could have been an ethos which disendorses acquisitiveness as such (see n. 32, and the digression at the end of Sect. III), other than on *behalf of* the worst off.

50   The distinction given above corresponds to that between the difficulty and the cost of actions: see my *Karl Marx's Theory of History* (Oxford: Oxford University Press, and Princeton: Princeton University Press, 1978), pp. 238–9.

51   See the sentence beginning "But once" [on p. 229].

52   It does not follow that they are not *laws* unless they enjoy such compliance: perhaps they are nevertheless laws, if they "satisfy a test set out in a Hartian rule of recognition, even if they are themselves neither complied with nor accepted" (Joshua Cohen, in comment on an earlier draft of this paper). But such laws (or "laws") are not plausibly represented as part of the basic structure of society, so the statement in the text can stand as it is.

53   That is because of Rawls's reasonable stipulation that, in a just society, the threat of coercion is necessary for assurance game reasons only: each is disposed to comply provided that others do, and coercion is needed not because, in the absence of its threat *to me*, I might not comply, but because in the absence of its threat to others I cannot be sure that *they* will comply (see *A Theory of Justice*, p. 315). This stipulation makes formal law less *essentially* coercive than one might otherwise suppose and therefore less contrastable with custom than I have supposed.

11

Justice across Cultures:
Animals and Accommodation

Paula Casal

I. Introduction

The cover of *Multicultural Citizenship*, Will Kymlicka's influential defence of special rights for cultural minorities, reproduces Edward Hicks's beautiful painting *The Peaceable Kingdom*.[1] Hicks's painting commemorates a treaty the painter saw as the beginning of the kingdom prophesied in Isaiah, where "the lion will lie down with the lamb" and "love will replace hostility and competition both amongst humans and in the natural world."[2] While seven Native Americans and eight white men sign the treaty in the background, the painting's main subjects are three children and twelve animals, peacefully enjoying themselves in an unspoiled environment.

There is a clear contrast between the content of Kymlicka's book and the prominence its cover accords subjects other than adult, male, human beings.[3] In the following, I revert to Hicks's focus on neglected subjects. There are sound reasons to do so since cross-cultural agreements may not merely partition resources between different cultural groups; they may also have profound effects on vulnerable members within minority groups. Feminist scholars have already highlighted the tension between granting certain group rights to cultural minorities and protecting female members of those minorities.[4] Similar problems arise in cases involving other vulnerable parties, including children, homosexuals, and, I shall suggest, non-human animals. More specifically, I shall argue against the claim that justice requires exempting cultural minorities from anti-cruelty legislation on either cultural or religious grounds.

The paper proceeds as follows. Section II distinguishes between *cultural accommodation* and a different culture-based legal practice, termed *cultural*

Paula Casal, 'Animals and Accommodation', revised by the author from her 'Is Multiculturalism Bad for Animals?', in *Journal of Political Philosophy*, 11:1 (2003), pp. 1–22.

mitigation. Section III distinguishes various views about the moral status of animals, and clarifies their relevance to distributive justice, and cultural accommodation in particular. Focusing on one paradigmatic case for the discussion of animals and accommodation, section IV describes the role ritual animal sacrifice plays within the Santería religion, and some recent legal disputes. The remaining sections distinguish two types of argument alleging that weightier considerations defeat any reasons to prohibit animal sacrifice. *Religious arguments* assume that special protection for religious activity is a basic civil liberty. *Fairness arguments* appeal to the fact that Santería sacrifices are performed by a disadvantaged minority, living within a larger society that uses animals in different but comparably objectionable ways. I contend that both arguments fail.

II.   Mitigation and Accommodation

There are at least two ways in which legal systems might grant exceptional treatment to members of cultural minorities. The first concerns the extent to which such individuals are held responsible when they violate legal norms. Suppose, for example, members of a minority culture kidnap a young woman not to obtain a ransom but a wife, or injure a child to save her from some allegedly greater evil.[5] Some might argue those individuals should receive less severe punishment than non-members because of the way in which pressures from their cultural background explain their motivation and actions. Such arguments for cultural mitigation do not attempt to justify their conduct, or the tradition that encourages it. On the contrary, they may stress the oppressive nature of a culture in order to portray the accused as yet further victims of some tyrannous tradition.

Cultural accommodation, the focus of this paper, involves a quite different form of exceptional treatment. Unlike arguments for mitigation, which grant certain actions should be prohibited and only question how severely members of certain cultural groups should be punished for performing them, arguments for accommodation address the prior question of what the law should prohibit. More specifically, the latter arguments claim that members should be exempt from legal prohibitions that justifiably apply to non-members. If the legal system accommodates minority cultures, then, their members can be confident that they will not be punished for certain actions associated with their cultures. Arguments for accommodation might be extended even further, and require not only legal exemptions but also various other forms of recognition or subsidy that ensure the relevant actions actually take place. In contrast, mitigation arguments do not rule out justifiable punishment, and may even give courts considerable discretion in deciding the implications to draw from a defendant's cultural background.

Arguments for cultural accommodation have been used successfully to restrict legislation protecting animal welfare. European Union anti-cruelty legislation, for example, does not apply to bullfighting and other Spanish *fiestas*. Thanks to cultural accommodation, Spaniards have the right to torture animals without fearing legal interference, while other Europeans performing exactly the same actions might be liable to prosecution.[6] Exemptions to domestic anti-cruelty legislation also exist within many European states. Perhaps the most common are those granted to *sechita* and *dhabh*, slaughter methods that result respectively in *kosher* and *halal* meat.[7] In order to prevent slow or painful deaths, abattoirs are normally required to stun animals before they are killed. Jewish and Muslim rituals, by contrast, require that animals are fully conscious when killed. In 1985 the Farm Animal Welfare Council expressed concern not only about the slow and painful way in which the ritual slaughter proceeded, but also about the way animals were forced into an unnatural position likely to cause them both discomfort and terror.[8] It also claimed the slaughter was often rushed, and that animals were sometimes shackled and hoisted onto the bleeding trail before they had fully lost consciousness.

The example I shall henceforth focus on, however, concerns the ritual animal sacrifices involved in the Santería religion. Santería provides an ideal test case to discuss accommodation because its practitioners constitute a *disadvantaged minority* whose claim to exceptional treatment is more plausible than that of larger, less vulnerable, groups. Moreover, animal sacrifice is not only part of the Santeros' culture but also part of their *religion*. Therefore, they can appeal to arguments about the free exercise of religion as well as cultural protection. Finally, animal sacrifice is not only linked to the practice of the Santería religion but a *required* part of it.

These combined features make the case for exempting Santería particularly strong. Compare the case for exempting bullfights, and other Spanish *fiestas*, from European Union animal welfare legislation. Although a minority in Europe, Spain has a thriving culture, and is not especially disadvantaged, or poor. Traditional Spanish forms of animal cruelty are often imbued with religious symbolism, and are part of religious festivals, but few believe the Virgin or saint they venerate demands they make *animal* sacrifices rather than some other offer. In contrast, Jews and Muslims may be described as disadvantaged minorities in some countries and some respects, and *sechita* and *dhabh* both possess religious significance. However, neither group is required by its religion to cause animals to suffer, since members are normally not required to eat, harm, or kill animals at all.

III. Animals and Ethics

Before criticizing arguments for accommodating traditional forms of animal cruelty it may be useful to emphasize that opposition to animal cruelty does not depend on certain ambitious assumptions; for example, that animals have rights, that killing animals is wrong, or that it is equally important to prevent the suffering of animals as that of humans. To reach my conclusion

I need at most the more modest assumption that the existence of anti-cruelty legislation is desirable because it is wrong to kill animals in painful ways when alternative less painful methods are available, and that there are sound moral reasons to enforce such a moral prohibition. I believe that the moderate view I adopt here accords with common sense morality, and is widely accepted by Western governments and citizens. Still, I shall attempt to dispel some common misunderstandings of that view before turning to Santería.

Some may reject my moderate view because they accept the following argument. Perhaps except where suffering takes a very extreme form, surely being killed is more harmful than being made to suffer. If so, then if producing the lesser harm of animal suffering is wrong, it must also be wrong to produce the greater harm involved in killing animals. Far from being moderate, then, my view implies we should not only oppose cruelty to animals but also make the whole world vegetarian. Since they think that conclusion is implausible, critics judge my view unsound.

One way to respond to this argument is to challenge its initial assumption that the relative harmfulness of death and suffering is constant across very different types of life. On reflection, it is more likely that the badness of either depends very much on the victim's identity. Thus, it seems plausible that there are weightier reasons to protect certain types of subjects from death than other types of subject, although there are not weightier reasons to protect them from pain. Even if people are not always aware of it, this moral asymmetry is one that common sense morality recognizes. A pregnant woman, for example, may endure great suffering for the sake of saving her foetus or baby the slightest pain, but when complications arise and doctors can only save one life, it is normally the mother that takes priority. War movies also illustrate the asymmetry. The entire supply of painkillers or cognac is reserved for the most gravely injured soldier, while the young and healthy resist unaided. However, when all but one can be rescued, or somebody has to stay behind to detonate a bomb, the most gravely injured soldier volunteers because he has least to lose by risking his life.

The same rationale may explain our attitude towards ending human or non-human lives. To avoid killing a person we may swerve the car and kill a dog because our victim has only a canine life to lose. Even so, this does not justify using a dog's paw to keep the elevator door open. For the fact that it is less bad to be killed for the dog (or the gravely injured soldier) than for the person (or healthy soldier), does not imply that it is also less bad for the dog (or injured soldier) to suffer pain.[9] The mere fact that an episode of suffering is part of a life which is shorter, or less valuable than another, does not automatically render that suffering less deserving of remedy. In fact, we may feel it is particularly urgent to relieve the pain of individuals who do not have long and wonderful lives ahead of them precisely because they do not. I conclude then, that it is fully consistent to enact legislation which prohibits causing unnecessary suffering to certain subjects, such as foetuses, animals, or the terminally ill, without being also committed to preventing, or maximally delaying, their deaths.

Even so, others may reject my view about animal cruelty because they assume that it requires a commitment to another controversial view in animal ethics which they reject, namely *anti-speciesism*.[10] The anti-speciesist claims that when deciding how to distribute burdens and benefits between different lives it is a serious moral vice, akin to racism, to take species membership into consideration. Instead, every case should be decided on its merits by appeal to each individual's characteristics.

Fortunately, there are several reasons to doubt that concern for animal cruelty requires a commitment to the doctrine. First, a speciesist may think that alleviating animal suffering, like alleviating the suffering of babies or injured soldiers, is *particularly important*, because members of those groups are more vulnerable. Secondly, she may think that species membership matters, but not very much, and that alleviating animal suffering is *extremely important*. Finally, she may believe that although alleviating human and animal pain have *equal objective importance*, species membership matters for other reasons. For example, it may matter because it explains why we celebrate chimpanzees with human-like intelligence, but lament the existence of humans with chimpanzee-like minds, and invest more in enhancing the capacities of the latter. We may also think that membership matters because feeling in certain ways towards other members of one's species is part of belonging to it: in our case, it is part of what it means to be human. Thus, we may endorse our special bond with other humans, like we endorse the bond with our friends, without thereby implying that the suffering of non-humans or non-friends objectively matters any less.

I conclude then that a commitment to anti-speciesism is not necessary in order to oppose animal suffering, nor to press the arguments of this paper. It is also worth noting that such a commitment is not sufficient. For example, given that for anti-speciesists, each case should be judged on its individual merits, the interests of individuals with greater capacities may be granted far more weight than the interests of less capable individuals. Following such an individualized ranking, while ignoring species boundaries, might result in the greatest importance being granted to the interests of the most gifted human beings, followed by the interests of the second most gifted human beings, and so on. Proceeding in this manner, by the time we come to ponder the interests of animals like cows and chickens, we may find that they hardly matter at all.

Since such a view is rather unattractive on several accounts, anti-speciesists might try to replicate the equalizing effect of the concept of *human* rights by introducing some other threshold, and affirming equal consideration for all those above it.[11] A boundary distinct from that delimiting the human species might be drawn, for example, at a high level that excludes human beings suffering cognitive misfortunes, or a low level that includes great apes. Anti-speciesism, thus reformed, would still be consistent with claiming equal rights for all those above the threshold, whilst denying rights, or perhaps any moral consideration, for all other animals.

There are, moreover, further ways in which similarly animal-unfriendly results can be derived from non-speciesist premises. Even the view that humans ought to give priority to fellow humans over animals can result from non-speciesist principles. For instance, we may believe that because (i) we owe obligations towards those capable of moral reasoning, (ii) we also owe derivative obligations towards their offspring, including those incapable of moral reasoning. The combination of these two types of obligation may yield a view that requires giving priority to human beings, but it is not based on a speciesist prejudice.[12]

On the whole, given that anti-speciesism is debatable and both unnecessary and insufficient to defend the interest of animals, there seems little reason to stake such defence on it. We return then to the more concrete and pressing issues raised by Santería ritual sacrifices, and the appeal of cultural accommodation.

IV.   The Case of Santería

Santería, a syncretic religion from the nineteenth century, originated when hundreds of thousands of the Yoruba people were brought as slaves from West Africa to Cuba, and conjoined Catholic iconography and sacraments to their traditional religion in order to escape persecution. Santería now counts on 50,000–60,000 practitioners in Dade County, Southern Florida, and has many more in other states and countries. Santeros worship *orishas*, living spirits of African origin that, they suppose, can help people fulfil their destinies. Orishas are powerful but not immortal, and their survival depends on animal sacrifices.

In the Florida town of Hialeah, where the building of a new Santería church gave rise to a great controversy, 15,000 to 18,000 animals are sacrificed annually to feed the orishas. The sacrifice proceeds as follows:

> the priest raises the animal's head with one hand and with the other hand inserts a knife about four inches long into the right side of the animal's neck and then pushes the knife through the entire neck...A veterinarian...testified that 'this method of killing is not humane because there is no guarantee that a person performing a sacrifice in the manner described can cut through both carotid arteries at the same time'. In addition, certain physiological events may occur in the animal, particularly in young goats and sheep, to prolong the experience of pain and distress prior to death. Moreover, chickens have four carotid arteries, which makes it more difficult to achieve success with one cut.[13]

Apart from the method of killing, there are also concerns about how animals are kept:

various species of animals are at times gathered in one room..., and exposed to the noise and bodily secretions produced by the nearby animal being killed...they may detect other animals' pain and fear, and may themselves experience fear and distress prior to their own sacrifice. Many of the animals killed in Santería ceremonies are raised specifically for sacrifice and may receive inadequate food, water, and housing during the course of their lives.[14]

Animals employed for healing and death rituals are killed but cannot be eaten. This gives Santeros little incentive to feed them properly, cure their diseases, or raise them in hygienic conditions.

Hialeah citizens complained about the health hazards posed by sacrificial leftovers, as piles of decapitated goats, sheep, guinea pigs, ducks and turtles were discarded in public places, often near riverbanks. They also expressed concern about animal suffering, and the "psychological effects the sacrifice procedures could have on children observing the ritual."[15] Two resolutions and four ordinances, unanimously approved, dictated criminal punishment of anyone who "unnecessarily or cruelly kills animals," and made it illegal to "sacrifice" animals.[16]

After many legal defeats, Pichardo, President of the Church of Lukumi Babalú Ayé, appealed to the Supreme Court, which unanimously found the ordinances unconstitutional. The press reported that jubilant Santeros planned to resume their rituals as "Top Court Okays Animal Sacrifice."[17] The headline, however, was misleading. The Court did not hold that Santería sacrifice itself enjoyed the protection of the First Amendment freedom of religion clause. Instead it rejected a particular way of banning them: one which, in a clearly discriminatory fashion, singled out a particular religious group, and tailored a set of ordinances so that they together applied to Santería – "mostly a religion of poor people, mostly Black Cubans"[18] – and nothing else.

The Court's actual decision applied the test used in *Employment Division v. Smith*, a 1990 Supreme Court case holding that a law burdening a religion need not be justified by a compelling governmental interest if it is *neutral and generally applicable*.[19] In *Smith* the Court upheld Oregon's refusal to exempt peyote, a hallucinogenic drug used in Native American religious ceremonies, from its anti-drug laws on the ground that these laws were both neutral and generally applicable. Their effect on religious practices was deemed incidental, and so consistent with the First Amendment. In the words of Justice Kennedy, who wrote the majority opinion in *Lukumi*,

> ...a law that is neutral and of general applicability need not be justified by a compelling governmental interest even if the law has the incidental effect of burdening a particular religious practice...Neutrality and general applicability are interrelated, and...failure to satisfy one requirement is a likely indication that the other has not been satisfied. A law failing to satisfy these requirements must be justified by a compelling governmental interest and must be narrowly tailored to advance that interest.[20]

Returning to the Florida ordinances, the Court found that they breached facial neutrality, as they employed terms like "ritual" and "sacrifice"; had been "gerrymandered," so that four different prohibitions banned Santería sacrifices exclusively,[21] and entirely; and had a history of prejudice and hostility towards Santeros.[22] In addition, they were *underinclusive* in pursuing their objective to prevent animal suffering,[23] and *overbroad* because they could have regulated how animals had to be raised, killed, and disposed of, without imposing a total ban on sacrifice.

According to Kennedy, having failed the neutrality test, the ordinances might have been acceptable if they passed an alternative test employed in *Sherbert v. Verner*. Mrs. Sherbert, a Jehovah's witness, refused to work on Saturdays, and was denied state unemployment benefits on the ground that she had refused suitable employment. Mrs. Sherbert won her case, because the Court followed a different test. It requires laws burdening religious conduct to be *justified by a compelling state interest, and to employ the least restrictive means of protecting that interest*. Justices Blackmun and O'Connor advocated the use of this test in *Lukumi*. Here, however, unlike in *Smith* or *Sherbert*, the choice of test did not make any difference. Since the Florida ordinances were both underinclusive and overbroad, they could not pass this alternative test either.

Having described Santería sacrifice and some legal background, I shall conclude this section by distinguishing two types of reasons for agreeing with the Court's verdict. Some may be moved by what I termed religious arguments. They may see the events leading to *Lukumi* as an instance of unfair competition between religions calling for legal intervention to oppose discrimination. Or, perhaps, they think that religious activities are special and should receive especially vigorous legal protection. Others may be exercised by quite different fairness arguments, and moved by convictions about comparative desert, or by a desire to side with the underdog.

Similarly, those who agree with the Court's verdict in *Sherbert* may do so for religious or fairness reasons. For example, those moved by religious arguments may argue that the state's interest in saving tax payers' money is not sufficiently compelling to justify burdening religious conduct. Those advancing fairness arguments may explain that people who prefer their society's common pause day to fall on Saturday rather than Sunday are the losers in a coordination problem forcing a society to choose one among seven equally good options. Fairness may require exemptions without making any appeal to the religious significance of any day. Similarly, individuals who have to adopt a second language to solve their country's linguistic coordination problem may also be entitled to compensatory treatment, irrespective of whether their language has any religious significance.

At least in *Sherbert*, fairness arguments have more promise than religious arguments insofar as they escape two powerful objections threatening the latter. First, it is unfair to force non-believers, or believers in rival faiths, as well as any Jehovah witness who works on Saturdays, to subsidize Mrs. Sherbert's religious pursuits: justice does not require subsidizing pilgrimages to Mecca.[24] Second, the religious argument is implausible because it would still apply even if Mrs. Sherbert believed she ought to have not one pause day, but two or more.

I shall now examine the relative force of the religious and fairness arguments that have been, or could be, employed to defend Santería sacrifice. The next section discusses religious arguments without questioning the assumption that religious practices should enjoy special protection. The following section then questions whether such an assumption is well grounded. A final section discusses fairness arguments for and against permitting animal sacrifice.

V. Neutrality and General Applicability

In addressing religious arguments to exempt Santería, it is useful to identify three positions concerning the legitimacy of political intervention in religious activity. The first affirms the special liability of religion to interference, the second regards it as especially immune to interference, whilst the third denies that it is special in either of these negative or positive respects.

To illustrate, note that examples of the first view arose throughout the Santería case. Many advocates of prohibition appeared to assume the Santería religion, even if not religion in general, was especially liable to interference because it provided such inadequate reasons to cause suffering. To them, killing animals in ways that causes easily avoidable pain merely to dump their carcasses on a riverbank seemed like a clear instance of "causing unnecessary suffering."[25] The killings appeared to be "done without any useful motive," and the easily avoidable pain was regarded as gratuitous.

This attitude has some appeal since demanding an intelligible reason to practice animal sacrifice appears to be a reasonable request. If an individual wishes to impose substantial suffering, or enjoy a legal exemption, surely she should at least offer grounds others can understand and find minimally credible. If so, what we owe to others includes the idea of being able to give a reasonable explanation to our victims, or their representatives, of why we are imposing certain losses on them. The explanation "I am feeding the *orishas* to gain their allegiance" arguably does not constitute such an explanation.[26] Neither does "bull-fighting is in my blood," or "painless killing is not *kosher*."

The second view was advanced by Justices Blackmun and O'Connor. They favored special protection for religious practices, and claimed they should be burdened only in ways required by compelling state interests. I shall return to discuss this view at length in the next section. It contrasts sharply with the third view, which denies that religious practices should be singled out for special treatment of either a favorable or unfavorable kind. As Locke argued,

> If some Congregations should have a mind to sacrifice Infants, or . . . lustfully pollute themselves in promiscuous uncleanness . . . is the Magistrate obliged to tolerate them, because they are committed in a Religious Assembly? I answer,

No. These things are not lawful in the ordinary course of life...and therefore neither are they so in the Worship of God...But indeed if any People congregated upon account of Religion, should be desirous to sacrifice a Calf, I deny that That ought to be prohibited by a Law...what may be spent on a Feast, may be spent on a Sacrifice. But if...the interest of the Commonwealth required all slaughter of beast should be forborn some while...who sees not that the Magistrate in such a case may forbid all his Subjects to kill any Calves for any use whatsoever? Only 'tis to be observed, that in this case the Law is not made about a Religious, but a Political matter: nor is the Sacrifice, but the Slaughter of Calves thereby prohibited.[27]

On Locke's view, the practice of animal slaughter should neither be liable to nor immune from interference because it is religiously motivated. The *Smith* doctrine resembles Locke's, although it still treats religion as special insofar as it makes laws burdening religion pass a special test that laws burdening other activities are not required to satisfy.

Applying *Smith* to *Lukumi* the Court decided the Florida ordinances could not legitimately prohibit Santería sacrifices because their history and wording indicated they were designed to target religious practice. The decision might have been different had the ordinances employed a generally applicable anti-cruelty statute, neutrally worded by an animal welfare group.

In fact, in 1983, Gary Francione successfully represented the American Society for the Prevention of Cruelty to Animals against the Santero Church of Changó.[28] Though Santeros argued that New York State anti-cruelty law – a neutral and generally applicable statute – violated the First Amendment, Francione won the case. In his opinion, if Hialeah had used a neutral statute, rather than some separate and purpose-made set of ordinances, the case would probably not have reached the Supreme Court. Indeed, in the *Smith* decision, the Court explicitly cited an anti-cruelty statute as an example of a neutral and generally applicable law that may legitimately curtail religious activities.[29] Kennedy did, however, cite various uses of animals explicitly permitted by Florida's laws as evidence of the ordinances' underinclusiveness, and Santeros could still appeal to this observation whatever the ordinances' history and wording. Nevertheless, two reasons limit this argument's force. First, Kennedy never claimed the absence of general applicability sufficed for non-constitutionality. Instead he claimed that it provided further evidence for the lack of neutrality – hence his observation about how both principles are "interrelated."[30] Second, it is possible to point at various ways in which Santeros' use of animals is different to other uses permitted by Florida law.[31]

As Francione explains,

There are completely legitimate reasons to be concerned about Santería sacrifices, which are far more brutal than most other methods of slaughter...Santería practitioners often completely saw the heads off larger animals, such as goats and sheep, and place the heads of birds and smaller animals under foot and then pull the animals until dismemberment occurs. Animals are allowed to bleed to death very slowly and do not lose consciousness for extended periods of time. They are often kept in filthy and inhumane conditions, and are deprived of food or water, for several days before the ceremony. Decomposing animal bodies are disposed of in public places. Moreover, Santería practitioners insist on the absolute secrecy of their sacrificial practices. Every use of animals in our society is regulated, and although such regulation is imperfect in many ways, there is at least an acceptance in principle that the taking of animal life is something that must be regulated. Santería practitioners wish to be the only group in our society that can kill animals without any supervision whatsoever. Surely, neither the First Amendment nor common sense requires such a result.[32]

The right Santeros claim amounts to *carte blanche* to kill animals as they see fit behind closed doors. Because granting such a right seems incompatible with securing animal welfare, the ordinances may appear not to be overbroad. Nevertheless, in targeting religion as such the ordinances were overbroad. If one wants to protect infants from pneumonia caused by submersion in cold lakes during baptism, one should not prohibit baptism, but submerging babies in cold lakes. Believers can devise less risky ceremonies, such as replacing the original bath by some symbolic drops on the forehead. Similarly, neutral anti-cruelty legislation, avoiding terms like "sacrifice," can protect animals while leaving it to the Santeros' imagination to devise ceremonies consistent with such laws.

In short then *Smith* does not rule out neutral laws that protect animals from ritual killings. The next section examines whether a test that offers greater protection to religion would have different implications, and whether such a test is defensible.

VI.   Cruelty and Compelling Interests

The Religious Freedom Restoration Act of 1993 attempted to overrule *Smith*, and achieve even greater protection for religion. Had it not been declared unconstitutional in 1997,[33] even perfectly neutral and generally applicable laws causing purely incidental inconvenience to religious activities could be struck down if the interest they protected, although strong, was not "compelling" or "of the highest priority," or if those laws could have been less restrictive without being less effective.[34]

In his concurring opinion on *Lukumi*, Justice Blackmun (joined by O'Connor) expressed his preference for the compelling interest, or strict scrutiny, test, and complained that *Smith* turned the free exercise clause into a mere anti-discrimination principle. Regarding the Florida ordinances, he stressed that they failed because they targeted religion as such, and added that the judgment does not "reflect this Court's views on the strength of a state's interest in prohibiting cruelty to animals." His opinion ends by recording that "the number of organizations [he cites 22] that have filed *amicus* briefs on behalf of this interest...demonstrates that it [the interest in preventing animal cruelty] is not a concern to be treated lightly."

This final point reminds us that the compelling interest test requires *evidence* of the degree to which protecting animals from cruelty constitutes an important interest. The test does not, however, explain what constitutes evidence. It would be implausible to conclude from the fact that the state had not been effective in protecting animals, or women, children, and racial minorities, from cruelty that doing so was not a compelling interest, and then employ such evidence to grant those groups even less protection. Counting the number of laws enacted to defend an interest at any point, or the number of organizations filing *amicus* briefs, as evidence of the interest's importance would be similarly worrying. It would rely on St. Matthew's principle: to those who have, shall be given. Such a method does not seem promising as a way of protecting the weak and vulnerable.

The compelling interest test is also problematic for three further reasons. First, its advocates must provide a way to distinguish religious from non-religious practices. Second, they must explain why religious practices, thus distinguished, merit the special protection of being liable to interference only in pursuit of compelling interests. Third, such explanation must be sufficiently discriminating that it does not also support special protection for non-religious practices.[35] These problems are difficult to solve either individually or jointly.

Polly Toynbee's challenge, "Moonies, Scientologists, Mormons, Brethrens – how could you differentiate between cults, cranks, fruitcakes and true believers?", highlights the first problem. Reviewing some failed solutions, she writes,

> Dating back to 1601, the advancement of religion was a legal charitable aim, but the law never specified what religion is. So...the Charity Commission decided that only a religion with a dominant deity would qualify. This led to delightful absurdities where tree-hugging pagans praying to the spirit of a place did not get charitable status, but Odin-worshippers did – because Odin is a chief god....Lord Ahmed offered his own definition: 'Religion is that system of belief and action centered around the worship of God, which is derived in whole or in part from a book revealed by God to one of his messengers'. What does it mean? It would provide a very enjoyable circus of court cases, trying to decide what had been revealed by which god to what bona fide messenger. The idea that God's words don't count unless a messenger writes them down is interesting too. Literacy was never before endowed with such supreme spirituality.[36]

As Toynbee indicates, it is difficult to demarcate religion in a way neither underinclusive nor overbroad, let alone one which is also suitably connected to a weighty reason to grant special protection to members of the demarcated class of activities. Such a connection, however, is essential for an adequate defence of the compelling interest doctrine. For even if, accidentally and counterfactually, all religions happened to have *one* book and *one* deity, there would be no clear connection between those features, and an argument for special protection. Finally, it is difficult to understand why religious activity has a unique claim to special protection since standard defences of its importance naturally extend to non-religious activity.

For example, if religion merits protection because it expresses convictions not merely about personal, but impersonal, or intrinsic, values, or because of the structural role it plays in individual lives, then it is implausible to deny similar protection to at least some other comprehensive doctrines; some forms of environmentalism, for example, may share these features.[37] Second, protection for religion cannot be based on the intensity of religiously based desires. Some religious convictions need not be especially intense. At present, for example, some environmentalists may be prepared to sacrifice more for their convictions than most religious believers, and bikers' preference to ride without helmets is probably as intense as that of Sikhs. Furthermore, there are also independent arguments against relating moral urgency to subjective intensity.[38] Two final claims often made to defend the claims of religion refer to the role it may play in the transmission of ethical values, or the formation of individual, or collective, identity. However, in order to teach ethics it is not necessary to teach religion, and many times both activities are in competition. Moreover, gender, race, language and many other aspects of culture are also comparably important sources of identity.

The case of Native American use of peyote illustrates the difficulties besetting the compelling interest doctrine. According to the doctrine, peyote should be permitted if anthropological investigation shows that peyote ceremonies can be described as religious even if it also reveals that the ritual is not of great importance to Native Americans. Peyote rights should be denied if the anthropologists discover that the ceremony is not religious, even if the same investigation proved that the ceremony is an ancient tradition, intimately connected with group membership and moral development, which participants value immensely.[39] Such a dogmatic position inevitably creates perverse incentives for minorities to "sacralize" whatever practice they wish to preserve.

Finally, some argue that religion must be protected in order to combat discrimination against minorities.[40] Advocates of the compelling interest doctrine, however, must explain why *Smith* is insufficient for this purpose. Furthermore, they cannot argue that defining religion poses no grave problem because clear cases can first be protected. Any such definition is likely to mirror the dominant creeds, and be disastrous for minorities: whilst their powerful rivals receive it immediately, they may be struggling for recognition as groups meriting protection.

The protection of minorities is more likely to be achieved by laws tailored for that purpose than by laws protecting religion, which may even make matters worse for minorities. Well-established churches, often extremely powerful already, are the institutions most likely to extract the greatest gains from any concession made to religion in general. As Toynbee indicates, in Britain dominant religions have employed their political influence to obtain self-serving tax exemptions, seats in the House of Lords, and blasphemy laws that protect only them. She reaches a very plausible conclusion: "the only way to treat all religions equally is to favor none of them."[41]

VII. Fairness Arguments

I now examine some arguments that appeal to the fact that some activities as inhumane as animal sacrifice persist in our society. Unlike religious arguments, they do not rely on this fact to establish that prohibitions on animal sacrifice violate neutrality, or that prevention of animal cruelty is not a compelling state interest. Instead, they draw upon various convictions about fairness.

To understand the first argument we need to distinguish judgments about *noncomparative* and *comparative* desert.[42] Such judgements differ in the relevance they attach to other individuals' levels of advantage and deservingness in determining what particular individuals deserve. For illustration, suppose a committed employee, Al, has worked extremely hard and productively for many years, and for that reason deserves promotion. If so, it is regrettable from the perspective of noncomparative desert when Al receives only a mean pay rise. Now consider an additional employee, Beth, who is as hard-working and noncomparatively deserving as Al but receives an even meaner rise. Some desert theorists argue Beth's treatment not only involves a second, and even larger, violation of noncomparative desert but is also regrettable from the distinct, and potentially competing, perspective of comparative desert. They claim that since Al and Beth are equally noncomparatively deserving considerations of comparative desert require that they both fare equally well. Ideally, Al and Beth should each be promoted, thereby satisfying the demands of both varieties of desert. However, if the only way to ensure that Al and Beth fare equally well is for Al to receive Beth's meaner pay rise such a distribution would, in one respect, be welcome since it would satisfy comparative desert.

Returning to our case, the *comparative desert argument* claims that to restrict one activity when similarly inhumane activities go unrestricted is a sufficiently serious comparative injustice that animal sacrifice should be permitted. Justice requires that the equally deserving should be equally rewarded or punished. Poulter's defence of legal exemptions for *sechita* and *dhabh* suggests this argument. He writes:

> After the legal repudiation of racism and sexism, the law may ultimately move on to outlaw 'speciesism'. The upshot of such reforms may be that, while killing animals painlessly for food would still be permitted, the infliction of any pain and suffering as part of this process would be regarded as legally wrong... At present, however, the case for removing the legal exemption accorded to *sechita* has not been sufficiently made out.[43]

To indicate the slow pace at which we are moving towards eliminating speciesism, Poulter notes, alongside other examples, that even "beating a hedgehog, a harmless creature held high in the affection of the general public, was only made an offence as recently as 1996."[44] Hedgehog beating, however, would not have been banned, had those deciding the case reasoned like Poulter recommends. For hedgehog beating was probably as inhumane as some other practice, which had not yet been outlawed in 1996. Under present circumstances, insisting that nothing be prohibited unless everything comparable is prohibited is tantamount to lifting all existing prohibitions on comparable forms of cruelty.[45] Such reasoning would oppose most gradual reforms and incapacitate incremental political change.

Despite this difficulty, bullfighting supporters often pursue similar lines of argument, stressing that eating factory-farmed meat causes at least as much suffering as *corridas*. After all, they argue, before entering the ring most bulls have much better lives than animals reared intensively. Moreover, bullfighting kills 70,000 cows and bulls every year in Spain, a country that also annually kills over 2 million cows in order to eat.[46]

A major difficulty with their argument becomes apparent when we note the subjects of comparative desert claims should be *individuals* rather than *practices*. Bullfighting appears in a better light only when comparing practices rather than the moral record of the individuals who engage in them. Considering fewer than 20% of Spanish people support bullfighting, killing 70,000 bulls and cows a year is not such a modest figure.[47] More importantly, the minority of individuals who kill so many bulls and cows also eat factory-farmed meat, and so probably have more painful animal deaths on their account than anyone else. Therefore, their opposition to the recent tendency to convert bullrings into concert halls can hardly claim the moral high ground. A group of vegetarians requesting permission to use only one inhumane animal product, would have a much stronger position.

For similar reasons, our convictions about desert may not be violated even if a practice comparable to animal sacrifice remains legally permissible. The Santeros' position is less likely to resemble that of vegetarians than that of the bullfight supporter, who not only takes advantage of familiar inhumane uses of animals but adds a further cruel practice.

Suppose, however, that there was another group, whose practices were as inhumane as those of Santería and whose global cruelty record was no better than that of Santeros. If so, banning only one activity would appear objectionable on grounds of comparative desert, even after we agree that, were it not for comparative considerations, those activities deserve to be prohibited.

One plausible response to this suggestion employs a distinction between *horizontal* and *vertical* inequity. To illustrate, imagine a group of hikers overlooking a badly injured man, who has slipped down a cliff and is now hanging on for his life. After the man shouts to one hiker for help, the potential rescuer refuses on the ground that it is unfair to be singled out when there are other similarly situated individuals who could also perform the rescue. Despite this complaint, most of us remain convinced it would be better for the rescue to take place. A plausible explanation appeals to the fact that it is so much worse for the man to risk death while the hikers continue their walk than for the rescuer to be inconvenienced while the other hikers proceed. The vertical inequity between the man and the hikers, which would exist if he were abandoned, is much greater than any horizontal inequity that would exist amongst the hikers if one of them performed the rescue.[48]

The distinction between horizontal and vertical inequity suggests various responses to comparative desert arguments. The first response points out that such arguments should not focus only upon horizontal inequities. Exemptions will result in animals suffering far more pain than they deserve, and this vertical consideration should be balanced against Santeros, or bullfighters, undeservedly being punished more than some other group. The second response points out that the horizontal inequity suffered by the former need not give them a *decisive* complaint.[49] Perhaps there is *a* reason not to punish one individual because a similar offender has escaped, but that reason may not possess much weight. The fact that some muggers escape punishment is not a decisive reason against punishing muggers, even when the horizontal inequality between arrested muggers and escaped muggers is greater than the vertical inequality between a mugger and his victim. One plausible explanation of this widely shared conviction is that when individuals engage in harmful actions they either forfeit their right to equal treatment or diminish the force of that right.

The third response involves a parallel criticism to the levelling down objection to strictly egalitarian principles.[50] That objection claims that such principles absurdly imply that if it is impossible for a hospital to provide sight-saving treatment for all its patients, the fact that they are all equally entitled to treatment provides a reason to not save any of them from blindness. Proponents of the objection deny there is even a *pro tanto* reason to tolerate more suffering in order to enhance equality. The parallel criticism claims there is no reason to tolerate violations of noncomparative desert in order to satisfy principles of comparative desert.[51] Thus, if nobody deserves to be blind, a world where everyone is blind is terrible from the point of view of noncomparative desert, and is not better in any respect than a world where comparative desert is violated because only some are blind. Similarly, the fact that many murderous dictators have escaped the punishment they deserve is no good reason not to try other dictators whenever feasible – let alone to create legal exemptions for other individuals engaging in comparable activities. If this view of the priority of noncomparative over comparative desert is sound, and there are noncomparative reasons to prohibit animal sacrifice, then the comparative desert defence of cultural or religious exemptions from anticruelty legislation fails.

The previous argument's appeal to the existence of comparable practices might be supplemented by focusing on the additional facts that Santeros are standardly poor, black, Cuban immigrants. Thus, prohibiting animal sacrifice not only risks inequity but also burdens individuals who already suffer from social and economic disadvantage and racial discrimination, as well as an unjust embargo on their homeland,[52] and live in an alien culture where they lack a fair share of political influence. The additional facts might be thought relevant because they make compliance with legal prohibitions on animal sacrifice especially burdensome (the *cost* argument), or because they partly explain why animal sacrifice is prohibited while comparably inhumane activities are permitted (the *influence* argument).

The *cost argument* rests on a valid concern, appropriate where poverty, disability, or other disadvantages make compliance with the law impossible or particularly costly. The poor, retired, or unemployed sometimes enjoy tax exemptions or reduced fees on this ground. However, that concern is inapplicable in the present case since the requisite causal relationship between cost and disadvantage is absent. Prohibitions on animal sacrifice are not particularly costly to Santeros *because* they are poor: refraining from animal abuse is not a luxury the poor can ill afford, nor a barrier to escaping poverty. The cost argument, therefore, is not applicable.

The *influence argument* also faces difficulties. First, the argument assumes treating animal sacrifice differently from comparably inhumane practices is objectionable when such a difference is a product of the Santeros' disadvantaged position. It is not obvious, however, that prohibitions on animal sacrifice exist because Santeros have less than a fair share of political influence. Other more powerful groups may get away with comparably inhumane activities because their share of political influence is unjustly large. Second, note the influence argument merely claims that if certain comparable practices are allowed, animal sacrifice should not be restricted due to its supporters' lack of fair political influence. Unlike the earlier appeals to religion, the argument does not attempt to establish that a just society would recognize a right to animal sacrifice. Thus, it fails to show the inequitable treatment of animal sacrifice is akin to other inequities connected to Santeros' politically disadvantaged position, such as poverty and racism. Since the latter involve the violation of rights that a just society would protect, they form the basis of powerful complaints. However, merely complaining about an inability to harm animals in ways prohibited for most, but available to some, is far less forceful. The influence argument is inconclusive because it fails to show that Santeros' political disadvantage has deprived them of any entitlement they would enjoy in a just world.

Finally, the fact that a minority lacks a fair share of wealth and political influence provides reasons to ensure they have more wealth and political influence. It does not, however, provide sufficient reason to allow them to harm those even more disadvantaged, such as minority women and children, or animals. Such a solution involves discharging our multicultural responsibilities in a way some hope to discharge their religious duties: by passing the costs to someone else.

VIII. Conclusion

I have criticized both religious and fairness arguments in favor of granting legal exemptions to anti-cruelty legislation. Unless arguments that are more powerful can be devised, my findings suggest that the cruel side of cultural or religious traditions should be reformed. We should not be alarmed by this conclusion. Cultural adaptation is possible, and as groups come to understand, adjust, and forget, eventually nobody will suffer, while if cruel practices remain intact, every year millions of animals will continue to do so. Note also three positions that my arguments do not entail.

First, my arguments do not imply that animal welfare groups should attach priority to eliminating culturally rather than economically motivated cruelty when campaigning for legal reforms or the enforcement of existing legislation. Questions of political practice require reflection on different considerations. Economic organizations, such as large corporations, are likely to be more powerful than minority religious communities, but imposing gradual reforms on them is often feasible. Since the meat and cosmetic industries cause the most prolonged suffering to the largest number of animals, even a modest reform could avoid more suffering than the total elimination of animal sacrifice, and this is one of the most important considerations animal welfare groups should take into account.

A second caveat concerns the implications of my arguments for practices harmful to women. Since women, unlike animals, clearly have the same fundamental moral rights as men, it may appear much easier to criticize exemptions harmful to women rather than to animals. This, however, is not always true since women, unlike animals, may freely consent to harmful practices. Assuming consenting adults should sometimes possess rights to act against their interests, perhaps some harmful sexist practices should be tolerated whilst animal cruelty is prohibited. If so, the defence of sexist cultures would depend on the degree to which they are, or can become, voluntary associations, and the burden of proof, in this case, should be considerable.[53]

Finally, concluding that we should deny minorities exemptions detrimental to women, children, or animals, does not imply that we should reject other forms of special consideration. It is unfair that cultural minorities are systematically outvoted, and always forced to comply with the majority's norms, values, and traditions, while their own are ignored. Correcting this asymmetry requires special measures. Granting exemptions does not eliminate this one-way street's unfairness; at best, it slightly reduces its traffic. Constructing the appropriate two-way street justifies more positive political changes, involving not only affirmative action plans, but institutional reforms securing the adoption of shared norms that reflect minorities' distinctive concerns. Increasing minorities' ability to impose their legitimate moral demands on larger groups, and raise majorities' moral standards, enhances political equality without sacrificing the welfare of vulnerable members of either group. Equality does not require levelling down moral conduct: we can level up instead.

Fairness to minorities is not the only ground for such reforms. Cultural plurality, like biological diversity, may also be a good in itself, or a collective resource that provides opportunities for self-examination and mutual improvement. These are plausible views, but neither the quest for equality, nor the desire to preserve diversity, commit us to tolerating practices harmful to vulnerable, non-consenting, third parties. In fact, there are two reasons to think that the most plausible formulations of our egalitarian and pluralist convictions deny such an inference. The very concern for the worst off which justifies our support for disadvantaged groups also prohibits sacrificing their weakest members. Moreover, what we should celebrate, and struggle for, is the existence of a multitude of practices that are both diverse *and* good, not a varied collection of cruelties and crimes.

Notes

I am very grateful for written comments from Jerry Cohen, Will Kymlicka, Peter Singer, Dennis Thompson, Peter Vallentyne, and Andrew Williams, and helpful discussions with Joseph Chan, Matthew Clayton, Amy Gutmann, Jesús Mosterín, Ingmar Persson, Thomas Pogge, Erik Rakowski, and Hans Roth. I have also benefited from audiences at the Center for Multicultural Research at Uppsala University, the Center for Human Values at Princeton University, and the Center for Ethics and the Professions at Harvard, where I wrote an earlier version of this paper: "Is Multiculturalism Bad for Animals?", *Journal of Political Philosophy*, 11.1, 2003, pp. 1–22. For further funding I acknowledge a Leverhulme Research Fellowship, and a British Academy Travel Grant.

1   Will Kymlicka, *Multicultural Citizenship* (Oxford: Clarendon Press, 1995).
2   Ibid., p. vii.
3   Note, however, that Kymlicka discusses discrimination against women, and their political representation, for example, at ibid., pp. 39–42, 132–4, 136–40, and 145–9.
4   See, for example, J. Cohen et al. (eds.), *Is Multiculturalism Bad for Women?* (Princeton: Princeton University Press, 1999).
5   See D. Lambelet Coleman, "Individualizing Justice Through Multiculturalism," *Columbia Law Review* 96 (June 1996), pp. 1093–1166, p. 1109, for various examples, including one involving a Japanese woman who, having drowned her children before trying to kill herself, claimed that she was following the ancient parent—child suicide tradition and spent only one year in prison, the year she was on trial.
6   Apparently, the accommodation was obtained by the Spanish Ambassador to the European Union, Francisco Javier Elorza Cavengt, who explained his achievement thus: "I have been in the European Union for 13 years and I have done two great things: obtaining Union funds for Spain and smuggling a clause protecting bullfighting...They wanted to ban bullfighting and I love bullfights passionately. Getting my way cost me a couple of dinners. I worked out a scheme with a great E.U. lawyer: where the E.U. said that it 'will protect animal welfare,' we added 'whilst respecting cultural traditions,' and this way we 'bullet-proofed' bullfighting!" See *La Vanguardia*, June 2, 1999. The amendment is recorded in Protocol 33 of the Amsterdam Treaty, 1997. Producers of fighting bulls already receive E.U. farming subsidies of up to €18,900 per annum, and groups like Proyecto Minotauro are campaigning to obtain E.U. funds earmarked for traditional *fiestas*.
7   In Britain, the 1974 Slaughterhouses Act and the 1967 Slaughter of Poultry Act exempt both *sechita* and *dhabh*. They still enjoy exemption despite being opposed by the Royal Society for the Prevention of Cruelty to Animals, Compassion in World

Farming, the Humane Slaughter Association, and at least six Private Members' Bills in Parliament since 1955. In 1990, relying on research comparing slaughtering methods, conducted since 1985 and published in veterinary journals, the Commission of the European Communities Scientific Veterinary Committee also recommended to the European Parliament that legal exemptions from stunning – which had already been abandoned in Switzerland, Norway, and largely in Sweden – should be abolished in all member states. See S. M. Poulter, *Ethnicity, Law and Human Rights* (Oxford: Oxford University Press, 1998), p. 139.

8 For discussion, see Poulter, ibid., p. 139. Poulter discusses research indicating that "some cattle slaughtered by means of *sechita* took over two minutes to lose evoked responses in the brain, whereas in those which had been stunned the loss of evoked activity was virtually instantaneous."

9 It is true that there is often a correlation between the capacities to suffer and to have a valuable life. For example, the same capacity for friendship which makes the life of a chimpanzee more valuable than the life of a fish makes chimpanzees vulnerable to a form of suffering fish cannot feel, that caused by mourning the loss of friends. But such a correlation does not always obtain. For example, the reduced capacities of a child, compared to an adult, may make the child not less but *more* vulnerable to suffering because of experiences that hardly affect adults, such as being alone, or in the dark, or getting lost. Illness and pain can be more distressful for individuals who do not understand what is happening to them.

10 The term "speciesism" was invented by Richard Ryder, and then adopted by Peter Singer and others. See *Animal Liberation* (New York: Avon Books, 1990), ch. 1.

11 The idea is suggested by Rawls's discussion of a "range property" in *A Theory of Justice*, rev. edn. (Cambridge, MA: Belknap Press of Harvard University Press, 1999), pp. 443–4.

12 This is T. M. Scanlon's explanation of why "the fact that a human being is 'of human born' provides a strong reason for according it the same status as other humans." See *What We Owe To Each Other* (Cambridge, MA: Harvard University Press, 1998), p. 185.

13 F. Barbara Orlans et al. (eds.), *The Human Use of Animals* (Oxford: Oxford University Press, 1998), p. 309.

14 Ibid.

15 Ibid., p. 310.

16 To "sacrifice" was defined as "unnecessarily to kill, torment, torture, or mutilate an animal in a public or private ritual or ceremony not for the primary purpose of food consumption." Breach of the ordinances was punishable with up to sixty days' imprisonment, or fines up to $500, or both.

17 This was the headline in the *New York Newsday* on June 13, 1993.

18 Orlans et al., *The Human Use of Animals*, p. 310.

19 The Court discussed the unemployment benefits of two Native Americans dismissed for peyote consumption from their jobs as alcohol and drug counselors in Oregon, one of the states with no special exemptions for peyote.

20 *Church of Lukumi Babalú Ayé v. City of Hialeah*, 508 U.S. 520, 113 S.Ct. 2217 (1993), II.

21 The ordinances were worded to be inapplicable to *kosher*, which enjoys an exemption granted by Congress, and accepted by Florida. See 7 U.S.C sec. 1902(b) (1988), and Fla. Stat. Ann. sec. 828.22, 828.23 (7)(b) (1976). As Kennedy noted, privileging

one religion over another by exempting only *kosher* could be "an independent constitutional violation." *Lukumi*, IIA1.

22 For example, the minutes and taped excerpts of the session of June 9, 1987, recorded that "When Councilman Martinez, a supporter of the ordinances, stated that in pre-revolutionary Cuba people were put in jail for practicing this religion, the audience applauded. The chaplain of the Hialeah Police Department told the city council that Santeria was 'a sin', 'foolishness', 'an abomination to the Lord', and 'the worship of demons'. He advised the City Council that 'We need to be helping people and sharing with them the truth that is found in Jesus Christ.'" *Lukumi* IIA2.

23 The Court noted that "fishing...is legal. Extermination of mice and rats...is also permitted. Florida law...sanctions euthanasia of 'stray, neglected, abandoned, or unwanted animals'...the infliction of pain...'in the interest of medical science'...and '...hunt[ing] wild hogs'." *Lukumi*, II3B.

24 For classic discussion of these issues, see R. M. Dworkin, *Sovereign Virtue* (Cambridge, MA: Harvard University Press, 2000), esp. pp. 48–59.

25 The Attorney-General of Florida had defined "unnecessary killing" as "done without any useful motive, in a spirit of wanton cruelty or for the mere pleasure of destruction, without it being in any sense beneficial or useful to the person killing the animal." *Fla. Op. Atty. Gen. 87–56, Annual Report of the Atty. Gen.* (1988), at 149, n. 11.

26 Brian Barry cites Rabbi Kimche as an advocate of "the notion that wants, however fantastic the beliefs on which they depend, should count as good currency in public policy." The Rabbi's argument for permission to erect an *eruv* (twenty-foot posts connected near the top with fishing line) in north London was this: "You don't understand, you won't understand it, and quite honestly, you don't need to understand it. The point is we want it, we consider it important and we ask you to respect that." C. Trillin, "Drawing the Line," *New Yorker* (December 12, 1994), p. 62 cit. in B. Barry, "John Rawls and the Search for Stability," *Ethics* 105 (July 1995), p. 897, n. 33.

27 J. Locke, *A Letter Concerning Toleration* (Indianapolis: Hackett Publishing Company, 1985), pp. 41–2.

28 See *First Church of Changó v. American Society for the Prevention of Cruelty to Animals;* 134 A. D. 2d 971, 521 N.Y.S. 2d 356 (1st Dept 1987), affirmed, 70 N.Y. 2d 616, 521 N.E. 2d 443 (1988).

29 G. Francione and A. Charlton, "Supreme Court did not Okay Animal Sacrifice," *Animal People* (July/August 1993).

30 See the first quotation from *Lukumi* (n. 20).

31 For example, euthanasia for strays is painless, and performed for the animals' sake, and medical research, and pest control arguably serve compelling state interests, and can also benefit animals. Such justifications are inapplicable to hunting wild hogs, but hogs, unlike sacrificed animals, enjoy a life of freedom until the day they are shot.

32 G. Francione, "Supreme Court did not Okay Animal Sacrifices," *The Houston Chronicle*, June 13, 1993.

33 For further discussion of the Act's constitutional status, see C. L. Eisgruber and L. G. Sager, "Why the Religious Freedom Restoration Act is Unconstitutional," *New York University Law Review* 69 (1995).

34   Apparently one of the reasons that led to *Smith* was that, in order to reach sensible verdicts, the terms "compelling" and "of the highest priority" were used so loosely that they became increasingly meaningless.

35   Some have also claimed that to "favor, by accommodating, religious practice *as such* – is for government, in violation of the non-establishment norm, to take action based on the view that, at least as a general matter, religious practices are, as such, better or more valuable than nonreligious practices." M. J. Perry, *Religion in Politics* (New York: Oxford University Press, 1997), p. 29. For further discussion, see C. L. Eisgruber and L. G. Sager, "The Vulnerability of Conscience: The Constitutional Basis for Protecting Religious Conduct," *University of Chicago Law Review* 61 (1994); S. Sherry, "Lee v. Weisman: Paradox Redux," *Supreme Court Review* 123 (1993); and W. P. Marshall, "The Religious Freedom Restoration Act: Establishment, Equal Protection, and Free Speech Concerns," *Montana Law Review* 56 (1995). See also L. G. Sager, "The Free Exercise of Culture: Some Doubts and Distinctions," *Proceedings of the American Academy of Arts and Sciences* 129:4 (2000).

36   P. Toynbee, "Rites and Wrongs," *The Guardian* (October 29, 1999).

37   See R. M. Dworkin, *Life's Dominion* (New York: Alfred Knopf, 1993), pp. 160–8.

38   See n. 24.

39   From a historical or anthropological perspective it is often difficult to separate religion from non-religion. Whether a practice, such as circumcision, is considered religious or not varies from one area to the next. Its status often depends on whether local leaders decided at some point to confer religious status on some practice to protect it, or to impose it on local dissidents. The idea that cows are sacred, for example, was invented by India's military elite to protect army stocks while traveling in a country of starving people. See P. Diener, D. Nonini, and E. E. Robkin, "Ecology and Evolution in Cultural Anthropology," *Man* (1980), p. 8.

40   This is M. Nussbaum's only argument against *Smith* and for the Restoration Act in her contribution to *Is Multiculturalism Bad for Women?* However, protecting minorities is precisely what *Smith* is designed to do – hence Blackmun's complaint about how *Smith* turned the Free Exercise Clause into an anti-discrimination principle.

41   Toynbee, "Rites and Wrongs."

42   For further discussion, see S. Kagan, "Equality and Desert," in L. Pojman and O. McLeod (eds.), *What Do We Deserve?* (New York: Oxford University Press, 1999), pp. 300–2.

43   Poulter, *Ethnicity, Law, and Human Rights*, p. 146.

44   Ibid., p. 145

45   Poulter may have intended to combine this argument with an appeal to the importance of religion. If so, he would have only recommended allowing all religiously motivated cruelty until all non-religious cruelty has been prohibited. Singling out religion in this manner, however, faces the difficulties described in the previous section, without escaping my current criticisms.

46   Sources: Alternativa para la Liberación Animal (ALA) y Asociación Nacional para la Protección y el Bienestar de los animales (ANPBBA). The number of animals killed annually by bullfighters was 50,000 a few years ago. See other relevant figures in my prologue to P. Singer, *Liberación Animal* (Madrid: Trotta, 1998).

47   An Intergallup survey indicated that 82% of Spanish respondents have never attended a bullfight, and 87% condemned animal suffering in spectacles. *El Mundo* (April 22, 1998).

48   For related reasons, most doubt the fact that some other similarly situated members of their society never contribute to any charitable cause, such as famine relief, gives them a *decisive* reason not to contribute to any such causes. In more technical terms, partial compliance need not provide overriding justification for non-cooperation, when the beneficiaries of collective action are much worse off than the donors, even if donors become worse off than non-donors. For further discussion of partial compliance, see the final chapter of G. A. Cohen, *If You're an Egalitarian, How Come You're So Rich?* (Cambridge, MA: Harvard University Press, 2000), and L. B. Murphy, *Moral Demands in Non-Ideal Theory* (New York: Oxford University Press, 2000).

49   As Kagan notes in "Equality and Desert," p. 302, "you can believe in comparative desert while still thinking noncomparative desert considerations are more significant".

50   See D. Parfit, "Equality or Priority?" and L. Temkin, "Equality, Priority and the Levelling Down Objection," in M. Clayton and A. Williams (eds.), *The Ideal of Equality* (London: Macmillan, 2000).

51   The criticism is suggested by Kagan's admission that "of course, not everyone believes in the existence of comparative desert. The reasons vary, but one important reason is the fact that (like strict equality) comparative desert can favor lowering those who are better off, even though this does nothing for those who are worse off, and even if the person being lowered has less than he absolutely deserves." "Equality and Desert," see p. 53.

52   This argument would be inapplicable if Santeros were, instead, the rich white Cubans whose inordinate political influence largely explains the existence of the current embargo.

53   For example, it should include exposure to a plurality of valuable options and exclude unacceptably high exit costs, childhood indoctrination into sexist or racist beliefs, and fears of eternal damnation if opting for equality. Until they become consenting adults, girls should not only be protected from clitoridectomy and forced marriage but also from patriarchal dogmas damaging their self-esteem and sense of equal moral worth.

Justice across Borders: Brief for a Global Resources Dividend

Thomas W. Pogge

Article 25: Everyone has the right to a standard of living adequate for the health and well-being of himself and of his family, including food, clothing, housing and medical care.

Article 28: Everyone is entitled to a social and international order in which the rights and freedoms set forth in this Declaration can be fully realised.

Universal Declaration of Human Rights

In two earlier essays (Pogge 1994, 1998), I have sketched and defended the proposal of a global resources dividend or GRD. This proposal envisions that states and their citizens and governments shall not have full libertarian property rights with respect to the natural resources in their territory, but can be required to share a small part of the value of any resources they decide to use or sell. This payment they must make is called a dividend because it is based on the idea that the global poor own an inalienable stake in all limited natural resources. As in the case of preferred stock, this stake confers no right to participate in decisions about whether or how natural resources are to be used and so does not interfere with national control over resources, or eminent domain. But it does entitle its holders to a share of the economic value of the resource in question, if indeed the decision is to use it. This idea could be extended to limited resources that are not destroyed through use but merely eroded, worn down, or occupied, such as air and water used for discharging pollutants or land used for farming, ranching, or buildings.

Proceeds from the GRD are to be used toward ensuring that all human beings can meet their own basic needs with dignity. The goal is not merely

Thomas W. Pogge, 'Brief for a Global Resources Dividend', revised and updated by the author from his 'Eradicating Systemic Poverty: Brief for a Global Resources Dividend', in *Journal of Human Development*, 2 (2001), pp. 59–77.

to improve the nutrition, medical care and sanitary conditions of the poor, but also to make it possible that they can themselves effectively defend and realize their basic interests. This capacity presupposes that they are freed from bondage and other relations of personal dependence, that they are able to read and write and to learn a profession, that they can participate as equals in politics and in the labour market, and that their status is protected by appropriate legal rights which they can understand and effectively enforce through an open and fair legal system.

The GRD proposal is meant to show that there are feasible alternative ways of organizing our global economic order, that the choice among these alternatives makes a substantial difference to how much severe poverty there is world-wide and that there are weighty moral reasons to make this choice so as to minimize such poverty. My proposal has evoked some critical responses (Reichel 1997; Kesselring 1997; Crisp and Jamieson 2000) and spirited defences (Kreide 1998; Mandle 2000) in the academy. But if it is to help reduce severe poverty, the proposal must be convincing not only to academics, but also to the people in governments and international organizations who are practically involved in poverty eradication efforts. I am most grateful therefore for the opportunity to present a concise and improved version of the argument in this volume.

I. Introduction: Radical Inequality and Our Responsibility

One great challenge to any morally sensitive person today is the extent and severity of global poverty. Among about 6,150 million human beings (in 2001), 815 million lack adequate nutrition, 1,100 million lack access to safe water, and 2,400 million lack basic sanitation (UNDP 2002: 21, 29), more than 880 million lack access to basic health services (UNDP 1999: 22), 1,000 billion are without adequate shelter and 2,000 million without electricity (UNDP 1998: 49). "Two out of five children in the developing world are stunted, one in three is underweight and one in ten is wasted" (FAO 1999: 11). 179 million children under 18 are involved in the "worst forms of child labour" including hazardous work in agriculture, construction, textile or carpet production as well as "slavery, trafficking, debt bondage and other forms of forced labour, forced recruitment of children for use in armed conflict, prostitution and pornography, and illicit activities" (ILO 2002: 9, 11, 18). Some 854 million adults are illiterate (UNDP 2002: 11). Roughly one-third of all human deaths, some 50,000 daily, are due to poverty-related causes and thus avoidable insofar as poverty is avoidable (WHO 2001: Annex Table 2; cf. USDA 1999: iii). If the US had its proportional share of these deaths, poverty would kill some 71,000 of its citizens *each month* – more than were killed during the entire Vietnam War. For the UK, the monthly death toll from poverty-related causes would be 15,000.

There are two ways of conceiving global poverty as a moral challenge to us: we may be failing to fulfill our *positive* duty to help persons in acute distress.

And we may be failing to fulfill our more stringent *negative* duty not to uphold injustice, not to contribute to or profit from the unjust impoverishment of others.

These two views differ in important ways. The positive formulation is easier to substantiate. It need be shown only that the poor are very badly off, that we are very much better off and that we could relieve some of their suffering without becoming badly off ourselves. But this ease comes at a price: some who accept the positive formulation think of the moral reasons it provides as weak and discretionary and thus do not feel obligated to promote worthy causes, especially costly ones. Many feel entitled, at least, to support good causes of their choice – their church or alma mater, cancer research or the environment – rather than putting themselves out for total strangers half a world away, with whom they share no bond of community or culture. It is of some importance, therefore, to investigate whether existing global poverty involves our violating a *negative* duty. This is important for us, if we want to lead a moral life and important also for the poor, because it will make a great difference to them whether we affluent do or do not see global poverty as an injustice we help maintain.

Some believe that the mere fact of *radical inequality* shows a violation of negative duty. Radical inequality may be defined as involving five elements (extending Nagel 1977):

1   The worse-off are very badly off in absolute terms.
2   They are also very badly off in relative terms – very much worse off than many others.
3   The inequality is impervious: it is difficult or impossible for the worse-off substantially to improve their lot; and most of the better-off never experience life at the bottom for even a few months and have no vivid idea of what it is like to live in that way.
4   The inequality is pervasive: it concerns not merely some aspects of life, such as the climate or access to natural beauty or high culture, but most aspects or all.
5   The inequality is avoidable: the better-off can improve the circumstances of the worse-off without becoming badly off themselves.

World poverty clearly exemplifies radical inequality as defined. But I doubt that these five conditions suffice to invoke more than a merely positive duty. And I suspect most citizens of the developed West would also find them insufficient. They might appeal to the following parallel: suppose we discovered people on Venus who are very badly off, and suppose we could help them at little cost to ourselves. If we did nothing, we would surely violate a positive duty of beneficence. But we would not be violating a negative duty of justice, because we would not be *contributing* to the perpetuation of their misery.

This point could be further disputed. But let me here accept the Venus argument and examine what *further* conditions must be satisfied for radical inequality to manifest an injustice that involves violation of a negative duty by the better-off. I see three plausible approaches to this question, invoking three different grounds of injustice: the *effects of shared social institutions, the uncompensated exclusion from the use of natural resources,* and *the effects of a common and violent history.* These approaches exemplify distinct and competing political philosophies. We need nonetheless not decide among them here if, as I argue, the following two theses are true. First, *all three approaches classify the existing radical inequality as unjust and its coercive maintenance as a violation of negative duty.* Second, *all three approaches can agree on the same feasible reform of the status quo as a major step toward justice.* If these two theses can be supported, then it may be possible to gather adherents of the dominant strands of Western normative political thought into a coalition focused on eradicating world poverty through the introduction of a Global Resources Dividend or GRD.

II.   Three Grounds of Injustice

II.1.   *The effects of shared social institutions*

The first approach (suggested in O'Neill 1985; Nagel 1977; and Pogge 1989: §24) puts forward three additional conditions:

6   There is a shared institutional order that is shaped by the better-off and imposed on the worse-off.
7   This institutional order is implicated in the reproduction of radical inequality in that there is a feasible institutional alternative under which so severe and extensive poverty would not persist.
8   The radical inequality cannot be traced to extra-social factors (such as genetic handicaps or natural disasters) which, as such, affect different human beings differentially.

Present radical global inequality meets Condition **6** in that the global poor live within a world-wide states system based on internationally recognized territorial domains, interconnected through a global network of market trade and diplomacy. The presence and relevance of shared social institutions is shown by how dramatically we affect the circumstances of the global poor through investments, loans, trade, bribes, military aid, sex tourism, culture exports and much else. Their very survival often crucially depends on our consumption choices, which may determine the price of their foodstuffs and their opportunities to find work. In sharp contrast to the Venus case, we are causally deeply involved in their misery. This does not mean that we should hold ourselves responsible for the remoter effects of our economic decisions. These effects reverberate around the world and interact with the effects of countless other such decisions and thus cannot be traced, let alone predicted. Nor need we draw the dubious and utopian conclusion that global interdependence must be undone by isolating states or groups of states from one another. But we must be concerned with how the rules structuring international interactions foreseeably affect the incidence of extreme poverty. The developed countries, thanks to their vastly superior military and economic strength, control these rules and therefore share responsibility for their foreseeable effects.

Condition 7 involves tracing the incidence of poverty in an explanatory way to the structure of social institutions. This exercise is familiar in regard to national institutions, whose explanatory importance has been powerfully illustrated by domestic regime changes in China, Eastern Europe and elsewhere. In regard to the global economic order, the exercise is unfamiliar and shunned even by economists. This is due in part, no doubt, to powerful resistance against seeing oneself as connected to the unimaginable deprivations suffered by the global poor. This resistance biases us against data, arguments and researchers liable to upset our preferred world view and thus biases the competition for professional success against anyone exploring the wider causal context of global poverty. This bias is reinforced by our cognitive tendency to overlook the causal significance of stable background factors (e.g., the role of atmospheric oxygen in the outbreak of a fire), as our attention is naturally drawn to geographically or temporally variable factors. Looking at the incidence of poverty world-wide, we are struck by dramatic local changes and international variations, which point to local explanatory factors. The heavy focus on such local factors then encourages the illusion, succumbed to by Rawls (1999: 108) for example, that they completely explain global poverty.

This illusion conceals how profoundly local factors and their effects are influenced by the existing global order. Yes, a culture of corruption pervades the political system and the economy of many developing countries. But is this culture unrelated to the fact that most affluent countries have, until quite recently, allowed their firms to bribe foreign officials and even made such bribes tax-deductible?[1] Yes, developing countries have shown themselves prone to oppressive government and to horrific wars and civil wars. But is the frequency of such brutality unrelated to the international arms trade, and unrelated to international rules that entitle anyone holding effective power in such a country to borrow in its name and to sell ownership rights in its natural resources (Wantchekon 1999; Pogge 2002: ch. 6)? Yes, the world is diverse, and poverty is declining in some countries and worsening in others. But the larger pattern of increasing global inequality is quite stable, reaching far back into the colonial era: "The income gap between the fifth of the world's people living in the richest countries and the fifth in the poorest was 74 to 1 in 1997, up from 60 to 1 in 1990 and 30 to 1 in 1960. [Earlier] the income gap between the top and bottom countries increased from 3 to 1 in 1820 to 7 to 1 in 1870 to 11 to 1 in 1913" (UNDP 1999: 3).[2] The affluent countries have been using their power to shape the rules of the world economy according to their own interests and thereby have deprived the poorest populations of a fair share of global economic growth (Pogge 2001) – quite avoidably so, as the GRD proposal shows.

Global poverty meets Condition **8** insofar as the global poor, if only they had been born into different social circumstances, would be just as able and likely to lead healthy, happy and productive lives as the rest of us. The root cause of their suffering is their abysmal social starting position which does not give them much of a chance to become anything but poor, vulnerable and dependent – unable to give their children a better start than they had themselves.

It is because the three additional conditions are met that existing global poverty has, according to the first approach, the special moral urgency we associate with negative duties, so that we should take it much more seriously than otherwise similar suffering on Venus. The reason is that the citizens and governments of the affluent countries – whether intentionally or not – are imposing a global institutional order that foreseeably and avoidably reproduces severe and widespread poverty. The worse-off are not merely poor and often starving, but are *being* impoverished and starved under our shared institutional arrangements, which inescapably shape their lives.

The first approach can be presented in a consequentialist guise, as in Bentham, or in a contractualist guise, as in Rawls or Habermas. In both cases, the central thought is that social institutions are to be assessed in a forward-looking way, by reference to their effects. In the present international order, billions are born into social starting positions that give them extremely low prospects for a fulfilling life. Their misery could be justified only if there were no institutional alternative under which such massive misery would be avoided. If, as the GRD proposal shows, there is such an alternative, then we must ascribe this misery to the existing global order and therefore ultimately to ourselves. As, perhaps surprisingly, Charles Darwin wrote in reference to his native Britain: "If the misery of our poor be caused not by laws of nature, but by our own institutions, great is our sin" (quoted in Gould 1991: 19).

II.2.   *Uncompensated exclusion from the use of natural resources*

The second approach adds (in place of Conditions 6–8) only one condition to the five of radical inequality:

9 The better-off enjoy significant advantages in the use of a single natural resource base from whose benefits the worse-off are largely, and without compensation, excluded.

Currently, appropriation of wealth from our planet is highly uneven. Affluent people use vastly more of the world's resources, and they do so unilaterally, without giving any compensation to the global poor for their disproportionate consumption. Yes, the affluent often pay for the resources they use, such as imported crude oil. But these payments go to other affluent people, such as the Saudi family or the Nigerian kleptocracy, with very little if anything, trickling down to the global poor. So the question remains: what entitles a global elite to use up the world's natural resources on mutually agreeable terms while leaving the global poor empty-handed?

Defenders of capitalist institutions have developed conceptions of justice that support rights to unilateral appropriation of disproportionate shares of resources while accepting that all inhabitants of the earth ultimately have equal claims to its resources. These conceptions are based on the thought that such rights are justified if all are better off with them than anyone would be if appropriation were limited to proportional shares.

This pattern of justification is exemplified with particular clarity in John Locke (cf. also Nozick 1974: ch. 4) [see chs. 1 and 4 in this volume, eds.]. Locke is assuming that, in a state of nature without money, persons are subject to the moral constraint that their unilateral appropriations must always leave "enough, and as good" for others, that is, must be confined to a proportional share (Locke 1689: §27 and §33). This so-called Lockean Proviso may however be lifted with universal consent (1689: §36). Locke subjects such a lifting to a second-order proviso, which requires that the rules of human coexistence may be changed only if all can *rationally* consent to the alteration, that is, only if everyone will be better off under the new rules than anyone would be under the old. And he claims that the lifting of the enough-and-as-good constraint through the general acceptance of money does satisfy this second-order proviso: a day labourer in England feeds, lodges and is clad better than a king of a large fruitful territory in the Americas (Locke 1689: §41 and §37).

It is hard to believe that Locke's claim was true in his time. In any case, it is surely false on the global plane today. Millions are born into poverty each month, in a world where all accessible resources are already owned by others. It is true that they will be able to rent out their labour and then buy natural resources on the same terms as the affluent can. But their educational and employment opportunities are almost always so restricted that, no matter how hard they work, they can barely earn enough for their survival and certainly cannot secure anything like a proportionate share of the world's natural resources. The global poor get to share the burdens resulting from the degradation of our natural environment while having to watch helplessly as the affluent distribute the planet's abundant natural wealth amongst themselves. With average annual *per capita* income of about $87, corresponding to the purchasing power of $347 in the US, the poorest fifth of humankind are today just about as badly off, economically, as human beings could be while still alive.[3] It is then not true, what according to Locke and Nozick would need to be true, that all are better off under the existing appropriation and pollution rules than anyone would be with the Lockean Proviso. According to the second approach, the citizens and governments of the affluent states are therefore violating a negative duty of justice when they, in collaboration with the ruling elites of the poor countries, coercively exclude the poor from a proportional resource share.

II.3.   The effects of a common and violent history

The third approach adds one condition to the five of radical inequality:

10   The social starting positions of the worse-off and the better-off have emerged from a single historical process that was pervaded by massive grievous wrongs.

The present circumstances of the global poor are significantly shaped by a dramatic period of conquest and colonization, with severe oppression, en-slavement, even genocide, through which the native institutions and cultures of four continents were destroyed or severely traumatized. This is not to say (or to deny) that affluent descendants of those who took part in these crimes bear some special restitutive responsibility toward impoverished descendants of those who were victims of these crimes. The thought is rather that we must not uphold extreme inequality in social starting positions when the allocation of these positions depends upon historical processes in which moral principles and legal rules were massively violated. A morally deeply tarnished history should not be allowed to result in *radical* inequality.

This third approach is independent of the others. For suppose we reject the other two approaches and affirm that radical inequality is morally acceptable when it comes about pursuant to rules of the game that are morally at least somewhat plausible and observed at least for the most part. The existing radical inequality is then still condemned by the third approach on the ground that the rules were in fact massively violated through countless horrible crimes whose momentous effects cannot be surgically neutralized decades and centuries later (cf. Nozick 1974: 231).

Some friends of the present distribution claim that standards of living, in Africa and Europe for instance, would be approximately the same if Africa had never been colonized. Even if this claim were both clear and true, it would still be ineffective because my argument applies to persons, not to societies or continents. If world history had transpired without colonization and enslavement, then there would perhaps now be affluent people in Europe and poor ones in Africa, much like in the Venus scenario. But these would be persons and populations quite different from those now actually living there. So we cannot tell starving Africans that *they* would be starving and *we* would be affluent even if the crimes of colonialism had never occurred. Without these crimes there would not be the actually existing radical inequality which consists in *these* persons being affluent and *those* being extremely poor.

So the third approach, too, leads to the conclusion that the existing radical inequality is unjust, that coercively upholding it violates a negative duty, and that we have urgent moral reason to eradicate global poverty.

III.   A Moderate Proposal

The reform proposal now to be sketched is meant to support my second thesis: that the status quo can be reformed in a way that all three approaches would recognize as a major step toward justice. But it is also needed to close gaps in my argument for the first thesis: the proposal should show that the existing radical inequality can be traced to the structure of our global economic order (Condition 7). And it should also show that Condition 5 is met because none of the three approaches involves denying that the status quo is unjust only if we can improve the circumstances of the global poor without thereby becoming badly off ourselves.

I am formulating my reform proposal in line with the second approach, because the other two would support almost any reform that would improve the circumstances of the global poor. The second approach narrows the field by suggesting a more specific idea: those who make more extensive use of our planet's resources should compensate those who, involuntarily, use very little. This idea does not require that we conceive of global resources as the common property of humankind, to be shared equally. My proposal is far more modest by leaving each government in control of the natural resources in its territory. Modesty is important if the proposed institutional alternative is to gain the support necessary to implement it and to sustain itself in the world as we know it. I hope that the GRD satisfies these two desiderata by staying close to the global order now in place and by being evidently responsive to each of the three approaches.

In light of the vast extent of global poverty today, one may think that a massive GRD would be necessary to solve the problem. But I doubt this is so. Present radical inequality is the cumulative result of decades and centuries in which the more affluent societies and groups have used their advantages in capital and knowledge to expand these advantages ever further. This vast gulf between rich and poor does not demonstrate that economic systems have irresistible centrifugal tendencies. Rather, it shows the power of long-term compounding when such tendencies are not continuously resisted (as they are, to some extent within most modern states). It is quite possible that, if radical inequality has once been eradicated, quite a small GRD may, in the context of a fair and open global market system, be sufficient continuously to balance those ordinary centrifugal tendencies of markets enough to forestall its re-emergence. The great magnitude of the problem does suggest, however, that initially more may be needed so that it does not take all too long until severe poverty is erased and an acceptable distributional profile is reached.[4]

To get a concrete sense of the magnitudes involved, let us consider an initial, maximal figure of 1 percent of aggregate global income. While affluent countries in 2001 actually provided $52.3 billion annually in official development assistance – a figure that declined throughout the 1990s – a 1 percent GRD would have raised $315 billion that year.[5] Such an amount, if well targeted and effectively spent, would make a phenomenal difference to the poor even within a few years. On the other hand, the amount is rather small for the rest of us: well below the annual defence budget of just the US alone, significantly less than the annual "peace dividend" enjoyed by the developed countries, and less than half the market value of the current annual crude oil production.[6]

Let us stay with the case of crude oil for a moment and examine the likely effects of a $2 per barrel GRD on crude oil extraction. This dividend would be owed by the countries in which oil is extracted, though most of this cost would be passed along, through higher world market prices, to the end-users of petroleum products. At $2 per barrel, over 18 percent of the high initial revenue target could be raised from crude oil alone – and comfortably so: at the expense of raising the price of petroleum products by about a nickel per gallon (0.8 pence per litre). It is thus clearly possible – without major changes to our global economic order – to eradicate world hunger within a few years by raising a sufficient revenue stream from a limited number of resources and pollutants. These should be selected carefully, with an eye to all collateral effects. This suggests the following desiderata: the GRD should be easy to understand and to apply. It should, for instance, be based on resources and pollutants whose extraction or discharge is easy to monitor or estimate, in order to ensure that every society is paying its fair share and to assure everyone that this is so. Such transparency also helps fulfill a second desideratum of keeping overall collection costs low. The GRD should, thirdly, have only a small impact on the price of goods consumed to satisfy basic needs. And it should, fourthly, be focused on resource uses whose discouragement is especially important for conservation and environmental protection. In this last respect, the GRD reform can produce great ecological benefits that are hard to secure in a less concerted way because of familiar collective-action problems: each society has little incentive to restrain its consumption and pollution, because the opportunity cost of such restraint falls on it alone while the costs of depletion and pollution are spread world-wide and into the future.

The scheme for disbursing GRD funds is to be designed so as to make these funds maximally effective toward ensuring that all human beings can meet their own basic needs with dignity. Such design must draw upon the expertise of economists and international lawyers. Let me nonetheless make some provisional suggestions to give more concreteness to the proposed reform. Disbursement should be made pursuant to clear and straightforward general rules whose administration is cheap and transparent. Transparency is important to exclude political favouritism and the appearance thereof. It is important also for giving the government of any developing country clear and strong incentives toward eradicating domestic poverty. To optimize such incentive effects, the disbursement rules should reward progress: by allocating more funds to this country and/or by assigning more of its allocation directly to its government.

This incentive may not always prevail. In some poor countries, the rulers care more about keeping their subjects destitute, uneducated, docile, dependent and hence exploitable. In such cases, it may still be possible to find other ways of improving the circumstances and opportunities of the domestic poor: by making cash payments directly to them or to their organizations or by funding development programs administered through UN agencies or effective non-governmental organizations. When, in extreme cases, GRD funds cannot be used effectively in a particular country, then there is no reason to spend them there rather than in those many other places where these funds can make a real difference in reducing poverty and disadvantage.

Even if the incentives provided by the GRD disbursement rules do not always prevail, they shift the political balance of forces in the right direction: a good government brings enhanced prosperity through GRD support and thereby generates more popular support which in turn tends to secure its position. A bad government finds the poor harder to oppress when they receive GRD funds through other channels and when all strata of the population have an interest in realizing GRD-accelerated economic improvement under a different government more committed to poverty eradication. With the GRD in place, reforms will be pursued more vigorously and in more countries, and will succeed more often and sooner, than would otherwise be the case. Combined with suitable disbursement rules, the GRD can stimulate a peaceful international competition in effective poverty eradication.

This rough and revisable sketch has shown, I hope, that the GRD proposal deserves serious examination as an alternative to conventional development assistance. While the latter has an aura of hand-outs and dependence, the GRD avoids any appearance of arrogant generosity: it merely incorporates into our global institutional order the moral claim of the poor to partake in the benefits from the use of planetary resources. It implements a moral right – and one that can be justified in multiple ways: namely also forward-lookingly, by reference to its effects, and backward-lookingly, by reference to the evolution of the present economic distribution. Moreover, the GRD would also be vastly more efficient. The disbursement of conventional development aid is heavily influenced by political considerations as is shown by the fact that only 21 percent of it goes to the least developed countries (UNDP 2003, 290). A mere $3.7 billion is spent on basic social services (http://millenniumindicators.un.org/unsd/mi/mi_series_results.asp?rowId=592), less than one cent per day for each person in the poorest quintile. The GRD, by contrast, would initially raise nearly 80 times as much exclusively toward meeting the basic needs of the global poor.

Since the GRD would cost more and return less in direct political benefits, many of the wealthier and more powerful states might be tempted to refuse compliance. Wouldn't the GRD scheme then require a global enforcement agency, something like a world government? In response, I agree that the GRD would have to be backed by sanctions. But sanctions could be decentralized: once the agency facilitating the flow of GRD payments reports that a country has not met its obligations under the scheme, all other countries are required to impose duties on imports from, and perhaps also similar levies on exports to, this country to raise funds equivalent to its GRD obligations plus the cost of these enforcement measures. Such decentralized sanctions stand a very good chance of discouraging small-scale defections. Our world is now, and is likely to remain, highly interdependent economically. Most countries export and import between 10 and 50 percent of their gross domestic product. No country would profit from shutting down foreign trade for the sake of avoiding its GRD obligation. And each would have reasons to fulfill its GRD obligation voluntarily: to retain control over how the funds are raised, to avoid paying extra for enforcement measures and to avoid the adverse publicity associated with non-compliance.

To be sure, such a scheme of decentralized sanctions could work only so long as both the US and the European Union (EU) continue to comply and continue to participate in the sanction mechanism. I assume that both will do this, provided they can be brought to commit themselves to the GRD scheme in the first place. This prerequisite, which is decisive for the success of the proposal, is addressed in Section 5. It should be clear however that a refusal by the US or the EU to participate in the eradication of global poverty would not affect the implications of the present section. The feasibility of the GRD suffices to show that extensive and severe poverty is avoidable at moderate cost (Condition 5), that the existing global order plays an important role in its persistence (Condition 7) and that we can take what all three approaches would recognize as a major step toward justice (second thesis).

IV.   The Moral Argument for the Proposed Reform

By showing that Conditions 1–10 are met, I hope to have demonstrated that present global poverty manifests a grievous injustice that can and should be abolished through institutional reform – involving the GRD scheme, perhaps, or some superior alternative. To make this train of thought as transparent and criticizable as possible, I restate it now as an argument in six steps. The first two steps involve new formulations, so I comment on them briefly at the end.

1   If a society or comparable social system, connected and regulated by a shared institutional order (Condition 6), displays radical inequality (Conditions 1–5), then this institutional order is *prima facie* unjust and requires justification. Here the burden of proof is on those who wish to defend this order and its coercive imposition as compatible with justice.
2   Such a justification of an institutional order under which radical inequality persists would need to show either
  2a   that Condition 10 is not met, perhaps because the existing radical inequality came about fairly: through an historical process that transpired in accordance with morally plausible rules that were generally observed; or
  2b   that Condition 9 is not met, because the worse-off can adequately benefit from the use of the common natural resource base through

> access to a proportional share or through some at least equivalent substitute; or
>
> 2c that Condition 8 is not met, because the existing radical inequality can be traced to extra-social factors (such as genetic handicaps or natural disasters) which, as such, affect different persons differentially; or
>
> 2d that Condition 7 is not met, because any proposed alternative to the existing institutional order either
>
>   —is impracticable, that is, cannot be stably maintained in the long run; or
>
>   —cannot be instituted in a morally acceptable way even with good will by all concerned; or
>
>   —would not substantially improve the circumstances of the worse-off; or
>
>   —would have other morally serious disadvantages that offset any improvement in the circumstances of the worse-off.

3 Humankind is connected and regulated by a shared global institutional order under which radical inequality persists.

4 This global institutional order therefore requires justification <from 1 and 3>.

5 This global institutional order can be given no justification of forms 2a, 2b, or 2c. A justification of form 2d fails as well, because a reform involving introduction of a GRD provides an alternative that is practicable, can (with some good will by all concerned) be instituted in a morally acceptable way, would substantially improve the circumstances of the worse-off and would not have disadvantages of comparable moral significance.

6 The existing global order cannot be justified <from 4, 2 and 5> and hence is unjust <from 1>.

In presenting this argument, I have not attempted to satisfy the strictest demands of logical form, which would have required various qualifications and repetitions. I have merely tried to clarify the structure of the argument so as to make clear how it can be attacked.

One might attack the first step. But this moral premise is quite weak, applying only if the existing inequality occurs within a shared institutional order (Condition 6) *and* is radical, that is, involves truly extreme poverty and extreme differentials in standards of living (Conditions 1–5). Moreover, the first premise does not flatly exclude any institutional order under which radical inequality persists, but merely demands that it be justified. Since social institutions are created and upheld, perpetuated or reformed by human beings, this demand cannot plausibly be refused.

One might attack the second step. But this moral premise, too, is weak, in that it demands of the defender of the status quo only one of the four possible showings (2a–2d), leaving him free to try each of the conceptions of economic justice outlined in Section 2 even though he can hardly endorse all of them at once. Still, it remains open to argue that an institutional order reproducing radical inequality can be justified in a way that differs from the four (**2a–2d**) I have described.

One might try to show that the existing global order does not meet one of the ten conditions. Depending on which condition is targeted, one would thereby deny the third premise or give a justification of forms **2a** or **2b** or **2c**, or show that my reform proposal runs into one of the four problems listed under **2d**.

The conclusion of the argument is reached only if all ten conditions are met. Existing global poverty then manifests a *core injustice*: a phenomenon that the dominant strands of Western normative political thought jointly – albeit for diverse reasons – classify as unjust and can jointly seek to eradicate. Insofar as advantaged and influential participants in the present international order grant the argument, we acknowledge our shared responsibility for its injustice: we are violating a negative duty of justice insofar as we contribute to (and fail to mitigate) the harms it reproduces and insofar as we resist suitable reforms.

V. Is the Reform Proposal Realistic?

Even if the GRD proposal is practicable, and even if it could be implemented with the good will of all concerned, there remains the problem of generating this good will, especially on the part of the rich and mighty. Without the support of the US and the EU, massive global poverty and starvation will certainly not be eradicated in our lifetimes. How realistic is the hope of mobilizing such support? I have two answers to this question.

First. Even if this hope is not realistic, it is still important to insist that present global poverty manifests a grievous injustice according to Western normative political thought. We are not merely distant witnesses of a problem unrelated to ourselves, with a weak, positive duty to help. Rather we are, both causally and morally, materially involved in the fate of the poor by imposing upon them a global institutional order that regularly produces severe poverty and/or by effectively excluding them from a fair share of the value of exploited natural resources and/or by upholding a radical inequality that evolved through an historical process pervaded by horrendous crimes. We can realistically end our involvement in their severe poverty not by extricating ourselves from this involvement, but only by ending such poverty through economic reform. If feasible reforms are blocked by others, then we may in the end be unable to do more than mitigate some of the harms we also help produce. But even then a difference would remain, because our effort would fulfill not a duty to help the needy, but a duty to protect victims of any injustice to which we contribute. The latter duty is, other things equal, much more stringent than the former, especially when we can fulfill it out of the benefits we continually derive from this injustice.

My second answer is that the hope may not be so unrealistic after all. My provisional optimism is based on two considerations. The first is that moral convictions can have real effects even in international politics – as even some political realists admit, albeit with regret. Sometimes these are the moral convictions of politicians. But more commonly politics is influenced by the moral convictions of citizens. One dramatic example of this is the abolitionist movement which, in the nineteenth century, pressured the British government into suppressing the slave trade (Drescher 1986). A similar moral mobilization may be possible also for the sake of eradicating global poverty – provided the citizens of the more powerful states can be convinced of a moral conclusion that really can be soundly supported and provided a path can be shown that makes only modest demands on each of us.

The GRD proposal is morally compelling. It can be broadly anchored in the dominant strands of Western normative political thought outlined in Section 2. And it also has the morally significant advantage of shifting consumption in ways that restrain global pollution and resource depletion for the benefit of all and of future generations in particular. Because it can be backed by these four important and mutually independent moral rationales, the GRD proposal is well positioned to benefit from the fact that moral reasons can have effects in the world. If some help can be secured from economists, political scientists and lawyers, then moral acceptance of the GRD may gradually emerge and become widespread in the developed West.

Eradicating global poverty through a scheme like the GRD also involves more realistic demands than a solution through private initiatives and conventional development aid. Even when one is certain that, by donating $900 per year, one can raise the standard of living of two very poor families by $400 annually, the commitment to do so is hard to sustain. Continual unilateral mitigation of poverty leads to fatigue, aversion, even contempt. It requires the more affluent citizens and governments to rally to the cause again and again while knowing full well that most others similarly situated contribute nothing or very little, that their own contributions are legally optional and that, no matter how much they give, they could for just a little more always save yet further children from sickness or starvation.

Helping to implement the GRD, by contrast, one would also lower one's family's standard of living by $900 annually, but one would do so for the sake of raising by $400 annually the standard of living of *hundreds of millions* of poor families. One would do so for the sake of eradicating severe poverty from this planet while knowing that all affluent people and countries are contributing their fair share to this effort.

Analogous considerations apply to governments. The inefficiency of conventional development aid is sustained by their competitive situation, as they feel morally entitled to decline to do more by pointing to their even stingier competitors. This explanation supports the optimistic assumption that the affluent societies would be prepared, in joint reciprocity, to commit themselves to more than what they tend to do each on its own.

Similar considerations apply to environmental protection and conservation, with respect to which the GRD also contributes to a collective solution: levels of pollution and wastefulness will continue to be much higher than would be best for all so long as anyone causing them can dump most of their cost on the rest of the world without any compensation ("tragedy of the commons"). Exacting such compensation, the GRD redresses this imbalance of incentives.

An additional point is that national development aid and environmental protection measures must be politically fought for or defended year after year, while acceptance of the GRD scheme would require only one – albeit rather more far-reaching – political decision.

The other optimistic consideration has to do with prudence. The times when we could afford to ignore what goes on in the developing countries are over for good. Their economic growth will have a great impact on our environment and their military and technological gains are accompanied by serious dangers, among which those associated with nuclear, biological and chemical weapons and technologies are only the most obvious. The transnational imposition of externalities and risks will ever more become a two-way street as no state or group of states, however rich and mighty, will be able effectively to insulate itself from external influences: from military and terrorist attacks, illegal immigrants, epidemics and the drug trade, pollution and climate change, price fluctuations and scientific-technological and cultural innovations. It is then increasingly in our interest, too, that stable democratic institutions shall emerge in the developing countries – institutions under which governmental power is effectively constrained through procedural rules and basic rights. So long as large segments of these peoples lack elementary education and have no assurance that they will be able to meet even their most basic needs, such democratic institutions are much less likely than explosive mixtures of religious and ideological fanaticism, violent opposition movements, death squads and corrupt and politicized militaries. To expose ourselves to the occasional explosions of these mixtures would be increasingly dangerous and also more costly in the long run than the proposed GRD.

This prudential consideration has a moral side as well. A future that is pervaded by radical inequality and hence unstable would endanger not only the security of ourselves and our progeny, but also the long-term survival of our society, values and culture. Not only that: such a future would, quite generally, endanger the security of all other human beings and their descendants as well as the survival of their societies, values and cultures. And so the interest in peace – in a future world in which different societies, values and cultures can coexist and interact peacefully – is obviously also, and importantly, a moral interest.

Realizing our prudential and moral interest in a peaceful and ecologically sound future will – and here I go beyond my earlier modesty – require supranational social institutions and organizations that limit the sovereignty rights of states more severely than is the current practice. The most powerful states could try to impose such limitations upon all the rest while exempting themselves. It is doubtful, however, that today's great powers can summon and sustain the domestic political support necessary to see through such an attempt to the end. And it is doubtful also whether they could succeed. For such an attempt would provoke the bitter resistance of many other states, which would simultaneously try very hard, through military build-up, to gain access to the club of great powers. For such a project, the "elites" in many developing countries could probably mobilize their populations quite easily, as the examples of India and Pakistan illustrate.

It may then make more sense for all to work toward supranational social institutions and organizations that limit the sovereignty rights of all states equally. But this solution can work only if at least a large majority of the states participating in these social institutions and organizations are stable democracies, which presupposes, in turn, that their citizens are assured that they can meet their basic needs and can attain a decent education and social position.

The current geopolitical development drifts toward a world in which militarily and technologically highly advanced states and groups, growing in number, pose an ever greater danger for an ever larger subset of humankind. Deflecting this development in a more reasonable direction realistically requires considerable support from those other 84 percent of humankind who want to reduce our economic advantage and achieve our high standard of living. Through the introduction of the GRD or some similar reform we can gain such support by showing concretely that our relations to the rest of the world are not solely devoted to cementing our economic hegemony and that the global poor will be able peacefully to achieve a considerable improvement in their circumstances. In this way and only in this way can we refute the conviction, understandably widespread in the poor countries, that we will not give a damn about their misery until they will have the economic and military power to do us serious harm. And only in this way can we undermine the popular support that aggressive political movements of all kinds can derive from this conviction.

VI.   Conclusion

We are familiar, through charity appeals, with the assertion that it lies in our hands to save the lives of many or, by doing nothing, to let these people die. We are less familiar with the here examined assertion of a weightier responsibility: that most of us do not merely let people starve but also participate in starving them. It is not surprising that our initial reaction to this more unpleasant assertion is indignation, even hostility – that, rather than think it through or discuss it, we want to forget it or put it aside as plainly absurd.

I have tried to respond constructively to the assertion and to show its plausibility. I do not pretend to have proved it conclusively, but my argument should at least raise grave doubts about our common-sense prejudices, which we must in any case treat with suspicion on account of how strongly our self-interest is engaged in this matter. The great moral importance of reaching the correct judgement on this issue also counsels against lightly dismissing the assertion here defended. The essential data about the lives and deaths of the global poor are, after all, indisputable. In view of very considerable global interdependence, it is extremely unlikely that their poverty is due exclusively to local factors and that no feasible reform of the present global order could thus affect either that poverty or these local factors. No less incredible is the view that ours is the best of all possible global orders, that any modification of it could only aggravate poverty. So we should work together across disciplines to conceive a comprehensive solution to the problem of global poverty, and across borders for the political implementation of this solution.

Notes

1 A Convention on Combating Bribery of Foreign Officials in International Business Transactions, which requires signatory states to criminalise the bribery of foreign officials, was finally drafted within the OECD under public pressure generated by the new non-governmental organization Transparency International (<www.trans parency.de>). The Convention went into effect in February 1999 (<www.oecd.org/ document/21/0,02340,en_2649_34859_2017813_1_1_1_1,00.html>).
2 For 2001, the corresponding ratio appears to have been 71:1 (World Bank 2002: 234–5, my calculation). Many economists reject this statistic as misleading, claiming that the comparison should be made in terms of purchasing power parities (PPPs) rather than market exchange rates. However, market exchange rates are quite appropriate to highlight international inequalities in expertise and bargaining power as well as the increasing avoidability of poverty, which is manifest in the fact that just 1 percent of the national incomes of the highest-income countries would suffice to raise those of the lowest-income countries by 74 percent.

   To compare standards of living, PPPs are indeed appropriate. But general-consumption PPPs, based as they are on the prices of all commodities weighted by their share in international consumption, substantially overstate the purchasing power of the poor relative to the basic necessities on which they are compelled to concentrate their expenditures. This is so because poor countries tend to afford the greatest price advantages for commodities (services and other "non-tradables") which their poor citizens cannot afford to consume. By using PPPs that average out price differentials across all commodities, economists inflate the nominal incomes of the poor as if their consumption mirrored that of the world at large. See Reddy and Pogge 2002 for a detailed critique.

   Even if one takes PPPs at face value, the increase in global inequality is alarming: Over a recent five-year period, "world inequality has increased…from a Gini of 62.8 in 1988 to 66.0 in 1993. This represents an increase of 0.6 Gini points per year. This is a very fast increase, faster than the increase experienced by the US and UK in the decade of the 1980's…. The bottom 5 percent of the world grew poorer, as their real incomes decreased between 1988 and 1993 by $\frac{1}{4}$, while the richest quintile grew richer. It gained 12 percent in real terms, that is it grew more than twice as much as mean world income (5.7 percent)" (Milanovic 2002: 88).
3 The World Bank estimates that, in 1998, 1,175 million out of 5,923 million human beings lived below the international poverty line, which it currently defines in terms

of $32.74 PPP 1993 per month or $1.08 PPP 1993 per day (Chen and Ravallion 2001; World Bank 2001: 17 and 23). "PPP" stands for "purchasing power parity," so people count as poor by this standard when their income per person per year has less purchasing power than $393 had in the US in 1993 or less purchasing power than $496 has in the US in the year 2003 (<www.bls.gov/cpi/>). Those living below this poverty line, on average, fall 30 percent below it (Chen and Ravallion 2001: 290, 293, dividing the poverty gap index by the headcount index). So they live on approximately $347 PPP 2003 per person per year on average. Now the $ PPP incomes the World Bank ascribes to people in poor developing countries are on average at least four times higher than their actual incomes at market exchange rates. Thus the World Bank equates India's per capita gross national income of $460 to $2,390 PPP, China's $840 to $3,940 PPP, Nigeria's $260 to $790 PPP, Pakistan's $470 to $1,960 PPP, Bangladesh's $380 to $1,650 PPP, Ethiopia's $100 to $660 PPP, Vietnam's $390 to $2,030 PPP, and so on (World Bank 2002: 232–3). Since virtually all the global poor live in such poor developing countries, we can then estimate that their average annual per capita income corresponds to at most $87 at market exchange rates. The aggregate annual income of the poorest fifth of humankind is then about $103 billion at market exchange rates or roughly one-third of 1 percent of the global product.

4   Since 1990, governments have been proclaiming their commitment to halve global poverty and hunger by 2015. In the 1996 Rome Declaration on World Food Security, 186 governments made the solemn promise "to eradicate hunger in all countries, with an immediate view to reducing the number of undernourished people, to halve their present level no later than 2015." More than half the 25-year period has passed with severe reductions in official development assistance and no reduction at all in the numbers of poor and undernourished people. But there is progress of a sort: the goal has been diminished. The UN Millennium Declaration promises "to halve, by the year 2015, the proportion of the world's people whose income is less than one dollar a day and the proportion of people who suffer from hunger." With world population estimated to increase by 36 percent in the 1990–2015 period, the sought reduction in the number of poor and undernourished people is now not 50 percent but merely 32 percent. In the face of 18 million poverty-related deaths per year, the official go-slow approach is morally unacceptable and the lack of effort toward implementing this approach appalling. It should also be said that the World Bank's severely flawed poverty measurement method leads to a gross understatement of the number of people living below its $1/day poverty line (Reddy and Pogge 2002). Moreover, this poverty line is, of course, grotesquely low. (Just imagine a family of four living on $1,984 per year in the US or on £1,250 per year in the UK.) The World Bank provides statistics also for a more adequate poverty line that is twice as high: $786 PPP 1993 ($992 PPP in 2003 or roughly $248 in the typical poor country) per person per year. 2,800 million people – nearly half of humankind – are said to live below this higher poverty line, falling 43 percent below it on average (Chen and Ravallion 2001: 290, 293, again dividing the poverty gap index by the headcount index). The aggregate annual income of these people is then about $396 billion at market exchange rates or about $1\frac{1}{4}$ percent of the global product. Their aggregate poverty gap is about $300 billion per year, under 1 percent of the global product. The GRD would thus suffice to bring all human beings up to the World Bank's higher "$2/day" poverty line.

5   Cf.   <http://millenniumindicators.un.org/unsd/mi/mi_series_results.asp?rowId =569> and UNDP 2003, 290. The annual global product (sum of all gross national incomes) was \$31,500 billion per year in 2001. Of this, 81.6 percent belonged to the richest countries containing 16 percent of humankind (World Bank 2002: 234–5). The US alone, with 4.6 percent of world population, accounts for 31.4 percent of global product (ibid. – and the US still managed to renegotiate its share of the UN budget from 25 percent down to 22 percent).

6   The end of the Cold War enabled the high-income countries to cut their aggregate military expenditure from 4.1 percent of their gross domestic product in 1985 to 2.2 percent in 1998 (UNDP 1998: 197; UNDP 2000: 217). The peace dividend these countries reap can then be estimated at \$477 billion (1.9 percent of their current aggregate annual GDP of \$25,104 billion in the year 2001 – World Bank 2002: 239). Crude oil production is currently about 78 million barrels daily or about $28\frac{1}{2}$ billion barrels annually. At \$25 per barrel, this comes to \$700 billion annually.

References

Aiken, Will and LaFolette, Hugh (eds.) (1996) *World Hunger and Morality*. Upper Saddle River, NJ: Prentice Hall.

Barry, Brian (1982) "Humanity and Justice in Global Perspective," in J. R. Pennock and J. W. Chapman (eds.), *Ethics, Economics, and the Law*. New York: New York University Press.

Beitz, Charles (1979) *Political Theory and International Relations*. Princeton: Princeton University Press.

Chen, Shaohua and Ravallion, Martin (2001) "How Did the World's Poorest Fare in the 1990s?," *Review of Income and Wealth*, 47, 283–300.

Crisp, Roger and Jamieson, Dale (2000) "Egalitarianism and a Global Resources Tax: Pogge on Rawls," in Victoria Davion and Clark Wolf (eds.), *The Idea of a Political Liberalism: Essays on Rawls*. Lanham, MD: Rowman & Littlefield.

Dasgupta, Partha (1993) *An Inquiry into Well-Being and Destitution*. Oxford: Oxford University Press.

Drescher, Seymour (1986) *Capitalism and Antislavery: British Mobilization in Comparative Perspective*. Oxford: Oxford: Oxford University Press.

Eichengreen, Barry, Tobin, James and Wyplosz, Charles (1995) "Two Cases for Sand in the Wheels of International Finance," *Economic Journal*, 105 (428), 162–72.

FAO (Food and Agriculture Organization of the United Nations) (1999) *The State of Food Insecurity in the World 1999* <www.fao.org/news/1999/img/sofi99-e.pdf>.

Gould, Stephen Jay (1991) "The Moral State of Tahiti – and of Darwin," *Natural History*, 10, 12–19.

ILO (International Labour Organization) (2002) *A Future Without Child Labour* <www.ilo.org/public/english/standards/decl/publ/reports/report3.htm>.

Kesselring, Thomas (1997) "Weltarmut und Ressourcen-Zugang," *Analyse und Kritik*, 19 (3), 242–54.

Kreide, Regina (1998) "Armut, Gerechtigkeit und Demokratie," *Analyse und Kritik*, 20 (3), 245–62.

Locke, John (1689) "An Essay Concerning the True Original, Extent, and End of Civil Government," in Peter Laslett (ed.), *John Locke: Two Treatises of Government*. Cambridge: Cambridge University Press.

Mandle, Jon (2000) "Globalization and Justice," *Annals of the American Academy*, 570, 126–39.

Milanovic, Branko (2002) "True World Income Distribution, 1988 and 1993: First Calculation Based on Household Surveys Alone," *The Economic Journal*, 112, 51–92.

Murphy, Liam (2000) *Moral Demands in Non-Ideal Theory*. Oxford: Oxford University Press.

Nagel, Thomas (1977) "Poverty and Food: Why Charity Is Not Enough," in Peter Brown and Henry Shue (eds.), *Food Policy: The Responsibility of the United States in Life and Death Choices*. New York: Free Press.

Nozick, Robert (1974) *Anarchy, State, and Utopia*. New York: Basic Books.

O'Neill, Onora (1985) "Lifeboat Earth" (1974), repr. in Charles Beitz, Marshall Cohen, Thomas Scanlon and A. John Simmons (eds.), *International Ethics*. Princeton: Princeton University Press.

Pogge, Thomas (1989) *Realizing Rawls*. Ithaca, NY: Cornell University Press.

Pogge, Thomas (1994) "An Egalitarian Law of Peoples," *Philosophy and Public Affairs*, 23 (3), 195–224.

Pogge, Thomas (1998) "A Global Resources Dividend," in David A. Crocker and Toby Linden (eds.), *Ethics of Consumption: The Good Life, Justice, and Global Stewardship*. Lanham, MD: Rowman & Littlefield.

Pogge, Thomas (2001) "Priorities of Global Justice," in id. (ed.), *Global Justice*. Oxford: Blackwell.

Pogge, Thomas (2002) *World Poverty and Human Rights: Cosmopolitan Responsibilities and Reforms*. Cambridge: Polity.

Rawls, John (1999) *The Law of Peoples*. Cambridge, MA: Harvard University Press.

Reddy, Sanjay and Thomas W. Pogge (2002). "How *Not* to Count the Poor," unpublished working paper <www.socialanalysis.org>.

Reichel, Richard (1997) "Internationaler Handel, Tauschgerechtigkeit und die globale Rohstoffdividende," *Analyse und Kritik*, 19 (3), 229–41.

Rome Declaration on World Food Security <www.fao.org/wfs/>.

Shue, Henry (1980) *Basic Rights*. Princeton: Princeton University Press.

Singer, Peter (1972) "Famine, Affluence and Morality," *Philosophy and Public Affairs*, 1 (3), 229–43.

Tobin, James (1978) "A Proposal for International Monetary Reform," *Eastern Economic Journal*, 4, 153–9.

UNDP (United Nations Development Programme) (1998) *Human Development Report 1998*. New York: Oxford University Press.

UNDP (1999) *Human Development Report 1999*. New York: Oxford University Press.

UNDP (2000) *Human Development Report 2000*. New York: Oxford University Press.

UNDP (2002) *Human Development Report 2002*. New York: Oxford University Press.

UNDP (2003) *Human Development Report 2003*. New York: Oxford University Press.

Unger, Peter (1996) *Living High and Letting Die: Our Illusion of Innocence*. Oxford: Oxford University Press.

UN Millennium Declaration <www.un.org/millennium/declaration/ares552e.htm>.

USDA (United States Department of Agriculture) (1999) *U.S. Action Plan on Food Security* <www.fas.usda.gov/icd/summit/usactplan.pdf>.

Wantchekon, Leonard (1999) "Why Do Resource Dependent Countries Have Authoritarian Governments?", working paper, Yale University <www.yale.edu/leitner/pdf/1999–11.pdf>.

World Bank (2001) *World Development Report 2000/2001*. New York: Oxford University Press. <www.worldbank.org/poverty/wdrpoverty/report/index.htm>.

World Bank (2002) *World Development Report 2003*. New York: Oxford University Press.

WHO (World Health Organization) (2001) *The World Health Report 2001*. Geneva: WHO Publications <www.who.int/whr/2001>.

13

Justice across Generations: The Non-Identity Problem

Derek Parfit

I. The Three Kinds of Choice

Unless we, or some global disaster, destroy the human race, there will be people living later who do not now exist. These are *future people*. Science has given to our generation great ability both to affect these people, and to predict these effects.

Two kinds of effect raise puzzling questions. We can affect the identities of future people, or *who* the people are who will later live. And we can affect the number of future people. These effects give us different kinds of choice.

In comparing any two acts, we can ask:

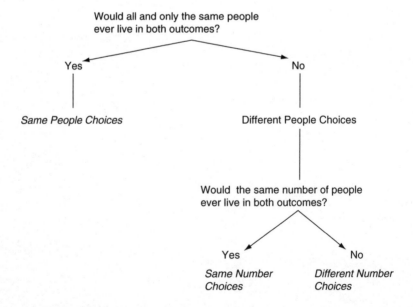

Derek Parfit, 'The Non-Identity Problem', from *Reasons and Persons* (Oxford: Clarendon Press, 1984), pp. 355–77 (sects. 120–6).

Different Number Choices affect both the number and the identities of future people. Same Number Choices affect the identities of future people, but do not affect their number. Same People Choices affect neither.

II. What Weight Should We Give To the Interests of Future People?

Most of our moral thinking is about Same People Choices. As I shall argue, such choices are not as numerous as most of us assume. Very many of our choices will in fact have some effect on both the identities and the number of future people. But in most of these cases, because we cannot predict what the particular effects would be, these effects can be morally ignored. We can treat these cases as if they were Same People Choices.

In some cases we can predict that some act either may or will be against the interests of future people. This can be true when we are making a Same People Choice. In such a case, whatever we choose, all and only the same people will ever live. Some of these people will be future people. Since these people will exist whatever we choose, we can either harm or benefit these people in a quite straightforward way.

Suppose that I leave some broken glass in the undergrowth of a wood. A hundred years later this glass wounds a child. My act harms this child. If I had safely buried the glass, this child would have walked through the wood unharmed.

Does it make a moral difference that the child whom I harm does not now exist?

On one view, moral principles cover only people who can *reciprocate*, or harm and benefit each other. If I cannot be harmed or benefited by this child, as we can plausibly suppose, the harm that I cause this child has no moral importance. I assume that we should reject this view.[1]

Some writers claim that, while we ought to be concerned about effects on future people, we are morally justified in being less concerned about effects in the further future. This is a common view in welfare economics, and cost-benefit analysis. On this view, we can *discount* the more remote effects of our acts and policies, at some rate of n per cent per year. This is called the *Social Discount Rate*.

Suppose we are considering how to dispose safely of the radio-active matter called *nuclear waste*. If we believe in the Social Discount Rate, we shall be concerned with safety only in the nearer future. We shall not be troubled by the fact that some nuclear waste will be radio-active for thousands of years. At a discount rate of five per cent, one death next year counts for more than a billion deaths in 500 years. On this view, catastrophes in the further future can now be regarded as morally trivial.

As this case suggests, the Social Discount Rate is indefensible. Remoteness in time roughly correlates with some important facts, such as predictability.

But... these correlations are too rough to justify the Social Discount Rate. The present moral importance of future events does *not* decline at a rate of *n* per cent per year. Remoteness in time has, in itself, no more significance than remoteness in space. Suppose that I shoot some arrow into a distant wood, where it wounds some person. If I should have known that there might be someone in this wood, I am guilty of gross negligence. Because this person is far away, I cannot identify the person whom I harm. But this is no excuse. Nor is it any excuse that this person is far away. We should make the same claims about effects on people who are temporally remote.

III.   A Young Girl's Child

Future people are, in one respect, unlike distant people. We can affect their identity. And many of our acts have this effect.

This fact produces a problem. Before I describe this problem, I shall repeat some preliminary remarks. I assume that one person can be worse off than another, in morally significant ways, and by more or less. But I do not assume that these comparisons could be, even in principle, precise. I assume that there is only rough or partial comparability. On this assumption, it could be true of two people that neither is worse off than the other, but this would not imply that these people are exactly equally well off.

'Worse off' could be taken to refer, either to someone's level of happiness, or more narrowly to his standard of living, or, more broadly, to the quality of his life. Since it is the broadest, I shall often use the phrase 'the quality of life'. I also call certain lives 'worth living'. This description can be ignored by those who believe that there could not be lives that are not worth living. But, like many other people, I believe that there are such lives. Finally, I extend the ordinary use of the phrase 'worth living'. If one of two people would have a lower quality of life, I call his life to this extent 'less worth living'.

When considering future people, we must answer two questions:

(1)   If we cause someone to exist, who will have a life worth living, do we thereby benefit this person?

(2)   Do we also benefit this person if some act of ours is a remote but necessary part of the cause of his existence?

These are difficult questions. If we answer Yes to both, I shall say that we believe *that causing to exist can benefit.*

Some people answer Yes to (1) but No to (2). These people give their second answer because they use 'benefit' in its ordinary sense. As I argued in Section 25 [of *Reasons and Persons*, eds.], we ought for moral purposes to extend our use of 'benefit'. If we answer Yes to (1) we should answer Yes to (2).

Many people answer No to both these questions. These people might say: 'We benefit someone if it is true that, if we had not done what we did, this would have been worse for this person. If we had not caused someone to exist, this would *not* have been worse for this person.'

I believe that, while it is defensible to answer No to both these questions, it is also defensible to answer Yes to both. . . . Since I believe that it is defensible both to claim and to deny that causing to exist can benefit, I shall discuss the implications of both views.

Consider

> *The 14-Year-Old Girl*. This girl chooses to have a child. Because she is so young, she gives her child a bad start in life. Though this will have bad effects throughout this child's life, his life will, predictably, be worth living. If this girl had waited for several years, she would have had a different child, to whom she would have given a better start in life.

Since such cases are, at least in the United States, becoming very numerous, they raise a practical problem.[2] They also raise a theoretical problem.

Suppose that we tried to persuade this girl that she ought to wait. We claimed: 'If you have a child now, you will soon regret this. If you wait, this will be better for you.' She replied: 'This is my affair. Even if I am doing what will be worse for me, I have a right to do what I want.'

We replied: 'This is not entirely your affair. You should think not only of yourself, but also of your child. It will be worse for him if you have him now. If you have him later, you will give him a better start in life.'

We failed to persuade this girl. She had a child when she was 14, and, as we predicted, she gave him a bad start in life. Were we right to claim that her decision was worse for her child? If she had waited, this particular child would never have existed. And, despite its bad start, his life is worth living. Suppose first that we do *not* believe that causing to exist can benefit. We should ask, 'If someone lives a life that is worth living, is this worse for this person than if he had never existed?' Our answer must be No. Suppose next that we believe that causing to exist *can* benefit. On this view, this girl's decision benefits her child.

On both views, this girl's decision was not worse for her child. When we see this, do we change our mind about this decision? Do we cease to believe that it would have been better if this girl had waited, so that she could give to her first child a better start in life? I continue to have this belief, as do most of those who consider this case. But we cannot defend this belief in the natural way that I suggested. We cannot claim that this girl's decision was worse for her child. What is the objection to her decision? This question arises because, in the different outcomes, different people would be born. I shall therefore call this the *Non-Identity Problem*.[3]

It may be said:

In one sense, this girl's decision *was* worse for her child. In trying to persuade this girl not to have a child now, we can use the phrase 'her child' and the pronoun 'he' to cover *any* child that she might have. These words need not refer to one particular child. We can truly claim: 'If this girl does not have her child now, but waits and has him later, *he* will not be the same particular child. If she has him later, he will be a different child.' By using these words in this way, we can explain why it would be better if this girl waits. We can claim:

(A) The objection to this girl's decision is that it will probably be worse for her child. If she waits, she would give him a better start in life.

Though we can truly make this claim, it does *not* explain the objection to this girl's decision. This becomes clear after the girl has had her child. The phrase 'her child' now naturally refers to this particular child. And this girl's decision was *not* worse for *this* child. Though there is a sense in which (A) is true, (A) does not appeal to a familiar moral principle.

On one of our familiar principles, it is an objection to someone's choice that this choice will be worse for, or be against the interests of, any other particular person. If we claim that this girl's decision was worse for her child, we cannot be claiming that it was worse for a particular person. We cannot claim, of the girl's child, that her decision was worse for *him*. We must admit that, in claim (A), the words 'her child' do not refer to her child. (A) is not about what is good or bad for any of the particular people who ever live. (A) appeals to a new principle, that must be explained and justified.

If (A) seems to appeal to a familiar principle, this is because it has two senses. Here is another example. A general shows military skill if, in many battles, he always makes his the winning side. But there are two ways of doing this. He might win victories. Or he might always, when he is about to lose, change sides. A general shows no military skill if it is only in the second sense that he always makes his the winning side.

To what principle does (A) appeal? We should state the principle in a way that shows the kind of choice to which it applies. These are Same Number Choices, which affect the identities of future people, but do not affect their number. We might suggest

The Same Number Quality Claim, or *Q*: If in either of two possible outcomes the same number of people would ever live, it would be worse if those who live are worse off, or have a lower quality of life, than those who would have lived.

This claim is plausible. And it implies what we believe about the 14-Year-Old Girl. The child that she has now will probably be worse off than a child she could have had later would have been, since this other child would have had a better start in life. If this is true, Q implies that this is the worse of these two outcomes. Q implies that it would have been better if this girl had waited, and had a child later.

We may shrink from claiming, of this girl's actual child, that it would have been better if he had never existed. But, if we claimed earlier that it would be better if this girl waits, this is what we must claim. We cannot consistently make a claim and deny this same claim later. If (1) in 1990 it *would be* better if this girl waits and has a child later, then (2) in 2020 it *would have been* better if she had waited and had a child later. And (2) implies (3) that it would have been better if the child who existed had not been her actual child. If we cannot accept (3), we must reject (1).

I suggest that, on reflection, we can accept (3). I believe that, if *I* was the actual child of this girl, I could accept (3). (3) does not imply that my existence is *bad*, or intrinsically morally undesirable. The claim is merely that, since a child born later would probably have had a better life than mine, it would have been better if my mother had waited, and had a child later. This claim need not imply that I ought rationally to regret that my mother had *me*, or that she ought rationally to regret this. Since it would have been better if she had waited, she ought perhaps to have some moral regret. And it is probably true that she made the outcome worse for herself. But, even if this is true, it does not show that she ought rationally to regret her act, all things considered. If she loves me, her actual child, this is enough to block the claim that she is irrational if she does not have such regret.[4] Even when it implies a claim like (3), I conclude that we can accept Q.

Though Q is plausible, it does not solve the Non-Identity Problem. Q covers only the cases where, in the different outcomes, the same number of people would ever live. We need a claim that covers cases where, in the different outcomes, different numbers would ever live. The Non-Identity Problem can arise in these cases.

Because Q is restricted, it could be justified in several different ways. There are several principles that imply Q, but conflict when applied to Different Number Choices. We shall need to decide which of these principles, or which set of principles, we ought to accept. Call what we ought to accept *Theory X*. X will solve the Non-Identity Problem in Different Number Choices. And X will tell us how Q should be justified, or more fully explained.

In the case of The 14-Year-Old Girl, we are not forced to appeal to Q. There are other facts to which we could appeal, such as the effects on other people. But the problem can arise in a purer form.

IV. How Lowering the Quality of Life Might Be Worse For No One

Suppose that we are choosing between two social or economic policies. And suppose that, on one of the two policies, the standard of living would be slightly higher over the next century. This effect implies another. It is not true that, whichever policy we choose, the same particular people will exist in the further future. Given the effects of two such policies on the details of our lives, it would increasingly over time be true that, on the different policies, people married different people. And, even in the same marriages, the children would increasingly over time be conceived at different times. As I have argued, children conceived more than a month earlier or later would in fact be different children. Since the choice between our two policies would affect the timing of later conceptions, some of the people who are later born would owe their existence to our choice of one of the two policies. If we had chosen the other policy, these particular people would never have existed. And the proportion of those later born who owe their existence to our choice would, like ripples in a pool, steadily grow. We can plausibly assume that, after three centuries, there would be no one living in our community who would have been born whichever policy we chose. (It may help to think about this question: how many of us could truly claim, 'Even if railways and motor cars had never been invented, I would still have been born'?)

Consider next

> *Depletion.* As a community, we must choose whether to deplete or conserve certain kinds of resources. If we choose Depletion, the quality of life over the next three centuries would be slightly higher than it would have been if we had chosen Conservation. But it would later, for many centuries, be much lower than it would have been if we had chosen Conservation. This would be because, at the start of this period, people would have to find alternatives for the resources that we had depleted. It is worth distinguishing two versions of this case. The effects of the different policies would be as shown below.

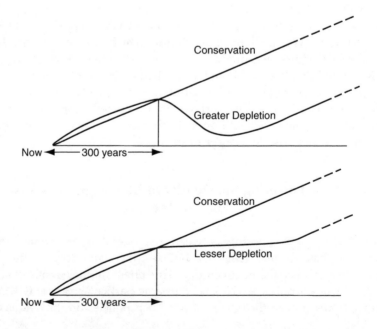

We could never know, in such detail, that these would be the effects of two policies. But this is no objection to this case. Similar effects would sometimes be predictable. Nor does it matter that this imagined case is artificially simple. The case raises the questions which arise in actual cases.

Suppose that we choose Depletion, and that this has either of the two effects shown in my diagram. Is our choice worse for anyone?

Because we chose Depletion, millions of people have, for several centuries, a much lower quality of life. This quality of life is much lower, not than it is now, but than it would have been if we had chosen Conservation. These people's lives are worth living; and, if we had chosen Conservation, these particular people would never have existed. Suppose that we do not believe that causing to exist can benefit. We should ask, 'If particular people live lives that are worth living, is this worse for these people than if they had never existed?' Our answer must be No. Suppose next that we believe that causing to exist can benefit. Since these future people's lives will be worth living, and they would never have existed if we had chosen Conservation, our choice of Depletion is not only not worse for these people: it *benefits* them.

On both answers, our choice will not be worse for these future people. Moreover, when we understand the case, we know that this is true. We know that, even if it greatly lowers the quality of life for several centuries, our choice will not be worse for anyone who ever lives.

Does this make a moral difference? There are three views. It might make all the difference, or some difference, or no difference. There might be no objection to our choice, or some objection, or the objection may be just as strong.

Some believe that *what is bad must be bad for someone*. On this view, there is no objection to our choice. Since it will be bad for no one, our choice cannot have a bad effect. The great lowering of the quality of life provides no moral reason not to choose Depletion.

Certain writers accept this conclusion.[5] But it is very implausible. Before we consider cases of this kind, we may accept the view that what is bad must be bad for someone. But the case of Depletion shows, I believe, that we must reject this view. The great lowering of the quality of life must provide *some* moral reason not to choose Depletion. This is believed by most of those who consider cases of this kind.

If this is what we believe, we should ask two questions:

(1) What is the moral reason not to choose Depletion?

(2) Does it make a moral difference that this lowering of the quality of life will be worse for no one? Would this effect be *worse*, having greater moral weight, if it *was* worse for particular people?

Our need to answer (1), and other similar questions, I call the Non-Identity Problem. This problem arises because the identities of people in the further future can be very easily affected. Some people believe that this problem is a mere quibble. This reaction is unjustified. The problem arises because of superficial facts about our reproductive system. But, though it arises in a superficial way, it is a real problem. When we are choosing between two social or economic policies, of the kind that I described, it is *not true* that, in the further future, the same people will exist whatever we choose. It is therefore *not true* that a choice like Depletion will be against the interests of future people. We cannot dismiss this problem with the pretence that this *is* true.

We partly answer question (1) if we appeal to Q. On this claim, if the numbers would be the same, it would be worse if those who live have a lower quality of life than those who would have lived. But the problem can arise in cases where, in the different outcomes, there would be different numbers of people. To cover these cases we need Theory X. Only X will explain how Q should be justified, and provide a full solution to our problem.

V.   Why an Appeal to Rights Cannot Wholly Solve the Problem

Can we solve our problem by appealing to people's rights? Reconsider the 14-Year-Old Girl. By having her child so young, she gives him a bad start in life. It might be claimed: 'The objection to this girl's decision is that she violates her child's right to a good start in life'.

Even if this child has this right, it could not have been fulfilled. This girl could not have had *this* child when she was a mature woman. Some would claim that, since this child's right could not be fulfilled, this girl cannot be claimed to violate his right. The objector might reply: 'It is wrong to cause someone to exist if we know that this person will have a right that cannot be fulfilled.' Can this be the objection to this girl's decision?[6]

Some years ago, a British politician welcomed the fact that, in the previous year, there had been fewer teenage pregnancies. A middle-aged man wrote in anger to *The Times*. He had been born when his mother was only 14. He admitted that, because his mother was so young, his early years had been hard for both of them. But his life was now well worth living. Was the politician suggesting that it would have been better if he had never been born? This suggestion seemed to him outrageous.

The politician was, implicitly, suggesting this. On the politician's view, it would have been better if this man's mother had waited for several years before having children. I believe that we should accept this view. But can we plausibly explain this view by claiming that this angry man had a right that was not fulfilled?

I believe that we cannot. Suppose that I have a right to privacy. I ask you to marry me. If you accept, you are not acting wrongly, by violating my right to privacy. Since I am glad that you act as you do, with respect to you I *waive* this right. A similar claim applies to the writer of the angry letter to *The Times*. On the suggestion made above, this man has a right to be born by a mature woman, who would give him a good start in life. This man's mother acted wrongly because she caused him to exist with a right that cannot be fulfilled. But this man's letter shows that he was glad to be alive. He denies that his mother acted wrongly because of what she did to him. If we had claimed that her act was wrong, because he has a right that cannot be fulfilled, he could have said, 'I waive this right'. This would have undermined our objection to his mother's act.

It would have been better if this man's mother had waited. But this is not because of what she did to her actual child. It is because of what she could have done for any child that she could have had when she was mature. The objection must be that, if she had waited, she could have given to some other child a better start in life.

Return now to the Case of Depletion. Suppose that we choose Greater Depletion. More than three centuries later, the quality of life is much lower than it would have been if we had chosen Conservation. But the people who will then be living will have a quality of life that is about as high as ours will on average be over the next century. Do these people have rights to which an objector can appeal?

It might be claimed that these people have a right to their share of the resources that we have depleted. But people do not have rights to a share of a particular resource. Suppose that we deplete some resource, but invent technology that will enable our successors, though they lack this resource, to have the same range of opportunities. There would be no objection to what we have done. The most that could be claimed is that people in each generation have a right to an equal range of opportunities, or to an equally high quality of life.[7]

If we choose Greater Depletion, those who live more than three centuries later will have fewer opportunities, and a lower quality of life, than some earlier and some later generations. If people have a right to equal opportunities, and an equally high quality of life, an appeal to these rights may provide some objection to our choice. Those who live more than three centuries later could not possibly have had greater opportunities, or a higher quality of life. If we had chosen otherwise, these people would never have existed. Since their rights could not be fulfilled, we may not violate their rights. But, as before, it may be objected that we cause people to exist with rights that cannot be fulfilled.

It is not clear that this is a good objection. If these people knew the facts, they would not regret that we acted as we did. If they are glad to be alive, they might react like the man who wrote to *The Times*. They might waive their rights. But I cannot assume that this is how they would all react. The appeal to these rights may provide some objection to our choice.

Can this appeal provide an objection to our choice of *Lesser* Depletion? In this case, those who live more than three centuries later have a much higher quality of life than we do now. Can we claim that these people have a *right* to an *even higher* quality of life? I believe that, on any plausible theory about rights, the answer would be No.

It will help to imagine away the Non-Identity Problem. Suppose that our reproductive system had been very different. Suppose that, whatever policies we adopt, the very same people would live more than three centuries later. The objection to our choice would then be that, for the sake of small benefits to ourselves and our children, we prevent many future people from receiving very much greater benefits. Since these future people will be better off than us, we are not acting unjustly. The objection to our act must appeal to the Principle of Utility.

Could this objection appeal to rights? Only if, like Godwin, we present Utilitarianism as a theory about rights. On Godwin's view, everyone has a right to get what the Principle of Utility implies that he should be given. Most of those who believe in rights would reject this view. Many people explain rights as what *constrain*, or *limit*, the Principle of Utility. These people claim that it is wrong to violate certain rights, even if this would greatly increase the net sum of benefits minus burdens. On such a theory, some weight is given to the Principle of Utility. Since such a theory is not Utilitarian, this principle is better called the *Principle of Beneficence*. This principle is one part of such a theory, and the claim that we have certain rights is a different part of this theory. I shall assume that, if we believe in rights, this is the kind of moral theory that we accept.

Return to the case where we imagine away the Non-Identity Problem. If we reject Godwin's view, we could not object to the choice of Lesser Depletion by appealing to the rights of those who will live in the further future. Our objection would appeal to the Principle of Beneficence. The objection would be that, for the sake of small benefits to ourselves and our children, we deny, to people better off than us, very much greater benefits. In calling this an objection, I need not claim that it shows our choice to be wrong. I am merely claiming that, since we deny these people very much greater benefits, this provides *some* moral reason not to make this choice.

If we now restore our actual reproductive system, this reason disappears. Consider the people who will live more than three centuries later. Our choice of Lesser Depletion does not deny these people *any* benefit. If we had chosen Conservation, this would not have benefited these people, since they would never have existed.

When we assume away the Non-Identity Problem, our reason not to make this choice is explained by an appeal, not to people's rights, but to the Principle of Beneficence. When we restore the Non-Identity Problem, this reason disappears. Since this reason appealed to the Principle of Beneficence, what the problem shows is that this principle is inadequate, and must be revised. We need a better account of beneficence, or what I call Theory X.

One part of our moral theory appeals to beneficence; another part appeals to people's rights. We should therefore not expect that an appeal to rights could fill the gap in our inadequate Principle of Beneficence. We should expect that, as I have claimed, appealing to rights cannot wholly solve the Non-Identity Problem.[8]

VI.   Does the Fact of Non-Identity Make a Moral Difference?

In trying to revise our Principle of Beneficence – trying to find Theory X – we must consider cases where, in the different outcomes, different numbers of people would exist. Before we turn to these cases, we can ask what we believe about the other question that I mentioned. Our choice of Depletion will be worse for no one. Does this make a moral difference?

We may be able to remember a time when we were concerned about effects on future generations, but had overlooked the Non-Identity Problem. We may have thought that a policy like Depletion would be against the interests of future people. When we saw that this was false, did we become less concerned about effects on future generations?

When I saw the problem, I did not become less concerned. And the same is true of many other people. I shall say that we accept the *No-Difference View*.

It is worth considering a different example:

> *The Medical Programmes.* There are two rare conditions, J and K, which cannot be detected without special tests. If a pregnant woman has Condition J, this will cause the child she is carrying to have a certain handicap. A simple treatment would prevent this effect. If a woman has Condition K when she conceives a child, this will cause this child to have the same particular handicap. Condition K cannot be treated, but always disappears within two months. Suppose next that we have planned two medical programmes, but there are funds for only one; so one must be cancelled. In the first programme, millions of women would be tested during pregnancy. Those found to have Condition J would be treated. In the second programme, millions of women would be tested when they intend to try to become pregnant. Those found to have Condition K would be warned to postpone conception for at least two months, after which this incurable condition will have disappeared. Suppose finally that we can predict that these two programmes would achieve results in as many cases. If there is Pregnancy Testing, 1,000 children a year would be born normal rather than handicapped. If there is Preconception Testing, there would each year be born 1,000 normal children rather than a 1,000, different, handicapped children.

Would these two programmes be equally worthwhile? Let us note carefully what the difference is. As a result of either programme, 1,000 couples a year would have a normal rather than a handicapped child. These would be different couples, on the two programmes. But since the numbers would be the same, the effects on the parents and on other people would be morally equivalent. If there is a moral difference, this can only be in the effects on the children.

Note next that, in judging these effects, we need have no view about the moral status of a foetus. We can suppose that it would take a year before either kind of testing could begin. When we choose between the two programmes, none of the children has yet been conceived. And all those who are conceived will become adults. We are therefore considering effects, not on present foetuses, but on future people. Assume next that the handicap in question, though it is not trivial, is not so severe as to make life doubtfully worth living. Even if it can be against our interests to have been born, this is not true of those born with this handicap.

Since we cannot afford both programmes, which should we cancel? Under one description, both would have the same effect. Suppose that Conditions J and K are the only causes of this handicap. The incidence is now 2,000 among those born in each year. Either programme would halve the incidence; the rate would drop to 1,000 a year. The difference is this. If we decide to cancel Pregnancy Testing, it will be true of those who are later born handicapped that, but for our decision, they would have been cured. Our decision will be worse for all these people. If instead we decide to cancel Pre-Conception Testing, there will later be just as many people who are born with this handicap. But it would not be true of these people that, but for our decision, they would have been cured. These people owe their existence to our decision. If we had not decided to cancel Pre-Conception Testing, the parents of these handicapped children would not have had *them*. They would have later had different children. Since the lives of these handicapped children are worth living, our decision will not be worse for any of them.

Does this make a moral difference? Or are the two programmes equally worthwhile? Is all that matters morally how many future lives will be lived by normal rather than handicapped people? Or does it also matter whether these lives would be lived by the very same people?

We should add one detail to the case. If we decide to cancel Pregnancy Testing, those who are later born handicapped might know that, if we had made a different decision, they would have been cured. Such knowledge might make their handicap harder to bear. We should therefore assume that, though it is not deliberately concealed, these people would not know this fact.

With this detail added, I judge the two programmes to be equally worthwhile. I know of some people who do not accept this claim; but I know of more who do.

My reaction is not merely an intuition. It is the judgement that I reach by reasoning as follows. Whichever programme is cancelled, there will later be just as many people with this handicap. These people would be different in the two outcomes that depend on our decision. And there is a claim that applies to only one of these two groups of handicapped people. Though they do not know this fact, the people in one group could have been cured. I therefore ask: 'If there will be people with some handicap, the fact that they are handicapped is bad. Would it be *worse* if, unknown to them, their handicap could have been cured?' This would be worse if this fact made these people worse off than people whose handicap could *not* have been cured. But this fact does not have this effect. If we decide to cancel Pregnancy Testing, there will be a group of handicapped people. If we decide to cancel Pre-Conception Testing, there will be a different group of handicapped people. The people in the first group would not be worse off than the people in the second group would have been. Since this is so, I judge these two outcomes to be morally equivalent. Given the details of the case, it seems to me irrelevant that one of the groups but not the other could have been cured.

This fact *would* have been relevant if curing this group would have reduced the incidence of this handicap. But, since we have funds for only one programme, this is not true. If we choose to cure the first group, there would later be just as many people with this handicap. Since curing the first group would not reduce the number who will be handicapped, we ought to choose to cure this group only if they have a stronger claim to be cured. And they do not have a stronger claim. If we *could* cure the second group, they would have an equal claim to be cured. If we choose to cure the first group, they are merely luckier than the second group. Since they would merely be luckier, and they do not have a stronger claim to be cured, I do not believe that we ought to choose to cure these people. Since it is also true that, if we choose to cure these people, this will not reduce the number of people who will be handicapped, I conclude that the two programmes are equally worthwhile. If Pre-Conception Testing would achieve results in a few more cases, I would judge it to be the better programme.[9]

This matches my reaction to our choice of Depletion. I believe that it would be bad if there would later be a great lowering of the quality of life. And I believe that it would not be *worse* if the people who later live would themselves have existed if we had chosen Conservation. The bad effect would not be worse if it had been, in this way, worse for any particular people. In considering both cases, I accept the No-Difference View. So do many other people.

I have described two cases in which I, and many others, accept the No-Difference View. If we are right to accept this view, this may have important theoretical implications. This depends on whether we believe that, if we cause someone to exist who will have a life worth living, we thereby benefit this person. If we believe this, I cannot yet state the implications of the No-Difference View, since these will depend on decisions that I have not yet discussed. But suppose we believe that causing someone to exist cannot benefit this person. If this is what we believe, and we accept the No-Difference View, the implications are as follows.

I have suggested that we should appeal to

Q: If in either of two possible outcomes the same number of people would ever live, it would be worse if those who live are worse off, or have a lower quality of life, than those who would have lived.

Consider next

The Person-Affecting View, or V: It would be worse if people are affected for the worse.

In Same People Choices, Q and V coincide. When we are considering these choices, those who live are the same in both outcomes. If these people are worse off, or have a lower quality of life, they are affected for the worse, and vice versa.[10] Since Q and V here coincide, it will make no difference to which we appeal.

The two claims conflict only in Same Number Choices. These are what this chapter has discussed. Suppose that we accept the No-Difference View. In considering these choices, we shall then appeal to Q *rather than* V. If we choose Depletion, this will lower the quality of life in the further future. According to Q, our choice has a bad effect. But, because of the facts about identity, our choice will be bad for no one. V does not imply that our choice has a bad effect. Would this effect be worse if it *was* worse for particular people? According to V, the answer must be Yes. Since we believe the No-Difference View, we answer No. We believe that V gives the wrong answer here. And V gives the wrong answer in the case of the Medical Programmes. Q describes the effects that we believe to be bad. And we believe that it makes no moral difference whether these effects are also bad according to V. V draws moral distinctions where, on our view, no distinctions should be drawn.

In Same People Choices, Q and V coincide. In Same Number Choices, where these claims conflict, we accept Q rather than V. When we make these two kinds of choice, we shall therefore have no use for V.

There remain the Different Number Choices, which Q does not cover. We shall here need Theory X. I have not yet discussed what X should claim. But we can predict the following. X will imply Q in Same Number Choices.

We can also predict that X will have the same relation to V. In Same People Choices, X and V will coincide. It will here make no difference to which we appeal. These are the choices with which most of our moral thinking is concerned. This explains the plausibility of V. This part of morality, the part concerned with beneficence, or human well-being, is usually thought of in what I shall call *person-affecting* terms. We appeal to people's interests – to what is good or bad for those people whom our acts affect. Even after we have found Theory X, we might continue to appeal to V in most cases, merely because it is more familiar. But in some cases X and V will conflict. They may conflict when we are making Same and Different Number Choices. And, whenever X and V conflict, we shall appeal to X *rather than* V. We shall believe that, if some effect is bad according to X, it makes no moral difference whether it is also bad according to V. As before, V draws a moral distinction where, on our view, no distinction should be drawn. V is like the claim that it is wrong to enslave whites, or to deny the vote to adult males. We shall thus conclude that this part of morality, the part concerned with beneficence and human well-being, cannot be explained in person-affecting terms. Its fundamental principles will not be concerned with whether our acts will be good or bad for those people whom they affect. Theory X will imply that an effect is bad if it is bad for people. But this will not be *why* this effect is bad.

Remember next that these claims assume that causing to exist cannot benefit. This assumption is defensible. If we make this assumption, these claims show that many moral theories need to be revised. On these theories, it must make a moral difference whether our acts are good or bad for those people whom they affect.[11] And we may need to revise our beliefs about certain common cases. One example might be abortion. But most of our moral thinking would be unchanged. Many significant relations hold only between particular people. These include our relations to those to whom we have made promises, or owe gratitude, our parents, pupils, patients, clients, and (if we are politicians) those whom we represent. My remarks do not apply to such relations, or to the special obligations which they produce. My remarks apply only to our Principle of Beneficence, or our general moral reason to benefit other people, and to protect them from harm.

Since my remarks apply only to this principle, and we shall have changed our view only in some cases, this change of view may seem unimportant. This is not so. Consider once again this (too grandiose) analogy: In ordinary cases we can accept Newton's Laws. But not in all cases. And we now accept a different theory.

VII. Causing Predictable Catastrophes in the Further Future

In this section, rather than pursuing the main line of my argument, I discuss a minor question. In a case like that of Depletion, we cannot wholly solve the Non-Identity Problem by an appeal to people's rights. Is this also true in a variant of the case, where our choice causes a catastrophe? Since this is a minor question, this section can be ignored, except by those who do not believe that Depletion has a bad effect. Consider

> *The Risky Policy.* As a community, we must choose between two energy policies. Both would be completely safe for at least three centuries, but one would have certain risks in the further future. This policy involves the burial of nuclear waste in areas where, in the next few centuries, there is no risk of an earthquake. But since this waste will remain radio-active for thousands of years, there will be risks in the distant future. If we choose this Risky Policy, the standard of living would be somewhat higher over the next century. We do choose this policy. As a result, there is a catastrophe many centuries later. Because of geological changes to the Earth's surface, an earthquake releases radiation, which kills thousands of people. Though they are killed by this catastrophe, these people will have had lives that are worth living. We can assume that this radiation affects only people who are not yet conceived, and that its effect is to give to these people an incurable disease that will kill them at about the age of 40. This disease will have no effects before it kills.

Our choice between these two policies will affect the details of the lives that are later lived. In the way explained above, our choice will therefore affect who will later live. After many centuries there would be no one living in our community who, whichever policy we chose, would have been born. Because we chose the Risky Policy, thousands of people are later killed. But if we had chosen the alternative Safe Policy, these particular people would never have existed. Different people would have existed in their place. Is our choice of the Risky Policy worse for anyone?

We should ask, 'If people live lives that are worth living, even though they are killed by some catastrophe, is this worse for these people than if they had never existed?' Our answer must be No. Though it causes a predictable catastrophe, our choice of the Risky Policy will be worse for no one.

Some may claim that our choice of Depletion does not have a bad effect. This cannot be claimed about our choice of the Risky Policy. Since this choice causes a catastrophe, it clearly has a bad effect. But our choice will not be bad for, or worse for, any of the people who later live. This case forces us to reject the view that a choice cannot have a bad effect if this choice will be bad for no one.

In this case, the Non-Identity Problem may seem easier to solve. Though our choice is not worse for the people struck by the catastrophe, it might be claimed that we harm these people. And the appeal to people's rights may here succeed.

We can deserve to be blamed for harming others, even when this is not worse for them. Suppose that I drive carelessly, and in the resulting crash cause you to lose a leg. One year later, war breaks out. If you had not lost this leg, you would have been conscripted, and killed. My careless driving therefore saves your life. But I am still morally to blame.

This case reminds us that, in assigning blame, we must consider not actual but predictable effects. I knew that my careless driving might harm others, but I could not know that it would in fact save your life. This distinction might apply to our choice of the Risky Policy. Suppose we know that, if we choose this policy, this may in the distant future cause many accidental deaths. But we have overlooked the Non-Identity Problem. We mistakenly believe that, whichever policy we choose, the very same people will later live. We therefore believe that our choice of the Risky Policy may be very greatly against the interests of some future people. If we believe this, our choice can be criticized. We can deserve blame for doing what we *believe* may be greatly against the interests of other people. This criticism stands even if our belief is false – just as I am as much to blame even if my careless driving will in fact save your life.

Suppose that we cannot find Theory X, or that X seems less plausible than the objection to doing what may be greatly against the interests of other people. It may then be better if we conceal the Non-Identity Problem from those who will decide whether we increase our use of nuclear energy. It may be better if these people believe falsely that such a policy may, by causing a catastrophe, be greatly against the interests of some of those who will live in the distant future. If these people have this false belief, they may be more likely to reach the right conclusions.

We have lost this false belief. We realize that, if we choose the Risky Policy, our choice will *not* be worse for those people whom the catastrophe later kills. Note that this is not a lucky guess. It is not like predicting that, if I cause you to lose a leg, this will later save you from death in the trenches. We know that, if we choose the Risky Policy, this may in the distant future cause many people to be killed. But we also know that, if we had chosen the Safe Policy, the people who are killed would never have been born. Since these people's lives will be worth living, we *know* that our choice will not be worse for them.

If we know this, we cannot be compared to a careless driver. What is the objection to our choice? Can it be wrong to harm others, when we know that our act will not be worse for the people harmed? This might be wrong if we could have asked these people for their consent, but have failed to do so. By failing to ask these people for their consent, we infringe their autonomy. But this cannot be the objection to our choice of the Risky Policy. Since we could not possibly communicate with the people living many centuries from now, we cannot ask for their consent.

When we cannot ask for someone's consent, we should ask instead whether this person would later regret what we are doing. Would the people who are later killed regret our choice of the Risky Policy? Let us suppose that these people know all of the facts. From an early age they know that, because of the release of radiation, they have an incurable disease that will kill them at about the age of 40. They also know that, if we had chosen the Safe Policy, they would never have been born. These people would regret the fact that they will die young. But, since their lives are worth living, they would not regret the fact that they were ever born. They would therefore not regret our choice of the Risky Policy.

Can it be wrong to harm others, when we know *both* that if the people harmed knew about our act, they would not regret this act, *and* that our act will not be worse for these people than anything else that we could have done? How might we know that, though we are harming someone, our act will not be worse for this person? There are at least two kinds of case:

(1) Though we are harming someone, we may also know that we are giving to this person some fully compensating benefit. We could not know this unless the benefit would clearly outweigh the harm. But, if this is so, what we are doing will be better for this person. In this kind of case, if we are also not infringing this person's autonomy, there may be no objection to our act. There may be no objection to our harming someone when we know both that this person will have no regrets, and that our act will be clearly better for this person. In English Law, surgery was once regarded as justifiable grievous bodily harm. As I argued in Section 25 [of *Reasons and Persons*, eds.], we should revise the ordinary use of the word 'harm'. If what we are doing will not be worse for some other person, or will even be better for this person, we are not, in a morally relevant sense, harming this person.

If we assume that causing to exist can benefit, our choice of the Risky Policy is, in its effects on those killed, like the case of the surgeon. Though our choice causes these people to be killed, since it also causes them to exist with a life worth living, it gives them a benefit that outweighs this harm. This suggests that the objection to our choice cannot be that it harms these people.

We may instead assume that causing to exist cannot benefit. On this assumption, our choice of the Risky Policy does not give to the people whom it kills some fully compensating benefit. Our choice is not *better* for these people. It is merely *not worse* for them.

(2) There is another kind of case in which we can know that, though we are harming someone on the ordinary use of 'harm', this will not be worse for this person. These are the cases that involve overdetermination. In these cases we know that, if we do not harm someone, this person will be harmed at least as much in some other way. Suppose that someone is trapped in a wreck and about to be burnt to death. This person asks us to shoot him, so that he does not die painfully. If we kill this person we are not, in a morally relevant sense, harming him.

Such a case cannot show that there is no objection to our choice of the Risky Policy, since it is not relevantly similar. If the catastrophe did not occur, the people killed would have lived for many more years. There is a quite different reason why our choice of the Risky Policy is not worse for these people.

Could there be a case in which we kill some existing person, knowing what we know when we choose the Risky Policy? We must know (*a*) that this person will learn but not regret the fact that we have done something that will cause him to be killed. And we must know (*b*) that, though this person would otherwise have lived a normal life for many more years, causing him to be killed will be neither better nor worse for him. ((*b*) is what we know about the effects of our choice of the Risky Policy, if we assume that, in doing what is a necessary part of the cause of the existence of the people killed by the catastrophe, we cannot be benefiting these people.)

Suppose that we kill some existing person, who would otherwise have lived a normal life for many more years. In such a case, we could not *know* that (*b*) is true. Even if living for these many years would be neither better nor worse for this person, this could never be predicted. There cannot be a case where we kill some existing person, knowing what we know when we choose the Risky Policy. A case that is relevantly similar must involve causing someone to be killed who, if we had acted otherwise, would never have existed.

Compare these two cases:

Jane's Choice. Jane has a congenital disease, that will kill her painlessly at about the age of 40. This disease has no effects before it kills. Jane knows that, if she has a child, it will have this same disease. Suppose that she can also assume the following. Like herself, her child would have a life that is worth living. There are no children who need to be but have not been adopted. Given the size of the world's population when this case occurs (perhaps in some future century), if Jane has a child, this will not be worse for other people. And, if she does not have this child, she will be unable to raise a child. She cannot persuade someone else to have an extra child, whom she would raise. (These assumptions give us the relevant question.) Knowing these facts, Jane chooses to have a child.

Ruth's Choice. Ruth's situation is just like Jane's, with one exception. Her congenital disease, unlike Jane's, kills only males. If Ruth pays for the new technique of in vitro fertilization, she would be certain to have a daughter whom this disease would not kill. She decides to save this expense, and takes a risk. Unluckily, she has a son, whose inherited disease will kill him at about the age of 40.

Is there a moral objection to Jane's choice? Given the assumptions in the case, this objection would have to appeal to the effect on Jane's child. Her choice will not be worse for this child. Is there an objection to her choice that appeals to this child's rights? Suppose we believe that each person has a right to live a full life. Jane knows that, if she has a child, his right to a full life could not possibly be fulfilled. This may imply that Jane does not violate this right. But the objection could be restated. It could be said: 'It is wrong to cause someone to exist with a right that cannot be fulfilled. This is why Jane acts wrongly.'

Is this a good objection? If I was Jane's child, my view would be like that of the man who wrote to *The Times*. I would regret the fact that I shall die young. But, since my life is worth living, I would not regret that my mother caused me to exist. And I would deny that her act was wrong because of what it did to me. If I was told that it *was* wrong, because it caused me to exist with a right that cannot be fulfilled, I would *waive* this right.

If Jane's child waives his right, this undermines this objection to her choice. But, though *I* would waive this right, I cannot be certain that, in all such cases, this is what such a child would do. If Jane's child does not waive his right, the appeal to this right may perhaps provide some objection to her choice.

Turn now to Ruth's choice. There is clearly a greater objection to *this* choice. This is because Ruth has a different alternative. If Jane does not have a child, she will not be able to raise a child; and one fewer life will be lived. Ruth's alternative is to pay for the technique that will give her a different child whom her disease will not kill. She chooses to save this expense, knowing that the chance is one in two that her child will be killed by this disease.

Even if there is an objection to Jane's choice, there is a greater objection to Ruth's choice. This objection cannot appeal only to the effects on Ruth's actual child, since these are just like the effects of Jane's choice on Jane's child. The objection to Ruth's choice must appeal in part to the possible effect on a different child who, by paying for the new technique, she could have had. The appeal to this effect is not an appeal to anyone's rights.

Return now to our choice of the Risky Policy. If we choose this policy, this may cause people to exist who will be killed in a catastrophe. We know that our choice would not be worse for these people. But, if there is force in the objection to Jane's choice, this objection would apply to our choice. By choosing the Risky Policy, we may cause people to exist whose right to a full life cannot be fulfilled.

The appeal to these people's rights may provide some objection to our choice. But it cannot provide the whole objection. Our choice is, in one respect, unlike Jane's. Her alternative was to have no child. Our alternative is like Ruth's. If we had chosen the Safe Policy, we would have had different descendants, none of whom would have been killed by released radiation.

The objection to Ruth's choice cannot appeal only to her child's right to a full life. The same is therefore true of the objection to our choice of the Risky Policy. This objection must in part appeal to the effects on the possible people who, if we had chosen differently, would have lived. As before, the appeal to rights cannot wholly solve the Non-Identity problem. We must also appeal to a claim like Q, which compares two different sets of possible lives.

It may be objected: 'When Ruth conceives her child, it inherits the disease that will deny it a full life. Because this child's disease is inherited in this way, it cannot be claimed that Ruth's choice kills her child. If we choose the Risky Policy, the causal connections are less close. Because the connections are less close, our choice kills the people who later die from the effects of released radiation. That we kill these people is the full objection to our choice.'

This objection I find dubious. Why is there a greater objection to our choice because the causal connections are less close? The objection may be correct in what it claims about our ordinary use of 'kill'. But, as I argued in Section 25 [of *Reasons and Persons*, eds.], this use is morally irrelevant. Since that argument may not convince, I add

> *The Risky Cure for Infertility.* Ann cannot have a child unless she takes a certain treatment. If she takes this treatment, she will have a son, who will be healthy. But there is a risk of one in two that this treatment will give Ann a rare disease. This disease has the following features. It remains dormant for twenty years, is undetectable, kills men but does not harm women, and is infectious. The following is therefore true. If Ann takes this treatment and has a healthy son, there is a chance of one in two that in twenty years she will infect her son with a disease that will kill him twenty years later, or when he is about forty. Ann chooses to take this treatment, and she does later infect her son with this fatal disease.

On the objection stated above, there is a strong objection to Ann's choice, which does not apply to Ruth's choice. Because the causal connections are less close, Ann's choice kills her son. And she knew that the chance was one in two that her choice would have this effect. Ruth knows that that there is the same chance that her child will die at about the age of 40. But, because the causal connections are so close, her choice does not kill her son. According to this objection, this difference has great moral relevance.

This is not plausible. Ruth and Ann both know that, if they act in a certain way, there is a chance of one in two that they will have sons who will be killed by a disease at about the age of forty. The causal story is different. But this does not make Ann's choice morally worse. I believe that this example shows that we should reject this last objection.

The objector might say: 'I deny that, by choosing to take the Risky Cure, Ann kills her son'. But, if the objector denies this, he cannot claim that, by choosing the Risky Policy, we kill some people in the distant future. The causal connections take the same form. Each choice produces a side-effect which later kills people who owe their existence to this choice.

If this objection fails, as I believe, my earlier claim is justified. It is morally significant that, if we choose the Risky Policy, our choice is like Ruth's rather than Jane's. It is morally significant that, if we had chosen otherwise, different people would have lived who would not have been killed. Since this is so, the objection to our choice cannot appeal only to the rights of those who actually later live. It must also appeal to a claim like Q, which compares different sets of possible lives. As I claimed earlier, the appeal to rights cannot wholly solve the Non-Identity Problem.

Notes

1 For the reasons given by Brian Barry in 'Circumstances of Justice and Future Generations', in I. Sikora and B. Barry (eds.), *Obligations to Future Generations* (Philadelphia: Temple University Press, 1978).
2 See Theodora Ooms [née Parfit] (ed.), *Teenage Pregnancy in a Family Context: Implications for Policy Decisions* (Philadelphia: Temple University Press, 1981).
3 This problem has been called by Kavka 'the paradox of future individuals': G. Kavka, 'The Paradox of Future Individuals', *Philosophy and Public Affairs*, 11:2 (Spring 1982).
4 I follow R. M. Adams, 'Existence, Self-Interest, and the Problem of Evil', *Noûs*, 13 (1979).
5 See T. Schwartz, 'Obligations to Posterity', in Sikora and Barry (eds.), *Obligations to Future Generations*.
6 This form of the objection is suggested in M. Tooley, *Abortion and Infanticide* (Oxford: Clarendon Press, 1983).
7 See Brian Barry, 'Intergenerational Justice in Energy Policy', in D. MacLean and P. G. Brown (eds.), *Energy and the Future* (Totowa, NJ: Rowman & Littlefield, 1983); see also Barry, 'Justice Between Generations', in P. M. S. Hacker and J. Raz (eds.), *Law, Morality, and Society: Essays in Honour of H. L. A. Hart* (Oxford: Clarendon Press, 1977).
8 For a further discussion, see J. Woodward, 'The Non-Identity Problem', *Ethics* (July 1986).
9 J. McMahan has suggested to me that, if the handicap greatly affected the nature of these people's lives, it may not be clear that someone with a lifelong handicap would have been better off if he had been born normal. Some may doubt whether, in the relevant sense, these two very different lives would have been lived by the same person. And R. M. Adams, 'Existence, Self-Interest, and the Problem of Evil', *Noûs*, 13 (1979), suggests that, even if such a person would have been better off, this need not imply that he has reasons to regret his handicap. If we accept either claim, the

example is not what we need. We can avoid these questions by supposing that the handicap affects these people only when they are adults. The handicap might be, for example, sterility.

10   There may seem to be one exception. If my life is worth living, killing me affects me for the worse, but does it cause me to be worse off, or to have a lower quality of life? As I use the phrase, I do have 'a lower quality of life'. This is true if my life goes less well than it could have gone, or if what happens in my life is worse for me. Both are true when, with a life worth living, I am killed.

11   One example is the plausible theory advanced in T. M. Scanlon, 'Contractualism and Utilitarianism', in A. K. Sen and B. Williams (eds.), *Utilitarianism and Beyond* (Cambridge: Cambridge University Press, 1982). Scanlon argues that the best account of moral motivation is not that given by Utilitarians, who appeal to universal philanthropy. Our fundamental moral motive is instead 'the desire to be able to justify one's actions to others on grounds that they could not reasonably reject'. Scanlon sketches an attractive moral theory built upon this claim. On this theory, an act is wrong if it will affect someone in a way that cannot be justified – if there will be some complainant whose complaint cannot be answered. On this theory, the framework of morality is essentially person-affecting. Unfortunately, when we choose a policy like Greater Depletion, there will be no complainants. If we believe that this makes no moral difference, since the objection to our choice is just as strong, we believe that it is irrelevant that there will be no complainants. The fundamental principle of Scanlon's theory draws a distinction where, on our view, no distinction should be drawn. Scanlon's theory therefore needs to be revised.

Similar remarks apply to many other theories. Thus R. B. Brandt, *A Theory of the Good and the Right* (Oxford: Clarendon Press, 1979), suggests that to the phrase 'is morally wrong' we should assign the descriptive meaning 'would be prohibited by any moral code which all fully rational persons would tend to support, in preference to all others or to none at all, for the society of the agent, if they expected to spend a lifetime in that society' (p. 194). It seems likely that, on the chosen code, an act would not be wrong if there are no complainants. Similar remarks apply to B. Gert, *The Moral Rules* (New York: Harper & Row, 1973), to J. Narveson, *Morality and Utility* (Baltimore: Johns Hopkins Press, 1967), and to G. R. Grice, *The Grounds of Moral Judgement* (Cambridge: Cambridge University Press, 1967), and they may apply to J. L. Mackie, *Ethics* (Harmondsworth: Penguin, 1977), D. A. J. Richards, *A Theory of Reasons for Action* (Oxford: Clarendon Press, 1971), G. Harman, *The Nature of Morality* (Oxford: Oxford University Press, 1977), D. Gauthier, *Morals By Agreement* (Oxford: Clarendon Press, 1986), John Rawls, *A Theory of Justice* (Cambridge, Mass.: Harvard University Press, 1971), and others.

Further Reading

General

Ackerman, Bruce, *Social Justice in the Liberal State* (New Haven: Yale University Press, 1980).

Barry, Brian, *Theories of Justice* (Berkeley: California University Press, 1989).

Buchanan, Alan, Dan W. Brock, Norman Daniels, and Daniel Wikler, *From Chance to Choice: Genetics and Justice* (Cambridge: Cambridge University Press, 2000).

Clayton, Matthew, and Andrew Williams, eds., *The Ideal of Equality* (London: Palgrave, 2000).

Daniels, Norman, *Justice and Justification* (Cambridge: Cambridge University Press, 1996).

Darwall, Stephen, ed., *Equal Freedom* (Ann Arbor: University of Michigan Press, 1995).

Hurley, Susan, *Justice, Luck, and Knowledge* (Cambridge, MA: Harvard University Press, 2003).

Kamm, Frances M., *Morality, Mortality*, vol. 1 (New York: Oxford University Press, 1993), pt. III.

Kymlicka, Will, *Contemporary Political Philosophy: An Introduction*, 2nd edn. (Oxford: Oxford University Press, 2002).

LaFollette, Hugh, ed., *The Oxford Handbook of Practical Ethics* (New York: Oxford University Press, 2003), pts. III–V.

Mason, Andrew, ed., *Ideals of Equality* (Oxford: Blackwell, 1998).

Miller, David, *Principles of Social Justice* (Cambridge, MA: Harvard University Press, 1999).

Murphy, Liam, and Thomas Nagel, *The Myth of Ownership* (New York: Oxford University Press, 2002).

Nagel, Thomas, *Equality and Partiality* (New York: Oxford University Press, 1991).

Okin, Susan Moller, *Justice, Gender, and the Family* (New York: Basic Books, 1989).

Roemer, John, *Theories of Distributive Justice* (Cambridge, MA: Harvard University Press, 1996).

——*Equality of Opportunity* (Cambridge, MA: Harvard University Press, 1998).

Scanlon, T. M., *What We Owe To Each Other* (Cambridge, MA: The Belknap Press of Harvard University Press, 1998).

Sen, Amartya, *Inequality Reexamined* (Oxford: Clarendon Press, 1992).

Temkin, Larry, *Inequality* (Cambridge, MA: Harvard University Press, 1992).

Vallentyne, Peter, ed., *Justice and Equality*, vols. 1–6 (London: Routledge, 2002).

Walzer, Michael, *Spheres of Justice* (New York: Basic Books, 1983).

Young, Iris Marion, *Justice and the Politics of Difference* (Princeton, NJ: Princeton University Press, 1990).

Locke

Locke, John, *Two Treatises of Government*, ed. P. Laslett (Cambridge: Cambridge University Press, 1988).

Simmons, A. John, *The Lockean Theory of Rights* (Princeton, NJ: Princeton University Press, 1992), chs. 5–6.

Sreenivasan, Gopal, *The Limits of Lockean Rights in Property* (New York: Oxford University Press, 1995).

Tully, James, *A Discourse on Property* (Cambridge: Cambridge University Press, 1980).

Waldron, Jeremy, *The Right to Private Property* (Oxford: Oxford University Press, 1988).

——*God, Locke, and Equality: Christian Foundations in Locke's Political Thought* (Cambridge: Cambridge University Press, 2002).

Hume

Barry, Brian, *Theories of Justice* (Berkeley: California University Press, 1989), ch. 4.

Gauthier, David, 'David Hume, Contractarian', *Philosophical Review*, 88 (1979), pp. 3–38.

Harrison, Jonathan, *Hume's Theory of Justice* (Oxford: Clarendon Press, 1981).

Hume, David, *An Enquiry Concerning the Principles of Morals*, ed. Tom Beauchamp (Oxford: Oxford University Press, 1998).

——*A Treatise of Human Nature*, ed. David Fate Norton (Oxford: Oxford University Press, 2000).

Mackie, John, *Hume's Moral Theory* (London: Routledge & Kegan Paul, 1980).

Miller, David, *Philosophy and Ideology in Hume's Political Thought* (Oxford: Clarendon Press, 1981).

Rawls, John, *Lectures on the History of Moral Philosophy*, ed. Barbara Herman (Cambridge, MA: Harvard University Press, 2000).

Justice as Fairness

Arneson, Richard, 'Primary Goods Reconsidered', *Noûs*, 24 (1990), pp. 429–54.

——'Rawls, Responsibility, and Distributive Justice', in Maurice Salles and John Weymark, eds., *Justice, Political Liberalism, and Utilitarianism: Themes from Harsanyi* (Cambridge: Cambridge University Press, forthcoming).

Cohen, G. A., 'Facts and Principles', *Philosophy and Public Affairs*, 31 (2003), pp. 211–45.

Cohen, Joshua, 'Democratic Equality', *Ethics*, 99 (1989), pp. 727–51.

Daniels, Norman, ed., *Reading Rawls* (Stanford, CA: Stanford University Press, 1989).

Freeman, Samuel, ed., *The Cambridge Companion to Rawls* (Cambridge: Cambridge University Press, 2003).

Parfit, Derek, 'Equality or Priority?', in Matthew Clayton and Andrew Williams, eds., *The Ideal of Equality* (London: Palgrave, 2000).

Pogge, Thomas, *Realizing Rawls* (Ithaca, NY: Cornell University Press, 1989).

—— 'Three Problems with Contractarian Consequentialist Ways of Assessing Social Institutions', in E. F. Paul, F. Miller Jr., and J. Paul, eds., *The Just Society* (Cambridge: Cambridge University Press, 1995).

Rawls, John, *Political Liberalism*, pbk edn. (New York: Columbia University Press, 1996).

—— *Collected Papers*, ed. Samuel Freeman (Cambridge, MA: Harvard University Press, 1999).

—— *Justice as Fairness: A Restatement*, ed. Erin Kelly (Cambridge, MA: The Belknap Press of Harvard University Press, 1999).

—— *The Law of Peoples* (Cambridge, MA: Harvard University Press, 1999).

—— *A Theory of Justice*, rev. edn. (Cambridge, MA: The Belknap Press of Harvard University Press, 1999).

Richardson, Henry, and Paul Weithman, eds., *The Philosophy of Rawls: A Collection of Essays* (New York: Garland, 1999), vols. 1–5.

Scanlon, T. M., 'Rawls's Theory of Justice', *University of Pennsylvania Law Review*, 121 (1973), pp. 1029–69.

—— 'The Diversity of Objections to Inequality', in Matthew Clayton and Andrew Williams, eds., *The Ideal of Equality* (London: Palgrave, 2000).

Sen, Amartya, 'Justice: Freedom versus Means', *Philosophy and Public Affairs*, 19 (1990), pp. 111–21.

Historical Entitlement Theory

Arneson, Richard, 'Lockean Self-Ownership: Toward a Demolition', *Political Studies*, 39 (1991), pp. 36–54.

Cohen, G. A., *Self-Ownership, Freedom, and Equality* (Cambridge: Cambridge University Press, 1995).

Freeman, Samuel, 'Illiberal Libertarians: Why Libertarianism is not a Liberal View', *Philosophy and Public Affairs*, 30 (2001), pp. 105–51.

Gorr, Michael, 'Justice, Self-Ownership and Natural Assets', *Social Philosophy and Policy*, 12 (1995), pp. 267–91.

Mack, Eric, 'Self-Ownership, Marxism, and Egalitarianism', pts. I and II, *Politics, Philosophy and Economics*, 1 (2002), pp. 75–108 and 237–76.

Narveson, Jan, *The Libertarian Idea* (Philadelphia: Temple University Press, 1987).

Nozick, Robert, *Anarchy, State and Utopia* (New York: Basic Books, 1974).

Otsuka, Michael, *Libertarianism without Inequality* (Oxford: Clarendon Press, 2003).

Paul, Jeffrey, ed., *Reading Nozick* (Oxford: Blackwell, 1981).

Reeve, Andrew, and Andrew Williams, eds., *Real Libertarianism Assessed* (London: Palgrave, 2003).

Steiner, Hillel, 'Capitalism, Justice, and Equal Starts', *Social Philosophy and Policy*, 5 (1987), pp. 49–71.

—— *An Essay on Rights* (Oxford: Blackwell, 1994).

Vallentyne, Peter, and Hillel Steiner, eds., *Left-Libertarianism and its Critics: The Contemporary Debate* (London: Palgrave, 2000).

Waldron, Jeremy, *The Right to Private Property* (Oxford: Oxford University Press, 1988).

Equality of Resources

Arnsperger, Christian, 'Envy-Freeness and Distributive Justice', *Journal of Economic Surveys*, 8 (1994), 155–86.

Burley, Justine, ed., *Dworkin and his Critics* (Oxford: Blackwell, forthcoming).

Clayton, Matthew, 'The Resources of Liberal Equality', *Imprints*, 5 (2000), pp. 63–82.

Dworkin, Ronald, 'What is Equality? Part 2: Equality of Resources', *Philosophy and Public Affairs*, 10 (1981), pp. 185–243.

—— *Sovereign Virtue* (Cambridge, MA: Harvard University Press, 2000).

—— et al., 'Symposium on Ronald Dworkin's *Sovereign Virtue*', *Ethics*, 113 (2002), pp. 5–143.

Lippert-Rasmussen, Kasper, 'Egalitarianism, Option Luck, and Responsibility', *Ethics*, 111 (2001), pp. 548–79.

McLeod, Colin, *Liberalism, Justice, and Markets* (Oxford: Oxford University Press, 1998).

Rakowski, Eric, *Equal Justice* (New York: Oxford University Press, 1991).

—— 'Who Should Pay for Bad Genes?', *California Law Review*, 90 (2002), pp. 1345–1414.

Roemer, John, *Egalitarian Perspectives* (Cambridge: Cambridge University Press, 1994), pt. II.

Vallentyne, Peter, 'Brute Luck, Option Luck, and Equality of Initial Opportunities', *Ethics*, 112 (2002), pp. 529–57.

Van Parijs, Philippe, *Real Freedom for All* (Oxford: Clarendon Press, 1995).

Williams, Andrew, 'Resource Egalitarianism and the Limits to Basic Income', *Economics and Philosophy*, 15 (1999), pp. 85–107.

Equality of Welfare

Arneson, Richard, 'Equality and Equal Opportunity for Welfare', *Philosophical Studies*, 56 (1989), pp. 77–93.

—— 'Liberalism, Distributive Subjectivism, and Equal Opportunity for Welfare', *Philosophy and Public Affairs*, 19 (1990), pp. 158–94.

—— 'Equality of Opportunity for Welfare Defended and Recanted', *Journal of Political Philosophy*, 7 (1999), pp. 488–97.

—— 'Welfare Should Be the Currency of Justice', *Canadian Journal of Philosophy*, 30 (2000), pp. 497–524.

Christiano, Thomas, 'Difficulties with the Principle of Equal Opportunity for Welfare', *Philosophical Studies*, 62 (1991), pp. 179–85.

Cohen, G. A., 'On the Currency of Egalitarian Justice', *Ethics*, 99 (1989), pp. 906–44.

Dworkin, Ronald, 'What is Equality? Part 1: Equality of Welfare', *Philosophy and Public Affairs*, 10 (1981), pp. 185–246.

—— *Sovereign Virtue* (Cambridge, MA: Harvard University Press, 2000), pp. 1–7, 11–16, 48–59, 65–73, 237–303.

Lippert-Rasmussen, Kasper, 'Arneson on Equality of Opportunity for Welfare', *Journal of Political Philosophy*, 7 (1999), pp. 478–87.

Rawls, John, 'Social Unity and Primary Goods', in Amartya Sen and Bernard Williams, eds., *Utilitarianism and Beyond* (Cambridge: Cambridge University Press, 1982).

Scanlon, T. M., 'Equality of Resources and Equality of Welfare: A Forced Marriage?', *Ethics*, 97 (1986), pp. 111–18.

—— 'The Moral Bases of Interpersonal Comparison', in Jon Elster and John Roemer, eds., *Interpersonal Comparisons of Well-Being* (Cambridge: Cambridge University Press, 1991).

—— *What We Owe To Each Other* (Cambridge, MA: The Belknap Press of Harvard University Press, 1998), ch. 3.

Williams, Andrew, 'Equality for the Ambitious', *Philosophical Quarterly*, 52 (2002), pp. 377–89.

Luck Egalitarianism

Anderson, Elizabeth, 'What Is the Point of Equality?', *Ethics*, 109 (1999), pp. 287–337.
Arneson, Richard, 'Egalitarian Justice versus the Right to Privacy', *Social Philosophy and Policy*, 17 (2000), pp. 91–119.
—— 'Luck Egalitarianism and Prioritarianism', *Ethics*, 110 (2000), pp. 339–49.
—— 'Why Justice Requires Transfers to Offset Income and Wealth Inequalities', *Social Philosophy and Policy*, 19 (2002), pp. 172–200.
Crisp, Roger, 'Equality, Priority, and Compassion', *Ethics*, 111 (2003), pp. 745–63.
Dworkin, Ronald, '*Sovereign Virtue* Revisited', *Ethics*, 113 (2002), pp. 106–43.
—— 'Equality, Luck and Hierarchy', *Philosophy and Public Affairs*, 31 (2003), pp. 190–8.
Fleurbaey, Marc, 'Equal Opportunity or Equal Social Outcome?', *Economics and Philosophy*, 11 (1995), pp. 25–55.
Frankfurt, Harry, 'Equality as a Moral Ideal', *Ethics*, 98 (1987), pp. 21–43.
Hinton, Timothy, 'Must Egalitarians Choose Between Fairness and Respect?', *Philosophy and Public Affairs*, 30 (2001), pp. 72–87.
Scheffler, Samuel, 'What is Egalitarianism?', *Philosophy and Public Affairs*, 31 (2003), pp. 5–39.
—— 'Equality as a Virtue of Sovereigns: A Reply to Ronald Dworkin', *Philosophy and Public Affairs*, 31 (2003), pp. 199–206.
Shiffrin, Seana Valentine, 'Egalitarianism, Choice-Sensitivity, and Accommodation', in Philip Pettit, Samuel Scheffler, Michael Smith, and R. Jay Wallace, eds., *Reasons and Values: Themes from the Work of Joseph Raz* (Oxford: Oxford University Press, forthcoming).
Temkin, Larry, 'Egalitarianism Defended', *Ethics*, 111 (2003), pp. 764–82.
Vallentyne, Peter, 'Brute Luck, Option Luck, and Equality of Initial Opportunities', *Ethics*, 112 (2002), pp. 529–57.
Wolff, J., 'Fairness, Respect, and the Egalitarian Ethos', *Philosophy and Public Affairs*, 27 (1998), pp. 97–127.

Desert

Feinberg, Joel, *Doing and Deserving* (Princeton: Princeton University Press, 1970).
Feldman, Fred, *Utilitarianism, Hedonism, and Desert* (Cambridge: Cambridge University Press, 1997).
Hurka, Thomas, 'The Common Structure of Virtue and Desert', *Ethics*, 112 (2001), pp. 6–31.
Kagan, Shelly, 'Equality and Desert', in Louis Pojman and Owen McLeod, eds., *What Do We Deserve?* (New York: Oxford University Press, 1999).
Miller, David, *Principles of Social Justice* (Cambridge, MA: Harvard University Press, 1999), chs. 7–9.
Olsaretti, Serena, 'Unmasking Equality? Kagan on Equality and Desert', *Utilitas*, 13 (2002), pp. 387–400.
—— ed., *Justice and Desert* (Oxford: Oxford University Press, 2003).
Rawls, John, *Justice as Fairness: A Restatement*, ed. Erin Kelly (Cambridge, MA: The Belknap Press of Harvard University Press, 1999), sects. 20–2.

Scheffler, Samuel, 'Justice and Desert in Liberal Theory', in *Boundaries and Allegiances* (Oxford: Oxford University Press, 2001).

Sher, George, *Desert* (Princeton: Princeton University Press, 1987).

The Family, Gender, and Justice

Arneson, Richard, 'Feminism and Family Justice', *Public Affairs Quarterly*, 11 (1997), pp. 313–30.

Cohen, Joshua, 'Okin on Justice, Gender, and Family', *Canadian Journal of Philosophy*, 22 (1992), pp. 263–86.

Lloyd, S. A., 'Family Justice and Social Justice', *Pacific Philosophical Quarterly*, 75 (1994), pp. 353–71.

Mason, Andrew, 'Equality, Personal Responsibility, and Gender Socialisation', *Proceedings of the Aristotelian Society*, 100 (2000), pp. 227–46.

Nussbaum, Martha, *Women and Human Development* (Cambridge: Cambridge University Press, 2000).

Okin, Susan Moller, *Justice, Gender, and the Family* (New York: Basic Books, 1989).

——'*Political Liberalism*, Justice and Gender', *Ethics*, 105 (1994), pp. 23–43.

Rawls, John, 'The Idea of Public Reason Revisited', *University of Chicago Law Review*, 64 (1997), pp. 765–807; repr. in Rawls, *The Law of Peoples* (Cambridge, MA: Harvard University Press, 1999), and in Rawls, *Collected Papers*, ed. Samuel Freeman (Cambridge, MA: Harvard University Press, 1999).

Russel, J. S., 'Okin's Rawlsian Feminism? Justice in the Family and Another Liberalism', *Social Theory and Practice*, 21 (1995), pp. 397–426.

The Market and the Site of Distributive Justice

Carens, Joseph, *Equality, Moral Incentives, and the Market: An Essay in Utopian Politico-Economic Theory* (Chicago: University of Chicago Press, 1981).

——'An Interpretation and Defense of the Socialist Principle of Distribution', *Social Philosophy and Policy*, 20 (2003), pp. 145–77.

Cohen, G. A., 'Incentives, Inequality, and Community', in Stephen Darwall, ed., *Equal Freedom* (Ann Arbor: University of Michigan Press, 1995), pp. 331–97.

——'The Pareto Argument for Inequality', *Social Philosophy and Policy*, 12 (1995), pp. 160–85.

——*If You're an Egalitarian, How Come You're So Rich?* (Cambridge, MA: Harvard University Press, 2000).

Cohen, Joshua, 'Taking People As They Are?', *Philosophy and Public Affairs*, 30 (2001), pp. 362–86.

Estlund, David, 'Liberalism, Equality and Fraternity in Cohen's Critique of Rawls', *Journal of Political Philosophy*, 6 (1998), pp. 99–112.

Murphy, Liam, 'Institutions and the Demands of Justice', *Philosophy and Public Affairs*, 27 (1998), pp. 251–91.

Pogge, Thomas, 'On the Site of Distributive Justice: Reflections on Cohen and Murphy', *Philosophy and Public Affairs*, 29 (2000), pp. 226–48.

Vandenbroucke, Frank, *Social Justice and Individual Ethics in an Open Society: Equality, Responsibility, and Incentives* (Berlin and New York: Springer, 2001).

Wilkinson, T. M., *Freedom, Efficiency and Equality* (London: Macmillan, 2000).

Williams, Andrew, 'Incentives, Inequality, and Publicity', *Philosophy and Public Affairs*, 27 (1998), pp. 226–48.

Justice across Cultures and Species

Barry, Brian, *Culture and Equality* (Cambridge, MA: Harvard University Press, 2001).

Carens, Joseph, *Culture, Citizenship, and Community* (Oxford: Oxford University Press, 2000).

Cohen, G. A., 'Multiculturalism and Expensive Tastes', in R. Bhargarva, A. K. Bagchi, and R. Sudarshan, eds., *Multiculturalism, Liberalism, and Democracy* (New Delhi: Oxford University Press, 1999).

Cohen, Joshua, et al., eds., *Is Multiculturalism Bad for Women?* (Princeton: Princeton University Press, 1999).

Gutman, Amy, ed., *Multiculturalism* (Princeton: Princeton University Press, 1994).

Kymlicka, Will, *Multicultural Citizenship* (Oxford: Clarendon Press, 1995).

Nussbaum, Martha, and Jonathan Glover, eds., *Women, Culture and Development* (Oxford: Clarendon Press, 1995).

Okin, Susan Moller, 'Feminism and Multiculturalism: Some Tensions', *Ethics*, 108 (1998), pp. 661–84.

Persson, Ingmar, 'A Basis for Interspecies Equality', in Paola Cavalieri and Peter Singer, eds., *The Great Ape Project* (New York: St Martin's Griffin, 1996).

Raz, Joseph, 'Multiculturalism: A Liberal Perspective', in *Ethics and the Public Domain* (Oxford: Clarendon Press, 1994).

Singer, Peter, 'All Animals Are Equal', in id., ed., *Applied Ethics* (Oxford: Oxford University Press, 1986).

Justice across Borders

Barry, Brian, 'Statism and Nationalism: A Cosmopolitan Critique', in Ian Shapiro and Lea Brilmayer, eds., *Global Justice* (New York: New York University Press, 1999).

Beitz, Charles, *Political Theory and International Relations* (Princeton: Princeton University Press, 1979).

—— 'Rawls's Law of Peoples', *Ethics*, 110 (2000), pp. 669–96.

Blake, Michael, 'Distributive Justice, State Coercion, and Autonomy', *Philosophy and Public Affairs*, 30 (2001), pp. 257–96.

Buchanan, Allen, 'Rawls's Law of Peoples: Rules for a Vanished Westphalian World', *Ethics*, 110 (2000), pp. 607–721.

Crisp, Roger, and Dale Jamieson, 'Egalitarianism and a Global Resources Tax: Pogge on Rawls', in Victoria Davion and Clark Wolf, eds., *The Idea of a Political Liberalism* (Lanham, MD: Rowman & Littlefield, 2000).

Miller, David, *On Nationality* (Oxford: Clarendon Press, 1995).

Miller, Richard, 'Cosmopolitan Respect and Patriotic Concern', *Philosophy and Public Affairs*, 30 (2003), pp. 202–24.

Pogge, Thomas, *Realizing Rawls* (Ithaca, NY: Cornell University Press, 1989), pt. 3.

—— ed., *Global Justice* (Oxford: Blackwell, 2001).

—— *World Poverty and Human Rights* (Oxford: Blackwell, 2002).

Rawls, John, *The Law of Peoples* (Cambridge, MA: Harvard University Press, 1999).

Satz, Debra, 'International Economic Justice', in Hugh LaFollette, ed., *The Oxford Handbook of Practical Ethics* (New York: Oxford University Press, 2003).

Scheffler, Samuel, *Boundaries and Allegiances* (Oxford: Oxford University Press, 2001).

Shue, Henry, *Basic Rights*, 2nd edn. (Princeton: Princeton University Press, 1996).

Steiner, Hillel, 'Just Taxation and International Redistribution', in Ian Shapiro and Lea Brilmayer, eds., *Global Justice* (New York: New York University Press).

Unger, Peter, *Living High and Letting Die: Our Illusion of Innocence* (New York: Oxford University Press, 1996).

Justice across Generations

Barry, Brian, *Theories of Justice* (Berkeley: California University Press, 1989), ch. 5.

—— 'Sustainability and Intergenerational Justice', in Andrew Dobson, ed., *Fairness and Futurity* (Oxford: Oxford University Press, 1999).

English, Jane, 'Justice between Generations', *Philosophical Studies*, 31 (1977), pp. 91–104.

Kavka, Gregory, 'The Paradox of Future Individuals', *Philosophy and Public Affairs*, 11 (1982), pp. 93–112.

Kumar, Rahul, 'Who Can Be Wronged?', *Philosophy and Public Affairs*, 31 (2003), pp. 99–118.

Laslett, Peter, and James Fishkin, eds., *Justice between Age Groups and Generations* (New Haven: Yale University Press, 1987).

McMahan, Jeff, 'Wrongful Life: Paradoxes in the Morality of Causing People to Exist', in Jules Coleman and Christopher Morris, eds., *Rational Commitment and Social Justice: Essays for Gregory Kavka* (Cambridge: Cambridge University Press, 1998).

Parfit, Derek, *Reasons and Persons* (Oxford: Clarendon Press, 1984), pt. IV.

Rawls, John, *A Theory of Justice*, rev. edn. (Cambridge, MA: The Belknap Press of Harvard University Press, 1999), sect. 44.

Roberts, Melinda, *Child versus Childmaker* (Oxford: Rowman & Littlefield, 1998).

Shiffrin, Seana, 'Wrongful Life, Procreative Responsibility, and the Significance of Harm', *Legal Theory*, 5 (1999), pp. 117–48.

Sikora, R., and Brian Barry, eds., *Obligations to Future Generations* (Philadelphia: Temple University Press, 1978).

Wolf, Clark, 'Contemporary Property Rights, Lockean Provisos, and the Interests of Future Generations', *Ethics*, 105 (1995), pp. 791–818.

Woodward, James, 'The Non-Identity Problem', *Ethics*, 96 (1986), pp. 804–31.

—— 'Reply to Parfit', *Ethics*, 97 (1987), pp. 800–16.

Index

Note: page numbers in *italics* refer to information in chapter notes.